Journeyings

By the same author:

Struggletown: Public and Private Life in Richmond 1900–1965

Journeyings

The Biography
of a Middle-Class Generation
1920–1990

Janet McCalman

MELBOURNE UNIVERSITY PRESS

First published 1993
Reprinted 1993 (twice)
First paperback edition 1995

Designed by Al Knight
Typeset by Syarikat Seng Teik Sdn. Bhd.
Printed in Malaysia by
SRM Production Services Sdn. Bhd. for
Melbourne University Press, Carlton, Victoria 3053

National Library of Australia Cataloguing-in-Publication entry

McCalman, Janet, 1948– .
Journeyings: the biography of a middle-class generation
1920–1990.

Bibliography.
Includes index.
ISBN 0 522 84675 0 (pbk.).

1. Private schools—Victoria—Alumni and alumnae—
Biography. 2. Middle class—Victoria—History.
I. Title.

305.550922945

Contents

Preface

Scholars have been rather shy of writing about the Australian middle class, especially of its history during the twentieth century (has it been too close to home?); and yet it has been, and remains, so important. To be fair, the middle class is elusive and treasures its privacy—its problems and private life receive far less exposure than do those of the working class. So if one wants to write about the middle class, where does one start? Private schooling, especially in Victoria and South Australia, has always been an important part of being 'middle-class' in this country: it is not a necessary condition, but it is a widely desired and practised one. It seemed, therefore, a good idea to collect a middle-class generation from private schools and to follow them from childhood to old age as a way of exploring middle-class life and manners. Schools also have an intrinsic poignancy in the stories of young lives being moulded, innocent of the fates awaiting them. But this book is not a collection of school histories: it is a group biography of a generation which, while rooted in the particular, may illumine the general. Some may decide, therefore, that it is not about 'their' middle class—I hope they will forgive the vignette in place of the grand portrait.

This book is about people, people who happen to share the experience of a particular private education. And I have written it first for the people it is about, because the practice of oral history imposes a special accountability on the historian: the people in this group biography are contributors and witnesses, historians of themselves and their times, not originators of texts to be deconstructed. They have contested, criticized and explicated my reconstructions of their experience; and they have remained in control of their contributions, for it is a fearful thing to expose one's life and feelings to the outside world. And because this is a group biography, a collection of stories of actual lives, it needs to unfold in the way real lives do—which is that none of us knows what lies ahead. Perhaps one of the most important functions of fiction is to permit us to escape that existential plight—it is a rehearsal for life; in writing history, however, we need to feel life's dreadful unpredictability, its untidiness, its ordinariness, its splendours. Art is under our control; history, like life, is not. And yet history is but our reconstructions, is but an artefact of the mind, conceived of differently by all of us, and differently by all of us at different times in our lives. It is individual, forever changing, never 'definitive'. We are incorrigibly historical beings: our inner histories of ourselves—private history—constitute our ever-evolving senses of identity—we are our own stories. But in constructing histories—whether private or public—we are torn between what we would like the story to be and what the evidence insists that it really is. The novelist enjoys a licence; the historian a responsibility. This book is written in the conviction that historians have a place in the broad culture of society: that we are among the last remaining members of the academy who can write for the outside world and not just for each other. We practise a profession that borders—in its written form—on art. History is both a scholarly discipline and a literary genre: it is creative writing in which the author is not in control of the plot.

The book is based on conventional archival research, oral history and the results of a detailed survey of six hundred and sixty-three people which was undertaken with the assistance of Dr Mark Peel. Eighty men and women from the four schools were interviewed and the extracts from those interviews quoted in the book have all been edited and approved by the contributors. Some have chosen to remain anonymous and they have pseudonyms in italics: any resemblance to the name of a former student of any of the schools is accidental and not intended. Those married women who have decided to use their names are in the book under their maiden names.

Appendix II includes the long statistical tables from the survey and an account by Dr Peel of its nature and procedures. Short tables from the survey have been placed in footnotes and material quoted from individual respondents is referred to by the questionnaire number.

Throughout the book 'private school' has been used to cover 'church school', 'independent school', 'corporate school' and 'public school'.

Acknowledgements

There are many people to thank. First, the contributors: without their words this book would be nothing. They have been generous, tolerant and welcoming. For some the experience of being interviewed was distressing, and the first sight of their words in hard-cold typescript traumatic. Oral history is not easy, either intellectually or emotionally, but it must surely be the most personally enriching for the historian. I only hope that I can do justice to them all.

I am grateful to the principals and staff of the schools who allowed me to work in their archives: from Genazzano College, Sister Margaret Mary Kennedy FCJ and Sister Dolores Kirby FCJ; from the Methodist Ladies' College, Mr David Loader, Mrs Joanna Day and Mrs Margaret Leslie; from Trinity Grammar School, Mr Don Marles and Ms Helen Reynolds; from Scotch College, Dr Gordon Donaldson and Mr Geoff Tolson; from MacRoberston Girls' High School, Miss Gabrielle Blood; from Melbourne Boys' High School, Mr Neville Drohan and from Essendon High School, Mr John Saltau. I must also thank the new principals of Genazzano College and Trinity Grammar School, Mrs Pat Fitzgerald and Mr Peter Crawley, and the four schools' directors of development—Brian Reid, Michael Thornton, Sue Lines, Ian Monro, Rohan Brown and Peter Crook. May I also express my gratitude to Mr Bruce Turner and his staff at the Prahran Mechanics Institute's Victorian and Local History Library: this is a remarkable collection, not just of formal histories, but of biography, memoirs, family history, business history and institutional history of all sorts, both in published form and in manuscript. The richness of that collection provided the bedrock for this book.

The five years of research and writing for this book were made possible first by the University of Melbourne, then the Australian Research

ACKNOWLEDGEMENTS

x

Council and, in 1992, an Ideas for Australia Fellowship through Deakin University. Many colleagues have helped and listened, but may I single out Professor Stuart Macintyre, Associate Professor Patricia Grimshaw and Dr Barbara Falk in the History Department of the University of Melbourne. I am particularly grateful to Dr Ailsa Thomson Zainu'ddin, whose marvellous history of MLC ignited the spark for this book; and she, along with Dr Brenda Niall, Dr Geoffrey Serle and Dr Ian Britain, read my drafts and listened and talked throughout the whole five years. Dr Judith Brett and Dr Graeme Smith, Dr Graham Little and Dr Peter Gronn have all provided ideas and support. To Dr Mark Peel I have a special debt: we worked together on the survey and on an analysis of *Who's Who in 1988* and it was a truly exciting collaboration. Laurie and Helene McCalman read my drafts; but my greatest debt of all is to my husband Al Knight, without whom none of this would have been possible.

The quotations in this book are reproduced with the permission of David Higham and Associates for the passage from *Land of Spices* by Kate O'Brien; of Pan Macmillan for the passage from *Robert Menzies' Forgotten People* by Judith Brett; of Curtis Brown for the passage from *A Radical Life* by Russel Ward; of Allen and Unwin for the passages from *The Paradise Tree* by James Murray and from *R. G. Menzies: a Portrait* by Sir John Bunting; of Weldon Publishing for the extract from Judith Armstrong's translation of *In the Land of Kangaroos and Goldmines* by Oscar Comettant; from Mrs Dorothy Adams for the extract from *Memories of Darling Road Methodist Church*; of the author for the passage from *Goodbye Melbourne Town* by Graham McInnes; and of Pan Macmillan for the passage from *A Suburban Girl* by Moira Lambert.

Journeyers over consecutive seasons, over the years, the curious
    years each emerging from that which preceded it,
Journeyers as with companions, namely their own diverse phases,
Forth-steppers from the latent unrealized baby-days,
Journeyers gayly with their own youth, journeyers with their
    bearded and well-grained manhood,
Journeyers with their womanhood, ample, unsurpass'd, content,
Journeyers with their own sublime old age of manhood or
    womanhood,
Old age, calm, expanded, broad with the haughty breadth of the
    universe,
Old age, flowing free, with the delicious near-by freedom of
    death.

Walt Whitman

'Song of the Open Road'

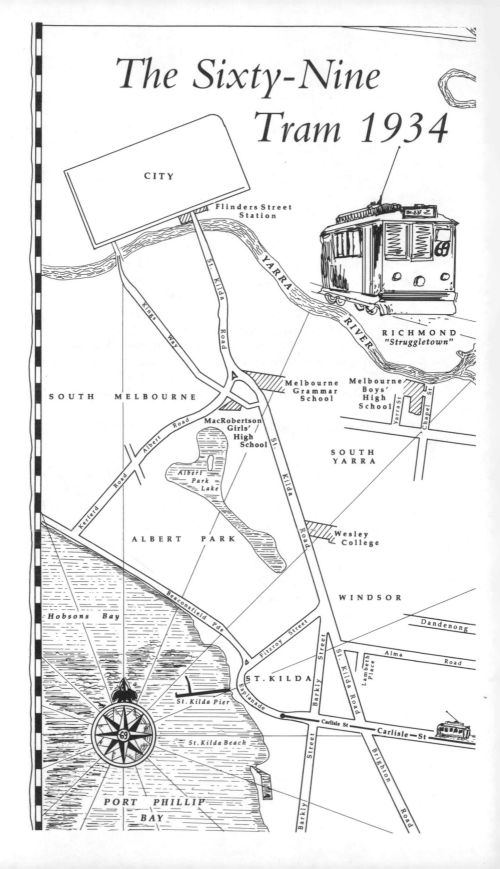

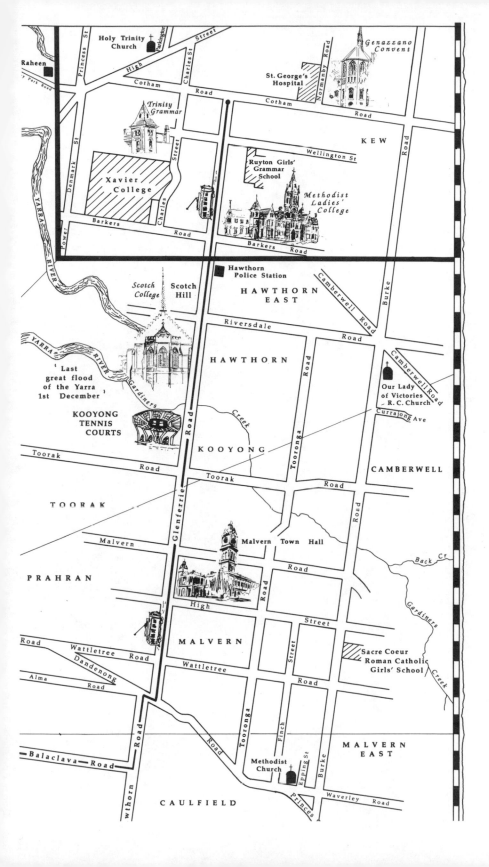

1
The Sixty-Nine Tram
1934

The Sixty-Nine Tram
1934

It's the first day of school for 1934, and the 69 tram begins its long journey along the spine of Melbourne's middle-class heartland, from St Kilda Beach to Cotham Road, Kew. This is a women's and children's tram, not a working-men's, and as it stops along Carlisle Street, the first college boys and girls climb aboard. Many of them are Jewish and wearing the cardinal caps of Scotch College or the star of the Methodist Ladies' College, for Jews are made welcome at these two schools at a time when many other private schools have a covert Jewish quota.[1] One boy has walked down from Lambeth Place to catch the 69 and he's early enough to secure his favourite seat—the middle place on the blind side. He begins to read, and to the fascination of his school mates, will not lift his head until he reaches Scotch's tram stop. His routine never varies. He is to become a distinguished academic lawyer, a public figure of immense charm and cultivation, and a healing governor general.

St Kilda has seen better days and its mansions have mostly declined into rooming houses or have been subdivided into flats. The Depression can still be felt in 1934, even if it has lost some of its sting, and it has hastened the erection of flats at the expense of villas on quarter-acre blocks. But as Carlisle Street becomes Balaclava Road the townscape is more recognizably surburban. George Johnston will later savage its 'horrible flatness' in his semi-autobiographical novel *My Brother Jack*; many others will recall Caulfield with less jaundice. It is a suburb much favoured by returned servicemen, and the Johnston family is only one of many where war-damaged men are distracted by their memories and

---

[1] Ailsa G. Thomson Zainu'ddin, *They Dreamt of a School: A Centenary History of the Methodist Ladies' College, Kew, 1882–1982*, pp. 300–1.

nightmares.[2] The college boys and girls begin to fill the tram as it swings around Balaclava Junction into Hawthorn Road. There are more than a dozen Protestant, Catholic and privately-owned schools on the 69 tram route and not one government high school. The nearest high schools are in South Yarra and Albert Park, Dandenong and Frankston, and it will be another twenty years before a government school will offer a full secondary education in the eastern suburbs. The middle class of Melbourne are 'College People' from both choice and necessity.[3]

The Scotch boys on the 69 tram play a game—'having on the connies'. Some of the conductors enjoy it; others do not. The favourite with many is one afflicted with a crossed eye, who tips his head amusingly to one side so that he can focus his good eye on the ticket before clipping it. A certain deference to college boys and girls is expected and frequently paid. These are good young people, however, a credit to their parents and teachers, and they will soon be mature enough to display courtesy to all. At home and at school they largely do as they are told and with little complaint. Their books of tram concession tickets state that they must always offer their seat to an adult and they do. The MLC girls are a little different. They have a remarkable headmistress (although she is to be mysteriously and unforgiveably dismissed before the end of the year), who runs the school under the supervision of a Methodist minister principal. She is an old collegian, a scholarship girl, and the school's most gifted scholar in its first half century.[4] She is still faintly common in speech and she has a certain softness for battlers:

> Mrs Landen used to say that we were the lucky ones during the Depression—we were still at school, while there were many people who were as important as we were—probably more so—and probably more clever, who were denied education. We were the lucky ones and she wanted us to remember it. And she used to tell us that on the trams we should stand for a working girl of our own age.[5]

Melbourne in 1934 is a sharply divided society, both in class and religion, and college people enjoy considerable prestige. The major events of the private school calendar are part of the civic culture in a way that will not survive the social upheavals of the 1960s. Adults as well as children flaunt school colours on Boat Race Day and the 'Milky Way' in Little Collins Street sells sundaes biliously concocted to match the colours of the six 'Public Schools'—the Anglicans' Melbourne and Geelong

---

[2] George Johnston, *My Brother Jack*, p. 32; James Murray, *The Paradise Tree*, p. 99.
[3] Box Hill Boys' High School had its first matriculation class in 1954, and the co-educational Camberwell High School did so in 1956.
[4] Zainu'ddin, *They Dreamt of a School*, pp. 207–35.
[5] Interview with Jean Cane, 25 October 1988.

Grammars, the Presbyterians' Scotch and Geelong Colleges, the Methodists' Wesley College and the Jesuits' Xavier College. The headmasters of these institutions are public figures whose Speech Day addresses are annually reported in the press. Even so, Protestants display a certain reserve towards Xavier in all things except sport. 'Black and red are the devil's colours', some mutter, and the Jesuits they find the most alarming of all the Catholic religious orders because they are clever and can indoctrinate a child by the age of seven.[6] But sport and the tram forge an unexpected alliance between Scotch and Xavier. They are the only two 'Public Schools' to travel on the 69, and they find common ground in their antagonism to Melbourne Grammar—if Scotch can't beat Grammar this time, then let's hope Xavier can.[7] Grammar boys sneer at Scotch as 'that high school'—an insult 'that speaks volumes'—but Scotch is the school they fear: 'They outnumber us, and there's something flinty and determined about them which we find hard to put down'.[8] It's a rivalry that will last a life-time: 'It's incredible that you can be in a party of men and women, and you can pick a Grammar bloke—you only have to have a few sentences with him to realize he's not a Scotch bloke'.[9]

There is a certain factual base to Grammar's hauteur towards Scotch, who are a more democratic bunch of boys. As the 69 tram moves up Hawthorn Road, it skirts other major subdivisions of the 1920s, where the grounds of great houses like Harleston, Labassa, Crotonhurst and Cantala have been sold off as building blocks.[10] And the fathers of the Scotch boys and MLC girls who come from these streets are engineers and small businessmen, sales representatives and accountants. The majority are new members of the middle class.[11] They are not poor, but neither do they have money to throw about. Those on government salaries have had to cope with a 10 per cent drop in their income as part of Victoria's Depression economies. Some in business have cut their workforce, trimmed their overheads, put their cars up on wooden blocks for the duration, and asked their womenfolk to darn their stockings and make do with less.[12] One of the few Scotch boys to come from Toorak has an unusual father—a brilliant musician and a Fabian Socialist, he is also a successful businessman and he has just taken advantage of the fall in property values to build a fine home in Melbourne's best suburb. One day

[6] Murray, *The Paradise Tree*, p. 102.
[7] Interviews with Geoffrey Tolson, 26 March 1990, and with *Walters Rhodes*, 27 September 1990.
[8] Interview with Geoffrey Serle, 27 October 1988; Chester Eagle, *Play Together, Dark Blue Twenty*, p. 21.
[9] Geoffrey Tolson.
[10] St Stephen's Presbyterian Church, Caulfield, *First Fifty Years*, p. 6.
[11] Scotch College Archives: records of the 267 boys who entered Senior School in 1934 ('Scotch 1934 Cohort'); MLC Archives: records of the 284 girls born 1919–20 ('MLC 1919–20 Cohort'). See Appendix I, tables 1, 2 and 3.
[12] Interview with *Gwenda Holtby*, 8 June 1988; Geoffrey Tolson.

the son overhears his father 'almost apologizing' for sending his son to Scotch in preference to Melbourne Grammar: 'It's a good thing it's so democratic', he insists to his Toorak neighbour, 'they come from everywhere there'.[13]

The tram cuts diagonally across the vastness of Dandenong Road and commences its spectacular journey along Glenferrie Road, through the ridges and dales of Malvern and Hawthorn. It is now amidst the established middle class. Much of Malvern was built in the land boom of the 1880s, but it also boasts some of the finest Edwardian houses in Melbourne. The shopping centre is genteel and prosperous enough, given the economic times, and it is certainly looking better than its equivalents in Richmond or Prahran. There is a real, if subtle, sense of community in Malvern, born of longtime residence and busy church life. Young couples often seek their first home near their parents, and East Malvern offers cheaper houses which are still within walking distance for a young mother pushing a pram. East Malvern is popular too with returned servicemen. The Protestant churches are full for every service: at Epping Street Methodist Church you can wait months just for an audition for the choir, and the very keen are well advised to take singing lessons.[14] Finch Street is perhaps Malvern's finest street, but the well-off of Malvern are homely rather than social and the church is the centre of their social whirl also. But as the tram pushes along Glenferrie Road, past the Malvern Town Hall which Sir Robert Menzies will adopt as the spiritual capital of his 'Forgotten People' after the war, it collects fewer Scotch boys and MLC girls. This is the eastern border of Toorak and the navy blue of the boys' and girls' Grammars is more apparent. Suddenly the tram takes a marvellous plunge into the valley of Gardiner's Creek at Kooyong. There are still Chinese market gardens on the flat, but there is also a new tennis stadium. It is, however, a flood plain and part of the Yarra's system, and on 1 December, travellers on the 69 tram will be stopped by an inland sea—the last great Yarra flood to devastate the eastern suburbs. The river has already been straightened near Richmond; now the backing-up of tide and floodwaters further upstream will have to be dealt with. The Scotch rowing shed will be swept away, the floodwaters will lap the steps of the Memorial Hall, and boys will boast for years of their swimming feats in the flood of 1934: 'I remember that flood very well. My cousin Mac swam from Tooronga Road, across the flats and right up to the chapel and back again'.[15]

---

[13] Interview with *Neil Ewart*, 11 December 1990.
[14] Lynne Strahran, *Private and Public Memory: A History of the City of Malvern, passim*; W. H. Bossence, *Epping Street*, p. 38; Dorothy Adams et al., *Memories of Darling Road Uniting Church*, p. 147.
[15] Interview with Archie Crow, 5 July 1990.

Rising up the escarpment to the left is Scotch College. It is a stunning site for a school. The playing fields are on the flats, and behind the school there is a frontage to the Yarra river itself. Already there are established trees, including exotic species; fifty years later there will be leafy avenues and romantic vistas. The buildings themselves are apt for a Melbourne middle-class school: displaying various workings of red brick and white stucco, topped with soaring tiled roofs—dignified but not quite beautiful, and perfectly in tune with the houses the boys' parents have been building for themselves in Camberwell and Caulfield since about 1910. For this is not Scotch's original location. It is by now eighty-three years old—old enough to be creating legends—and very proud to be Victoria's oldest Associated Public School: 'In those early days, when the gold fever had entered into men's blood, the Presbyterians of Melbourne, with all the Scotsman's passion for education, desired that their children should have the advantages of a good secular and religious training'.[16] The Presbyterian Church first built the school on two acres of land granted by the government in Eastern Hill. Under two great headmasters, both Scots, it has established itself as the leading private institution in Melbourne. It has been innovative, democratic and responsive to the modern world of science and technology, history and literature; but perhaps its most prized achievement has been to have 'formed a public opinion amongst the boys, whereby they [are] enlisted on the side of orderliness, honour and truth'. Foreseeing the growth of the eastern suburbs, the school began the move to Hawthorn in 1915 and now claims to be 'one of the largest schools in the Empire'.[17] The editor of the *Scotch Collegian* for 1934 will expound the meaning of 'Scotch' in his August issue:

Cardinal, gold and blue, colours which are held in respect throughout the Empire, are *your* colours, a common link between you and countless Old Boys scattered throughout the world today. They set before you ideals which, when coupled with the lettering around the badge, mean a full life's work living up to. Think of it—Beauty, Goodness and Truth. Cardinal, purity and richness of colour reflecting the depth and beauty of high ideals; gold, a symbol of goodness surviving fire and water, age, and even the very acid test of life; and blue, truth in everything, fidelity to all, the old British 'true blue' . . .

'Deo, Patriae, Litteris'—for God, Country, Learning. You should bow down your heads before her with humility and, with bursting heart, receive these her most precious gifts, to guard them with your very life.

Do you wonder *now* that our boys went away to shell-torn France singing 'We're fighting for the Cardinal, Gold and Blue'? Who wouldn't fight for Scotch, for beauty, goodness and truth, the finest things in life?[18]

---

[16] *Scotch College Prospectus*, 1934, p. 8.
[17] G. H. Nicholson, *First Hundred Years: Scotch College, Melbourne, 1851–1951*, p. 155.
[18] Henry I. Marshall, *Scotch Collegian*, August 1934, pp. 121–2.

The feelings of most of the boys walking through the gates of Scotch on this first day of school for 1934 are somewhat more prosaic, although most are very proud to be wearing the cardinal, gold and blue. They know they are privileged to be going to such a good school, and they are proud too for their parents, for this marks their going up in the world. There are 267 boys entering Senior School this year and only twenty of them are the sons of Old Boys. Almost three quarters of them come straight from state schools, and four-fifths will be at Scotch for four years or less.[19] Their families cannot afford more than a 'finishing' at a private school. The fees are 11 guineas a term, so that a £50 legacy can comfortably buy a year at Scotch; and there are crude folk who boast that a year at Scotch or Grammar is all you need for the old school tie and a foot on the ladder. Grandparents and maiden aunts often help out financially; the prudent have invested in insurance policies; a cheeky few will send their boy for a year and never pay at all.[20]

The 69 tram is bringing boys from the north as well—in fact as many come from the north as from the south—for while half the boys come from the heartland which extends from Caulfield to Kew, others are coming from all over Melbourne. There are six from Moonee Ponds and only five from nearby Toorak; there are four from Footscray and one from Kooyong; there's a doctor's son from Windsor and a bank manager's son from Richmond; there's a furrier's son from Carlton and a hairdresser's boy from Newmarket. The business of most Scotch fathers is business, but very few own big companies. The majority are men on salaries and the most common qualification is in accountancy. They are not an educated class overall, and there are only eight doctors, four lawyers, three clergymen and fourteen engineers. About one-fifth are in small business, from grocers and butchers, to garage proprietors and builders; from radio dealers and contractors to furriers and tailors. Just one-eighth are 'senior managers', and there's a handful of investors, merchants, importers and senior bankers. And there are clerks and sales representatives, and a solitary 'railway employee'. Twenty-one boys are the sons of farmers and graziers, but not all are boarding at the school, for the Depression has hit them hard and some can only afford to stay with city relatives and attend as day boys. Perhaps the most vulnerable are the fatherless, and they will have the shortest time at Scotch; only six of the twenty-seven lone mothers admit they are working, and two of those are shopkeepers and a third a Chinese herbalist.[21]

---

[19] Scotch 1934 Cohort: 69% came from state schools, 25% had had some time at other private schools, and just ten boys (4%) had been at Scotch since starting school. Thirty-six per cent of the boys were to stay one or two years; 79% for four years or less.

[20] Scotch College Archives, Account Books, 1932–36.

[21] See Appendix I, table 2; Scotch 1934 Cohort: Parents' Occupations by Boys' Academic Attainment.

As these boys start their education in the Senior School, they are also taking their first steps towards manhood and independence. The school is now as important as the family, and its task is to train the boys in the mental skills and moral habits which will enable them to join the middle class in their own right and remain there securely and honourably. But the school is also the guardian of middle-class culture and standards: is this boy worthy in mind and character of belonging to the world of Scotch? The school will judge the boys' performances, and some, especially those whose families are new to the middle class and to booklearning, will not make the grade. Those who are good enough and who embrace the school, will find themselves embraced in return by a school family which can be theirs to the day they die, if they wish it. Ahead of these thirteen- and fourteen-year-olds lie great tests and trials. The war will claim the lives of twenty-eight of them, and fracture the health of many more. Most will lead steady lives as good citizens and conscientious providers; only a few are destined for fame, distinction or great wealth. But all of this is far from the minds of the boys as they make their way to the Memorial Hall for their first Senior School assembly.[22]

Relieved of much of its load, the 69 tram crests 'Scotch Hill' and reaches the intersection of Riversdale Road. This corner is a flirt's paradise and the cradle of many a marriage, as the college boys and girls of a dozen schools wait for their respective trams:

> One gradually developed one's 'Thrills' and 'Big Thrills' among the travellers. It seldom got any further than 'eye games' (for which I was still too shy). These had special categories: you could 'recognize', that is smile and perhaps say 'hello'; 'cut dead' (look away); and if they winked, it was permissible, if you were interested, to give the glad eye, a sideways come hither look like a slow wink.[23]

Not a lot wink. Many a youthful heart is crushed by shyness and fear of disapproval. The girls from the Methodist Ladies' College, especially, find flirting difficult, for most come from tight-knit church communities which frown on dancing and 'fast' behaviour. One MLC father, a Methodist of Northern Irish origin, will not allow his daughter to go out with Scotch boys, for even Presbyterians have their moral weaknesses.[24] The MLC uniform is drab and unflattering, the black lisle stockings make their legs itch, and too many are plump—early victims to the English

[22] Scotch College Archives: lists of ex-servicemen, 1939–45; Mark Peel and Janet McCalman, *Who Went Where in Who's Who 1988*, Melbourne University History Research Series No. 1, 1992, pp. 24–35.
[23] Moira Lambert, *A Suburban Girl, Australia 1918–1948*, p. 51.
[24] Interview with *May Featherstone*, 7 December 1990.

teetotaller's compensatory addiction to cakes and pastries.[25] The girls do try, however, to make something of themselves:

> I had a great crush on Miss Hill and Miss Dewhurst—they were young and they were pretty. Miss Dewhurst had a piece of floppy hair down her forehead, and all the girls cut their hair to be like her. I started putting a few bobby pins in the front of my hair, trying to curl it up, and one day it hadn't turned out very well, and I was standing at the basin in North House with a comb and some water, trying to comb it out. Miss Luke came out and asked me what I was doing, and I said, 'Oh my hair's awful'. And she said, 'I've been thinking how nice your hair's been looking lately my dear, and what trouble you've been taking with it'. It's a simple remark, but I remember it, and that shows a kindliness that wasn't evident in many of the other teachers.[26]

Most teachers think poorly indeed of girls who make eyes at boys: 'precocious', 'conceited, personal appearance, boys etc main joy', 'loiters in streets', 'self-satisfied' they note on the girls' record cards at the school. But most girls are still untroubled by the heats of their desires:

> It was not a very religious school, but it was a very moral one. We were terribly innocent really, but it was a nice wholesome innocence. As far as I know there was only one girl who lost her virginity all the time I was there. And she disappeared and they said, 'She's going to have a baby . . . she's going to have a baby'. She was a boarder. We had one lass who liked boys, and we used to look at her with great awe really, to think that she had advanced to that stage. But nobody talked about marriage—they had other things on their minds.[27]

If the MLC girls lack what the popular song calls 'IT', they are still very nice girls. They are not quite as snobbish as many other college girls, but then at least a quarter of their fathers are 'in trade', and there are girls' schools which will not admit those in trade.[28] The MLC families are not showy, for Nonconformists believe that beauty comes from within, and are mindful of what Christ had to say about the difficulties a rich man may encounter on attempting to enter the Kingdom of Heaven. Methodists can make money as well as anyone, but they cannot enter 'society' without imperilling their principles. They are scorned as 'wowsers' and disliked for their rigidity; while privately they cherish kindness and shrink from unpleasantness. And there are times when these careful and controlled people are flooded with the joy of faith as they sing in church:

---

[25] Interviews with *Betty Thomas*, 18 July 1988, and with Fred Eager, 6 September 1990.
[26] Interview with Lurline Keck, 9 May 1989.
[27] Interview with Betty Blay, 7 March 1988.
[28] Marjorie R. Theobald, *Ruyton Remembers, 1878–1978*, p. 94; A. D. Pyke, *The Gold, the Blue, a History of Lowther Hall*, Melbourne 1983, pp. 71–3.

Visit then this soul of mine;
Pierce the gloom of sin and grief;
Fill me, Radiancy divine;
Scatter all my unbelief;

People notice now nice the MLC girls are. A constable at the Hawthorn Police Station has been watching them, and he has decided to send his daughter there—just for a couple of terms—to be 'finished'. She is to do 'Home Training and Domestic Science', music, commercial art and no examinations. Her mother can make the uniform (some mothers do, sometimes to their daughters' embarrassment), she will need 18 shillings for her hat and tie, but only 1s 7d for books; and with the extra Home Science fees, the whole investment will cost the constable £35.[29] Further down Glenferrie Road, a woman is renting the house behind her brother's shop, so that she can care for her demented mother. Her husband manages a bookstall on Flinders Street Station:

> Gran was senile, and she didn't know who she was, so we had to keep the door locked; and Mum lived through incredible sadness because this was her mother who didn't know her own daughter—she called Mum 'that woman'. I was thirteen at the time—I thought it was fun, because Gran thought that Sel, her son, was a man trying to marry her for her money, and my father was doing the same thing, so she'd nick behind doors and hide. We children were involved in everything. I got Gran up in the morning—I got her dressed. I coped with Gran while Mum coped with the whole family, cooking and washing. And I wouldn't have dreamt of saying 'I don't want to', because I was part of the family and this was my job. Fortunately Gran died before Mum had a nervous breakdown.[30]

The mother watches the MLC girls also, as every day they pass the shop, and they look so nice in their uniform that she vows, 'My daughter is going there if it kills me'.

The tram reaches the intersection of Barkers Road, and the MLC girls swarm towards the side gate where the prefects check that their hats and gloves are in place. The school is just over half a century old. The front building, with its restrained tower, is suburban Gothic in stuccoed brick (the Anglicans, Presbyterians and Catholics built their first establishments in real stone). MLC was founded by prosperous Wesleyans at the dawn of the booming 1880s, to be a 'modern school of the first order, a collegiate institution for girls, unsurpassed in the Colony'.[31] The Presbyterian Ladies' College is eight years older, and the two schools have

[29] MLC Archives, Account Books, 1932–36.
[30] Interview with Elaine Corran, 26 September 1990.
[31] Zainu'ddin, *They Dreamt of a School*, p. xix.

always enjoyed a ladylike, but no less deadly, rivalry. Both ladies' colleges were to provide an education as good as that offered in their brother colleges; and both now, in 1934, are the only two private girls' schools accredited to conduct their own Intermediate and Leaving examinations. Their academic reputations are high, but their performance is equalled and sometimes surpassed by the government high schools. Both ladies' colleges promote themselves as the first modern secondary church schools for girls in Victoria, and they forget the convent schools of the Mercy and Presentation orders, whose popularity with Protestant families was a not insignificant reason for their own foundation.[32] The Methodists chose 'Deo Domuique'—'For God and for Home'—as their motto, but in 1934 the school sends the girls mixed messages about womanhood and the life of the mind: 'the teachers were all feminists in their own way—a very controlled feminism, feminism within a system that was controlled by men'.[33] The teachers are strict, but all schools are strict in 1934. MLC has its quota of chatterers and gigglers, who amass detentions and opprobrium, but serious-mindedness is encouraged because Methodists pride themselves on being 'Christianity in Earnest'.

The school is more Methodist and English than Scotch is Presbyterian and Scottish, and Cornish and north country names abound on the school register. The school's founder, the Rev. Dr W. H. Fitchett, was one of the most eloquent champions of British grit, and his popular histories—Deeds that Won the Empire and Fights for the Flag—have made him a household name around the Empire ('Old Bleeds' the disenchanted call him). Methodists hold dear their English connections and their loyalty shapes their disapproval of Irish Catholicism and its political manifestations. Just last year (1933), the editor of MLC's Silver and Green, blessed with a Celtic name of great antiquity, reflected on the glories and duties of British blood:

> We were born into an uneasy world. The war, which a history of innumerable wars calls 'Great' until the end of time, hands on its penalties and its new sense of values. So much depends on us, so much in this present struggle between sublime idealism and crude, giant facts. Because it is difficult, it is great, and because we have British blood strong in our veins it is not only great, it is inevitable.
>
> The force which we call 'House Spirit' is at the roots of patriotism. Are we to follow the small band of English students who have denied patriotism in its noblest sense, or shall we stand for the greatness of our race, its honours, its magnanimity, its tradition, its ideals? They are not ideals to dazzle, but to steady us. May we be worthy of our responsibility, and may we find fulfilment in 'lives obscurely great'.[34]

---

[32] Ibid., pp. 3–4.
[33] Betty Blay.
[34] Wynwode Macdonald, Silver and Green, December 1933, p. 3.

The school buildings are grey, the stucco walls around the school are grey, the girls' uniform is soon to be changed to grey, relieved with dark green. The buildings are cold, and both girls and staff suffer miseries with chilblains. The front garden is coming to life, however, and soon a young landscape gardener called Edna Walling is to create a romantic 'Crab-apple Walk'. While some vital and gifted girls are favoured with special interest from some remarkable teachers, the majority—as in all schools—are a little neglected: the slow, like the poor, will always be with us. 'If Dorrie can't do algebra, then she should leave the classroom'; if a girl 'cries about school', then she 'needs a strict form mistress'.[35] As everywhere, women teachers are paid a pittance, many are caring for frail elderly parents, too many know little of the arts of teaching and have forgotten what it is like to be fifteen:

> I'm sure that many of the teachers were unhappy women, and I wonder if they were those whose fiancés and boyfriends were killed in the war. And it was Depression time and people weren't marrying. There seemed to be a lot of single ladies around everywhere—in the churches and in the schools. Probably most of them were sexually repressed, because there wasn't the freedom there is now; and lonely and caught up in that atmosphere of being responsible for discipline—which perhaps went to their heads.[36]

And yet the school has a magic which touches many. There are teachers filled with that 'Radiancy divine', and one in particular is a young singing mistress on the threshold of a career in school music that will win her international recognition. All of Methodism is contained in its hymn book, and music more than transcends the mundane and the ugly—it can even transfigure. Often they sing at school or in church:

> Finish then Thy new creation,
> Pure and spotless let us be;
> Let us see Thy great salvation,
> Perfectly restored in Thee,
> Changed from glory into glory,
> Till in heaven we take our place,
> Till we cast our crown before Thee,
> Lost in wonder, love and praise.

As the 69 tram draws away from Barkers Road and MLC, its journey's end at Cotham Road is in sight at the top of the hill. On the ridge which extends west to the Yarra perch noble houses, once graced by spacious grounds, but now built-in and obscured by more modest dwellings. And in every dale huddle workers' cottages, erected amid the

[35] Interview with Dorothea Cerutty, 16 March 1988; MLC Archives: 'MLC 1919–20 Cohort'.
[36] Lurline Keck.

drainage run-off from the rich on the hills. If the immediate economic crisis is evident, so too is that of the terrible crash of the 1890s. The decaying mansions of 'Marvellous Melbourne' now seem incongruous—exuberant and sensuous, vulgar even, built by another race of men who had no misgivings about growing rich on other people's money. They are immigrants' palaces of dreams, where the adventurous, lured to Australia by the gold rush only to make fortunes in more conventional ways, played, ever so briefly, at being lords and ladies. Not many of these palaces are private homes now, for few can afford the army of servants needed to make them habitable—just keeping them warm in winter requires at least a brood of biddable sons who enjoy chopping wood.[37] Some are boarding houses and flats, many are seminaries and training colleges, private hospitals and children's homes. Private schools also have converted their vast formal rooms into classrooms, and splendid staircases and noble proportions charm new members of the middle class. Three such early great houses constitute the core of Trinity Grammar School in Wellington Street, Kew, two tram stops up from MLC.

There are not many Trinity boys on the 69 tram for it is very much a local school, with two-thirds of the ordinary day boys coming from Kew and Hawthorn.[38] Many can walk to school:

> Trinity boys living in the western part of Hawthorn would normally have had a long walk to school *via* Power Street and Wellington Street. A much shorter walk was through what we used to refer to as the 'Xavier Park'—the quite sylvan paths parallel to the main drive-way, commencing at the Xavier College gates in Barkers Road—and permission was granted to do this. The main path emerged near Charles Street and was liberally covered by the overhanging branches of many trees—and wound its way through quite thick shrubs. It was really a lovely place to walk, and it abounded in bird life. At times one would encounter one of the Fathers of the College staff, usually immersed in reading from his breviary—and never at all surprised at seeing a 'foreign' school cap in the midst of these pleasant glades—now, alas, no longer in existence.
>
> What remains, never to be lost, is the memory of the melodious carolling of the magpies, . . . and, less frequently, but equally memorable, the quaint and haunting call of the pallid cuckoo.[39]

The local Trinity boys live in the smaller villas which have filled the gaps left by the disasters of the 1890s, and their fathers do much the same things as the Scotch and MLC fathers. Few are well-off; most have to live

---

[37] Kathleen Fitzpatrick, *Solid Bluestone Foundations*, pp. 1–8; Brian Lewis, *Sunday at Kooyong Road*, pp. 15–23.

[38] Trinity Grammar School Archives: Records of the 118 boys born 1919–20 ('Trinity 1919–20 Cohort'), see Appendix I.

[39] Robert Trumble, *The School on the Hill*, p. 52.

carefully; some are in desperate straits. The boys wear their olive green caps correctly and behave well, but many are in shiny, second-hand suits which don't quite fit. One boy arrives at school wearing sandshoes, because his only pair of leather shoes is being mended. The school offers many scholarships and its fees are lower than Melbourne Grammar's, so most see Trinity as a 'second best' to the 'Public Schools'. Almost a third of the boys who start at the school in the 1930s use it as a preparatory school for Scotch or Grammar, but its 'inferiority' in no way diminishes its commitment to 'Public School spirit'.[40]

The Depression has brought hardship to Trinity and its constituency. The school is still small—fewer than 300 boys will be on the roll this year—and many families are behind in their fees. The school is kept afloat by the energy and dedication of its headmaster, who has even been seen mowing the oval during the Christmas holidays.[41] The headmaster has been in harness since 1917, and his personality and passions dominate the school. Trinity was founded in 1903 by the vestry of Holy Trinity Church, Kew, as a parish grammar school, and it was the first new Anglican school since the establishment of Melbourne and Geelong Grammars. In 1934 it is still distinctively Anglican and parochial, and many clergymen send their sons there in preference to Melbourne Grammar. Vicarage families are often very poor, for some vicars have received almost no stipend from the collection plate since the Depression, and have been almost as dependent on charity as their parishoners.[42] The headmaster is a devout churchman, soon to be a lay canon of St Paul's Cathedral; but he is also a devoted student of the English language and its literature. The passages of the school year are all celebrated in a language steeped in the King James Version and the Book of Common Prayer. He reads poetry to the boys in morning assemblies, some of it modern stuff by a T. S. Eliot and somebody Auden; and he openly 'descends into tears' at beloved lines. He has an excellent voice which he delights in using, and he concludes each school year with a reading from the final chapter of Revelation:

> . . . and let him that heareth say, Come.
> And let him that is athirst, come. And whosoever
> will, let him take the water of life freely.[43]

Many of these callow suburban youths are moved, even though they laugh behind the headmaster's back and call him 'Grease' because of his

---

[40] See Appendix I, table 6; interview with *Richard Stanton*, 25 September 1990.
[41] Interviews with Dr Robert Trumble, 16 August 1990; and with Kelvin Emmett, 18 December 1990.
[42] Dorothea Cerutty, and interview with Ken Tolhurst, 21 November 1990.
[43] Trumble, *The School on the Hill*, p. 58.

'Uriah Heepish mannerisms'.[44]   One small boy in Form IV this year will learn Blake's *Jerusalem*, and half a century later will write a poem about that day in 1934:

> Blue covered books were set about the classroom,
> Jerusalem the object of our wonder,
> The words by Blake, the music Parry
> The learning short for boys of nine or ten,
> By lesson's end, the melody remembered,
> Chariot of fire, satanic mills,
> What can it mean? Our young minds ponder.
> With choral sweep and organ swelling
> The Hymn in great emotion welling
> Blake and Parry built between them
> Such a song of praise o'erwhelming
> *Con maestoso largamente*
> All the signatures of time
> Blend together in performance
> Everlastingly sublime.[45]

This boy is a singer, and in two years time he will be good enough to win a chorister's scholarship and join St Paul's Cathedral Choir. The St Paul's Choir boys have been at Trinity since 1929, and the subsidy they bring with them from the Archdiocese has helped the school survive the Depression. But for young boys it is a punishing routine: 'the conduct of the St Paul's Choir was a bloody tyranny'.[46] Every week-day morning they practise at the cathedral from 9 to 11, and then take the train to Kew. At 3.30, when the ordinary boys go home or play sport, the choristers return to the cathedral for more practice and then Evensong. Saturday is their only free day, but they do get home for lunch on Sundays. At school it's difficult for the 'choir scrags' also, for they don't play proper sport, only lacrosse among themselves. Even worse, many of them are 'common':

> I suspect that Dr A. E. Floyd [the cathedral organist] believed the quality of treble voices to be directly correlated with need. Those who had to sing for their supper sang sweetest and best and with a commitment to the long after-school hours and loss of weekend and holiday. The price of a private school education was indeed high, but none of us from the northern, western or southern suburbs complained until we were old enough for our voices to break and to think about other things we might have been missing.[47]

---

[44] Interview with James Austin, 12 and 13 September 1990.
[45] George Morcom, 'On Learning Jerusalem, 1934', unpublished MS. in possession of the author.
[46] Ken Tolhurst.
[47] Letter to author from Dr Max Kemp, 21 September 1990.

Not all find it difficult, and one whose father will be unemployed throughout his son's years at Trinity will thank the school for sticking to its motto of '*Viriliter Agite*' or 'Act Manfully': 'As I look back now, we got just as good a treatment from [the headmaster] as Bob Menzies' boy'.[48]

Bob Menzies is already one of Kew's most famous residents, and later this year he will be elected to federal parliament as the member for Kooyong. In 1960, at the height of his second prime ministership, he will be invited to write a foreword to a centenary history of Kew:

> I am, as you know, a reasonably bigoted Kew citizen, proud of the history of the City and delighted with its constant development. There are, no doubt, those who think Kew is a quiet corner of Greater Melbourne, and that this takes it out of the main stream of events. There could be no greater error. A quiet corner we may be, but the quietness is one which has nourished thoughtful people, good citizens and great schools. There is a charm about Kew which nothing can take away from it.[49]

There are, however, two Kews—no different in wealth, or lack of it, no different in thoughtfulness or good citizenship, but utterly opposed in religion. The two Kews operate in parallel, each providing a structure of identity and community from the cradle to the grave—and Beyond, although they disagree as to who will be admitted There. There is little need for Protestant Kew or Catholic Kew to have anything to do with each other, and mostly they don't. They rub shoulders every now and again, politely, but rarely do they connect. The Trinity boys officially enjoy cordial relations with the Xavier boys, whose magnificent Renaissance-style college overshadows theirs, but they know nothing of 'what goes on in there'.[50] Protestant distrust is fuelled by Catholic withdrawal from the secular and the hostile; Protestants speculate about secret practices and there are many for whom the rooting out of Papist perfidy provides an indispensable *frisson* to their otherwise quiet and charitable lives. Catholics are, of course, taught from childhood that since Protestants are outside the Church, they are 'full of sin'. There are many who have no friends and but few acquaintances of 'the other faith', but there has been more intermarriage than most would care to admit.[51] Middle-class Catholicism is more visible in Kew than in any other part of the heartland: Archbishop Mannix lives in the palatial Raheen in Studley Park Road, and two of Melbourne's leading Catholic schools declare their

[48] Interview with Walter Stone, 11 November 1990.
[49] R. G. Menzies, foreword to W. D. Vaughan, *Kew's Civic Century*.
[50] Interview with Keppel Henty-Wilson, 29 October 1990.
[51] Survey (see Appendix II): 'Was there any intermarriage in your extended family between Catholic and Protestant before 1940?' Yes: Scotch, 14%; Trinity, 15%; MLC, 17%; Genazzano, 48%. N/A: Scotch, 8%; Trinity, 5%; MLC, 13%; Genazzano, 14%.

presence from Kew's best hills. At the corner of Glenferrie and Cotham roads stands Sacred Heart Church, an 'anatomical dedication' according to the Aunt Polly of a mischievous local Scotch boy:

> The bravest thing we could do was to run into Sacred Heart Church and dip our fingers in the holy water. Wet hands were the required proof. Though we never went right inside the church itself, our hearts pounded with fear that a black apparition might unexpectedly block our exit.
>
> One day we deposited frogs in the holy water stoups and ran away breathlessly as some innocent intercessor, blessing herself on leaving, was confronted by a pop-eyed amphibian.[52]

The 69 tram has now reached its terminus at Cotham Road and unloaded nearly all the college boys and girls it has collected since it left St Kilda beach an hour ago. The only ones left are a small number of girls, very quiet and ladylike, in navy blue but with a stylish, wide hat band that adds a touch of elegance. Their brothers, wearing the 'devil's colours', got off at Wellington Street with the Trinity boys. The sisters perhaps cast a longing glance at Lilley's milk bar which they are forbidden to enter (for in milk bars lurk confectionery and boys), and cross Cotham Road to catch the tram going east. Cotham Road is a handsome thoroughfare, lined with Victorian and Edwardian villas to match Malvern's Finch Street. In six years time, at the beginning of the war, a young English-woman will also make this journey down Cotham Road. Her husband is in the British Colonial Service as a prison officer in Singapore, and she has come to Melbourne to find a boarding school for her young daughter. They have investigated MLC and PLC and found neither welcoming, for even though they are a Protestant family, the daughter has had a happy time at a multiracial Catholic school in Singapore. Then:

> My mother happened to be visiting St George's Hospital in Cotham Road one day with my aunt, and they passed this impressive-looking fence with a high cypress hedge, and my mother said,
> —What's that? And my aunt said,
> —That's a toffy convent.
> —Well, we'll go and have a look at it.
> —You'll never be able to afford that Win, forget it.
> —Oh, I'll just go and have a look.
>
> So she walked up the massive long drive and wondered if she'd ever get to the front door. She was ushered into the parlour and this lovely, lovely nun, Mother Winifred Dando, came and spoke to her. Mother told her she was going back to Malaya and she needed to put me into a

---

[52] James Murray, *The Paradise Tree*, pp. 137–9.

boarding school, but somewhere where I was happy. I was eight at the time. Mother Winifred said, 'My dear, bring Thelma up, and if she likes the school, she is to come'. There was no mention of fees at that stage.

A couple of weeks later I came and they brought down this tiny little tot, Marie Mahony, who was the youngest boarder they'd ever had. She started boarding at four because her mother had rheumatoid arthritis. Marie showed me over the convent—she showed me the refectory, the dormitories, the bathrooms, the class rooms and the garden—which was another thing I loved. We had the boarders' garden—a little plot where we used to grow flowers, and they had these little gnomie things and malformed jugs we used to do in pottery. And I thought—oh, this is lovely. It was a gentle atmosphere. And that's how I went.[53]

She will stay at the 'toffy convent' right through the war, with her mother working in Melbourne and her father a prisoner of war in the Changi prison where once he had been the gaoler. And her fees will never rise beyond the junior boarder rate.

Genazzano Convent commands the best site in Kew, a brick Gothic bastion overlooking formal gardens, playing fields and a rough private park, and protected from prying Protestant eyes by the hedge. It looks European, not British, and that is intentional. It is one of the few Melbourne schools to be designed by a great Australian architect, and in William Wardell, the creator of St Patrick's Cathedral, the nuns of the Faithful Companions of Jesus (FCJ) found one who could build them a convent redolent of the Order's aristocratic and French origins. Wardell's magnificent conception has been only half realized, however, for the building was commenced in 1890, just before the nuns, like everybody else, lost all their money in the 1890s depression. The Faithful Companions of Jesus is a comparatively recent order, coming 'to birth in the heart of the foundress, Marie Madeleine, Madame D'Houet, on Holy Thursday in 1820'; and the nuns' habit retains the simple nineteenth-century widow's bonnet that Madame D'Houet wore.[54] The Faithful Companions of Jesus is entirely a teaching order, founded to educate both the daughters of gentlemen and the children of the poor, and in Victoria they are teaching working–class children in Richmond and country girls in Benalla. The Genazzano fathers are mostly gentlemen, better heeled and very much better educated than the Scotch, MLC and Trinity fathers. The money comes from the land, contracting and hotels; the education comes from the medical and legal professions.[55] Genazzano is unofficially the sister school of Xavier College, and from the time of the foundress,

[53] Interview with Thelma Squire, 15 November 1990: 'I was never to know or feel a charity child'.
[54] Sr Maria Bell FCJ, *And the Spirit Lingers . . . Genazzano . . . One Hundred Years, 1889–1989*, pp. 18–19; Sr M. Clare O'Connor FCJ, *The Sisters Faithful Companions of Jesus in Australia*, pp. 139–45.
[55] See Appendix II, table 4b: Fathers' Occupations at the age of Fifty.

the FCJs have drawn deeply on Jesuit spirituality. The Jesuits are their confessors, and the religious, familial and educational ties with the Society of Jesus extend to the university and beyond. Despite all this, Genazzano is ranked only third on the social ladder of Catholic girls' schools, and is considered 'not as wealthy as Mandeville, nor as aristocratic as Sacre Coeur'.[56] This is not a large Catholic ascendancy, however, for each convent school is very small, between them educating fewer girls than MLC does on its own. Catholic professional families congregate in Kew just so that their children may attend Xavier and Genazzano and, with large families intermarrying within a select and confined community, a social network of daunting complexity confers a rich sense of belonging and no privacy whatsoever. The Catholic settlement is densest in Studley Park Road around Raheen, and in one Genazzano-Xavier family, the task of conveying messages from Genazzano to Dr Mannix will be entrusted in turn to mother and daughter, and for each—thirty years apart—there will be cordial and fruitcake. Their world changes very little in these three decades; but that cannot be said for the subsequent thirty years.[57]

By now, 1934, the Faithful Companions of Jesus is an Australian community, but the French traditions are not lost. French hymns are sung and French prayers are uttered, and in the boarding school, 'we had coffee and rolls for breakfast and we had to speak French at the table—pretty terrible French, I can tell you,—'Passez-moi le butter'.[58] The school plays an exotic French version of rounders called 'Catte', but interschool competition is restricted to the few other convents which indulge in Continental sports.The Irish Australians find it enchanting, and they fall in love with the starched white linen, the marble, the high-polished floors, the paintings, the candles and the shining brass. The excitement of each feast day is to see what the colours of the flowers on the altar will be. All the domestic labour to create this daily beauty is carried out by lay sisters—nuns who do not teach and who may not advance to positions of authority within the Order, but who are suited to a contemplative life. They cook and scour and polish, sweat drenching their black serge in the summer heat. They converse with no one, for the Order holds dear its rule of silence and the nuns may speak only about their duties and with permission.[59] Their spiritual self-discipline is ferocious, but with the girls they are gentle, if reserved, and most girls feel cherished. One will later recall only one rebuke in all her time at the school, 'Please don't put your elbows on the desks—it does so spoil them for ballgowns'.[60] The girls,

[56] Bell, *And the Spirit Lingers*, pp. 19 and 106; interview with *Elinor Doyle*, 20 September 1988.
[57] *Elinor Doyle*.
[58] Interview with Mary Thompson, 24 October 1990; and interview with *Helen Browne*, 24 November 1990.
[59] *Helen Browne*.
[60] Mary Thompson.

especially the boarders, are secular members of the religious community rather than mere students; and they are withdrawn from the world while the nuns shape a faith in them which will withstand the temptations and shocks that adult flesh is heir to. The convent has been dedicated from the beginning to the Virgin, and the name 'Genazzano' comes from a village near Rome where a painting of 'Our Lady of Good Counsel' hangs miraculously without earthly support. Many Old Girls make a pilgrimage to Genazzano, and some even poke their umbrellas up behind the painting to confirm its miraculousness. Two recent Genazzano girls have left for Brussels to enter the novitiate (as postulants awaiting their journey they were dubbed 'Brussel sprouts'). More than half a century later they will recall the ideals of the school put before them on their first day: 'We were to be good Catholics (we'd say Christians now); we were to be ladies and finally we were to be students, but that was definitely the lowest category'.[61]

In 1934, however, the school and the order are poised to enter a new phase of spiritual life. At Genazzano there is a new mistress of studies—she is a rigorous scholar and will be remembered as 'an exceptional religious'.[62] The school is becoming stricter and more academic, and along with the wider Catholic community, affected by new currents and their oppositions moving through the Church. This year the Catholic Church will mount a National Eucharistic Congress to coincide with the centenary of the founding of Melbourne. It will bring to Australian Catholicism the first call for Catholic Action, a new role in the Church for the laity and the seedbed of the transformations that lie far ahead in Vatican II. At Genazzano there will be a garden party to honour the papal legate, Cardinal MacRory, hosted by a committee of fathers because the nuns, unlike those at Sacre Coeur, will not break their rules of silence and enclosure, even for a papal legate.[63] In 1941 the Irish novelist Kate O'Brien will publish in London *The Land of Spices,* a thinly disguised depiction of the Faithful Companions of Jesus and their legendary Irish convent, Laurel Hill. It will cut close to the bone:

But—*Mère Générale* loved the Order as she found it and as she proposed, quixotically, to have it remain. She loved its stiff, polite and predominantly pious tradition. It may be that she foresaw somewhat the twentieth century assault of 'progress', guessed at new fevers of theory and experiment, in nationalism, in education, in social science, which, threatening the institutions of the Church with extinction, might force them in self-defence to unpredictable adaptations and vulgarities. Perhaps she foresaw that the awkward, finicky *bourgeois* instrument forged by an eighteenth century lady

---

[61] Interview with Sister Anthony Buckley FCS and with Sister Dolores Kirby FCS, 1 September 1989.
[62] *Helen Browne.*
[63] Rev. J. M. Murphy SJ and Rev. F. Moynihan, eds, *The National Eucharistic Congress,* p. 280.

for the pious training of girls throughout the world would soon be made to seem, by the nimble and the expeditious, an absurd and deplorable curio. Wrongly or rightly, *Mère Générale* would hold these theorists to be short-sighted fools, and would desire *La Compagnie de la Sainte Famille* to hold its prim, Christian way, as long as possible, amid the lures of progress. '*La pudeur et la politesse, mes Enfants*'. Already *Mère Générale* and had seen some forward-marchers smile at those two amusing words—and had expressed herself aghast at the risks which she saw the informed preparing to take with human nature.[64]

It will be uncannily, though subtly, prophetic. The nuns will be forbidden to read it 'because there is a bad page in it';[65] the few girls who do can scarcely guess at the changes in the Church and in society which will visit their generation. The girls who pass through the convent door on this first day of school for 1934, are still secure in a world where everyone they know believes in Heaven, and almost everyone in Hell. But time is against them. In October, Judge Alf Foster in a General Sessions case will question a boy to make sure that he understands the taking of the oath. The boys replies that if he lies, he knows he will go to Hell. Judge Foster, the rationalist, will have none of that talk in his court: 'Do not believe in it sonny. There is no hell. It is a shame that children should be taught such things'.[66]

This book is a biography of that generation of college boys and girls on their way to school in 1934. It is the story of their making as individuals, as middle-class men and women, as believers and doubters, as Australians; it is the story of the historical forces and the families, churches, schools and society that worked to shape them. It is the story of how they fared; and how, in turn, they shaped the country they inherited and the genera-tions that succeeded them. It is the story, therefore, of their journeyings—both of the body and the mind—and of the cultural baggage they set out with and which they accumulated on the way. And we are drawn, as they are themselves, to those pathways which came upon stony ground, where the going became difficult, for it is in the challenges of life that we are are tested and judged and ultimately forged. Finally, it is a story that they will in part tell for themselves, for this book is not so much a history as a meditation—upon life and upon this country as it is remembered by some particular people from a particular place.

---

[64] pp. 56–7.
[65] Remark remembered by *Elinor Doyle*.
[66] Constance Larmour, *Labor Judge, the Life and Times of Judge Alfred Foster*, p. 127.

2

Inheritances
1850–1919

Inheritances
1850–1919

Memory

When this generation of college boys and girls were born in the first years of peace after the 'war to end all wars', European settlement in Victoria was not yet a century old. The gold rush was just within living memory, and everywhere among old people, soft brogues and flat vowels bespoke the pioneering past. The great adventure of emigration and survival in a new land was still very close—in fact close enough to be a commonplace; and as the old people died, too often their stories went with them. Some grandchildren were interested, however, as Winsome Walklate was:

> I always enjoyed asking questions and perhaps it was not quite polite, but it wasn't that I was being curious—I was interested and I wanted to get the feel of the past. I knew that you didn't just pop into the world as a single person. I was always very conscious of the fact that you represent so much that is past in thought and it's passed on. And I found my granny (who didn't die until I was eight) and her sisters very interesting women. They were so British. I once asked my great aunt, 'What am I?', and she looked at me for a while and thought about it—'You're British dear'.[1]

The tales taught identity—the dual identity of a colonial society and, if later generations sometimes deplored those who spoke of Britain as 'Home', they failed to understand that for many it was indeed 'Home'. *Veronica Keogh*'s English granny never looked back, however:

> I remember Granny saying to me, 'I never regretted coming out and I never wanted to go back. And I never had any fear coming out on a sailing ship'. And Auntie Annie used to talk about the captain on the

[1] Interview with Winsome Walklate, 11 December 1989.

sailing ship finding her wandering about during a storm and asking, 'Have you had your burgoo?' [porridge]. And how in rough weather the kids used to love to sit on one side of the dining room floor and slide to the other. The day they arrived, Annie was holding my mother (who was one) and my mother broke her arm on the railings. Then they all went down with measles, so they rented a room in Port Melbourne and they were all on the floor with measles.[2]

Kate Morgan's daddy came out from Ireland aged twenty-three: 'I came to Australia in 1881, and I never seen a man I'd seen before', poetically recording the awful aloneness of it.[3] And *Monica O'Farrell* was acutely affected by her great-grandfather who was also very Irish:

He told stories of seeing men stood up against walls and shot. He had a wonderful library—he must have been a man of some learning. He was blind when I knew him, but he still had an Edwardian goatee which my mother used to trim. He was a beautiful man.[4]

The pioneers who succeeded were often deeply impressive human beings. Archie Crow's grandparents came out from Glasgow in the 1890s. Landing with £5 in his pocket, one grandfather survived the 1890s depression and founded first a large building firm and, later, a porcelain insulator factory for those of his sons who returned from World War I. Archie's father was of the same mould, but he was only one of many strong characters on the Williamstown Council:

They were a very fine body of people on the council, and I think that was characteristic of the day too—men of great character, quite apart from the sea captains who most certainly were. It was character-building, establishing themselves in a strange land. Everything was different about it—especially for the women, especially up-country. One woman many years ago spoke to me of her grandmother who'd come out from a castle in Scotland and she lived in a little humpy with a corrugated iron roof up in the centre, with the sand hissing over the top. And the women who saw their menfolk go out in the morning and perhaps never come back, or come hanging from the stirrup.

Grandfather—he was a strong person. He was wise, he was kindly; and one of the things he was remembered for was the help he gave to British migrants coming out to this country, finding them jobs and getting them established. I was eight when he died and I remember the funeral cortege going out to the Footscray General Cemetery—it was about a mile long. I have very kindly memories of him and the family, and of the atmosphere in the home and the people who dropped in.[5]

---

[2] Interview with *Veronica Keogh*, 13 November 1989.
[3] Interview with Kate Morgan, 11 and 13 October 1989.
[4] Interview with *Monica O'Farrell*, 26 November 1990.
[5] Interview with Archie Crow, 5 July 1990.

Few immigrants did so well; in fact for some the great adventure concluded in a loss of gentility. *Philip Hardwicke*'s grandfather came from a London family which owned a substantial hat business, but he had poor health and was sent to New Zealand under the care of a doctor. On board ship, he fell in love with a young lady who played the squeezebox and they married on landfall; whereupon the family cut him off and ordered the doctor back to England. Eventually they made their way to Melbourne, 'and went through a series of hatting businesses and residences—they shifted every twelve months just about—the Fitzroy area and East Kilda'. By the time *Philip* won his scholarship to private school, the *Hardwickes* had been outwardly working class for two generations and his father was off work:

> It's odd. My father's father came from a presumably wealthy London family and they were in a way gentlefolk. My father had a library—a beautiful, elaborate bookcase with really a wide selection of books. Looking back, it was a remarkably good, diverse selection. He had read them, and he used to read the newspaper and Hansard from cover to cover. We were allowed to browse in the library and we picked up literature through reading those books.
>
> My mother was more working class, even though her father was self-employed, because she had worked as a young woman at sewing. Her sister had also worked in a sewing establishment, but she married someone who became a wealthy man, so we had a connection with them too.
>
> We were a mixture because Dad was politically Labor, but we had this connection with middle-class Malvern people and this inheritance of the people in London.[6]

If the Melbourne middle class of the 1920s had a short history, it was none the less both full and troubled. This generation of college boys and girls inherited a metropolitan society which was complex, strained, prejudiced and divided. And if there were colonial achievements to trumpet, there were also embarrassments to conceal, and the silences in family lore could be telling. The libraries today are full of people searching for their lost family histories, and the paradox is that there must have been so many stories to tell—tales of perilous voyages around the rim of the world before the 'roaring forties'; epics of fire and flood; romances of parted and reunited lovers; sagas of fortunes won and lost—yet there are many who have no idea of why their ancestors came ten thousand miles. In some cases the stories fell victim to lower-class diffidence; in many others the daily round of making livings and futures blotted out the past; and there were those who needed to forget. When Winsome Walklate rediscovered her family history she found a convict, John Wolfe Walklate,

---

[6] Interview with *Philip Hardwicke*, 24 August 1990.

who was already a Methodist lay preacher when he was found guilty of
stealing a glass jug and tumblers from his employer and was transported to
Van Diemen's Land.[7] The descendants of English and Scottish convicts
lacked the nationalist legends which were the Irish salve to shame. In the
family of Sister Anthony Buckley FCJ, convict ancestry was remembered
and understood: 'My great-grandfather came to Australia at His Majesty's
expense, sent out by the Essex Assizes for a public house brawl; and because he was an R.C. he got a life sentence'.[8] Betty Blay has traced her
father's English Protestant family from two convicts in Van Diemen's
Land and followed their 'quiet rise into the lower middle class'. They
were saddlers and shoemakers, but by 1890 her grandparents had moved
to Melbourne and secured their new respectability by owning a sweet
shop in Toorak Road, South Yarra. There her grandmother—'Mater'—
ruled her unmarried offspring mercilessly: 'She was really a dreadful old
woman, and yet she was very intelligent; she should never have married—
she married to get away from the family'. 'Mater' had no religion except
that she hated Catholics, and she loved no one other than Betty's father.[9]

What was being concealed more often was not shame so much as
ordinariness. The families which had risen from rags to riches had a dramatic story and were usually proud of it. But far more numerous were
those who, once the great adventure of emigration was over, slipped into
obscurity and the steady disciplines of suburban respectability. Betty
Blay's family was typical:

> Dad was a clerk and a very good clerk. They were definitely lower
> middle class. You never aspired to anything higher, you never married
> out of your class—that was foolish. In fact Mum's family thought her
> sister Nellie was foolish to have married a commercial traveller because he
> was just a little bit more classy.
>
> My parents were very respectable. It was a matter of doing the right
> thing—always well groomed. As soon as you got up in the morning, you
> had to clear your lounge-room, because if you had visitors, you could
> shut the bedroom door. But you had to make the bed too.
>
> They drank but they drank 'pale'. Women liked a little glass of sherry
> or port wine. The youngest boy was the biggest drinker, but with most of
> them drink was out. Aunt Annie's Irish husband liked a drink—loved
> wakes—a real gent but hopeless with money and I can remember Annie
> covering up for him when he was snoring away.
>
> Part of being respectable was always looking clean, looking nice. Very
> modest—I never saw my mother dressing although I shared a room with
> her for sixteen years. She always dressed under her nightie and she

---

[7] Winsome E. Matenson, *Sullivan Bay and Beyond: A Short History of Two Port Phillip Bay First Families and Some of their Descendants*.
[8] Interview with Sr Anthony Buckley FCJ, 1 September 1989.
[9] Interview with Betty Blay, 7 March 1988.

emerged with her corsets and petticoats on, ready to put on her dress.

Once you were married, you'd made your bed and you had to lie in it. There was never any thought of divorce and yet there were a number of unhappy marriages in the family—you stuck by your man. You never let him go on the pension while you could still work—that was a form of respectability.

One of my aunts got pregnant when she was unmarried and told her Ma:

—I've got news for you—I'm pregnant.

—Who's the man? Tell him I want to see him . . .

—Will you marry her?

—No, not unless she marries me in a Catholic church.

—Oh we'll have none of that. Give me £25 for an abortion.

And it was done in two days by somebody she knew.

If many of the family histories were forgotten or refashioned, it did not rob them of their power. This generation of college boys and girls were, as we all are, both products and captives of their pasts and, as they grew up and created their own histories, they took both the remembered and the hidden past with them.

Seekers and Saints: 1850–1870

The solid foundation of the Melbourne middle class came with gold—not in the fortunes made by diggers, but rather in the vast migration and the attendant economic activities that it enticed to the Colony of Victoria. Between 1851 and 1861 more than half a million men and women arrived in Victoria, and among the transients and the adventurers, the old colonials, the Americans and the Chinese, there were a quarter of a million permanent settlers from the United Kingdom. They had enough money to pay their way; or if they were assisted, they could afford the greater outlays required for the long voyage to Australia. The destitute went to America, and the only potato famine victims to reach Victoria were Scots from the Highlands and Islands who were imported to replace the shepherds who had run off to the diggings. The new settlers were unusually literate, making Victoria briefly the most educated society of the Empire, and they brought with them yearnings for the wealth and significance that was beyond their reach in the Old Country. A common prejudice claimed that the only people who went to Australia were 'adventurers, invalids and failures' and it was true in part.[10]

---

[10] Donna Hellier, ' "The Humblies": Scottish Highland Emigration to nineteenth century Victoria' in Patricia Grimshaw, Chris McConville and Ellen McEwen, *Families in Colonial Australia*, p. 11; John Wischer, ed., *The Presbyterians of Toorak, A Centenary History of the Toorak Presbyterian Church, 1876–1976*, p. 36.

They came from a society that was divided not only by class, religion and ethnicity, but also by the gulf between the respectable and the rough. You could be rich and a rogue and few would want to know you; you could be poor but honest and find yourself kept on in the slack season and entrusted with responsibility—perhaps. Much was made by moralists and preachers of the rewards in this world of sobriety, cleanliness, thrift, civility, reliability and manly independence: 'self-help'—they insisted—was the only honourable help. Yet one of the great dynamic forces of nineteenth century society was the frustration of the poor but honest: they kept the rules of respectability, hard as those rules were, but still the world failed to grant them the security they deserved and the respect they craved.

The poor but honest were ripe for religion and radicalism, and their energy and imagination fuelled the explosion of religiosity in the early nineteenth century and powered the secular movements which worked to better life on earth.[11] But they also filled the emigrant ships to the new worlds to the west and to the south. Edward Gibbon Wakefield called them 'the anxious class' and recognized their suitability as colonists: they had trade or clerical skills, they were thrifty, they were law-abiding, but they were also aggrieved just enough to have an edge of desperation to their ambitions.[12] Emigration offered the chance to reinvent themselves, to become somebodies in a new land where no one knew they had once been nobodies: 'labouring people, who would be unpretending people at home, assume such airs here', complained an impoverished governess of Sydney in 1868, 'they call each other Mr and Mrs so and so, and speak of each other as ladies and gentlemen'.[13]

The anxious class had reason to be so. In good times their regular earnings gave their lives stability and order, and they appeared far removed from the condition of the 'rough', casual poor who lived from day to day, even from hour to hour. But one bad winter could change everything. If a clerk or a tradesman missed weeks or months of work, his savings or his Friendly Society could not keep him out of debt for long, and once his clothes became shabby, he was immediately under suspicion: was he drinking? was he gambling? was he losing his self-respect? Respectability was hard on men, for it depended on their being prepared to tolerate decades of tedious and exhausting work without the relief of the pub or the diversions of sin. It was an unforgiving society and they could not afford to make mistakes either at work or in leisure. *Ron Pearson*'s bank manager father once showed him a nineteenth-century ledger where a clerk had made an error: the unfortunate's slip was memo-

[11] Janet McCalman, Respectability and Working-class Politics in Victorian London.
[12] Keith Sinclair, *A History of New Zealand*, p. 99.
[13] Patricia Clarke, *The Governesses: Letters from the Colonies, 1862–1882*, p. 100.

rialized by being circled in red ink, with the name of the perpetrator, the date and the signatures of the clerk and the manager.[14] The capital the respectable man had to guard and invest wisely was in fact himself: it was social capital, not financial. And under the direction of his wife, domestic order, personal cleanliness and obedient children proclaimed the respectable man's good character—his social capital—to the watching world. There was little margin for error.

And so they had great hopes of Australia. But in reviewing that gold rush generation, Geoffrey Serle has argued that just as significant as the talents and energy they brought to Victoria is the likelihood that most of them did nowhere near as well as they had hoped. It was the already established colonists who were on hand to take advantage of the easy alluvial finds and to profit from the new immigrants' need for provisions, accommodation and alcohol.[15] The common experience of the 1850s and 1860s arrivals was dislocation, disappointment and resignation to the certainty that ahead lay only more hard work, frustration and impecuniosity. But the anxieties and disappointments of class and caste were only part of the cultural baggage they brought with them. If the new colonists came as men and women, rich, middling or poor, they also came as English, Scots and Irish, and their first point of identity was ethnic before it was social. And symbiotically attached to ethnic identity was religion.

In the melting pot of an immigrant society, organized religion became the readiest means of bonding the respectable, and thus was born the distinctive role of the Australian churches in the preservation of ethnic loyalties and in the instilling of division.[16] This did not mean that the new Australians were a notably religious people. Church-going in the colonies remained, as it was in the Old Country, a mark of gentility and, being religious was not just the possession and enrichment of a spiritual life, it was also integral to the social performance of being serious-minded and responsible. English and Scottish Dissenters came in their droves to the gold rush, increasing in the gold decade almost three times as fast as those who adhered to the Church of England.[17] And if there was one church which stood above all others on the Ballarat Flat and among the deep lead miners of Bendigo, it was the Methodists. Methodism travelled well. Its theology was poetically transcribed in its hymn book, and its system of lay preachers and class meetings needed no church or ordained clergy. The class meeting defined church members as distinct from mere church attenders, and members met weekly, with perhaps ten others to pray, to confess their sins and to find guidance and support for the leading of a

[14] Interview with Ron Pearson, 3 September 1990.
[15] Geoffrey Serle, The Golden Age, pp. 374–5.
[16] David Hilliard, 'God in the Suburbs: the Religious Culture of the Australian Suburbs in the 1950s', Australian Historical Studies, no. 97, October 1991, pp. 401–2.
[17] Hugh Jackson, Churches and People in Australia and New Zealand, 1860–1930, pp. 5–15 and 21.

Christian life. It taught that all men and women—in contrast to the Calvinists' elect—could be saved, and in the lush diction of eighteenth-century poetry, it sang of a passionate personal relationship with Christ:

> Thou Shepherd of Israel, and mine,
> The joy and desire of my heart,
> For closer communion I pine,
> I long to reside where Thou art:
> The pasture I languish to find
> Where all, who their Shepherd obey,
> Are fed on Thy bosom reclined,
> And screened from the heat of the day.

and of the believer, plucked from a maelstrom of sin by the power of Christ's love:

> To the haven of Thy breast,
> O Son of Man, I fly;
> Be my refuge and my rest,
> For O the storm is high!
> Save me from the furious blast,
> A covert from the tempest be;
> Hide me, Jesus, till o'er past
> The storm of sin I see.

It was perfect for pioneers. It preached the disciplines of self-care and hard work which made the difference between success and failure. It advocated abstinence in a society soaked in alcohol, and where teetotalism was one of the few ways a man or woman could exercise some control over bodily and mental health. Its sense of community and its vivid evocation of a personal Saviour protected the immigrant and the pioneer against the terrible loneliness of the bush. But it also gave people practical skills, for its class meetings and lay preaching trained men and women in organization, literacy and confident speech. Above all, it provided a schema for daily living, suffusing the believer with spiritual power; and its great historical moment was to be on the gold diggings. Mr James Wood was already established as a timber merchant in Geelong when he was called to join a party of 'Christian companions' on the flat at Ballarat, where 'these good men, and true, held open air services near their own camp, and also in other parts of the diggings, with the substantial results of checking Sabbath breaking and open immorality; and it is hoped, bringing some sinners acquainted with Christ as a personal Saviour'.[18]

Thus they withstood the temptations and backsliding of the diggings and when disappointed miners turned to shopkeeping and small farming,

[18] Thomas Williams, *Memoir of Mr James Wood*, p. 51.

the Methodists were often the first to erect a place of worship in the new settlements and towns, establishing themselves in Victoria as the 'religion of the bush'.[19] Other Protestants found themselves attending Methodist services in the absence of their own, and Sir Robert Menzies' family was one of many where Methodism blended with Presbyterian origins. The gold fields and the new hamlets were still relatively free of ordained clergy, and in their absence, sectarianism fell victim to the camaraderie of the frontier, as Catholics and Protestants worked together in the 1850s and 1860s to build towns and communities. Catholic publicans made donations towards the building of chapels and churches, and Methodists and Presbyterian shopkeepers and farmers returned the compliment. Even more alarming to the clergy was the eagerness of Catholics and Protestants to marry each other. Irish immigration in the 1850s had consisted of single men and women, who had quickly melted into the wider community.[20] Irish girls showed a distinct preference for Protestant husbands with good prospects, but Irish men also captured Protestant hearts, as happened with Sister Anthony Buckley's grandparents:

> Grandfather Moore married Jeannie McCreith who was born in Australia (I think) but whose parents were definitely Scotch. She was Scotch Presbyterian and she stayed Scotch Presbyterian right to the end of her days. She went to church *every* Sunday and you didn't have high jinks on Sunday either—it wasn't done. There were some on one occasion, but she got such a fright and everyone got upset about it and it didn't happen again. The boys, home from Xavier, had a tin tray and they came down the stairs on the tin tray and it nearly frightened the wits out of her.
>
> She stuck to her religion, but she educated us in our faith.

The Methodists were themselves divided, for a gulf of class and temperament separated the legalistic and more urbane Wesleyan Methodists from their Cornish Bible Christian and Primitive Methodist brethren. The Cornish were not all respectable—they were notorious for picking fights with the Irish on the gold fields, and not a few gave way to the consolations of the bottle.[21] *Betty Thomas* has written of the Bible Christian inheritance, 'transported from the wilds of Cornwall by lay men and women and wandering preachers':

> The Bible Christians were more 'wild' than the legally-minded Wesleyans, who were prone to stress the advantages of formal schooling. The Bible Christians were more democratic, having been founded by lay participation

---

[19] Ross Terrill, *Australians: in Search of an Identity*, pp. 2–3.
[20] Jackson, *Churches and People*, pp. 35–6.
[21] Jim Faull, *The Cornish in Australia*, pp. 54–5.

as a major emphasis, and certainly in Cornwall having always included women preachers.

The inspiration of this and other 'founding streams' of Victorian Methodism was not education but 'blessed assurance', the doctrine that each individual received grace from God, and that this personal experience of salvation is the essential factor in building the new church. By the twentieth century it was conventionally agreed that education in the worldly sense is necessary—but *not sufficient*—and there was enough of the influence of the nineteenth century traditions still living and forceful in local congregations across the state, to give effect to a sentiment that schooling is part of the bureaucratic structure of the modern world and the modern church, and that it now has to be included in regulations for candidates for the ministry, but the REAL QUALIFICATIONS AND PRE-REQUISITES LIE ELSEWHERE AND ARE NOT OF THE WORLD.[22]

While *Betty*'s mother came from the Bible Christians, her father was Wesleyan Methodist, from a family linked with traders in Fiji and flawed by an aptitude for bankruptcy. The *Thomases* had a shop in Ballan and a string of unsuccessful small businesses. *Betty*'s grandmother at one stage opened a ribbon shop in Bendigo: 'she was a woman of great charm, but even her charm and the ample bosom drooping over the ribbons couldn't save that shop and they became bankrupt again'. There was no doubt, however, that in marrying a Bible Christian, her son had let the family down:

> I can still remember my grandmother walking into the house for the
> annual visit and saying, 'Ida, my dear, how lovely to be here'. And then
> she would say in that incomparably fruity tone which I realized afterwards
> was the Fiji accent, 'Of course I'll have a lovely time—it would be
> terrible if two Christian women couldn't get on together', and with a
> sinking feeling in my childish heart, I knew there would be a row before
> the end of the day, and of course there was. Instinctively I took my
> mother's part, and although I had a lot to say for myself, I felt all the time
> that she wasn't having a fair go.[23]

Betty's Bible Christian great grandmother had been in charge of the music for the congregation on the gold fields, leading the singing with the aid of a tuning fork, before the family took up a selection at Elmore. It was a closed but emotionally rich community. On Sundays they all went into town for church in the morning, Sunday school in the afternoon and church again at night, 'then they'd have to go home and feed the cows'. On the Sunday following the eucharist, many Methodists held love

---

[22] Manuscript in possession of the author.
[23] Interview with *Betty Thomas*, 28 July 1988.

feasts—the partaking of a simple meal of bread and water and where various members of the congregation would relate their religious experiences.
It was difficult not to become embattled, a community of godly people
beset on all sides by temptation and sin. There was much intermarriage
between the Cornish families: 'and you could see why—you couldn't
marry an Anglican, which was a class above you, and anyway you didn't
go to race meetings or the pub; and you certainly couldn't marry a
Catholic'. But the years of hard work and self-discipline paid off once the
superphosphate came, and *Betty*'s grandfather, being 'a good farmer who
of course wouldn't waste his money on riotous living', was able to sell up
and take his daughter to Camberwell and into urban Methodism. It was a
common family history. Gwen Garside, another old collegian from MLC,
testified:

> My grandfather came from Cornwall and took up land in Victoria when it
> was opened up. They were allotted too small an amount of land, which was
> purchased at £1 an acre and had to be cleared and fenced within a year, and
> so they lived in a tent. He started the first Methodist church in the area and
> he preached and his wife played the organ—portable, which they took
> with them. His daughters were taught painting and music which they later
> taught. My father in the late 1920s built another modern church in the country
> district. In those days everyone worked together. My father was an out-
> standing man—a councillor in the town for forty years.[24]

The paths to social improvement for these gold-fields Methodists
were primarily shopkeeping, small farming and night school. Ballarat and
Bendigo remained great centres of Methodism, and in the Ballarat
Eisteddfods that musical legacy lives on today. The Schools of Mines in
each city provided a ladder of opportunity, enabling clever young men
like *Gwenda Holtby*'s father to become engineers. And once there were
high schools and scholarships, the university was within reach. *Betty Thomas*'
father was the first boy from Ballan for eight years to pass the Merit Certificate and he went on to Bendigo High School. From there he won a
scholarship to Wesley College, with an 'implied scholarship to the university'; 'but his daddy goes bankrupt again, so what does good, honest, serious, responsible elder brother do? He goes back and gets a job on the
Bendigo Advertiser in daytime and studies accountancy at night. It took
him four years and he was propping up the family'. It was a noble act of
loyalty because bankruptcy brought expulsion from the Methodist
Church until the stewards were satisfied that the debts had been paid, and
it remains a source of bitterness that *Betty*'s father shouldered the blame
while another, richer partner was spared disgrace. *Betty*'s mother was

[24] Survey No. 437: MLC, born 1910, real estate agent, married, Methodist<agnostic.

clever at school also, but the family was too frightened of her getting into 'bad company' to permit her to go to Bendigo High School. She then won a scholarship to MLC and she was safely educated among fellow Methodists. Forbidden to learn typing ('the implication was that it was vulgar'), she became a teacher of singing and speech, and with her sister who taught music (as in Gwen Garside's family) 'they would travel around in a horse and buggy teaching these refinements to the farmers' children'.

And so Methodists began to make money as grocers and drapers, accountants and engineers, farmers and orchardists, teachers and bank managers. Methodists preferred to do business with other Methodists and the habits of intermarriage continued unabated in the city. But as they made money, their Methodism came under strain. *Betty Thomas* again:

> In fact, as you study the history of the Church, you find success brings respectability, and the more exciting—and I would say the more attractive attributes of spontaneity and praying before the Lord—these tend to be toned down in later years. But there were always Bible Christians who were respectable because they'd seen the Lord, but who were travelling around and maybe never had really good jobs. And the wandering preachers were in a way not respectable—there was always that tension.

The paradox was that Methodism was a recipe for worldly success—self-improvement of the soul inevitably flowed on to improvement of the whole man and woman. Thrift and self-discipline enabled Methodist shopkeepers to prosper while their careless competitors went to the wall; but Methodism needed fire—'See how great a flame aspires'—and gentility found that embarrassing. There had always been a double side to correct Methodist behaviour: the Wesleys had taught that godly people should be sober, restrained and methodical in everyday life; but in church, praising the Lord, they should be emotionally free. John Wesley was himself a gloriously happy man who bubbled with the joy of a personal Christ. Methodism depended on the believer having a conversion experience, of moments of transfiguration, and *Betty Thomas* has seen them: 'the ones who are transfigured like that—they look like *angels*'. Transfiguration needed innocence and unself-consciousness—qualities difficult to preserve in an urbane life—and the Rev. Dr A. H. Wood, one of the last of the truly great Methodist preachers, had no doubt that Methodism began its decline in the 1850s, 'as it became respectable'.[25] Singing became the only enduring medium of collective religious intensity in worship. *Betty Thomas* again:

> This transfiguration, when it comes, is from the hymns. Even now—I shouldn't be unfair—when you get the older men singing that lovely Welsh

---

[25] Interview with the Rev. Dr A. H. Wood, December 1988.

hymn. But I'm sure they'd be transfigured while they were singing, but they'd have had to go back to the farm, the grocer's shop. So music has the power to transfigure you and get you into a higher world, a better world, the world of the emotions, the world of feeling that God cares for you and is close to you and all that. Then you go back to your secular life, and I think that a lot of men believed that God was boss of the whole world and if you did your grocer's job honestly, He would care for you. My uncle who had a grocer's shop in Bendigo was a person who felt the reality of God all this life and I think a lot of men did then. But it involved a view of the world which put a high value on individual piety, on doing your duty and obviously on getting it straight and being comfortable with your conscience—'I can't do anything to solve the problems of the poor beyond generosity'—and I know they'd let people run up credit in hard times. But you wouldn't necessarily be a socialist because that's not a necessary part of being a Methodist for everybody. It is for some, but not for all.

John Wesley had predicted all this: 'religion must necessarily produce both industry and frugality, and these cannot produce but riches. But as riches increase, so will pride, anger and love of the world'; and as he observed the Methodist people doing just that, he confessed that 'although the form of religion remains, the spirit is swiftly vanishing away'.[26] Urban Methodism came to terms with its past by building legends, and idealized its Celtic brethren as 'true Methodists'—impressive but also quaint, and at a comfortable distance in both time and class. The Rev. Irving Benson wrote in 1935 of Victorian Methodism's seed-time:

> There were many Cornish and Irish miners aflame with the fire of Methodism, and by their frank and fearless piety they won a singular respect among wild and reckless men who abounded at the diggings. They maintained religious services in many a gully and on many a creek side, where on Sunday, the sound of singing, the voice of prayer and the proclamation of the Gospel was heard, and companies of rough, bearded, earth-stained diggers gathered round and shared in worship. Companies of Methodists held their classes and prayer meetings in each others' tents. There was a leavening influence amid the riot of gambling, drinking and moral havoc.[27]

There was a sense of loss and for a hundred years after there were longings that great revivals would re-ignite the flame of Methodism, but its historical moment had passed, even as its history as a great institutional church in Victoria was just beginning.

---

[26] E. P. Thompson, *The Making of the English Working Class*, p. 391.
[27] C. Irving Benson, *A Century of Victorian Methodism*, pp. 98–9.

The Greedy and the Good: 1870–1890

The gold-rush generation had been conspicuously fertile, and during the 1870s and 1880s their offspring were seeking jobs and a place to settle. The mining towns had little to offer, and the focus of economic growth and social energy turned to the metropolis. Melbourne presented the odd—and perilous—phenomenon in that urbanization preceded industrialization, and the economic engine house became the building of the city itself. The population of Melbourne grew from 283 000 or 33 per cent of the colony's population in 1881, to 491 000 or 43 per cent in 1891, and the explosion in building was extraordinary. Residential investment almost doubled between 1883 and 1888, and more than half the estimated private capital formed in the city was absorbed just in building houses. At the peak in 1889–90 it rose to 70 per cent. The amount of trees felled and sawn, of bricks made and laid, of mortar mixed and spread, of timber turned and fashioned, of decorative iron lace cast, of slates cut and of leadlight windows assembled, was breathtaking. It was in those twenty years that Melbourne was given an extent and physical fabric that endured until the 1950s. Even today the vision and grandeur of 'Marvellous Melbourne' distinguishes the city: most of its public buildings, the theatres, the two cathedrals, are creations—even if left unfinished—of the 1870s and 1880s; so too are the suburbs—as far north as Essendon; as far west as Footscray, even Sunshine; as far south as Brighton and (incredibly) as far east as Ringwood. When the Rev. E. H. Sugden arrived from England in 1886 to become Master of the Methodists' new university college, he was dazzled: 'The city is enormous and as big in extent as Paris', he wrote home; and he climbed to the top of the Exhibition Building so that he could survey the whole city:

> It lies flat so that you can see it all, and the view is most impressive. In front, the sea; behind, the Dandenong Hills; and all around as far as the eye could reach, the city. When we remember that fifty years ago this was an uninhabited marsh, we feel with truthful James, 'Is this what they seems or is visions about?'. . .I don't think that people at home have the least idea of its magnificence and extent. It's a world wonder.[28]

In less than a lifetime, the European invaders had made one of the great cities of the nineteenth-century world.

But even more significant than the built environment was the complex metropolitan society those edifices housed and served. Graeme Davison's *The Rise and Fall of Marvellous Melbourne* wonderfully traces the

---

[28] Mary Florence Sugden, *Edward H. Sugden*, p. 22.

expansion of business, the organization of trades, the growth of the administrative classes, the formalization and development of the professions and the coming to power of a confident bourgeoisie. In all aspects of public and private life, institutions responded to the expanding need for organization, for the dissemination of knowledge and culture, for the bonding of peers, for entertainment and social intercourse. And there was a lot of money about waiting to be spent. It had come first from the profits of the golden decade, from the capital amassed not by miners so much as by shopkeepers and publicans and merchants. Then, as the boom gathered momentum, in came the little people—the skilled workmen, the small shopkeepers, the growing army of commercial and government clerks. The rising real incomes of the early 1880s saw deposits in savings banks and Post Office savings banks treble both in the number of accounts and in the value of the deposits. But the flood of capital which financed the crowning madness came from Britain, as the Victorian Government, the municipalities, the pastoral and mining companies, building societies and land finance companies offered foreign investors apparently safe returns at unusually high rates of interest. From the middle of the 1880s, foreign capital was imported into Victoria on a scale never matched again until our own times a century later. And as in the 1980s, the boom was made possible not just by the greed of the lenders, but also by the greed of the borrowers. J. K. Galbraith sees the origin of all great booms and busts as the delusion suffered by ordinary people that they are 'pre-destined by luck, an unbeatable system, divine power, access to inside information, or exceptional financial acumen to become rich without work'. For Geoffrey Serle the chaotic morals of the gold rush, the corruption of the selection acts in the 1860s, 'even the common practice of presenting fake invoices to the Customs officers which a protective system cultivated' all encouraged a 'permissive commercial ethic'. In the land boom was the pot of gold for which so many had emigrated in the 1850s, but which had so far eluded them. Now, it seemed, it was theirs if they were bold enough to speculate.[29]

And they were. In 1891 there were sixty-five 'banks' in Australia, and three stock exchanges in Melbourne alone, but also in the speculative swim were building societies, land investment companies and mortgage banks. Henry Gyles Turner, historian and manager of the Commercial Bank of Australia, later described them as the 'swarm of land-jobbing, financial and mortgage agencies and property investment companies, which by the misleading use of the word "bank", made a large haul of borrowed wealth, and upset all business calculations by their prodigal

---

[29] Graeme Davison, *The Rise and Fall of Marvellous Melbourne*, passim; J. K. Galbraith, *The Great Crash, 1929*, p. 13; Geoffrey Serle, *The Rush to be Rich*, p. 271; this brief account of the Land Boom owes much to Serle's.

expenditure of it'. But this was a judgement in retrospect; the banks did not want to be left out of the 'rush to be rich' and so, in competition, they had begun making advances on the security of urban land—thereby breaking with established British practice. Sir Matthew Davies' Mercantile Bank, James Munro's Federal Bank and Gyles Turner's own Commercial Bank were equally prodigal in imploring their customers to take out loans. So the respectables and the small savers, who once kept their nest-eggs in the savings banks, joined the speculators and the crooks in the intoxicating pursuit of wealth without work. The Rev. Dr W. H. Fitchett was only one of many Nonconformists—both lay and clerical—who persuaded themselves that speculation did not constitute a sophisticated form of gambling. By late 1888 speculation had moved from shares to land. The market value of suburban land rose five, ten, twenty times in five years, and there are blocks of land in Hawthorn which have never since regained the relative value they achieved at the height of the land boom a hundred years ago. Land came to change hands so rapidly that sometimes there was a chain of four or five vendors between the still unpaid holder of the title and the latest purchaser. Wealth had become fantasy. In Michael Cannon's memorable words: 'the big speculators were selling to the medium speculators and the medium speculators were selling to the small speculators, and madness was in the air'. 1888 was dubbed 'that insane, miraculous year' and Serle estimates that the extent of small investment was such that possibly every third man in Melbourne bought a block of suburban land. By 1904 Gyles Turner remembered with pain the speculative fever which had infected the city: 'The talk of the streets, the clubs, the trains, the luncheon rooms and the dinner-tables centred round the rise or fall of stocks, the chances of subdivision sales, or the wonderful luck that had followed the operation of divers well-known leaders in the arena of competitive finance'. And as it got madder, the trade deficit ballooned, so that in 1889 exports were barely half the value of imports, and much of that was imported capital.[30]

Fantasy money paid for fantasy living. The mansions along the Toorak ridge and those surveying the rest of the metropolis from its best hills appalled the retired banker who once had lent money to some of their builders:

An immense sum was spent during that decade on the internal embellishment of splendid mansions, many of which passed in a few years into the hands of mortgagees for less than half their cost, and were unsaleable at that. Liveried indoor servants, hitherto almost unknown beyond portals of Government House, were soon common enough to be taken for granted. Entertainments were devised on a costly scale, armorial bearings were discovered and displayed, and men whose market value had been but a few

---

[30] Serle, pp. 251–2; Michael Cannon, *The Land Boomers*, p. 97; Henry Gyles Turner, *A History of the Colony of Victoria*, vol. II, p. 261.

years before appraised at a salary of £250 per annum considered it necessary to have a retinue and a stable which many a landed aristocrat in England would have found difficulty in supporting.

Gyles Turner had no doubt that this sapped the moral fibre of the colony:
'In a country where all men are workers, and where there was practically
no wealthy leisured class, this servile copying of an older social system was
prejudicial to the manly independence and healthy simplicity associated
with the idea of colonial life'.[31]
    Less conspicuous but far more numerous were those below the level
of the wealthy for whom the Boom brought comfort, perhaps
pretension, but certainly a new standing in society. Fairlie Taylor's father
was an auctioneer and estate agent in Cheltenham. She remembered him
then as a short, slim man with jet black hair which was always beautifully
brushed, and a well-trimmed short black moustache. 'His skin was
swarthy, his hazel eyes alert, and his speech rapid.' He dressed well for
work 'in a dark coat with small revers and the top button done up. The
edges of the coat were braided and it had slit pockets. He always wore a
watch-chain across his waistcoat. With this attire he wore a boxer hat,
but for more sporting occasions he had a peaked cap'. He was away a lot
and always pre-occupied, but the family moved into a new house, and
hired an excellent servant who liked the children and played with them
while their mother took to holding 'at home' days: 'They happened
about once a month, and Percy and I didn't like them much. The
atmosphere in the house seemed rather tense beforehand. Mum wore her
best dress, with leg-of-mutton sleeves, a high ruffled collar, and a tight-
fitting bodice fastened with a long row of buttons'.[32] It was to be a short-
lived gentility.
    In the 1880s suburban life came into its own. A French visitor, Oscar
Comettant, was charmed by middle-class married life in Melbourne:

It is a pleasure to see the railway trains leaving at short intervals every
evening, all filled with husbands returning to stay with their wives and children, until the next morning, when their work in the city recalls them. In
their pretty well-furnished houses, each with its flower-garden, large or
small, the heads of families enjoy their rest (so beneficial to mind and body)
in an atmosphere of sincere and sweet affection. They forget their disappointments and renew their strength for the morrow's struggles. The
out-of-town family house is a sanctuary of pure joy, a respite from all the
troubles, pre-occupations, worries, and sadnesses of which life is woven.[33]

---

[31] Turner, pp. 263–4.
[32] Fairlie Taylor, *Bid Time Return*, pp. 4 and 36.
[33] Oscar Comettant, *In the Land of Kangaroos and Gold Mines*, p. 173.

But too much money was being made too quickly, and even more was being borrowed too recklessly. The new rich had to find ways to establish their distinctiveness and 'breeding'; and those whose 'breeding' went back a few or more generations made much of it. Paul de Serville has discerned how 'an inherited historical past' was 'more potent than a knighthood', because for the well-born, it was 'something which no self-made man, no matter how rich or successful, could buy or enjoy'.[34] On the other hand, many who had done well were individuals of great intellectual capacity and considerable self-education, despite little formal schooling: Sister Anthony Buckley's grandmother had only eighteen months schooling 'but don't go away with the idea that she wasn't a cultured woman'. Speech and accent were not yet reliable indicators of origins and destinations; even in England provincial accents still abounded in the upper and upper-middle classes. In the colonies the marks of class and caste were even more confusing, and England remained the touchstone of 'breeding' and recognition. But the colonies also followed the English example where private schooling endowed the aspirant with membership of the caste. The 'old school tie' could obliterate the taint of trade and eradicate the solecisms of the 'common'. The 'old school tie' could survive even impoverishment or imprisonment: if educated to be a gentleman, then always, technically at least, a gentleman he would be. The colonial Etons and Harrows longed to join the magic circle, but they never quite made the grade. The lawyer, P. A. Jacobs, came to Scotch from St Paul's School, London, and as much as he loved his Australian school, it was not the same: the boys spoke differently and even called each other by their Christian names. (Percival Serle, who was Jacobs' contemporary at Scotch, remembered with pride that 'all through the years Scotch has had a reputation for the absence of snobbery and racial discrimination'.)[35]

Those with education and gentle birth rarely tired of criticising the manners of the social newcomers, and colonial awkwardness exercised the talent for snobbery of foreign visitors for decades to come, Beatrice Webb, the Fabian Socialist, being among the more shameful practitioners (in 1898 she dismissed the members of the Victorian Legislative Council as 'a mean undignified set of little property owners, with illiterate speech and ugly manners').[36] But not all high-born foreign visitors were as rude. Paul Bibron arrived in Melbourne in 1886 and his daughter is Eleonore:

> Apparently the Lord Mayor was the butcher and so on and so forth, and
> it was just a young uncouth sort of place, and my father, coming from
> Europe, seeing all this, thought it could be remedied. With another

---

[34] Paul de Serville, *Pounds and Pedigrees: the Upper Class in Victoria, 1850–1880*, p. 196.

[35] P. A. Jacobs, *A Lawyer Tells*, p. 17; G. H. Nicholson, ed., *First Hundred Years*, p. 29.

[36] A. G. Austin, ed., *The Webbs' Australian Diary, 1898*, p. 66.

Frenchman he started a dancing and deportment class, then Lady Clarke asked him if he would do a class at 'Cliveden'—the cotillions and all those dances which were very complicated.

M. Bibron liked Australians—he was not critical of them, just helpful, and he made a good living teaching dancing and social graces before opening a popular nightclub, 'Admiralty House' in 1925. He remained incorrigibly and charmingly French:

> His accent was fairly strong and I remember my husband laughing one day and I said, 'What's the funny thing?' And he said, 'Pa just said to me—Old chap, when I first came out here, I could say only ZIS and ZAT, and *now* I can say ZIS and ZAT. He was quite sure he was saying 'this' or 'that'.[37]

Beatrice Webb met her match during her visit to Melbourne in Dr Constance Stone, the city's leading woman doctor. Married with a young daughter, Dr Stone had only four years to live before being claimed by tuberculosis. She would not acquiesce in Mrs Webb's 'unfavourable opinion of the Australian rich women', but she had a theory of her own for the visiting social critic:

> [Dr Stone] said that Australian women had far stronger passions than English or American ; that illegitimacy was of constant occurrence even among the wealthier classes of women, and that the growing practice of artificial restraint meant more self-indulgence in sexual intercourse between husband and wife, not less. On this ground she opposed restriction and preached temperance; also she was firmly convinced that the means adopted by women induced chronic irritation in those parts and made them susceptible to cancer and other diseases. Her impression was that artificial restriction was practised chiefly by the lower middle class, not so much by the labourers and the rich.[38]

Oscar Comettant admired the dutiful husbands filling the trains to the suburbs each night, because, unlike the French, if they did not love their wives, they at least pretended to: 'which is almost like loving them. They respect them and live with them in the house'.[39] Married love was difficult, because married love produced babies—more than most women could cope with and more than most men could afford. W. S. Robinson's father would growl at his sons as they walked to and from church, 'Lift your feet boys'. 'Years later I understood why every scrape of the leather on the path way almost seared his soul; he had a big family who made his salary look small.'[40]

---

[37] Interview with Eleonore Bibron, 26 November 1990.
[38] Austin, *The Webbs' Australian Diary*, pp. 75–6.
[39] Comettant, *In the Land of Kangaroos and Gold Mines*, p. 173.
[40] W. S. Robinson, *If I Remember Rightly*, p. 6.

The ability to prevent conception reliably and safely has been an immense biological change for mankind. Sex had always been a fearful problem for human beings, especially for those who were poor, and for those who were passionate. It was dangerous because not only did it bring too many babies into the world, it could kill. It killed young women in their first confinement and it killed older women with other children to care for, but whose tired bodies failed them. It was dangerous because it passed on diseases which were disgusting, disfiguring and essentially incurable, and which could blight the innocent next generation. People who decided that they wanted to stay within the ranks of the respectable had to commit themselves to a strict control of their sexuality. They could not have sexual intercourse outside marriage and, as many discovered, they could not have much sexual intercourse even within marriage. Many respectable women, both affluent and poor, married in complete sexual ignorance only to be appalled by the carnality of the marriage bed. Many respectable men, both affluent and poor, soon faced the painful truth that they were destined for sexual frustration for the rest of their married life. We are not to know how many of the suburban husbands Oscar Comettant admired sought relief in the arms of prostitutes or in those of widows of reduced circumstances and warm disposition. Certainly in England it was the aspiring bourgeoisie who led the use of birth control in the 1870s and 1880s, but in the Australian colonies the very prosperity of the 1880s may account for the later practice of family limitation.[41] There were primitive mechanical and chemical contraceptive devices, but they were not easy to obtain, especially by the shy and unworldly. Many men practised coitus interruptus, despite its unpleasantness, high failure rate and the Biblical injunctions against the sin of Onan. Many others, it seems, saw no alternative to abstinence. Frederic Eggleston was only one of many sensitive young men whose mental health was imperilled by their burgeoning sexuality. If, in its terrors of the 'loss of vital bodily fluids' and of the madness that must surely engulf the masturbator, the nineteenth century displayed symptoms of collective sexual neuroticism, it had reason to be disturbed.[42]

There were other anxieties that the flesh brought into everyday life. The body was as much a locus of anxiety and suffering as of activity and delight. Premature death was part of life for rich and poor: small cuts turned fatally septic; chest infections advanced to pneumonia and, even as late as the 1930s, school friends fell ill and 'never came back'; tuberculosis struck down the young with all the ruthlessness of AIDS and, once Robert Koch had identified the bacillus in 1882 and proved it to be contagious, the way was open for society to incarcerate its victims and deprive them of their liberty until they died. And for those with dental

---

[41] Survey: Appendix II, table 9: Family sizes over three generations.
[42] Serle, *The Rush to be Rich*, p. 172; Hugh Jackson, 'Fertility Decline in New South Wales', pp. 260–73; Warren G. Osmond, *Frederic Eggleston*, pp. 20–44.

abscesses, arthritis, injuries, burns, ulcers, kidney and gall stones and the corrosive agony of cancer, there were only opiates and alcohol to relieve them. The nineteenth-century record of human suffering is full of otherwise temperate people who became addicted to the alcohol and opiates prescribed them in sickness. The body could almost be an enemy—a source of danger both to life and to the soul.

The history of the rise of the 'individual'—the consciousness of self as separate from kin and community—has been more written of by the French than the British historians.[43] Christianity had always demanded that the believer take great care of his or her soul, but the believer was born full of sin, so that the self was innately tainted and worthless. The new conception of the individual was therefore a secular one, a discovery of innocence and natural virtue. This new interest in the individual offered the opportunity for experimental and exciting existences, but it also implied the possibility of failure. The long story of social rising, self-improvement and emigration throughout the nineteenth century meant that literally millions of men and women took large risks, broke away from family and village networks, moved to cities and to new parts of the world. They were very much on their own, and their success depended on talent, hard work and sheer luck. But success could be dangerous to the psyche: once the long haul of making a fortune was accomplished, what was to be done now that obsessive structure for daily existence was no longer needed? Durkheim looked for exotic reasons for the rise in suicide in France during times of prosperity, and identified 'anomie'—a state of paralysis induced by prosperity, where the multiplicity of life choices overwhelmed the fortunate. Above all, when it came within the reach of many men of humble origin to escape poverty and insignificance and when the new industrial and bureaucratic society provided abundant jobs for men with social capital but little else behind them, it became possible in a new and terrifying way to fail. In the century of individual enterprise, failure and ruin lurked in the shadows. And those shadows fascinated the respectable classes of Marvellous Melbourne, who read avidly the reports from the abyss of the 'Vagabond' and the tragic mulatto John Freeman, and who even took voyeuristic expeditions through the back streets of the city to view the sinful.[44] 'Boys', intoned Dr Alexander Morrison of Scotch College, 'a boy never stops at smoking. Smoking leads to drinking, drinking leads to gambling, and gambling leads to the gallows'.[45] Beneath the surfaces of colonial vitality and success, fears, guilts and frustrations nagged and corroded.

Religion supplied the dominant moral structure of public and private life, and its conspicuous practice signalled that the family, with its male head, deserved membership of both the congregation and the

---

[43] Alain Courbin, 'Backstage', *passim*.
[44] Graeme Davison and David Dunstan, 'Images of Low Life', pp. 29–57.
[45] Scotch College, *Diamond Jubilee, 1851–1911*, Melbourne, 1911, p. 22.

respectable classes. But religion was also one of the great pleasures and solaces of nineteenth-century life. It protected against the terrors of mortality and isolation; it injected high emotion into quiet lives; it brought music, art and drama into mundane existence. Valerie East is a psychologist who has watched much religious life as a minister's wife, and she believes that people in the nineteenth century read sermons partly for similar emotional reasons that they read about sex today.[46] Religion held believers and their world together: it was psychic, moral and social cement.

The 1870s and 1880s were great years for institutional religion. In May 1851 there had been thirty-nine churches and chapels of all sorts in the colony; in December 1871 there were 2602, of which almost two-thirds had been built in the previous ten years at a completion rate of over three a week.[47] For the next five years an average of five places of worship were being consecrated each week. And as the suburbs grew and the handsome churches went up, the Anglicans and the Presbyterians began to claw back some of the defectors who had joined up with the lay preachers or the secularists in the bush. Prosperity also brought the discreet self-elevation of successful Nonconformists to the Anglican fold of the perceived Establishment, although rich Presbyterians proved to be more resistant to the temptations than rich Methodists.[48] But the Anglicans and Presbyterians who actually went to church had become overwhelmingly middle and upper class: on the Sunday census of 1887 only 12 per cent of Anglicans in the northern suburbs went to church, and 26.5 per cent of the Presbyterians; the Methodists by contrast scored a healthy 78 per cent. In the more affluent southern suburbs almost a quarter of Anglicans attended, and almost a third of Presbyterians. The Methodists significantly dropped to 63.7 per cent.[49] More striking with the growth of the middle-class suburbs and the establishment of vigorous congregations became the incidence of 'in-marriage' for both Catholics and Protestants. The local church became the dominant social network of the middle-class young, and Victoria's brief flirtation with religious tolerance fell victim to these new structures of urban life. Most people worked part of Saturday so that Sunday was the only day a family could be together. Good Protestants made their way to the church three times on Sunday: for the morning service, then home for lunch and the weekly roast, Sunday school attendance and teaching in the afternoon, and the whole family returned for the evening service. For the poorer classes, where shortage of space forced young children to share the parental bedroom, Sunday school was a welcome opportunity for couples to make love; however,

---

[46] Interview with Valerie East, 12 October 1988.
[47] J. M. Freeland, *Architecture in Australia*, p. 130.
[48] J. R. Poynter, *Russell Grimwade*, p. 46.
[49] Jackson, *Churches and People*, pp. 105 and 83.

Brian Lewis, growing up in the world of the Armadale Presbyterian Church, came to suspect that many serious Protestants believed that even married love was inappropriate to the Lord's Day.[50]

In the new suburbs the local churches quickly became the hub of community, providing the social and economic networks that were characteristic of the middle class. By contrast, in working-class districts, the street, the corner store and the pub built the bonds between people that sustained them in good times and bad, in happiness and sadness. Good character mattered for the working class also; but it was essentially a secular ethic that recognized kindness, diligence, decency and courage. The middle-class ethic was intertwined with religious practice and doctrine, and required a complex performance of duties and demeanours. W. S. Robinson's father once almost ruined his reputation with just one slip at St Jude's Church of England, Carlton:

> 'Dad' was a pocket-sized man with any amount of guts. He was a church warden and the slightest noise during the service annoyed him intensely. He was also keen on being first with the responses, but virtually wrecked his reputation when one Sunday he came an easy first with 'Lord have mercy upon us miserable sinners'—instead of the less incriminatory response that was called for. His lone confessional rocked the adult congregation and won giggles and cheerful smiles from the faces of the young.[51]

The social discipline provided by the church was powerfully reinforced by its economic role. Church families found their doctors, lawyers, dentists, account shopkeepers and master tradesmen through the local church. Men and youths starting out in the world found jobs through 'someone at the church', and the clergyman and the elders or wardens supplied character references. Methodists did business with Methodists, Anglicans with Anglicans, and Catholics with Catholics, although the Presbyterians seemed to do business with everyone. Moral ruin could bring financial ruin.

Prosperity and social rising amid the variety and energy of a colonial society forced the stricter Nonconformists to bend with the wind if they were to continue to attract adherents. The Presbyterians of Hawthorn in the 1860s still stood to pray and sat to sing, and sang only psalms, unaccompanied but for a tuning fork (hymns were 'mere human compositions'). They prided themselves on their 'Presbyterian reverence' and 'expression was limited to what was natural and spontaneous, and in a large measure the volume of singing was maintained at a constant level throughout'. But in 1871 they called a new minister, who abandoned the

---

[50] Lewis, *Sunday at Kooyong Road*, pp. 41–2.
[51] Robinson, *If I Remember Rightly*, p. 6.

strict adherence to the Westminster Confession of his predecessor and es-
poused a new faith more suited to the temper of his Hawthorn parishioners, who were 'a generation increasingly dominated by the idea of
progress . . . Hence there developed an unbounded belief in the possibilities and goodness of man'. This was not a phenomenon exclusive to Presbyterians, according to F. Maxwell Bradshaw: '[rather it was] the growing
external pietism of the age, the use of language garbed with religiosity
(tending to cover the fundamental change that was occurring), and the
fact that accepted doctrine was not so much denied as rendered irrelevant
by a gospel that stressed life and practical matters instead of faith as the
springs of conduct'.[52] And by the end of the century, Presbyterians sat to
pray and stood to sing, and sang hymns as well as the psalms.

Prosperity distracted many ordinary Anglicans and Presbyterians
from the intellectual and theological ferment which now threatened the
cosmos as they conceived of it. Presbyterianism was a church of the Old
Testament, and as the Bible was the only authentic link between the
earthly world and God, every Christian had to be able to read. Literacy
became a touchstone of Presbyterianism and Scottishness, and in the
traditions of Scotch College the Scottish respect for learning has probably
been more powerful than the beliefs of the Presbyterian Church. All
Presbyterians were proud of their educated clergy, and disdained
Methodists for their reliance on 'blessed assurance' at the expense of scholarship. The Scots were proud, too, of their universities which were
broader and more philosophical than those of England; Scottish law was
based on principles not precedents, which provoked debate on the
human condition and Calvinism itself encouraged metaphysical enquiry.
In the words of Malcolm Prentis, it had been a cardinal point of the Ref-
ormation that 'every parish should have a school, so that all might be able
to read the Bible and better themselves', for 'the aim and achievement of
the parish school was to help to create an ideal of citizenship that was
relatively classless'. Presbyterians were therefore particularly vulnerable (as
were all liberal, intellectual Protestants and Anglicans) to the attack on the
literal truth of the Bible unleashed by the evolutionary theories of Charles
Darwin. The Higher Criticism, which interpreted the Scriptures as
metaphor and morally significant myth, found its way into the sermons of
even the most remote Presbyterian ministers. Uncomplicated fundamen-
talist belief was becoming difficult to sustain and to teach; and, if that was
in many ways a liberation, there was also an acute sense of loss. The
consolations of Heaven and the certainty of God's supernatural power
now eluded many rational minds, and perhaps the most potent image of
the crisis of Christian belief in the nineteenth century is of George Eliot,

---

[52] F. Maxwell Bradshaw, *Rural Life to Urban Surge: a History of the Presbyterian Congregation at Hawthorn,
Victoria*, pp. 34–5.

tears streaming down her cheeks as she translated Strauss' *Life of Jesus*, grieving for the Loss of Heaven and supernatural belief.[53]

The persecution of Dr Charles Strong, of Scots Church Collins Street, by Free Kirk fundamentalists who accused him of being a covert Unitarian, shocked and divided Presbyterian Melbourne, and the controversy signalled the parting of the ways between the old world and the modern. But the raw energy of Protestantism came from the Evangelicals, the Sabbatarians and the Temperance Movement. If Dr Strong was inclined to see sin in the existence of poverty, the Evangelicals saw it in the morally weak individual, and the surplus funds of the successful were poured into fabulous coffee palaces which would save the weak from themselves. The Sabbath too had to be kept quiet, pure and devoted to worship, and it was in the 1880s, argues Hugh Jackson, that the character of Protestantism which would mark Melbourne for the next eighty years was impressed upon the city.[54] Wowserism and sectarianism rushed to fill the spiritual vacuum left by the Loss of Heaven.

By the outbreak of World War I, all the major Protestant sects had lost their distinctive doctrine. The terrors of Hellfire and Eternal Damnation had almost disappeared from the Protestant preacher's repertoire and the ordinary believer's eschatology. Science had so undermined the literal truth of the Scriptures that increasingly belief demanded more intellectual subtlety and experiences of intense spirituality which could over-ride scepticism.[55] Individuals of powerful belief could be found in every congregation, and clergy with a radiant, expressive faith and a fluent tongue continued to reach their materialistic and rationalistic parishioners who longed to believe but who were finding it increasingly difficult to do so. Being Methodist or Presbyterian or Anglican now depended to a large degree on family history, and, for not a few, being a Methodist had come down to feeling British, enjoying singing and being a teetotaller. Religious excitement for many by the turn of the century, was to be found in the competition each Hospital Sunday as to which church contributed the most. At the Toorak Presbyterian Church great pride was taken each year in coming top, even if hurried calls went out at the last minute to boost the plate lest St John's Church of England overtake them.[56] But by then the Presbyterians of Toorak included some guilty consciences, and in 1909 Macrae Stewart had found it necessary to formulate a Presbyterian pioneering myth to distance the church from the guilty deeds of some of its most prominent adherents:

[53] Malcolm Prentis, *The Scottish in Australia*, p. 12; Lewis, *Sunday at Kooyong Road*, pp. 39–40; C. R. Badger, *The Reverend Charles Strong and the Australian Church*, pp. 66–9.
[54] Charles Strong D.D., *Christianity Re-interpreted and Other Sermons*, pp. 71–2; Jackson, *Churches and People*, pp. 110–15.
[55] Jackson, pp. 125 and 73; Strong, *Christianity Re-interpreted*, pp. 13–16.
[56] Wischer, *The Presbyterians of Toorak*, p. 54.

They belonged to an older day, and carried into their new surroundings a simple faith in God that criticism had not yet loosened, and lust for gold had not yet grown strong enough to darken and destroy.[57]

Penitents: 1890–1900

After that 'insane, miraculous year' of 1888, the price of land in Melbourne suddenly collapsed. The supply of housing had outstripped the demand, and the acres pegged out amidst the farms and orchards around the rim of the metropolis returned to their real worth as residential land which was next to nothing. The web of failed interlocking deals and loans then destabilized the rickety financial structure of the city. In the middle of 1890 there was a big maritime strike; over the New Year big losses in Argentina stung the British investors and they passed their pain on to their Australian borrowers. Financiers had most of their recent short-term loans sunk in now-depreciated real estate or in long-term residential accommodation, so they were helpless in the face of a sudden crisis of confidence. The financial institutions tried everything to halt the march towards disaster, but first building societies, then the mortgage companies and land banks were forced to suspend operations. And with them fell their architects, including the Premier, James Munro, the Speaker of the Legislative Asssembly, Sir Matthew Davies, and the biggest boomer of them all, Benjamin Fink.

In 1893 down came the banks—not just in Victoria but throughout the country. In 1891 there had been sixty-five banks in Australia; two years later, fifty-four of them had closed, thirty-four of them permanently. No savings bank in the City of Melbourne closed, but business was devastated, and Geoffrey Blainey maintains that he can find no banking crisis in the United Kingdom, Germany, France, Holland— possibly even America—which can match our crash of 1893. But it was bank shareholders rather than depositors who lost in the end, because nearly all deposits were eventually repaid, and with interest. To have pressed the borrowers too leniently would have lowered economic confidence even further.[58]

The 1890s depression was catastrophic, but we are only just beginning to know how catastrophic and for whom. There are even fewer statistics than for the 1930s depression, but generally it is accepted that at least one in three men in Melbourne was out of work at the worst of the crisis. Fifty-six thousand Victorians abandoned the colony, robbing Melbourne of its pre-eminence over Sydney as Australia's largest city—a

---

[57] D. Macrae Stewart, *Growth in Fifty Years: The Presbyterian Church of Victoria Jubilee History*, p. 2.
[58] Geoffrey Blainey, *A Land Half Won*, pp. 318–31.

pre-eminence it has never regained. Thousands went to Western Australia in search of gold, among them many young middle-class men whose immediate prospects had been dashed. Some went further afield to South Africa: in fact the flight from Victoria was so dramatic that one Melbourne private school added a verse in its Old Boys' song dedicated to those in South Africa and Kalgoorlie. The private schools were a useful barometer of the effects of the crash on the better-off: new enrolments at Scotch College fell from 125 in 1890, to 35 in 1895, and at Melbourne Grammar from 122 to 47. PLC was plunged into debt. The Commercial Bank had been popular with Methodists and its failure contributed to the halving of the enrolment at MLC between 1888 and 1893. As for Wesley College, the total number of boys collapsed to 106, including just thirteen boarders, and the school would have been sold had the Methodist Church been able to find a buyer. The 'Public Schools' were at their lowest ebb, and their place was taken by the cheaper and more commercially-oriented private academies such as South Melbourne College and the original University High School. Melbourne Grammar averaged only eight matriculation passes a year in the mid-1890s.[59]

Those who came of age in the 1890s were something of a blighted generation. Many had to leave school earlier than planned, and Frederic Eggleston was one of a number of budding intellectuals who were denied university education. John Blanch's father was the one in the family who 'missed out' on going to Scotch, and instead left school at fourteen and started work in a wholesale grocery. Kathleen Fitzpatrick was the grand-daughter of the real estate agent J. R. Buxton, and she never doubted that the 1890s depression was one of the great turning points in Australian history. The bleak lesson learned by the young as they listened to their fathers pacing the floor at night, agonizing over their debts, was that there was no security on earth: 'the worst effect of all, because it lasted for life, was . . . a dread that things were not as they seemed and that something terrible might happen any moment'.[60] Economically the crash ushered in more than forty years of stagnation, where the Australian economy was among the most depressed of the developed world.[61] Victoria was left with a sophisticated infrastructure it would be paying off—in the case of the railways—until after World War II. Melbourne was a noble city of handsome homes, fine private schools, clear lines of class distinction and hardly any money.

[59] Bruce Scates, 'A Struggle for Survival', pp. 41–63; Jenny Lee, 'The Marks of Want and Care', in Verity Burgmann and Jenny Lee, eds, *Making a Life*, Melbourne, 1988, pp. 194–204; Davison, *The Rise and Fall of Marvellous Melbourne*, p. 227; Zainu'ddin, *They Dreamt of a School*, pp. 79–91; Kathleen Fitzpatrick, *PLC Melbourne*, pp. 104–12; Blainey, *A Land Half Won*, p. 334; *Liber Melburniensis*.

[60] Interview with John Blanch, 27 January 1989; Kathleen Fitzpatrick, *PLC*, p. 112.

[61] N. G. Butlin, 'Some Perspectives of Australian Economic Development, 1890–1965', in C. Forster, ed., *Australian Economic Development in the Twentieth Century*, pp. 266–327.

The victims were legion and they came in all sizes. It was a fearful lesson on the folly of 'getting above yourself'. A. E. Hocking's good Methodist father Harry, at the age of fifty in 1889, had seen his chance to make a fortune. He sold his two shops in Carlton for £3000 and invested the lot in a speculative venture, the Premier Building Association. He was offered a return of a dazzling 15½ per cent which would bring in £400 a year—more than enough to retire on. But he received only one dividend before the company crashed and he lost the lot. The son never forgot that, and as he studied accountancy at night and moved up in the financial world, he never gambled or invested in anything more adventurous than government bonds. Hocking abandoned the Methodist teetotalism in middle life after he observed that it hindered his acceptability in the business community, but he never abandoned the caution impressed on him by his father's financial ruin.[62] As for Fairlie Taylor:

> The first I heard of it was when I found Annie crying in the kitchen one day. 'I've got to leave here, love, and I'm going to miss you terribly. The home has been sold, and so has most of your mother's beautiful furniture. Your Ma's very upset, I'm sorry for her—best leave her alone just now'. I felt I was in some other strange world and began to cry too, but Annie dried my tears and said, 'Don't fret about it, love. Your Pa will get on top again, you'll see!'[63]

Family mythologies which grew out of the disaster sought to soften the blow to self and public esteem. Many who had blossomed in the boom borrowed against over-valued assets and their halcyon days were brief. Dorothea Cerutty's mother came from a family of Ascot Vale engineers who did so well that they bought a large Hawthorn home which had been 'built by convicts'. They lost it again, but that brief interlude changed the family's identity; it conferred a sense of being 'quality' and nourished a lively interest in the arts which enriched their lives ever after. The Cerutty family history was more modest. Her grandfather had been one of five brothers to emigrate in the 1850s from Tavistock in Devon. (The Ceruttys or Cerruttis had been converted Protestants who made an exodus from Genoa in 1797.) Her grandfather was 'a charming gentleman' who rose to be in charge of the pilot service for the Port of Melbourne; his wife, Mrs Bessie Morphett Cerutty, had an irascible temper which inflicted 'a strange loneliness' on the rest of the family. However, Mr Cerutty brought home various 'sea captains and strange people from overseas' and 'the stories of the sea gave Dad some sort of romantic background to an otherwise sad existence'. Of the three sons, one died

---

[62] Patricia Hocking, *Stormy Petrel: a Biography of Albert Edward Hocking, 1885–1969*, pp. 8–9, 15–17.
[63] Fairlie Taylor, *Bid Time Return*, p. 72.

young, one became an engineer and her father worked in a draper's business before entering theological college to train for the Anglican ministry. Of the daughters

> one was a virtuous virgin who passed away unshattered at the end of a long life; the other was a naughty lady called *Aggie*, who, after many love affairs, eloped with a gentleman friend who later married her and she was never seen in the home again.[64]

Another casualty of the 1890s depression was the marriage rate. Amongst the large families of the newly impoverished genteel there were many young men and women who had to choose between remaining single or marrying down. Of the Rev. Duguld McCalman's ten children, only two sons married, and one of those settled in South Africa. The other sons were unable to sustain themselves as middle-class men and Willie and Alec were both dead from the drink before they were forty. Many a marriage was delayed or never embarked upon, and the generation of women who came of child-bearing age in the 1890s was the least married and the least fertile in our history. The men were not quite so deprived, for many were able to delay marriage until later in life; even so not a few came to prefer the bachelor state. But if there was sadness at being left single, the army of middle-class spinsters, as in England, nurtured not a few feminists and brought into education, church and community life a fresh and cultivated feminine energy. Their financial plight was often appalling, but their impoverished gentility sharpened wits and honed self-discipline more often than it crushed spirits.[65]

Dashed hopes and lowly futures were just some of the consequences of the crash; as painful were shame and disgrace. Nineteenth-century society was predicated on good character, therefore grievous loss and the taint of impropriety could bring about the disintegration of a man's entire personality. This was a difficult time for many middle- and upper-class Protestants, and probably no church was more shaken than the Toorak Presbyterian Church. In the 1880s it had been the 'Land Boom at prayer', for six of its elders and nine members of its board of management were prominent boomers. Not all of them were rogues, but at least two of the Davies brothers were and Sir Matthew was lucky indeed to avoid conviction and imprisonment. What must have been far worse was the grief suffered by all the trusting fellow parishioners who had sunk their nest-eggs in the financial ventures promoted by men they worshipped with every Sunday. Many suburban churches were left half-finished and hopelessly in debt and St John's Presbyterian Church, Elsternwick, was one of many

---

[64] Interview with Dorothea Cerutty, 16 March 1988.
[65] Constance Tisdall, *Forerunners: the Saga of a Family of Teachers*, pp. 96–7, 154–5; Beverley Kingston, *Glad, Confident Morning*, p. 120.

where 'these financial troubles had an unsettling effect on the minds of those connected with the Church, and had unfavorably affected the congregation'.[66]

The churches were chastened and the Presbyterians never recovered their position within the Victorian élite. In 1892 the Free Presbyterians undertook a solemn fast, although somehow 'the insidious advances of Romanism' were nominated as part of the cause of the financial disaster. (A century later Sacred Heart Church, St Kilda, remembers with pride that its lone speculator, Timothy Kelly, 'proudly resolved not to declare himself bankrupt so as to pay only a fraction of his debts'.)[67] The Wesleyans set aside a week of denial as penitence for 'some hasting to get rich, and entering unjustifiable speculations little less than gambling', and in May 1893 the Protestant churches combined for a Special Day of Humiliation and Prayer and held an ecumenical service in the Melbourne Town Hall. The minister of Scots Church exemplified the difficulties many felt when he shrank from condemning the practices of some of his most prominent laymen.[68] Few uttered prayers for the poor, especially for the always poor, whose sufferings this time were certainly no fault of their own.

A veil of discretion and deceit was pulled over the disgraces of the boomers by respectable society. An odd provision in Victorian law enabled a bankrupt to make a 'Composition by Arrangement' with his creditors, pay trifling amounts on his debts such as a penny or halfpenny in the pound, and be discharged from insolvency without the knowledge of anyone other than his creditors. Not until 1966 when Michael Cannon published *The Land Boomers* were those lists of briefly bankrupted boomers made public. For decades, those who 'knew' had done the 'decent thing' by each other—so many were scorched that it was in everyone's interest not to name names; and into the 1950s the historical record of Melbourne life went on as though the Land Boom had never happened.[69] The damage control was astonishingly effective, but it was also terribly unjust, because the small punters, the amateurs, did not have access to slick solicitors, and their losses and disgraces were made public. Some churches expelled bankrupts, and bitterness in some families continues to this day. Religion did help some, however. Joan Rennick's 'Auntie' Katie Longmuir lived in a street near the old South Yarra picture theatre. Her husband had met a tragic end after 'some banking fiasco' which was never explained. Left widowed and penniless, she was none

---

[66] N. G. McNicol, 'St John's Presbyterian Church, Elsternwick, 1887–1962', p. 3; Wischer, *The Presbyterians of Toorak*, pp. 138–41.

[67] David Moloney, *From Mission to Mission*, p. 11.

[68] Davison, *Rise and Fall of Marvellous Melbourne*, p. 249.

[69] O. G. A. Colles and M. Dew, *History of Hawthorn Jubilee Year 1910*, pp. 56 and 59–62; R. H. Croll, *I Recall*, pp. 20–1; A. H. Chisholm, *Scots Whe Hae, History of the Royal Caledonian Society*, pp. 48–9.

the less cheerful: 'Years later we found out she had joined the Salvation Army. She kept it a secret because belonging to the Salvoes would almost certainly have been scoffed at among the prosperous and well-connected people she knew. It was her Salvation Army bonnet that gave the secret away. Someone noticed it on top of her wardrobe and word got out.'[70]

The 1890s were terrible years in Victoria. The Protestant churches saw their congregations shrink, the middle class was stricken with a failure of nerve, and a new chastened Puritanism overtook the suburbs. For ever after, people acknowledged the virtue of living carefully, for as Macrae Stewart passed judgement in 1909: 'Worldly prosperity has caused the hearts of some of its children to wax gross [and] for this state of things, life's inexorable laws are working out a grim remedy'.[71] But two later historians were to see in the 1890s new hope. Geoffrey Blainey detected in that decade the first signs of the social conscience among the university students which would become so characteristic of Melbourne's young intellectuals half a century later. Brian Fitzpatrick saw an even greater moment of truth for a chastened people who took possession of that final responsibility of maturity—'the "recognition of necessity"; that is to say, perception of realities that had to be faced, and undismayed attention to them'.[72] In the 1890s was born the careful and moral Melbourne middle class; and for many, suddenly dispossessed of their savings, their property and their businesses, the long slow climb to comfort and security had to begin all over again.

Patriots: 1900–1919

But for rising and declining Protestants there were new and promising antagonists. The Free Presbyterians' endeavour to heap the blame for the Land Boom and the crash on the 'insidious advances of Romanism' was ominous. Even though sectarianism had been part of White Australia's history from the beginning, it was now that Protestantism was in spiritual decline that the churches looked increasingly to bigotry to bolster congregational solidarity. At the same time there was no question that Romanism was on the advance, and by 1900 Catholicism was more disciplined and effective than it had ever been before in Australia's short history. As Protestants drifted into secularism, more and more Catholics

---

[70] Elizabeth Rennick, ed., *Sketched from Memory*, p. 36.
[71] Stewart, *Growth in Fifty Years*, p. 81.
[72] Geoffrey Blainey, *A Centenary History of the University of Melbourne*, pp. 96–7; Brian Fitzpatrick, *The Australian People*, pp. 217–8; see also Don Watson, *Brian Fitzpatrick*, pp. 194–5.

were attending Mass and sending their children to the new parish and secondary schools. And the Catholic Church was succeeding where the Protestants had largely failed—they were reaching the urban poor as Catholic schools became the centre-piece for the training and bonding of the flock. Australian Catholics drank deep of the rise of Irish pietism among the psychically shattered survivors and witnesses of the Irish famine. In the 1830s there had been an acute shortage of priests and places of worship in Ireland, so that the drastic fall in population through both death and emigration enabled the Church to spread its limited resources more effectively. But the horror of the Great Hunger itself made people more receptive to the promise of Heavenly release from this 'valley of tears', and the labouring poor, who had been still attached to ancient pagan magic and mystery, began attending Mass in force. A reforming episcopy tightened its control of the dioceses, and in the parishes, devotions which were new to most Irish Catholics, including the Rosary, the forty-hours adoration, blessed altars, benediction and vespers, and devotion to the Sacred Heart, became popular. A rush of vocations swelled the ranks of priests, brothers and nuns, providing a steady supply of religious for the New World, and thereby restoring Irish sentiment in distant new societies where it was in danger of being forgotten. By the end of the nineteenth century an extraordinary 90 per cent of Catholics attended Mass regularly—a figure no Protestant church in the British Isles ever even approached.[73]

By 1900, not just 'Romanism' had advanced in Australia: so too had the Irish and their numerous descendants. The Irish who had come here were a little better off and rather more literate than those who had fled to the United States of America, and over 70 per cent of the Irish immigrants to Victoria after 1850 could read and write. Most came as single men and women. They were sexually moral; they drank no more than the Scots and the 'secular' English; they were just as lax in their attendance of church services as Presbyterians and Anglicans while churches and clergy were few; and they were happy to marry Protestants and did so in great numbers. As Patrick O'Farrell has pointed out, they came from a society steeped in deference to 'the Quality', and in the colonies, the lowly made loyal and cheerful servants while the more successful were eager to please their Protestant neighbours and the local gentry. Mother Mary McKillop wrote to Rome in the early 1870s of her fear that the Catholic spirit was being weakened by the fact that Catholics were afraid of losing favour with their Protestant employers. On the 'frontier' Catholic and Protestant reached out before the 1860s, so that episodes of sectarian ill-feeling were infrequent in larger towns, and virtually unknown outside them.[74]

---

[73] Jackson, *Churches and People*, pp. 12–15.
[74] Patrick O'Farrell, *The Irish in Australia*, pp. 63 and 126; Jackson, *Churches and People*, pp. 35–7.

And many Irish who came here did well, even though a seminal Irish-Australian myth was that they have lacked a Catholic aristocracy 'to give status to their pleading'.[75] But the young Brian Lewis, growing up through World War I, Presbyterian, middle-class and patriotic, knew of an Irish 'aristocracy' in Melbourne: Sir Redmond Barry, Sir John Madden, Gavan Duffy, the Higgins brothers and the gallant Captain 'Joe' Lalor who was the first to fall at Gallipoli. And some of these were even Catholic. Moreover, for the young Lewis, all his folk heroes were Irish: Ned Kelly, Peter Lalor and Robert O'Hara Burke. Ned Kelly was far too good to be allowed to remain the preserve of the Catholics: 'there were a lot of things about Ned Kelly we liked [and] it may have some significance that when Ned's gang came upon the police party, they allowed the Scottish trooper to get away but killed the three Irish policemen, and that Ned was condemned to death by an Irish judge, one of the Irish gentry'.[76] There was prejudice of course. E. M. Clowes, excusing herself on the grounds that she was half Irish, spoke for many when she averred, 'Generally speaking, Australia can do little with the Irish. The summit of the ambition of most Irish colonists is to attain the dignity of owning a public house'. She was conscious of admirable exceptions, but such were 'not often the case'.[77] That ambition to own a pub was a sound one, however. Hotels, well run by efficient and abstemious families, could make a lot of money quickly, and the capital amassed could provide a launching pad into education and prosperity. Nancy Naughton comes from a family of Melbourne hoteliers:

> My paternal grandfather was born in Kerry in 1845 and arrived in Melbourne in 1863. And he would say, 'I arrived on the Station Pier with £12 in my pocket'. He was as Irish as Paddy's pigs and he went into the hotel industry.
> When the Irish people first came out here they were largish in their personality, they were tolerant, they were good entertainers. There was a hotel-keeper who would sing 'Mother Machree' and 'Danny Boy' and any of the Irish songs up and down the bar. It was like a bit of theatre while he was serving. That drew people in. They weren't 'time and motion' efficiency—they were personality, and to me, Irish people have that; and a sense of hospitality. So it seemed natural that they should go into an industry where they could play on their personalities, and at the same time, make a few shillings.[78]

Mary Thompson's son now runs the family's elegant hotel in Cobden which cost £6000 to build in 1904: 'most of the cost was the cartage from

[75] Niall Brennan, *John Wren: Gambler*, p. 142.
[76] Brian Lewis, *Our War*, pp. 80–1.
[77] E. M. Clowes, *On the Wallaby*, p. 176.
[78] Interview with Nancy Naughton, 22 November 1990.

Ballarat—the bricks were made locally'. Mary's two grandfathers came out during the gold rush, one having already been to the Californian gold fields:

> My uncle married an English girl who became a Catholic, and my grandmother was a very bigoted Irish Catholic—she was always 'that black Protestant' to her—and she wouldn't go to the wedding. And my aunt Teresa was so infuriated that she went off and married a lovely man who'd been wanting to marry her and he had a hotel in Cobden. And my mother went up and met the hotelkeeper from the other hotel and she said he was the most beautiful thing she'd ever seen, and married him.[79]

The other ways that the Irish made money were in carrying and contracting, and many families combined all three: the O'Keefe clan started in hotels on the goldfields, began contracting, building railways and irrigation channels, and finally entered the Riverina squattocracy; *Mary Geoghegan*'s maternal grandfather was a contractor on the irrigation channels in the Goulburn Valley who also invested in rural property.[80] And Kate Morgan's lovely Irish daddy who came here at twenty-three and 'never seen a man I'd seen before', got started, lost everything in the 1890s depression, began again as a contractor, married in his forties, bought the bluestone house Niddrie on 249 acres of land, and retired to become a father and a part-time farmer. The Irish love and knowledge of horses drew many into carrying, and again, the able found it lucrative. *Veronica Keogh*'s father was a 'master carrier':

> He wanted the best for his kids. He went to school on a horse. He started at St Ignatius's Primary School in Richmond—he was taught by the FCJ nuns, then by the Brothers. Did secondary at Christian Brothers' College, Parade, and he matriculated. He was interested in French—he read Dumas' *Three Musketeers*. He told us once that he wanted to do Med., but because he was the only boy and his mother was 'a strong character', he had to go into the family business.

It took a lot of money to erase the stigma that hotel-keeping and common trade suffered in a nominally Protestant society, and for the Irish the only sure path to esteem and dignity was through education. Protestants might revile Catholics' religion and ridicule their social ambitions, but they could not mock a fine doctor, a sound solicitor or an eloquent barrister. And for Victorian Catholics the two Jesuit colleges, Xavier and St Patrick's, East Melbourne, became the focus of educational ambition. The Scots did not

---

[79] Interview with Mary Thompson, 24 October 1990.
[80] Mary Healy, *Railways and Pastures: the Australian O'Keefes*; *passim*; interview with *Mary Geoghegan*, 9 October 1990.

have a monopoly on reverence for education for many Irish families placed the education of their children before all else. *Mary Geoghegan's* contractor grandfather even 'bought the desk from the state school that he'd attended— the desk he'd sat in at school'. Yet however hard they tried, the Protestants shut them out. Brian Lewis, reminiscing about the courting rituals between 'Public School' boys and girls, put it bluntly: 'A Xavier boy admittedly goes to a public school, but even a member of the Xavier crew would find it impossible to pick up a Protestant hatband and would be forced to make-do with that of a convent school, or even with something anonymous without a hatband at all'.[81]

The Catholic élite grew quietly and independently, and in Melbourne clustered around the schools in Kew and Glen Iris and the Catholic churches in the other suburbs, where the better-off, often having raised much of the money to build the church, became 'the Quality' of the parish.[82] It had its own rules and exclusivity for, while publicans' daughters were welcome at Genazzano, they were not at Sacre Coeur. That French orders and the Jesuits ran the most prestigious schools was significant, and the Irish-Australian ambience was enriched by European religious and by the presence of the sons and daughters of French, German, Italian and Spanish visitors and settlers. There developed a different visual aesthetic—European rather than English. And a high standard of manners and social style was expected and maintained, both in the schools and in the homes: at the O'Keefes' Riverina station Yamma the men 'wore a collar and tie at all times when on the job. The only worker not attired so formally was the cook'.[83] But the unspoken discrimination persisted in even the best circles. *Elinor Doyle*:

> My mother said of her country district, where her father's property was probably as good as most, that there were certain houses to which they were not invited. They could be in the tennis club but they mightn't be asked to the picnic races. There was a whole pecking order (rather like Mary Gilmore's 'chalk line') of the things Catholics could be in and a kind of inner circle they were *not* in. But it was not a question of money.[84]

Sectarianism was less genteel in Cobden if you were a Catholic publican's daughter as was Mary Thompson: 'If I laughed I was drunk and if I looked at a boy I was pregnant'. Australian Catholicism's best defence lay in its puritanism—its strictness and moral harshness, argues Edmund Campion, enabling its practitioners 'to feel superior to other Christians in this, if in

---

[81] Lewis, *Sunday at Kooyong Road*, p. 123.
[82] *Xaverian*, 1911, Catalogue of Students, 1878–1910; *Genazzano*, 1911 and 1920, Catalogue of Past and Present Students.
[83] Healy, *The Australian O'Keefes*, p. 146.
[84] Interview with *Elinor Doyle*, 20 September 1988.

nothing else'.[85] Methodists would have been astonished to know that there were Catholics who considered themselves purer in heart, but all Protestants' lapses and hypocrisies were duly noted: Mary Thompson's mother 'used to get furious with ladies who'd come to the hotel to buy a bottle of brandy "to make puddings with". And when a local postmaster who was a lay preacher ran away with somebody else's wife and left a note for his wife weighed down by a brandy bottle, my parents laughed with the most wicked glee for weeks afterwards'. But if the Catholic élite had a fatal flaw it was more that it had little appetite for hard-nosed commerce. Catholic spirituality—especially that of the Jesuits—did not fit a man for commercial life—the 'Other' was more important; money was no more than a means to an end and that end was gentility, culture and service to the Church. Not a few proved nonchalant stewards of their inherited wealth: the mighty O'Keefe fortune was dissipated by inefficient management and a taste for cultivated living.[86] For the Irish their ideal was the leisured Irish ascendancy—cultured, charming and bored by business. And the dearest hope of many a successful Catholic family was not that the cleverest sons should join the Melbourne Club, but that they should enter the Society of Jesus. If they lacked a vocation, then medicine or the law—but not speculative secular disciplines like philosophy or science which might imperil faith—were the preferred destinies. But as Catholics settled, succeeded and made their mark, men in higher places were about to change all that.

The force which finally drove the wedge between Catholic and Protestant was not religion but war. It has taken a long historical distance to appreciate how shameful was the behaviour of the middle and upper classes of all of the combatant nations at the outbreak of World War I. Here the 'Public Schools' delighted in the great chance for war glory and there was nothing less than a frenzy of blood sacrifice: the Collegiate School of St Peter in Adelaide is reputed to have prayed to God that it should end the war with the longest list of war dead of any Australian school. At Anglican schools the pressure to enlist was almost obligatory on leaving school, and at Wesley College the young Brian Lewis witnessed the daily glorying in each new Old Boy who had paid the supreme sacrifice until the tragedy and the hideousness of it defeated even the patriotism of the headmaster, L. A. Adamson. Lewis' *Our War* is a compelling testament to the fact that it was more a middle-class war; for while the romantic patriots were thrilled to be able to serve, in the back streets of Richmond cannier Australians watched and waited before committing themselves.[87]

---

[85] Edmund Campion, *Rockchoppers*, p. 63.
[86] Healy, *The Australian O'Keefes*, pp. 213–14.
[87] Janet McCalman, *Struggletown*, pp. 83 and 96–7.

The Melbourne middle class needed the war: here was their historical opportunity to recover self-respect after the psychic and financial disasters of the 1890s; and because it was a grand patriotic enterprise, and
not a conscripted defence of the homeland, the war offered a path to acceptance. An ambitious lower-class Methodist from Richmond had much
to gain in later life from a good war record. The fact that the Anzacs were
good soldiers and that they and their officers acquitted themselves well
made it all the easier. War conferred on schools like Scotch College and
Trinity Grammar a new social role in the production of loyal troops and
fine officers, but as the death toll mounted, the schools' Imperial and
military mission was their best defence against the guilt at having worked
so hard at persuading young men to lose their limbs, their wits or their
lives. The record of Scotch College's and Trinity Grammar's war sacrifices for decades after were bathed in the glow of 'valiant hearts' whose
'knightly virtue' had been 'proved'; but there was also heartsick grief.[88]
Four thousand seven hundred Old Boys from the six 'Public Schools'
served, although that was not many more than the lads who enlisted just
from Richmond. Unlike their English equivalents, less than half received
commissions (although that was far more than from Richmond); and an
appalling 756 lost their lives. Old boys poets wrote movingly of 'Service'
and 'Courage' and a son of the manse from Scotch, J. D. Burns, is still re-
vered for writing:

FOR ENGLAND

The bugles of England were blowing o'er the sea,
As they had called a thousand years, calling now to me;
They woke me from dreaming in the dawning of the day,
The Bugles of England—and how could I stay?

The banners of England, unfurled across the sea,
Floating out upon the wind, were beckoning to me;
Storm-rent and battle-torn, smoke-stained and grey,
The banners of England—and how could I stay?

O, England, I heard the cry of those that died for thee,
Sounding like an organ-voice across the winter sea;
They lived and died for England, and gladly went their way,
England, O England, how could I stay?

Burns was one of the too many promising young men who died. But the
war converted Scotch into 'one of the great schools of the Empire' and it
began to see itself taking its place with the Great Public Schools of England: the new generation had washed away the sins of their fathers and

---

[88] D. T. Merrett, 'The School at War: Scotch College and the Great War', pp. 209–33.

grandfathers with their sacrificial blood. And yet the grief which hung over the survivors and the bereaved shadowed Australia for the next twenty years: it was a second 'recognition of necessity' and it was that rather than daring and pluck which made a man.

At the beginning Xavier College was quite as enthusiastic about the war as were the Protestant schools and was deeply gratified that the first casualty at Gallipoli was their Captain 'Joe' Lalor, grandson of the hero of the Eureka Stockade.[89] The fathers of the girls at Genazzano during the 1930s were just as likely to have served in the war as the Protestants.[90] The Convent mounted patriotic pageants and sang *God Save the King* and *Rule Britannia* when Lady Stanley, the Governor's wife, paid a visit to the school in November 1916. War service offered the Irish Catholics full membership of the new nation and the 'Public School' world, except that Easter 1916 and Archbishop Mannix had changed everything utterly. This was the great divide that forced Catholics to follow the Church into its enclosed political fold and into total separateness. The conscription battles and the Irish cause drove the Catholics into the Labor Party and the Scots out of it.[91] And among the Catholics there were a number for whom that pressure was intolerable. Sir David Hennessy, Lord Mayor of Melbourne, discreetly removed his daughters from Genazzano Convent because of its close relationship with the new archbishop.[92] Other middle- and upper-class Catholics were not even Irish and at Genazzano there were conflicting loyalties. Connie Gorman was a boarder during the war:

> Some of the day girls would tell us stories they heard about Dr Mannix signalling from the upstairs windows of *Raheen* to German submarines in Port Phillip Bay. We did not believe them, nor did those who told them, but it was a feeling of the time that Catholics were mostly Irish and therefore not loyal. My own ideas were not clear. With an Irish background on one side, but a brother at the war, I probably agreed with my mother that Ireland's freedom ought to wait, and that it was unfair that only young men with a sense of duty should have to fight.[93]

For Protestants, however, there was no conflict: 'We have turned against the Catholics in recent years', recorded Brian Lewis, 'as a patriotic attitude all over Australia'. As the Australian Catholic Church became more Irish, the keener the bigotry: 'European Catholicism has an air of jolly fantasy; the Irish form is humourless and dripping with black hatred'.

---

[89] G. M. Dening, *Xavier: A Centenary Portrait*, p. 109.
[90] Survey: 'Did your father serve in World War I?': Yes: Scotch, 29.3%; Trinity, 38%; MLC, 26.6%; Genazzano, 30%.
[91] Malcolm Prentis, *The Scottish in Australia*, p. 68.
[92] Sister Maria Bell FCJ, *And the Spirit Lingers . . .*, p. 104.
[93] Ibid., p. 105; see also Elizabeth Rennick, *Sketched from Memory*, pp. 7–9.

There were regrets, however, about the gulf that had now emerged between Catholic and Protestant in the élite: 'Those families of Catholics
who have produced leaders in law, medicine and politics from the past
days of the state, we fully approve of and would be glad to have as friends.
That minority is just as patriotic as we are . . . They are the Brahmins of
the Church, the rest are untouchables'.[94] A step down in the social ladder,
the Methodist *Spectator*, reviewing the coming St Patrick's Day march for
1919, condemned Archbishop Mannix as 'a limelight-loving, egotistical,
rebel-promoting priestly egoist', and set the tone for what was to become
the most virulent sectarian decade in Australian history.[95]

More important, but less written about because of the difficulty of
evidence, was the psychic legacy of the war brought back to the homes
and workplaces by the returned men. They had seen hell, but they came
back to a society which had no comprehension of what it had really been
like. They did not talk about the battles, the fear and the pain because they
could not, although wives glimpsed it when their men screamed out their
nightmares. They had been through so much so young that many returned as grey men, old before their time, drained of their idealism and
adventurousness. These grey men wanted only a quiet life and a return to
the certainties and securities they remembered, or idealized, of life before
the war. There were, of course, marvellous exceptions, but those who
shrank from personal and intellectual growth probably outnumbered
those who grasped the challenges history had thrown out to them. Instead, the conservative majority imposed their deadened and deadening
spirit on the nation and its institutions.[96] But in Melbourne the losses and
casualties of the war had been a second blow. The depression of the 1890s
and the losses of the war—not just in lives but also in the damaged men
who survived it—amounted to a lost middle-class generation. There were
lots of empty places in the offices of the city which new men could fill.

This was the complex, prickly and anxious middle class that this generation of college boys and girls inherited. *Dick Wallace* was born in 1920, the
youngest of three children, and grew up in a two-bedroomed weatherboard house (with sleep-out) in Jersey Street, Balwyn.[97] His grandfather
had had 'a few quid' and *Dick*'s father went to Brighton Grammar School
until grandfather lost his importing business in the 1890s depression,
grandmother walked out and his father left school. *Dick*'s father worked
his way to England as a steward, 'for which I admired him—that he had
the guts to do that sort of thing'. Then 'he got into the insurance game—

[94] Lewis, *Sunday at Kooyong Road*, pp. 81–2.
[95] *The Spectator*, 22 January 1922, p. 50.
[96] Hugh Stretton, 'The Quality of Leading Australians', pp. 217–19.
[97] Interview with *Dick Wallace*, 7 November 1987.

he was an inspector' and he stayed there for the rest of his life. His only interest was competitive shooting: 'Father was a very stern, authoritarian sort of bloke—he was an angry little man who seethed through life'.

Dick's mother had been a teacher and was from a 'staunch Presbyterian family'. It was a big family—'eight or nine of them and all called Lillian and Myrtle and Ethel—all those old-fashioned names'. 'We were very proud of Grandpa Trend—he was in charge of religious instruction—I've no idea where or for what'. Grandpa Trend was 'very Prince Albert with a pointy beard, and we've got a photo which the family are very proud of—of him talking once to the Archbishop!' Dick's father didn't go to church but his mother sometimes did, and the children went to Sunday School. Football was a shared passion, however, and when asked about her team, Dick's mother would say:

> 'Of course Melbourne—they're such a decent sort of chap'. And she was convinced that a lot of doctors and lawyers and university men played for Melbourne. Then some rotten person pointed out to her that there were more doctors and lawyers playing for Collingwood than for Melbourne. It broke her heart.

In politics, the Wallaces were 'conservative of course':

> There was an enormous amount of class snobbery in our family. They wore collars and ties damn it. And very formal in their relationships. I don't think that it ever occurred to them to call their neighbours by their Christian names. Our neighbours, the Hobbs, he was a baker, so that made a social gap. If you wore a coat and tie or had a white-collar job, you were of that class, even though you hardly had a cracker. You didn't mix with the plumber—he might be making three times as much money as you, but he was a working-class type of man and he probably voted Labor!
>
> My parents drank not at all. The Irish did—they became the deservedly poor. They were a different species. I think you were born poor and you just stayed that way. We were probably poor by today's standards—if you counted the amount of spare money, we were—but you wouldn't have said that to my parents and got away with it. 'Genteel poor' does it. There was no way my father could amass any capital to go into business on his own—I don't think he had any particular desires to do that. He never expressed it. I think he and another bloke built a house once—raised the money and built a house. That was the only capitalistic venture I heard of.
>
> I remember as a kid, I was rather scared of Richmond—if I had to walk through Richmond at night, I wouldn't have fancied that.
> I don't think that a lot of people—like our family—were dissatisfied with their lives. It was—that's it and that's the way it goes.

The 'recognition of necessity'.

3

The Lessons of
Innocence
1920–1939

The Lessons of Innocence
1920–1939

Hearts and Homes

Our house was in Currajong Avenue, Camberwell, and it faced south.
There were hydrangeas up the easterly side. And in the front lawn we
had a type of cypress tree which was called *Cryptomerea Elegans*—it was a
beautiful thing with pink tips to it, that my brother put a match to when
my parents were away.

We had a drive—we didn't have a car—and where we eventually had a
garage, there was a fernery. Going up that drive we had standard roses—a
rose that stands on a stalk—quite ugly I feel—like an umbrella on the top.
We had the Velvet of black, Black Boys and pink. In the back garden we
had fruit trees and a bit of a vegetable garden; and Dad used to have beds
of annuals in front of the house which I've never gone in for like zinnias,
asters, stocks and petunias. Begonias would have been in the fernery.

The lawn was buffalo grass and we had a red gravel drive and a wire
fence—crinkly and the top turned over. And you had a tradesmen's
entrance because they came every day—'Here's today's meat and what
would you like tomorrow? (We didn't have an ice-chest.) That was black
asphalt—the path the tradesmen went up. The red brick house was built
about 1921—it was where they broke up the Sunnyside Estate, and the
homes were not uniform but they were of uniform quality.[1]

Marjorie O'Donoghue and her family of Currajong Avenue, Camberwell,
were part of the suburban frontier of the early 1920s. It was a carefully
managed middle-class frontier, because since 1898 the Camberwell City
Council had been restricting the styles of buildings to preserve the

---

[1] Interview with *Marjorie O'Donoghue*, 11 December 1990.

municipality's social character and in 1923 went so far as to declare it a 'brick area'.[2] *Marjorie*'s father was also a 'new man': one of the growing number of Commonwealth public servants. He had joined the Public Service straight from school, and in between his work, his fathering and his gardening during the 1920s, he was completing a university degree; once graduated, he was made head of the department.

The *O'Donoghues* were unusual for Camberwell, however, in that they were Catholics, for Camberwell was the showpiece of the Protestant middle class, home to the lowest proportion of Catholics in the metropolis. Even so, the Catholics had risen to the challenge and built Our Lady of Victories Church on the Burke Road hill as a glowing Triumphalist statement which would 'rival some of the noblest structures of the old land, and tell us by its very presence . . . the ancient glories of the ages of the faith'. Seventy thousand had turned out for its opening in 1918, many of them Protestants both awed and slightly shocked by the richly veined marble, the 'graven images' and the gilt.[3] On another Camberwell hill lived *Margaret Power,* near the St Dominic's church her parents had raised much money to build. Opposite them dwelt a retired Methodist teacher:

> He used to come over and tell my father how fortunate he should consider himself that he was the only Catholic he ever spoke to. He'd also come over every time he'd read some item in the paper such as there were more Catholics in gaol than of any other religion. I can remember father telling him that that was because they all took Irish names.[4]

In Currajong Avenue, however, Catholic and Protestant children mixed cheerfully: the boys playing 'footie' and cricket in the street; the girls playing mostly in each other's homes and gardens.[5] *Marjorie* started school at the parish school behind the church before going on to Genazzano, and when her parents went to London in 1938, the four children became boarders: 'I can remember the nuns pumping Dad for what he thought about Neville Chamberlain and the prospects of war'. The transition from home to boarding school was effortless—she felt loved and secure both at home and with the nuns. Hers was a happy childhood.

When the *O'Donoghues* walked to Mass, just round the corner in Burke Road they passed the home of Betty Jackson and her family. Her father was also a public servant—an inspector for the Postmaster General's Department, earning £500 a year. Betty's mother was also of Irish stock,

---

[2] Chris McConville, 'At Home with Sandy Stone', p. 92; Hocking, *Stormy Petrel*, p. 45.

[3] Mary Sheehan, *Our Lady of Victories*, p. 24.

[4] Interview with *Margaret Power*, 17 October 1989.

[5] Middle-class Catholic children were less sectarian in their playmates than the Protestants, possibly because of their lower concentration in middle-class suburbs: Survey: 'Did you have Catholic playmates?': MLC: Yes, 40%, N/A, 3%. 'Did you have Protestant playmates?' Genazzano: Yes, 85%; N/A, 2%.

but Methodist. And theirs was another happy family: 'My vision of child-hood is a big table and sitting around it with lots of people for meals, and there were a lot of laughs, a lot of jokes, a lot of stories'. Her mother was a niece of Joseph Furphy, and had grown up in Shepparton where she had become a pupil teacher:

> She became intensely interested in teaching and didn't want to get married because she was so interested in what she was doing. And I always remember her statement about when she got married at thirty— 'Everyone else was doing it, so I thought I'd better get married'.
>
>   But as children we were brought up with the stories of what happened at her school—we'd know the names of the teachers and headmasters. Every Sunday morning my two brothers and I would get into bed with her for about an hour, and she would talk about when she was young. I can remember her reciting stories from the school reader which she knew by heart.

Homework was almost a family game as they all sat around the dining room table with their mother, and Betty followed her brothers' progress in spelling tests: 'It was probably frightfully competitive, but somehow it was part of the games of childhood'. Their mother never seemed busy—there was *always* time for children: 'I can remember sitting at the table with mother teaching us all to play the mouth organ'. Their mother was instinctively tolerant:

> My second brother and I were never christened, which in those days was something! And I remember my mother saying to someone who asked why, 'Well I always thought that if they went to a country town, they mightn't want to go to a Methodist church, they might even want to become Catholics'. And *that* was considered shocking. She was very tolerant of Roman Catholics and she was thought to be a bit odd. I can remember her saying to someone, 'I'd rather my children were Catholics than nothing'.[6]

She made her Methodist principles 'very palatable'.

  Security, both emotional and material, was not always the lot of middle-class children. Within private schools in the inter-war years there was a wide range of income and status, but it was Genazzano which stood out among the four schools as having the most established, best educated and most prosperous constituency. Among the fathers there were double the proportions of doctors and lawyers than at Scotch and six times the proportions at Trinity and MLC; by all tests of income and status, Genazzano was ahead of the other three.[7] What is even more telling is that, if we take a wholly state-school education as an indicator of lower-class origins, then half the 'Survey' fathers at Scotch and Trinity and

---

[6] Interview with Betty Jackson, 2 August 1988.
[7] See Appendix II: tables 4a and 4b.

almost three-quarters at MLC were new members of the middle class by the 1920s and 1930s. But of the full cohorts of boys and girls at the three Protestant schools in the 1930s, the number of newcomers was probably higher still: at Scotch and Melbourne Grammar in the early 1930s no more than 10 per cent were the sons of Old Boys.[8] The middle class, depleted by the long depression of the 1890s and the war, was in the process of remaking itself. And the Genazzano fathers, a more select bunch from the Catholic middle and upper class, were a generation ahead of these Protestants in the acquisition of equity and higher education.

The mechanisms of social rising are not hard to detect: half the 'Survey' Scotch and Trinity fathers had been in low status occupations in their twenties and half of those were in trades or manual occupations. Among the petty clerical and sales workers, there were some with 'good prospects' who were doing their commercial apprenticeship, but a good proportion never got any further. At MLC 'trade' was even more prominent, and it was a painful way to rise as the 'tradesmen's entrance' for the homes of the suburbs reminded them daily of their marginality. MLC was noted for its willingness to admit 'trade' and, as a result, the young ladies from nearby Ruyton Girls' School disdained MLC as no better than a high school.[9] The other mechanisms were educational: entering accountancy by night school; engineering by technical college; pharmacy by apprenticeship; the law by articles only; the public service by examination; teaching by pupil teaching and college; the church by theological college. Very few of the Protestants had been to university: in fact the majority of the Scotch and Trinity fathers had no qualifications of any sort—they were men who had only reputation and experience.[10] They had got there by hard work. This was not a class born with 'a silver spoon' in its mouth: rather it was a class of self-made men and women and, whether by study or business, they rose because they had worked for it. *Gwenda Holtby*'s father was an engineer, from a Bendigo Methodist family. In 1919 he had a brick house built for them by an architect in Caulfield. As in Camberwell, this was a subdivision of a land boom estate with covenants which decreed that the house had to be brick and to the value of £750. The *Holtby* family led a steady, conscientious existence:

My father was a tremendous worker. He'd come home, walk up the side path at twenty past five. He'd have his dinner ready and start eating at half-past five; and at about ten to six he'd be out gardening or doing

---

[8] See Appendix I: Scotch 1934 Cohort and Melbourne Grammar 1934 Cohort; Survey: Fathers and Mothers who attended the same school: Scotch, 17%; Trinity, 4%; MLC, 13%; Genazzano, 19%. Mothers and Fathers who attended sister/brother school: Scotch (PLC), 8%; Trinity (an Anglican girls' school), 22%; MLC (Wesley) 10%; Genazzano (Xavier), 22%.

[9] Theobald, *Ruyton Remembers*, p. 74.

[10] See Appendix II, table 3.

carpentry or something. My mother *had* to be a tremendous worker and always 'do-it-yourself'. One of my first memories of them is in the lounge-room, putting double doors where there had been a single door. And my mother, who was about five foot two, was holding up a concrete beam while Dad did something to the side to put it in place. Absolutely hair-raising things that went on from 'do-it-yourself Methodists'.[11]

For many, becoming middle-class was precarious and their children remain deeply affected by their doggedness and courage. *David Miller.*

My father was an absolutely fascinating man. He was one of four children of an impecunious minister of religion in Hobart Town, Tasmania, who had gone to Moore College at Sydney University. And when he came back to Van Diemen's Land, they told him that they didn't like that qualification from those Heathens in Sydney, so he became Hobart City Missioner for the Baptist Church. My father remained an Anglican.

My father, through economic circumstances, had to go to work at the great old age of eleven years. Then my grandfather was silly enough to die and my father had to become the mainstay of the family. He was in the Public Service and did well. He had a very inquisitive mind. When my eldest son was doing his matric., he asked me about some English literature and I said. 'Listen son, I'm pretty full-bottle on music and visual arts, but I'm not as good on English literature as I should be. Go round and talk to your grandfather'. He went round and came back a couple of hours later, 'Gee Dad!' 'And did you see his library?' 'Yes.' 'Now I'll tell you something—he left school when he was eleven: that's education because the man wanted to be educated.'

My father came to the mainland as a public servant and hated it. And when he was thirty and had three or four children—he was an artistic man—he opened a furnishings, fabrics and designs business which hit the 1924 semi-recession. He did not go broke. He saw the writing on the wall and so he walked around to all his creditors and said, 'I will pay you and I'm closing the business'.

He then took two jobs—he was manager during the day of antiques and fine furnishings for a city store and at night he was manager of a public fun park. He had a great affinity for people and my mother used to get horrified when Dad would bring home some young man from the fun park who'd been in trouble with the law and Dad would say, 'Come on Ethel—he's got to come home and live with a normal family'. He stood in court and bonded him. And Dad did this to the extent that a man in England during the war stood with tears in his eyes and said, 'I owe it all to your father'.

He was a man much loved by people, with a brilliant artistic sense. He did the interior decorating of 'Ripponlea'. I nearly followed in his footsteps—he used to take me down as a schoolboy.[12]

---

[11] Interview with *Gwenda Holtby*, 8 June 1988.
[12] Interview with *David Miller*, 13 December 1990.

Tom McCaw's father finished his long working life as an industrial chemist, and the account of his career reveals much about the vagaries of social rising through the depressed 1890s into the twentieth century:

> He was one of the last of the self-made men. He married quite late in life—he was born in 1867 and he didn't marry until 1920. During that period when he was single, he moved around the country a lot—it was a growing state at that time. He had a wide range of experience, starting, I think, as a grocer's boy in Collingwood with a relative. The whole family moved with the construction of the railway lines to the north-east and to Gippsland. He was the eldest and the succeeding members of the family were born all the way up the line—places like Wallan and Chiltern and so on. Then they went on the Gippsland line down from Sale and he went to school in Nar Nar Goon. His father was a construction worker.
>
> My father had been an agricultural inspector in north-east Victoria when the phylloxera plague was on and he gained some scientific training from that. He had some time at the West Australian gold fields, came back and *somehow* became laboratory manager in the Melbourne University department of Physiology and was there about ten years. Then he went as a working hand to Maize Products when it was established as a starch and glucose factory for the confectionery industry, but he soon rose to assume importance in the place because of his scientific knowledge. I'm fairly certain he had done something at the Workingmen's College in single subjects and he was a member of the Chemical Society of Victoria and the Chemical Institute. He retired finally in 1948, so he had very long working life.

By the time he married in 1920 he had made enough to buy a house, and Tom and his wife live there still. He was able to send Tom to Scotch for seven years; but he could not afford a car until 1931.[13]

Tom McCaw's father was earning around £600 a year in the 1930s and the salaries of most middle-class managers and semi-professionals ranged between £500 and £700. The Richmond City Council paid its town clerk, C. C. Bleazy, £673 a year in 1937; but there was a large gap down to the city treasurer who received £364. Big money was not easy to make. In 1921 a survey of legal incomes revealed that in the two branches of the profession only forty practitioners were making over £1000 a year. One Scotch boy's father earned £1250 as a company director. Presbyterian ministers remained the best paid of the clergy with salaries of £500 a year in the suburban churches and more for the prestigious congregations in Toorak or the city. Supreme Court judges earned £2500 in 1920, and a truly rich man like Russell Grimwade had an income of between £15 000 and £26 000 a year during the 1920s and in those years never paid more than £5000 in tax (he did not face heavy

---

[13] Interview with Tom McCaw, 11 December 1990.

taxation until World War II). The families settling in the suburbs in the 1920s expected to pay £1575 for a seven-roomed brick villa in Camberwell or Canterbury and £795 for a five-roomed wooden house on a quarter-acre block. In respectable but still proletarian East Prahran a double-fronted weatherboard 'in perfect order' cost £435 to buy. At the other end of the scale Dr and Mrs *Frank Doyle* were able to build an elegant two-storey, five-bedroomed house with tennis court in Kew for £5000 in 1935.[14]

The deliberations of Judge Alf Foster at the Royal Commission into the Basic Wage provide a guide to the comparative real income of the middle and upper classes. The actual basic wage reckoned to be sufficient for a man supporting a wife and three children was just over £200 a year but, to the employers' horror, Judge Foster found that it needed to be a hundred pounds higher.[15] The lawyer, F. F. Knight, recorded that running a house with a cook cost him £44 11s 6d a month; by 1937, with a cook and a housemaid, his monthly bills came to £55, which he considered revealed how low was the cost of middle-class living.[16] The lower middle class on £300 to £400 a year were not exactly affluent, and there were many at the four schools whose parents were renters, not owners, of property. Geoff Tolson's parents lived in rented flats for most of the time he was at Scotch, sacrificing a home of their own so that the boys could have a good education. He suspects now that his mother 'envied—in a way—ladies who were in a much better position, who'd never be seen more than once in an evening frock'.[17] Elaine Corran sees her parents as 'salt of the earth—entirely unspectacular people—"grocers who gave you honest weight"'. Her father managed a bookstall on Flinders Street Station, and they were renters:

> My mother worked very hard—she loved her garden and we always improved the house we lived in—we felt that was proper. I helped Dad paint the outside. I helped put the carpets down. Mum did the washing and I helped her; and if she wasn't well enough, she expected me to do it, even though I was twelve or thirteen. She'd say, 'You can if you want to'. She was a very strong woman—she scrubbed floors and thought nothing of it. And she cooked beautiful meals.[18]

One father at MLC who was earning good money was the accountant Oswald Barnett, who as a specialist in insolvency was making £1000 a year in the 1930s. Like so many at the Protestant schools, he was self-made: the son of a Cornish quarryman who lost his job in the 1890s

---

[14] F. F. Knight, *These Things Happened*, pp. 263–4; *Richmond Chronicle*, 25 March 1937; J. Gray Robertson, *Golden Jubilee of St John's Church, Elsternwick*; J. R. Poynter, *Russell Grimwade*, p. 191; conversation with Mr Pettigrew.
[15] Constance Larmour, *Labor Judge*, pp. 89–94.
[16] F. F. Knight, *These Things Happened*, p. 313.
[17] Interview with Geoffrey Tolson, 26 March 1990.
[18] Interview with Elaine Corran, 26 September 1990.

depression and never worked again. Barnett grew up in the rich culture of Brunswick Methodism, where, according to Renate Howe, 'there was some overlap between the Methodist discussion groups' and the local socialists. He was deeply influenced by his brother-in-law Frank Hyett, who was active in the Victorian Socialist Party and secretary of the Victorian Railways' Union at the time of his tragic early death from Spanish Influenza in 1919.[19] Barnett also provided a home always for his sister May, who had paid for his education and pleaded his cause with the family, as he rose through pupil teaching, public service examinations and night study into practice as an accountant. He never lost his loyalty to the poor, and preached and put into practice a commonsense Christian socialism. And in private life he revealed the blending of working-class and middle-class ways which came with social rising. In 1913 he moved his family from the cramped respectability of Brunswick to the bracing heights of Balwyn, and the future father of the Victorian Housing Commission had definite ideas about ideal living. His second daughter, Betty:

> We were brought up with having a parlour where only visitors went and we children practised the piano. It was called the sitting room. And there was the best bedroom, to be slept in only by visitors. The second bedroom was Auntie May's room. We slept in a large, louvred sleepout and used an adjoining dressing room which had wardrobes and chests of drawers. Father was mad about fresh air—they had both been brought up in small, poky little houses—so fresh air, coming out to Balwyn—it was almost like a religion. Mother and Father slept in the double bed in the middle, and Joy and I were in beds each end, and when June was born she slept in the cot. Then she shared my bed for some years. When Le was born she had the cot, and when Mother's last baby, Brian, was born, Joy and I had our own bedroom—a glassed-in back veranda. When I was twenty-one Father gave up his workshop so I could have my own room.
>
> We all got up at half past six. There were no fires in the house until four in the afternoon, and Mother had a protégée in me in cold showers before we had a hot water service. She'd have her cold shower, then I'd hear her thumping down the passage, making noise so as to wake me, strip my bed, take me and grab a few clothes into the bathroom, undress me and put me under the shower with a big, wet, cold facewasher on my back, soapy and wet, and leave it to me. Everyone had a shower once we had a hot water service when I was twenty-one, otherwise everyone had a bath once a week, using the bath heater.[20]

Oswald Barnett was unusual for a Methodist in that he had a strong love of visual arts, which he passed on to his children. Betty was taken to the National Gallery for the first time when she was five:

---

[19] Renate Howe, 'Reform and Social Responsibility', pp. 22–6.
[20] Interview with Betty Barnett, 17 July 1990.

My parents were very much on improving themselves and their children. We couldn't go to the gallery on Sunday because we couldn't go on a tram and spend money—we were very Methodist—but the art gallery I was very familiar with—and the Botanic Gardens and rowing on the Yarra. Our father had pursued culture from a very poor family, and I've still got his English poets. He wrote a great deal of poetry himself and was an amateur painter. We were brought up with a great feeling for painting and Father bought pictures of Australian artists which were well chosen. He was always illustrating cards, and my copy of his memoirs—which he did for me—has illustrations going all through it. And envelopes had beautiful drawings of gum trees or violets on the front. I think that one of the reasons I was geared to go to Swinburne to do art was a fulfilment of his own wishes that he had had some training in it.

Social rising involved far more than acquiring nice homes, motor cars and smart clothes: there was also changes in speech and deportment, habits and ideas. The unconfident were often anxious about making mistakes or looking foolish, and for ever fretting over 'what will people SAY?' (Ministers' wives, particularly among the Methodists where lower class origins were more frequent, were among the most vulnerable—anxious that the minister's family set a good example of a Christian home, but also that the more affluent parishioners did not catch them out).[21] Joyce Thorpe's mother approached the task of social rising hard-headedly. She was the daughter of a country station master and one of ten children. She hated children and housework, so came to the city—'got a job as a salesperson, was paid a pittance, taught herself to type, got a job at ten shillings a week, and stayed at this little place in Carlton at 2s 6d a week, lived on 2s 6d and saved 5s'. She married D. W. Thorpe who had done well in the book and stationery trades, and after their marriage he founded a trade magazine which became very successful. They moved from Northcote to Burke Road, Kew, where the little girl next door was going to a private school: 'And my mother, who was a very acute person, knew nothing about private schools, but she was determined that I should be equal to the little girl next door, and she was actually able to pay for my fees at MLC out of her housekeeping which was only £3 a week':

> My mother was a very good manager but she was also a rather selfish
> woman. She was a complex character, because she was obviously
> unselfish in letting Dad start his own business, but Dad waited on her hand
> and foot. She was very intelligent, but why she didn't ever use her intelli-
> gence I don't know. She was extraordinarily lazy. She used to stay in bed all
> day and read if she could. But she would make me two dresses a year and
> she would do everything she could to see that I got the right social

---

[21] Interveiws with Lurline Keck, 9 May 1989, and with Nancy Batt, 6 October 1988.

upbringing. She was not interested in my education. She worked hard to
see that my brother passed his exams and got a scholarship to Wesley and
later to the university, whereas I was encouraged to leave school. But
basically the housework was never done. I couldn't take anybody home
because I was always worried that the dishes wouldn't have been washed.
But she always came good when it was important. She didn't want to have
children, but Dad was so keen on them that she did it as a wifely duty. She
had an enormous influence on him and he adored her, really worshipped
her. In fact the relatives used to say that Dad did everything for the children
except breastfeed us. He really did the most amazing things for us as
children and kept doing it for all his grandchildren—looked after them, put
them to sleep—he adored children.

Joyce found herself rather embarrassed by her mother's large family who were
'a bit agin the law': 'I was brought up as a fairly strict Methodist, honest,
honourable person and I was always shocked at my mother's relatives who
tried to beat the government—for example, they thought they were very
clever to get more tea and butter than the rations allowed them in the war'.[22]
    Mothers' ambitions for their children's schooling were often, as in the
Thorpe family, the more influential. While 61 per cent of the other MLC
mothers were state-school girls, around 10 per cent could be said to have
'married down', as did 10 per cent from Scotch. Trinity parents were more
equal in their social origin, but at Genazzano 20 per cent more of the
mothers than the fathers had been to Catholic schools: a reflection partly of
the degree of mixed marriages where the Catholicism became the dominant
religion and of the tendency for rising men to marry later and 'up'.[23] Quite
often the mothers' parents or childless siblings paid for the college education
of the next generation. The mothers too had a little longer at school than the
fathers, and the Genazzano mothers the longest of all. The Genazzano
mothers were also the most likely to have worked for their own living, nearly
half in office work and a sixth in trades or unskilled work. But if there were
subtle patterns, the Scotch and MLC mothers included the most teachers,
Genazzano and MLC the most office workers, Genazzano the most nurses
and Trinity and MLC the most manual workers.[24] Around 11 per cent from
MLC and an average of 20 per cent of those from the other three schools
worked after marriage. And only a minority brought a private income into
the marriages.[25] There was a wide diversity in these college families between
the wars—blendings of class, religion and culture which belied the monolithic image of the private-school world.

---

[22] Interview with Joyce Thorpe, 25 May 1988.
[23] See Appendix II, table 1b.
[24] Ibid: tables 2b, 5a and 5b.
[25] Survey: 'Did your mother work after marriage?' Yes: Scotch, 22%; Trinity, 22%; MLC, 11%;
Genazzano, 19%; 'Did your mother have an independent income?' Yes: Scotch, 29%; Trinity,
17%; MLC, 19%; Genazzano, 31%.

One of the subtle distinctions within the middle and upper classes was in the use of servants, and again Genazzano reported the highest incidence of paid domestic help.[26] Much of this domestic service in middle-class homes was simply the 'woman who came in to do the washing' on Monday morning—'a species that disappeared with World War II', recalls Tom McCaw. For those who could afford servants in the 1920s the problem was that working-class women saw domestic service as 'a last resort', and the National Council of Women prophetically resolved in 1920 that 'the solution of the present-day distaste for domestic work is for the better-off middle-class women to do their own work and to put the money saved from hiring assistance into better household equipment'.[27] Domestic service became the refuge of the otherwise unemployable: the widow, deserted wife or divorcee with children, the morally disgraced, even the simple. Prominent church families often provided a home and a wage to inmates of girls' homes or the unlucky-in-life. *Mary Geoghegan*'s father was a doctor in a working-class suburb: 'he loved the people and he was very kind to them' and did house calls day and night:

> He'd sit with people till they died—there was that feeling of family about it. People would give you things—food—because they couldn't pay.
> When I was old enough to take messages, I always thought that 'P' stood for Patrick and 'L' for Leo because those were his initials; but 'P' was for private and 'L' for Lodge and you were supposed to write that down. He had very few private patients—the Lodge was a marvellous thing—you paid very little and then you had unlimited care.
> And we had a maid and nursemaid—but they weren't paid much. They lived in—usually country people. We had one who was the daughter of a nun at the Abbotsford convent. I think that she had to go into the convent as a lay sister, doing the housework, and that way the two girls were brought up and looked after. Later we took one as a cook and she married the painter (and painters in those days came on pushbikes). All the people who worked for us still came to see my mother years after they left her employ. I think they were very grateful to be given a roof and meals, even though they didn't get much time off—half a day a week and Sunday after lunch.

Kate Morgan grew up at 'Niddrie'—a bluestone homestead with French windows in the drawing room, and bluestone stables and dairy—'I can still see the big milk pans'. There was no reticulated water, only tanks and an underground well, so baths were once a week with water heated in a kerosene tin on the stove. The two maids eased the burden of raising six lively children:

---

[26] Survey: 'Did your mother have domestic help?' Yes: Scotch, 57%; Trinity, 45%; MLC 55%; Genazzano, 72%; Yes—qualified: Scotch, 4%; Trinity, 5%; MLC, 13%; Genazzano, 12.5%. The 'qualified' was largely those who indicated that the help was only with laundering.

[27] Ada Norris, *Champions of the Impossible*, p. 43.

And I should be ashamed to say it, but we had Nellie and Nellie came when Dick and I were three months old, and we were fourteen, going on fifteen when she left to be married, and I couldn't put my school tie on. She was wonderful—she did everything. I think she had been with the nuns at Abbotsford and that was how Mother got Nellie.

The *Doyles* had a well staffed, smoothly ordered house in Studley Park Road, but their mother was anxious that her privileged children should not think of themselves as superior:

My mother's experience of living in London and Vienna while my father did post-graduate study had developed in her a strong social conscience; and when she became an employer in Depression Melbourne, she was determined to be a good one. The household routine was designed to respect the servants' privacy and free time as well as my father's work—meals were always on time; the kitchen was mostly out-of-bounds to the children, and politeness and consideration were absolutes. Probably for that reason, relations between the children and the servants were not close: only for the gardener-handyman (whom we called Mr Dudley—never Jack) was there real affection. And he was a source of muddled embarrassment: when on wet days he would offer to drive the girls to Genazzano—would anyone think us ostentatious for having a chauffeur? Or, embarrassing in another way, would this man in khaki overalls be mistaken for our father?

Their father had a busy practice as a consultant physician in Collins Street, and he also worked long hours at St Vincent's Hospital:

Every evening after dinner, my father would start his telephone calls, discussing patients who had been referred to him; then he would read his medical journals or write reports. There wasn't much family entertainment. We listened to the news and *Dad and Dave*, and that was about all. We would either go and do homework, or sit by the fire in the study, reading. I would listen to the telephone calls, picking up intriguing words like 'ventricular fibrillation' and wondering how you would spell 'emphysema'.

The war changed all that: when the women went into munitions, there was no more live-in help. The family relaxed its timetable and reclaimed the kitchen: their father learned 'survival cooking' and did a very good Sunday breakfast after eight-o'clock Mass.

Winsome Walklate was one of the minority at MLC to grow up in a large home with live-in servants. Her mother had a private income, the result of successful family property investments which had recovered after the 1890s crash, and her father, the brother of a prominent Methodist minister, was a commercial traveller. They were frugal: 'they certainly despised anyone who lived over their income', and her father felt it was his duty to pay off the family home, and did so before the 1930s depression; her mother's income paid for the school fees, children's clothing and 'extras'. Tanti was a lovely house in a glorious setting, built on a block subdivided from the Canonbury estate in Barnsbury Road, off Mont Albert Road, Canterbury:

> I remember the pleasures of playing in the garden. Mother never told us not to get dirty and we adored playing with mud and mud pies. We used to make cakes with mud and decorate them with flowers from the garden, and Mother would come and purchase them. We had an old table in the back garden for our amusement and we used our imaginations quite a lot and we'd turn it upside down to be a ship. We didn't venture from our garden much. We climbed trees. We had a married couple—the man was full-time doing the garden and we had full-time help in the kitchen. And we loved her—we used to get on her back when the dear soul was washing the floor. Earlier we had a maid-of-all-work and she was not the slightest bit down-trodden. Her name was Muriel and she cared for me and I remember her quite clearly. The birth of my sister Audrey eighteen months later was a joy to me and I never remember life without my sister Audrey. We did everything together and we were dressed alike.

It was, like so many, a very loving childhood: 'I was always conscious of being surrounded with love and caring and the beauty of the garden':

> My parents had been engaged for some years and they joyfully married. They practised birth-control because I asked Mother. My mother used to put her arms around me and say 'I *do* love you so' and they came and said goodnight and we said our prayers. But I didn't actually like physical contact—I didn't like kissing and one thing we weren't taught to do was to kiss each other as children. My uncle (an old Scotch boy) was a dentist in Harp Road and my aunt and he had five children. They were a very loving family and they were forever kissing. They kissed when they left the house and they kissed when they returned. Dr Kennan suggested that they shouldn't kiss so much because they were passing on infections.
> My mother and father tenderly kissed—I never kissed so much in front of my children in case they might feel jealous. I felt they might feel jealous of the relationship between husband and wife, which children sense very early, so I didn't do much kissing.

These youthful hearts were shaped and trained by the love and example of their parents. The first experiences of love and rejection were the building blocks of the adult to be, and there is no doubt that many commenced life with that most valuable of all assets—unconditional love. *Helen Browne* 'never doubted that [she] was loved—always'.[28] And *Doug*

---

[28] Interview with *Helen Browne*, 24 November 1990.

Gordon only once came from school to find his mother not at home waiting for him, and that was because he had left school early with a migraine
headache.[29] For many families the children were the centre of their existence. Sister Anthony Buckley was a country girl boarding at Genazzano:

> The whole life of the family centred on the children. My grandmother left
> Yarram to come to live in Melbourne so that there could be somewhere we
> could go on Sundays. And every Sunday there was a special dinner cooked
> for the children. It wasn't what my grandmother wanted—I'm sure she
> didn't want to come to Melbourne and leave her friends—but we were at
> boarding school. And it's only when we look back now that we realized
> how fortunate we were that she always had the door open.

But not all families found joy in parenthood. *Frances Costelloe*'s father was
a hard-working general practitioner in the northern suburbs and, at the
age of six, *Frances* was sent as a boarder to Genazzano; on holidays she had
to stay with cousins in the country. At eighteen she left school and entered nursing:

> I think now that I must have been very silly—I accepted what happened.
> I think back now—that boarding school was a horror really, for small
> children. They should have been in their own homes. The nuns were
> very good—I had no problems that way. I don't criticize but I wouldn't
> like that to happen to anyone I knew. I think a home's essential—I don't
> care if it's a shack by the river.[30]

There were dutiful parents, especially fathers, who loved their children
but who found intimacy difficult. Lawrence Cohn came from a secure family,

> but in those days I don't think that children had much of a relationship
> with parents in the way we would talk about relationships today. I'm
> sorry there wasn't more. My father—it would be fair to say—was a bit
> distant. He was a great walker and we'd go for walks, and the only thing
> that would stop him was a cat on a gatepost—he could never resist that.[31]

Geoff McKee hardly knew his bank officer father because 'night after
night, after dinner he'd be out at a Freemasons' Lodge'.[32] But hidden in
homes all over Australia were men who had gone to World War I and
who were never the same again.[33] For most the disabilities were physical,

---

[29] Interview with *Dr Doug Gordon*, 25 July 1990.
[30] Interview with *Frances Costelloe*, 1 November 1989.
[31] Interview with Lawrence Cohn, 21 September 1990.
[32] Interview with Geoff McKee, 24 May 1990.
[33] Survey: 'Did your father serve in World War I?' Yes: Scotch, 29%; Trinity 38%; MLC, 27%;
Genazzano, 30%. 'Did he suffer any lasting disabilities?' Yes: Scotch, 56%; Trinity, 54%; MLC,
49%; Genazzano, 50%.

but there were plenty who were by turn remote or morose or who shouted all the time. For the worst affected, family life became punctuated by sudden rages, drinking bouts and black depressions, but even for the most stable, there was always a shadow. One Genazzano woman recorded:

> My father was in both wars. I didn't think they had any effect on him until I sat with him in his last illness. He cried for his friends in the trenches at Gallipoli and told of his fears. I realized as children we had only been told the funny bits.[34]

The Repatriation hospitals and nursing homes were full of broken men. *Doug Gordon* can remember being taken by his mother to visit 'the rows and rows and rows of chronic bronchitics'. James Austin's father survived Gallipoli but was wounded and buried alive in 1917 by a shell on the Western Front. His shell shock went untreated and he was repatriated home to Australia with his young English bride. His own father had been killed in an industrial accident and so he had had little schooling, but the family rented a house in Abbotsford and he found a job in the nearby Kodak factory. When James was two and a half, and his brother just twelve months old, their father was struck in his turn by an industrial accident and his mind disintegrated. He spent the rest of his life in a psychiatric hospital:

> All he knew was that we were someone who was known to him—he wasn't aware of it. He could not speak rationally. He was never violent. He was in a dream world, and the dream was everything that had happened to him up to the point when the world finished for him in 1917. Quite amazing really. He lived on until he was seventy-two—he was there for forty-one years. The others in the ward were just walking around, staring into space, talking to themselves.[35]

At first they visited him once a week, then once a month and finally once every three months, 'almost like a pilgrimage in my earliest memories. My brother and I regarded it as a chore. We sort of understood what it was about and we sometimes made up stories about it because as kids you do'. Their mother coped, found some paid work, raised the two boys and got them to Trinity Grammar for a few years each, even though her pension was just one-third of the basic wage and the Public Trustee held her husband's pension in trust, sending her only £4 a week. Her husband outlived her, and when the boys divided his forty-one years of

---

[34] Survey No. 81: Genazzano, born 1928, daughter of public servant, primary teacher married to engineer.
[35] Interview with James Austin, 12 and 13 September 1990.

accumulated pension between them, there was enough for James to take his wife and four children to England to visit their relatives.

In recalling the emotions of childhood, women are better than men, because they have been permitted more emotional expressiveness; but for both sexes a high premium was placed on emotional control. Few of this generation were brought up to express strong emotion rather than routinely to suppress it, but women fared better than men, and the Catholics better than the Protestants.[36] This was more an emotional style than a pathology, however, and for many it became a source of strength in times of crisis: Valerie East, as a psychologist, doubts that 'letting it all hang out' necessarily makes it any easier to cope with grief or danger or anxiety: in fact it often makes it worse. It is possible that in those families where things were not as they should be, these constraints limited the incidence of domestic violence. One MLC respondent expresses the complexities well:

> I was taught to repress strong emotions as in 'sounding off' about someone or something.
> I now find it difficult to express strong personal emotions such as love, care, pity—verbally (though I feel these), but I find it easy to 'sound off' on other matters about which I feel strongly.[37]

There was, certainly, a set of constraints about the expression of feeling, the display of the naked body and the physical expression of affection. Many families were very loving, loyal and happy, but rarely kissed or cuddled, even with young children: 'you had to be going overseas to get a kiss', some remember. Many women would endanger their life rather than undergo an internal examination by a doctor, so that pregnancy and childbirth were an agony of shame. The Barnetts' mother was examined by her doctor for the first time in each of her five pregnancies when she was already in labour: 'she wouldn't let herself be touched by a stranger'. 'Mother never used the word "pregnant" and she disappeared socially after about three months—she just didn't go to church again. And then with shining face, produce the baby and expect everyone to be surprised.' She breastfed, but only in private, and her daughters never once saw her undressed (and they doubt that their father ever did either). Home births hold no romance for the Barnetts, for their mother's 'screaming and wailing' from the best bedroom rings still in their ears. *Anne Sullivan* was astonished while studying anatomy for nursing when her mother, who

---

[36] Survey: 'Were you brought up to express or repress strong emotions?'

	Scotch	Trinity	MLC	Genazzano
Express (per cent)	15.8	13.3	15.0	20.0
Repress (per cent)	51.9	57.8	52.8	51.7
Not answered (per cent)	32.4	28.9	32.2	28.3

[37] Survey No. 485: MLC.

had borne three children, asked ' "How do you have a baby? What happens?" And I had to give her a little lesson on the reproductive system'.[38]

Excessive modesty, religious prohibition and sexual ignorance were enough without the fear of pregnancy. The middle-class families of the 1920s and 1930s clearly wanted to have fewer children than their parents. The family sizes fell, both for Protestants and for Catholics and somehow these couples were practising birth control.[39] Even at Genazzano families of five or six were unusual in the 1930s. There is some evidence that even Catholics were using devices and pessaries and one doctor's wife worked out the rhythm method and used it to space a large family.[40] How many were as advanced for their time as were the Walklates we are not to know; how many restricted their families by not having sexual intercourse we can only suspect. Certainly a number of their children were later to realize that their parents had ceased to have sex. *Mary Geoghegan*, as the only daughter in a family of five, was her mother's unwilling confidante:

> My mother had fibroids and she used to talk a lot about it and I wish she hadn't—how she feared to have my youngest brother. And I think my father paid dearly for that. As we get older we can't judge as much—how painful it was; how she was always frightened having the last two children because she haemorrhaged so much. And they didn't have the care—they didn't do the transfusions and things that they do now. She was scared she would die and leave orphan children and I think it wasn't altogether selfish.

She found relief, as did many middle-class Catholic women, in a hysterectomy. Others, of all religions, shut their husbands out of their bedrooms.

Worst of all, some children knew they were never meant to be. Jean Cane's father—a man of strong independent and agnostic views—was not highly-sexed, but 'he was red-blooded enough to want sex occasionally'. But 'my mother hated it—hated it—you could tell by the way she talked about it'. She was 'an ardent Presbyterian', 'very righteous and self-righteous':

> . . . but I soon got to know when my mother was in 'the' mood and that I'd have to keep out of her way, because I was the one that actually took the flak. It's interesting: later on as a group of social workers we were talking about scapegoating in families, and I could see I was the scapegoat in ours and that I was the scapegoat quite young.
>
> I was unwanted, and I was told in adolescence once when my mother was very cross with me, that she had *never* wanted to have me and that she had gone to the doctor and actually asked for an abortion. I was about

---

[38] Interview with *Anne Sullivan*, 24 September 1990.
[39] See Appendix II, table 9: Family Sizes over three generations.
[40] Lambert, *A Suburban Girl*, p. 49.

thirteen—the phrase used was 'get rid' of me. It didn't surprise me by then, but having it said was very unpleasant. Admittedly my mother had had six children—she'd lost two—they did in those days. She was forty-odd and the year before she had nearly died because of undiagnosed gallstones, so she had some physical reasons for not wanting me, although she was told that it was probably quite good for her to have another baby at that stage.

But I think it spelt the end of any relationship between my parents. I think they didn't know how to prevent having children. They would never have discussed it anyway—Mother being so narrow-minded about those sort of things. No separate rooms though, and what's more, they continued to share a bed for quite a long time. And when she said she wanted a bed of her own, he really cut up properly. He was a man who used to hang on to his feelings until he could stand it no longer and then it would erupt in the most shocking temper tantrums. We grew up with those temper tantrums every now and again erupting and we never knew what they were about. They *terrified* us. He would go on for a couple of hours with it, and then it was all over and done with and things would be as they were. And my father blamed me for all this. He did not say so, but I believe my presence in the home was really painful to him, and he treated me quite differently from his other children. He never spoke to me or of me except to criticize.[41]

Divorce was a disgrace and resort to love affairs or prostitutes unthinkable. James Murray, growing up with a violent father, noted 'that all the women we knew seemed to have trouble with their husbands, but none ever thought of leaving them', and he blamed the war, the Depression and general defeat; but how many chafed at the prospect of a celibate life?[42] As a young Presbyterian minister in the late 1950s, Alan Reid was amazed at the number of old married couples he counselled who had not had sex for years.[43] 'Not all the families that stayed together were happy', remembers *Mary Geoghegan*, 'and a lot of people can remember very strange sets of parents. But they didn't actually abuse the children and they were not screaming at each other'. Despite everything, however, there were men and women who found their way, as did Betty Blay's aunts:

'Sex' was a no-word—you never mentioned that. My mother just blushed if you said 'sex'. But you could talk to them later on when they were old. Ginny would talk sex and so would Polly. Polly once said to my husband, John, 'Do you enjoy your sex life?' 'Yes, I do.' 'Oh, I'm glad of that—I did too.'

And there are people who remember their parents as 'adoring' each other and one wonders whether these were the fortunate who had found fulfilment in each other's arms.

---

[41] Interview with Jean Cane, 25 October 1990.
[42] Murray, *The Paradise Tree*, p. 99.
[43] Interview with the Rev. Dr Alan Reid, 3 December 1990.

Hearts had also to be trained to be brave, to be able to endure suffering. Boys of course had to learn to be brave and never cry, but the learning of self-control and endurance was just as important for girls. Valerie East's father was openly disappointed in only having daughters, but he made do:

> My father wanted us to have lots of courage and all the rest of it. I was naturally timid of heights, so my father would make me cross bridges over chasms, go round cliffs and things like that. And there'd be these terrible, panicky, screaming scenes where he'd try to make me do it. When he wasn't there, when I was about twelve, I'd make myself go off the high diving board at the Olympic Pool—always twice.

Childhood asthma was a still rare but even more dangerous condition than it is now and a severe attack could keep a child in bed for weeks, dictating a life of unrelenting physical and emotional restraint. Lurline Keck was afflicted with osteomyelitis, but after surgery for three years the wound would not heal. The pain was constant, the suppurating wound had to be dressed daily and at school 'some of the girls were curious, some were revolted by it'. It did not begin to heal until she was taken to the seaside for the first time in her life and 'I ran in with all my clothes on, I was so excited, and it healed up in that fortnight. Why I wasn't given salt baths or something beforehand I don't know'. The Rev. Harry Keck's family was a happy one and they led 'a rich family life', but

> None of us were allowed to cry—to have a few quiet tears. If I fell over I always got into trouble in case I hurt my leg. And the loud sobs that children do—you just had to learn to control them—you were not to cry.

She was loved and knew she was, but despite all that suffering, she has not one memory of being on her mother's knee and having a hug. The prohibitions on tears were even harsher for boys: 'There was no encouragement to express emotion', recalls Geoffrey Serle, 'one had to crack hardy and suppress'; and for Hugh Stretton: 'I only began to cry after I had a dose of cerebral encephalitis in later life which increased my capacities considerably'.[44]

Almost as important as love in the forming of hearts was play. In play imaginations, energies and aggressions were released; in play children rehearsed the adult life to come; in play children escaped temporarily the expectations and strictures of the adult world. Yet what is striking about these middle-class boys and girls is how good they were—or at least how good they *remember* themselves to have been. They relate little of the

---

[44] Interviews with Geoffrey Serle, 27 October 1988, and with Hugh Stretton, 16 September 1988.

devilment of the working-class children of *Struggletown*, who were full of pranks, schemes, and lurks. They have not known the pleasures of a street 'gang', of sitting in the gutter on hot summer nights under the street lamp telling ghost stories, of whole days of glorious freedom from adult supervision. A few of these middle-class boys threw stones at street lamps, or chased people they should not have like the Chinese greengrocers or got lost in storm-water drains, but most were like Geoff McKee—'a regular little boy'—and the 'games' they remember are cricket and football. There was no shortage of violence in the boys' world, for the short or the bespectacled were bullied both in school and outside it; and sport, especially football, incorporated and legitimated a degree of violence. Geoff Tolson and his playmates transformed a vacant block of land up the street into a battleground by digging trenches. But many middle-class boys had more toys and facilities for structured play: the Cohn boys played trains and one of Lawrence's friends had an 'enormous number of lead soldiers'. Middle-class children often had the room to play at home, and they therefore probably played more frequently with their siblings than could working-class children, so that a significant difference in middle-class life from working-class life may be more intense relationships between siblings, especially between brothers and sisters. But it is only *Philip Hardwicke*, growing up in a semi-working-class street, who tells of a childhood like the *Struggletowners'*—who has a fund of neighbourhood lore, who remembers the 'characters' among the neighbours, who played in the street with local kids. Country children, however, did enjoy more physical freedom, as did Hugh Stretton, growing up in semi-rural Beaumaris: 'When I was ten and my sister eight, we rode our ponies to Warrandyte for the holidays on our own, though there were folk there when we got there'.

This city was not a dangerous place. It was quite safe for *David Miller* when he was nine to return from choir practice at ten o'clock at night. And only the temporary incursion into Hawthorn of the petty gangster Squizzy Taylor made it risky for Elaine Corran to walk home from Girl Guides after dark; otherwise women and girls were reasonably safe at night—although not quite as safe as they would be in working-class suburbs where there were more people walking the streets. Many girls were not venturesome either physically or mentally and played 'school' or 'mothers and fathers'—rehearsing the serious business of being good and winning adult approval. But some girls were tomboys—the Barnetts were all good at sport and tree climbing; and *Betty Thomas* went in for rough games like wrestling, cops and robbers, and exploring Gardiner's Creek—but these were both families which retained some of that uninhibited energy of older, lower-class Methodism. *Betty Thomas* also had to do a lot of childminding and she could cook a roast dinner by the time she was twelve.

Where quiet boys and girls found freedom was in their heads and with books. Betty Blay read as addictively—and indiscriminately—as children today watch television, and once she had exhausted the library at Spring Road Central School, she began writing her own stories. *Margaret Power* and her brother had a hide-away behind their hedge where on holidays they went through two library books a day each: 'Mother didn't believe in us reading all day like that—you had to be busy some of the time—so if we needed to finish a book, one would go up there and the other would keep watch and do whatever was to be done. Yet Mother was herself an avid reader with catholic tastes'. Some childhood reading exerted a powerful influence. Valerie East:

> I think that probably the biggest influence in my life was Arthur Mee's *Children's Encyclopaedia* which I could read at the age of six. I used to sit on the back steps at home and other children would come round and I'd read them stories out of Arthur Mee. And because I read it so young— give me a child before he's seven—I think I was very strongly influenced by the moral values—not the jingoism—the underlying moral values.

Betty Thomas was also deeply affected by the books she read and the possibilities they offered her imagination:

> Books were the great outlet and safety valve for me. I read everything and I probably in my fantasy acted out all the men's and boys' parts as well as the girls' parts, which helps to explain why I didn't feel left out of anything. It took me a while to grasp the point made by the feminists that if one of your sisters feels left out by the Bible or the hymns or anything, then you should take her part—because I've never felt left out. I've always written myself in, or spoken myself in, or heard myself in there.
>
> And I think that's partly thanks to my upbringing—my parents always treated me as a very important person. Maybe they never thought they'd have boys. But to be fair to them, in their religion, which was Protestant—Methodist tinged with Bible Christian—a girl was just as important in God's eyes as a boy, and I never had any doubt of that. And of course, MLC reinforced that.

Once her reading got her into trouble:

> On the evening of my eighth birthday I was naughty and I got caught. My father borrowed books from the library that I was not allowed to read unless he had lent them to me. Anyway, I was reading behind the sofa a book my father had brought home from the library in the city. It had a picture of a young lady not wearing very much and a pistol, so it must have been a detective story with a seducer. I remember thinking I had a good place to read it. And was caught and got a thrashing on the evening of my eighth birthday.

It was desperately important to be good, and one of the great terrors of parenthood—alongside whooping cough, diphtheria and sexual perversion—was that children might be *spoiled*. Lurline Keck was an only girl with seven brothers:

> My life at home—even though it was a loving family atmosphere—was oppressive. I was near the end of a large family and my eldest brothers were fairly serious young men and took their work and their religion very seriously. They acted as another set of parents and they were determined that I would not be too spoilt. (I must have been indulged a bit because of my illness.) So they were down on me a lot, as well as my parents. I must have been about nine and went round saying 'Oh good—it's my birthday next week—I wonder what I'll get?' I must have overdone it a bit. Anyway, when my birthday came, those two brothers didn't give me anything, to teach me a lesson. I thought that was an awful thing to do. My parents would support them and defer a bit to the older children, who were a bit better educated and who knew what was right.

Physical punishment was common, but hardly universal and rarely excessive. Some families were simply biddable and orderly—the *Doyles* now think they were too good for their own good; but being sent to one's room in disgrace worked well enough. Only children had to be especially good. *Gwenda Holtby* was very good: 'Oh you had to be GOOD—goodness was a requisite: being honest, working hard, being kind to other people, being thoughtful, not too NOISY'. She longed for the companionship and adventure of Girl Guides: 'I asked my parents every day for eighteen months till they agreed, then I joined the Guides and was patrol leader in the end. I thought it was absolute heaven because it was in groups; but I don't think I ever went to camp—that was too adventurous'. If there was a danger, it was in the inability to cope with 'unpleasantness'. The striving to be Christian made the expression of anger difficult, even when it was justified. Lurline Keck was getting into trouble all the time, yet there were never arguments in her house:

> I sometimes wonder whether it was a good idea. All of us, I think, would feel physically ill at any raised voices or any dissension. We just weren't allowed to argue. I don't remember hearing any angry voices in the house. There was never any swearing—naturally—in a house like that. I don't recall any unpleasant atmosphere. There must have been tensions beneath the surface and I wasn't mature enough to be aware of them.

May Featherstone remembers no family conflicts either, and she is grateful that they did not learn to argue and 'to get things out of their system':

We were brought up in a society where you did accept strictness. I had it from my parents. You did as you were told. It didn't worry me at all. When I look back now, I think it was easier because I didn't have to make any decisions. We thought our elders were very strict, but we thought that was the world. And I think that if you don't learn to accept discipline when you're young from those near you, then you can never have self-discipline.[45]

The pursuit of goodness, and the goodness of the heart, had another dimension. This was not just a struggle between parent and child, instinct and training, impulse and restraint: for most it was a struggle between God and the forces of darkness, between salvation and original sin. Religion dramatized and defined the great struggle to attain goodness, and it spelt out the meaning of evil and the awfulness of eternal punishment. *Marina Graham*:

> There was my mother. I loved her very much and my father too. We lived on a remote farm just the three of us—and Betty, the maid, a local girl, one of a family of Welsh Baptists. There were eighteen of them. When Betty left I had no young company at all. My parents were both deeply religious and Mother used to go on a lot about the Fourth Commandment, and it seemed I was the worst young offender in this respect it had been her misfortune to encounter in all her years of teaching.

On the other hand, later she could be 'amazingly wise and good':

> When I was about fifteen—long after we had come to live in Melbourne and I was going to Gen.—there was the idea that you went to confession every Saturday. I used to start breaking out in a cold sweat on Thursday nights, dreading the Saturday confessional. I would be a quivering wreck, and I would come out with a wonderful feeling of relief after the pain and suffering. When I finally told my mother about this she said, 'Oh this is ridiculous—a good little girl like you! You've never done anything wrong in your life. I think we'll cut that confession back to once a month'.[46]

Hearts, nourished with love or starved of acceptance, had to be tamed and shaped into souls, and churches joined homes in imparting the lessons of innocence.

---

[45] Interview with *May Featherstone*, 7 December 1990.
[46] Interview with *Marina Graham*, 18 December 1990.

Souls and Churches

From the time he was eight years old, John Jamieson knew he was going to be a Presbyterian minister. He came from a strong church family but, if his vocation was predictable, it was accepted joyfully. His family could not afford to send him to university, so at the age of fourteen he transferred from St Stephen's Church, Caulfield, where his father was session clerk, to Gardiner Presbyterian Church. Here classes were held for a scholarship—the Allen Bequest—which enabled him to spend two years at Scotch College, as a candidate for the ministry before going on to university and the Theological Hall at Ormond College. Old Mr McPherson, a retired schoolmaster, coached the candidates: 'You had to learn copious portions of the scripture and the Shorter Catechism and what it meant—and it was a marvellous training in logic'. Mr McPherson himself had a 'high sense of duty' to the Church: 'He had been saving up for years to go to Scotland, until Edith Kerr wrote from Korea about the need of a village for a school, and he didn't take his trip'. But the dominant influence was that of the Gardiner church's minister, Eric Owen:

> Eric was a Welshman with the gift of the gab, so you had to go to church twice on Sunday because you never knew which sermon was going to be better. He really was an orator. But Eric was also a scholar; and he was a pacifist and very much interested in world affairs. He was chairman of the Mission Board and he always related the Bible to what was going on in the world. He had a tremendous influence. I think that fifteen of us from his congregation became ministers or deaconesses from that period.[1]

Winsome Walklate also found firm faith in early childhood:

> Two things stand out from my childhood—the happiness and love with which I was surrounded and my health. And I did have a lot of sickness. But my health made me very conscious of God and prayer and being sustained by God. One year I had five operations and I always prayed. And I used to wonder whether Dr Winifred Kennan knew how hard this little girl used to pray, but it sustained me and gave me a wonderful trust.

The teaching of religion and the shaping of souls were for many Protestants and certainly for most Catholics, the most important tasks of all in the raising and education of the young; and few middle-class families went about the business of private life without contact with organized religion in some form. Attendance at Protestant churches was

---

[1] Interview with the Rev. John Jamieson, 22 March 1991.

quietly falling off, especially among men, but it seemed none the less that the churches were still at the centre of middle-class life: they defined morals and they bonded society. If a chap was a 'good Methodist' or a 'staunch Presbyterian' or a 'devout Catholic' or a 'strong Anglican'—high, middle or low—you knew what to expect of him: you knew where he stood and what he stood by. And the chap himself knew where he stood and what he stood for. If to later generations the church communities appeared narrow and intolerant, they failed to comprehend the strength, the comfort and the guidance that organized religion could bestow.

Churches also brought fun, friendship and happiness into thousands of suburban lives. For *Gwenda Holtby* 'church was a great centre' to her life where she found 'tremendous fun'. Close congregations became an extended family, and in those churches founded in new suburbs by young families, a generation of parents and children progressed through life stages together. The intrusions of economic hardship, war and social change into private life were shared within the congregation, and people remember the outbreak of war or the coming of peace as a church community as well as a family. And when life was good, there was so much fun. The Methodists of Darling Road, East Malvern, had a wonderful life together. In addition to the football, cricket, tennis, and gymnastics teams, the Men's Club and Ladies' Guild and clubs for boys and girls of all ages, the congregation had a flair for theatre. At the Ladies' Guild concerts women dressed up as men and had the audience 'in stitches'; at the Men's Club concerts Dave Martin's 'rendition of "The Sergeant-Major's on Parade" always 'brought the house down'. Rex Carey and Tom Hicks, alias 'Rex and Tex', were 'natural comedians who could ad lib out of any situation' and 'shrieks of laughter' greeted the 'leading lady in a tight-fitting costume, teetering on high heels with falsetto voice and a trace of five-o'clock shadow'. If Methodists were required to abstain from dancing, gambling and alcohol, they still enjoyed themselves hugely and discharged the tensions of life effectively. All this did wonders for the children:

> [The children's concerts] taught us musical appreciation and expression,
> and to sing and speak clearly, and to face an audience; we blossomed,
> giving of our utmost. Who could forget the fairy wings falling off as she
> bowed; the prince's breeches splitting knee to thigh as he knelt to his
> princess; the loud promptings when nerves grabbed your tongue, and the
> wonderful sound of applause when it was all over.[2]

And yet this was not how John Wesley had advised that children should be raised. Instead:

---

[2] Adams, *Memories of Darling Road Uniting Church*, pp. 94–6.

Break their will betimes. Begin this work before they can run alone, before they can speak plain, perhaps before they can speak at all. Whatever pain it costs, break the will if you would not damn the child. Let a child from a year old be taught to fear the rod and to cry softly; from that age make him do as he is bid, if you whip him ten times running to effect it . . . Break his will now, and his soul shall live, and he will probably bless you to all eternity.[3]

Beneath the fellowship, the charity and the pursuit of Christian love, there was a darkness in popular religion. Lurline Keck's parents only once punished her physically and never raised their voices at her, but she knew that they believed that a child's will had to be broken before it could be handed over to God. Most Protestants had abandoned images of Hell with lakes of fire and brimstone, as would most Catholics by the next generation, but the concept of original sin was a thread that ran through both religious and secular culture. The 'mechanization' of infant care, in its most grotesque manifestation as the Truby King method of baby feeding, started from the assumption that the newborn must be 'broken' and tamed to conform to four-hourly feeding schedules. 'Excessive cuddling' would 'spoil' the baby and therefore ruin the adult to come.[4] In kindergartens, schools, churches and, of course, homes, an immense amount of time went into training children to be still, silent and spotless. They had to learn that there were parts of their bodies which were unclean and must not be touched except in the unavoidable duties of nature. To the young James Murray the Misses Wymond of 'Clarence' preparatory school, revealed the world to be 'divided into nice and nasty, proud and humble, clean and dirty, male and female, polite and uncouth'.[5]

Christians and secularists were divided over the nature of childhood innocence. Since the Enlightenment, the possibility of innate innocence in either children or 'noble savages' challenged the Christian doctrine of the Fall, where Adam and Eve, made in the image of God, but tempted by the devil to taste of the fruit of the tree of knowledge of good and evil, had alienated themselves from God. Each child of Adam and Eve was born thus alienated, and could only return to the Kingdom of God by becoming, through prayer, meditation, contrition and discipline, an 'empty vessel which could be filled by God'. Christianity was not just about belief in God and in his Only Son, it also required that each believer remake himself or herself in character. Christians were people who changed themselves, and if people—especially children—were to be able

---

[3] Quoted in Robert Southey, *Life of Wesley and Rise and Progress of Methodism*, vol. II, pp. 520–1. These phrases were drawn from a letter from his mother Susannah written on 24 July 1732. See *The Works of John Wesley*, vol. 1, pp. 387–9.

[4] See Philippa Mein Smith, Reforming Mothers and Babies: Aspects of Infant Survival in Australia, 1890–1945.

[5] Murray, *The Paradise Tree*, pp. 78–9.

to hear God, they had to learn to be still and be silent. The turbulence, egotism, sensuousness and exuberance of children had to be quelled if they were to be saved. Even more, if children were to be taught Christian goodness they had to be taught about evil; and if they were to want to be saved, they needed to be taught that they needed saving. Anglican children sang at Sunday school:

> He did it for me, He did it for me,
> A sinner as guilty as any could be,
> O, how I love Him, now that I see,
> He suffered, He died and He did it for me.

Sister Pauline Grutzner, in her child's understanding of the Redemption, used to feel very angry with God the Father for making Jesus Christ suffer as He did.[6] It was a difficult theology which too often became deformed in the teaching, so that Christianity appeared to be a religion of obedience and renunciation rather than of love. 'Vanity of vanities, and all is vanity, but to love God and serve Him alone' Thomas à Kempis had taught six centuries before, 'This is the highest wisdom, by despising the world, to make progress towards the Kingdom of Heaven'.

Churches and church schools sought to change children, but they did so slightly differently for boys and girls. Girls' schools took more seriously the task of controlling the movement and appearance of bodies, and worked harder at teaching the beauties of silence. On 21 November 1934 E.C. Pallot from the Methodist *Spectator* was invited to report on the annual voting by the girls at MLC for the conduct prizes. He was deeply impressed:

> It is difficult, however, to convey something of the charm and sanctity with which the ceremony of voting is carried out. Take, for example, the Seniors. When the time for voting arrives, the Senior School and staff assemble in Fitchett Hall. Then with quiet dignity, the Principal and Vice-Principal enter between rows of standing girls, and take their place upon the dais. With due impressiveness the Principal then outlines the purpose of the Asssembly and the method of procedure.
>
> The girls are reminded that not popularity, nor personal friendship must weigh with them, but worth. The girls chosen are to be the representatives of the School product in the outer world. On a quiet review of the year's conduct, what girl from among them do they think best carries the school standard and traditions? The silence is impressive, beyond that of many a church service. The address ended, the girls have the names presented to them, and must sit silently for a few moments ere they record their votes on the papers prepared for the occasion. Voting finished, the papers are gathered by the prefects and duly handed in. The results are not disclosed until

---

[6]Interview with Sister Pauline Grutzner, 30 January 1992.

prize night. Neither the girl selected nor the school assemblage could ever forget the importance of the occasion, nor the dignity and responsibility that the prize carries. It must, therefore, have great value in the moulding of their characters. The whole atmosphere is sacramental. The best traditions of a church school are made real.[7]

This was worship at the shrine of perfect behaviour: 'Christian children all must be/mild, obedient, good as He'.

It was a severe regime, and some perfectly normal children suffered childhoods of guilt and inadequacy visited upon them by parents and teachers filled with the best of intentions. Lurline Keck:

At MLC because there were so many ministers' daughters we were noticeable in class. There were some who were very well behaved and who did all their work and everything that was expected of them. And there were others who rebelled, and because you were a minister's daughter you were noticed more. There was always that rider on your behaviour that because you were a minister's daughter, you should know better, and I did resent that.

I know I did go through a phase where I was reading a lot of girls' books (the equivalent of *Billy Bunter* —I used to read all the boys' books too), and a few of us had the idea that it was really smart to be slightly naughty. There'd be books called *The Form Rebel* and we'd think we were one of them and think it was rather exciting. But it was brought home to me that I was far worse than that. In IVc I got two conduct marks in one term: one was when my friend and I had been talking after we'd been told and told to stop; the other was for telling lies.

Lurline had left some handwork at home and knew that she would get a detention without it, so she told her class teacher that she needed to go home for lunch. The teacher, ever vigilant, rang her mother and inspected her school bag with its packed school lunch, and Lurline returned to be confronted with the accusation that she had been 'telling falsehoods'. She was stood before the class and given her second conduct mark (three resulted in automatic expulsion), and the Vice-Principal, Dr Gladys Wade, told her she was 'an absolute disgrace to the class—and you, a minister's daughter—telling lies'. The next morning:

. . . the first hymn at assembly was 'In the strife midst truth and falsehood' and everyone turned round and looked at me. It was very traumatic that experience. And being my second conduct mark for the term, there was probably talk about whether I'd be expelled or not. It took me years to get over my feeling of shame and that I really was a bad girl. I'm very truthful.

[7] *Silver and Green*, December 1935, p. 4.

Order without suggested order within. Tidiness of uniform and neatness of work attained the potency of a cult, and ill-co-ordinated and messy children suffered agonies over their unacceptable appearance and disgraceful work books. For some teachers, exactly-ruled margins and blotless pages were almost more important than the work itself. Boys were given a little more latitude, but still standards of personal tidiness and of clean and accurate work were high. A phrase much used was 'attention to detail' and Joyce Thorpe excelled at it:

> I was so good at it—it's almost a liability to have this absolutely, overwhelming concern for detail. That's why I've got so far in life, I realise that; but at the same time, it's a great burden. I fuss so about details.

And of course, that was the point. The ability to control yourself, to learn tasks quickly and correctly, to pay attention to detail did make for success in the world and good management within the home.

The culture of Protestant girls' schools owed something to the first model of girls' academics—the convent school—so that   MLC was to some extent in the same tradition as   Genazzano. But the Faithful Companions of Jesus were a French order so that Genazzano was also a French tradition in another country. *Elinor Doyle*:

> There was a weekly ceremony called 'Marks' at which your progress was observed. The punishments were really just those psychological ones. Everyone would assemble, sit down in neat rows, class by class in the concert hall. The Mistress of Studies would say, 'Will someone go and get Reverend Mother'. A good girl would would be chosen to go to Reverend Mother's room and say, 'Everybody's ready for you Reverend Mother' and escort her to sit down beside the Mistress of Studies. The Mistress of Studies would then read out in a fairly formidable tone, with each girl standing as her name was read. And she would say, '*Elinor Doyle*—no marks lost', which would generally be what I would get; but if I had a particularly bad week it might be Silence—one, Exactitude—one (broken silence—talked during a lesson; exactitude would be late for class). They had Deportment, which was getting a bit more serious; Application—not doing your homework. Deportment would be whistling or something. Then there was Courtesy, which was a worse failing than Deportment. The final one, which was pretty bad, was Conduct, and that could cover practically anything—wearing lipstick or something—Gross Moral Turpitude of some kind. It wouldn't have had to be very 'gross', but the legend was that if you got three conduct marks, you got expelled. Those who lost more than three marks of any kind didn't have their names called, so didn't get Reverend Mother's approving smile and nod. *That* was the punishment—not being recognized.

To give some examples of naughtiness—which don't seem very spectacular—things like stamping a foot and saying, 'I hate you Mother Angela'. Did someone actually shut Mother Marcella in the Art Room cupboard?—I have a feeling something like that might have happened. Getting out at lunchtime and going down to Kew and smoking. Things like that. It was very hard to be naughty because the structure was so complete.

There was also a sequence of sodalities, marking stages of spiritual growth, each one rewarded with medals and ribbons:

They began with the Infant Jesus, at the age of seven or eight, which had red ribbons, and there were four steps so that if you were good and doing everything you should, then you would get your first step, second step, etc—medal. At each step the name of each applicant would be passed around all the nuns who were teaching us and they would tick or cross or comment 'not ready yet', 'immature', 'was seen chewing gum' or 'was rude'. And when you wrote for your next step, you'd say: 'Dear Reverend Mother, May I have my first degree or second degree in Holy Angel Sodality etc. I have tried very hard to get it'. Then she would interview us all and say, 'Well, you're not quite ready for that because Mother Marcella says your needlework is careless. And you really aren't trying very hard and you've been crossed by Mother Carmel for music and you'll have to wait for next time'.

Medals were given out each year after you had been through the three steps. You'd get a medal with a red ribbon and the Rector of Xavier would come and read out the successful applicants and pin the medals on. There was red—Infant Jesus, yellow—Holy Angels, green—St Aloysius— which was less important because people were bored with it by that time, which was the age of fourteen or fifteen.

The final one was Child of Mary which was a very broad pale blue ribbon worn right around the neck. I think that anyone who didn't get the Child of Mary would be a bit devastated because that was felt to be a big thing. And from the first, as a child of five, seeing the big girls with their broad blue ribbons sitting on the stage at Marks, they did seem pretty important.

A convent school was part of a convent, not a separate institution, and the students in the boarding house lived a convent life as lay members of the religious community. The core of the school was the boarding house, and the boarders were joined by the day girls for lessons. It was still common in the 1930s and 1940s for girls whose families lived in Melbourne to board at Genazzano—*Mary Geoghegan* boarded at Genazzano as a war precaution, but in her second last year, she refused to return to school at all if she was still forced to board:

It was the silence. We worked out that we could talk for an hour and a bit a day. We had readings at breakfast, and if you talked before the bell went—I was up to three hundred-plus meals where I wasn't allowed to talk when the bell went—and I think they wiped the slate clean and started again. I don't know why we couldn't talk at meal times—I suppose when you think of families, the noise is pretty dreadful—but you got about five minutes chat.

Kate Morgan vividly remembers the refectory:

In the refectory there was an honour table—and oval table, then small tables of four came down to the junior table—a long rectangular one. You had to be a Child of Mary before you sat at the honour table, and one of the honour girls would sit and supervise the little ones while they had their meal.

We had white damask cloths, and if you put a mark on a cloth, you got newspaper for the next meal. And we were taught that you don't fold your serviette, you only crease it. And one of my friends—if she didn't like something, she'd bring a piece of paper, wrap it up and throw it over the fence. But we had good meals.

The nuns themselves were a great mystery to the girls. Some had mothers who had been schoolfriends of a few of them, but little was known of most. Some were Australian, some were Irish and some were European, and there was a tendency for romantic young minds to imagine aristocratic origins or dashing—but rejected—suitors. The Faithful Companions of Jesus were exceptionally strict for a teaching order, and the rule of silence made the development of personal friendships impossible. The nuns could speak with each other only about their duties, and religious life separated them from their families: they were even forbidden to attend family funerals. Therefore the nuns' sole human relationships were with their students; and even there they were caring and kind but always reserved. They possessed a concentrated spiritual integrity which affected their pupils for life. *Monica O'Farrell*:

The Gen nuns had tremendous integrity. It was obvious even to a young girl the sacrifices they were making for what they believed was a real vocation to serve God. I can see them in class, moving their wimple with their fingers—it must have been hell in summer.

Mother Angela—a fantastic woman—loved sport, encouraged us all the time. She managed to establish associations with non-Catholic schools—we played against Lauriston and that was a very big break-through. She really was a friend. I remember her saying when we were reading one of those silly books about the French Revolution, 'the man is the lover, the woman is the beloved'—an extraordinary thing for a nun to say. She was all crooked with arthritis—in winter she'd have mittens on her hands. She really was a living saint, and never anything but sweetness from her.

Mother Gerda Prytz—a true teacher—anything she taught you, you'd remember; a martinet but a kind one. I suppose you remember the ones who loved you, and I always felt there was love coming from them.

Yet, even though the discipline was so complete, few girls felt oppressed by it; numerous compulsive talkers survived the experience of boarding at Genazzano and have happy memories. Thelma Squire was not even a Catholic:

> I was always a talker and I always lost my shield at Marks. I could get six marks for silence in a week and you were allowed three before you lost your shield, so I was always underbreath, whispering. I didn't really mind.
>
> Angelus bell rang at six and Mass was at seven. I used to hear the Angelus bell and that would rouse me. And then the nun would come in, and if it was winter time, turn the light on and say, 'Praise be to Jesus' and we would murmur, 'And holy be Thy name'. Then we'd struggle out. The older girls were allowed to have showers—cold water; the juniors and mediums weren't. And we used to go up to this bathroom which had a whole line of marble basins—I thought they were antiquated then; now I'd give my eye teeth to have one in my house. We used to have to take down our dressing gowns, tie them around our middle, and put a towel around our developing boobs and wash that way—underarms and face. The crutch and knees never got done.

Females of all denominations were brought up to be acutely modest about their bodies, but the association of personal cleanliness and sexual modesty with Christian purity was relatively new. For Catholics the association of cleanliness coming with godliness began with the De La Salle Brothers when their founder, Jean-Baptiste de La Salle, published his *Rules of Propriety and Christian Civility* in 1703.[8] The constraints on the body were part of a total programme of re-ordered behaviour, but, complicated by the tensions prompted by the libido and unwelcome bodily sensations, they became the most troublesome and the most bizarre. Nancy Naughton:

> In all Catholic schools great importance was placed on modesty, chastity and humility, both in thought and in action. Bathing was strictly supervised and many times I felt that the sight of the naked body was an offence against purity. (I had to reason all this out later—that God made you and made you for a purpose, and that the physical body is magnificent. But I didn't realise that until I had children of my own.) That modesty didn't help self-esteem.

---

[8] Roger Chartier, ed., *The Passions of the Renaissance: A History of Private life*, vol. III, pp. 177–88.

Neither did the nuns' emphasis on Christian diffidence. *Monica O'Farrell* has never forgotten the pretty little nun with new shoes:

> Someone must have dared to say. 'What nice shoes', and she said, 'Aren't they nice—I really like new shoes'. We all remembered that because they never spoke about themselves. They were totally self-effacing—there was no cult of personality at all. And I think, too, that if you had an ebullient personality, they didn't like that very much. The girls who conformed—pliable but good—they were the ones who had positions in the school.

The discipline was all part of the religious practice—control of body and mind was integral to the correct spiritual life, and the most important function of the convent school was to train and prepare souls for life. Religious life—the Order's rule and culture—made living for God part of every second of the day: there were not separate, special times for God, leaving the rest of existence free. And the convent in every aspect of its life was dedicated to God. The nuns cultivated the physical beauty of the building and the gardens because a beautiful environment honoured God and elevated the sensibilities of the inhabitants—for some, the excitement of feast days was to see what the flowers on the altar would be. Feast days also saw long devotional processions, around the convent building, up and down the magnificent stairs, enacting the spiritual journey of pilgrimage, honour and worship. Thelma Squire can smell still the smoky fires in the dormitories on winter nights and 'the rafters in the Immaculate Conception dormitory, went on for ever—you could almost think it was going up to God'. And everywhere, the mute lay sisters cleaned and cooked and washed: 'they used to polish the floor with a brick tied up in woollen things on a long stick and strew tea leaves to catch the dust'.

The convent was not part of the world, but separate, enclosed, at peace and living for God. By the time *Marjorie O'Donoghue* was there, the war was on:

> We did not see the newspapers, we did not have the radio, we had no idea of what was going on in the world. One weekend in four we were allowed to go out on the Saturday and stay overnight, so those times were the only ones where we knew what was in the newspapers. We only read what books were in the glass cabinets—Mary Grant Bruce and L. M. Montgomery, and we were read to a lot in the refectory and while we were doing our mending.

Marjorie was acutely receptive, and the seclusion of convent life built an inner spiritual life which has never left her:

> That seclusion is similar to what is called in our religious life—a retreat—which we used to do every year. During a retreat we would be in silence completely and we had a lot of periods of silence at school. So I enjoy

social life, but I find it very tiring because I'm perhaps more attuned to not talking than to always talking. And I really feel I have the Lord just behind my shoulder all day. I would be forever putting the children, or my husband or ourselves at His feet and saying, 'Look after this or that or the other, or just give me strength to cope'. I don't really ask for favours—I just ask for support.

In church I like weekday Mass better than Sunday Mass, because weekday Mass is always quiet, and those who are there are there because they really want to be and are praying. There's much more distraction at a Sunday Mass, and more things happening with the music and the children would be noisy, and the collections and notices.

To learn to hear God, she had to learn to turn aside from the clamour of the outside world and quell the noise from within.

In Australian Catholicism it has been the duty of the schools rather than the parish church to educate the young in the faith, so that children made their first communion and went to confession from school. In Mary Thompson's eyes this had damaged Catholic parish life since those who attended schools run by strong religious orders became attached to the religious community rather than to the local parish. This was largely a loss of middle-class parish members, because working-class children attended parish schools only. Certainly the Genazzano mothers and their daughters have been slightly less involved in parish life than their equivalents at MLC, because old Genazzano girls often devoted their church work to the FCJs and for decades after leaving it many went on retreat at the school.[9] Kate Morgan has bought a flat opposite the main gates of the school, 'and I am privileged to be allowed to attend daily Mass in St Raphael's Chapel at Genazzano'.

In *Marina Graham*'s case it was her father who had formed a spiritual relationship with the FCJ nuns. His mother had been one of Genazzano's first pupils and he had himself attended the school as a small boy. (As at most convents, boys were admitted as preparatory school pupils.) His daughter *Marina* began her education at a country convent boarding school:

At this convent there were a lot of Protestant day scholars because anyone who was 'naice' in the town sent their daughters to the convent. (And I think this is where I tended to make so many Protestant friends.) We were aged nine and ten. And the day scholars started coming to school with the most fascinating stories of how babies were born—we didn't seem to have much idea of how they got there. So we were swapping information and, inevitably, the nuns found out and literally all hell broke loose. We were all rounded up—there were about eight of us—and I and

---

[9] Survey: 'Did your mother do church or charity work?' Yes: MLC, 77%; Genazzano, 64%. 'Have you done church or charity work?' Yes, MLC 87%; Genazzano, 64%.

a friend were named as ring-leaders. And we were read some of the suffering of St Theresa of Avila—we were in grade five, which probably accounts for my claustrophobia to this day: how she felt she was in a very, very narrow tunnel leading into the lasting bonfire. So we were prepared for wickedness, for of all sins, the worst were ones against Holy Purity. So the local parish priest (I hope he had a sense of humour) was notified that a large number of little girls were coming down to confession. We had to make a general confession of the sins of our whole lives. We were ten. And we confessed these hideous sins that we'd talked about immodest things. I don't remember feeling any great trauma about that in particular, but it must have been about this time that I was down the street with the boarders on Saturday afternoon, and we passed the Paramount Picture Theatre and there was a Hedy Lamarr film showing. There was a photo of Hedy with a very low-cut gown and I inadvertently glanced at it. And Mother De Sales had told us that any sin against Holy Purity was a mortal sin—there was no such thing as a venial sin when it came to Holy Purity—so the next day was Mass and I couldn't go to Holy Communion because I was in a state of mortal sin, and everyone else was looking at me. The same thing happened on Monday and I couldn't wait to get into the confessional on Tuesday afternoon to clear my soul of mortal sin. And this is not exaggerated—I had already made an act of Perfect Contrition in case I died in my sleep—that's how scrupulous I was.

But when *Marina* transferred to Genazzano:

My first vivid memory as a very immature thirteen-year-old (I was only as big as a ten-year-old and I was in year ten) was when I didn't have an essay ready. And Mother Angela said, '*Marina*, dear'—I remember the 'dear'—'Have you got your essay here?' And I waited for my first big row at Gen, 'I'm sorry Mother, I haven't finished it'. And she said, 'That's all right dear—do you think you could finish it by Wednesday'. And I couldn't believe it—it was the gentleness and the courtesy and the lovely smile. The nuns—except for the formidable Mother Philomena Douglas who was always dignified—treated us all with such courtesy, and I loved Genazzano because of that.

I began to see the more beautiful side of religion. The chapel was lovely, and the devotion to Our Lady was stronger than ever, and I liked that, being a romantic and a sentimentalist. I loved the old-fashioned habit and the French customs they followed. I only wish they had retained more of it.

Religion at school was different for Protestants. Trinity Grammar and Scotch College each had chaplains and MLC had a Methodist minister as principal, but the schools were not the primary instrument of teaching the faith. Only a minority of Presbyterian, Anglican or Methodist children were ever able to attend a church school, so it was the

Sunday school which bore the full burden. Very few middle-class children did not go to a Sunday school of some sort at some time. Sunday school was 'functional religion': parents felt they were doing their duty even if they did not attend church themselves. Most parents believed that children needed religious training: Joyce Thorpe's mother 'hated church' but went 'because of the children' (Joyce's father was an active and devoted Methodist layman). Boys were involved in adult Anglican church life through the choirs: James Austin was singing in a church choir at seven and still does so. But John Jamieson thinks the Sunday school helped drive people away from religion: 'The Sunday school movement inoculated our generation against faith, I reckon. I think there's still something to be said for the experience of being at worship—children have to feel part of the show and not just that they belong to it when they grow up'.

The schools had different problems. Many students were not 'of the faith'— just over half at Scotch were Presbyterian, and around 60 per cent at MLC were Methodist. Trinity was three quarters Anglican, however, and many boys were the sons of clergy who on the average stipend of the 1920s and 1930s had no hope of sending their boys to Melbourne or Geelong Grammars. There were also at Scotch and MLC a significant Jewish minority. Jews were accepted and their religious differences respected. At Scotch Zelman Cowen confronted the school with the horrors of anti-Semitism, winning the Moyle Short Story Prize in 1935 with 'Pogrom':

> The girl with the babe, demented with terror, made a wild rush. A Cossack, drunk with vodka, took out his sabre and flashed it downward. A gaping hole appeared in the infant's head. The woman uttered a horrible, deathly shriek and dropped with the babe in the snow. The crowd shrieked with laughter. The soldier drained his vodka . . .[10]

Hein Altman came out as a refugee from Germany: within six weeks he could speak English, he was good at sport and loved football and his family were not religious—'father went through the motions'. The more orthodox Jews at Scotch were dubbed 'the football team' because 'they stuck together', but *Hein* integrated quickly and soon had more in common with middle-class Anglo-Celts than he had with his co-religionists.[11] At MLC also Jews were made welcome, especially in 1945 when St Michael's Church of England Girls' Grammar School in East St Kilda began to insist that its rapidly growing Jewish population observe the Christian practices of the school. The Rev. Dr A. H. Wood argued publicly for full toleration of Jewish students in Christian schools and

---

[10] *Scotch Collegian*, December 1935, p. 257.
[11] Interview with *Hein Altman*, 13 September 1990.

earned the gratitude of the Jewish community for inviting to MLC all those who wished to come. Many private and church schools had an unspoken quota for Jewish students, as *Valerie Golding*'s mother discovered when she tried to enrol her daughter at one of the more select establishments; but even at MLC *Valerie* was asked to relinquish two years of a three-year scholarship 'to give a Christian child a chance'. She loved MLC none the less: 'there were lots of Jewish girls; but not only that, there were lots of girls you could make friends with because there weren't any snobs'.[12] Genazzano also had a few Jewish girls, and as with the Protestants at the school, the nuns put them to good use. *Elinor Doyle*:

> There was one Jewish girl who boarded from an early age, who was a special favourite of the nuns. As with the other non-Catholic girls, we were expected to give 'good example' to those who didn't have the Faith. How could they see the beauty of the Faith if we didn't show it to them in our daily behaviour? There was no attempt to convert them, but of course the nuns hoped that the atmosphere of prayer and good example might do the trick.

Trinity Grammar was founded as a parish school of Holy Trinity Church, Kew and still by the 1930s that sense of being a parish school endured. But the religious ethos of the school came more from the headmaster, Frank Shann, who was a devoted Anglican. The morning assemblies of prayers, the saying of the Apostles' Creed and Bible readings began the day with a sense of worship so that, for Robert Trumble, 'Christianity was part of the ethos, part of the teaching even'.[13] James Austin now sees a private church school as 'a contradiction which should not be allowed'; and believes that the only valid grounds for the Anglican Church to have its own schools is to produce priests; but he was another receptive boy at Trinity:

> We had chapel every morning and the sixth form took it in turns to read from the good book. I can still see a fellow named Davey, who was a country boy—he'd come to the end of the page and give his thumb a big lick—the things that stick in your mind. And all the kids laughed. Frank Shann shot a look at us—'Stand up that boy!'
> You had chapel, and if you wanted to be confirmed it was down at the local church. Divinity was a subject right through to year ten, and it had some value because it was a good history-type subject. A lot of good was done there if it comes out in the number of priests who came from Trinity—two bishops and I can name four priests.

---

[12] Zainu'ddin, *They Dreamt of a School*, pp. 300–1; Susie Ehrmann in John Foster, ed., *Community of Fate: Memoirs of German Jews in Melbourne*, p. 166; interview with *Valerie Golding*, 14 December 1990.
[13] Interview with Dr Robert Trumble, 16 August 1990.

At Scotch also the lay headmasters were as important as the chaplains in the religious life of the school. The boys were difficult to reach spiritually; most of them, being Nonconformists, lacked an experience of liturgy which could lessen inhibitions about being moved by 'the beauty of holiness'. At Scotch, the more casual the approach, the more effective it proved. John Blanch was a believer and a fine school captain, and it was the headmaster's intimate boarders' evening services which touched him most: 'he'd discuss things with us—not too formal; I think formalities put people off—they like to take part'. The evangelical Crusader Union and the Student Christian Movement drew in the more religious and serious boys, but they were very much a minority. John Blanch, for one, was unimpressed by the calibre of the S.C.M.: 'we used to think they were too goody-goody; a few of them in later life showed that—they became too pious, not men of the world'. Colin Gilray ignited a spiritual chord in the young Alan Reid, but Scotch also had chaplains who deeply affected some boys. The Rev. Rowan MacNeil is fondly remembered by Archie Crow, but it was the Rev. Steve Yarnold who was the most controversial: for many he was a muddled, impractical communist; for others he was an inspiring Christian Socialist. Yarnold was chaplain at Scotch until almost the end of the war when he enlisted, and he was succeeded by a much loved and more conventional chaplain, the Rev. Alec Fraser. But Steve Yarnold and Colin Gilray, perhaps at first sight unlikely allies, together worked some spiritual magic at Scotch in the late 1930s and during the war. And when the security organization showed a close interest in his chaplain's political tendencies, the headmaster stood by him to the end. As a team they touched only a minority of the boys, but in the 'Public School' tradition, they were the boys who mattered—the gifted ones who were already aware that they were destined for a serious life. The school taught a Christianity of social action which was absorbed not just by the believers, but also by some who would become 'secular Christians'.[14] Hugh Stretton was one:

> Yarnold had no coercive religious authority really, and compulsory chapel was only for the boarders. I had no belief at all—ever—but I used to go to chapel each Sunday for aesthetic reasons, because I thought it was beautiful.
> I don't have a sense of any of them preaching in the ordinary hostile sense of the world, saying 'You shouldn't'. They would come up with projects which were interesting, which you could do. On formal occasions there would be sermons. A very practical religion, but always with layers of ordinary political leftism—howling at injustice and wondering whether capitalism would survive. And it was producing a lot of ministers—Arthur Burns and George Yule and so on. And from

---

[14] Nicholson, *First Hundred Years . . .* , pp. 249–50.

conversations we had, they thought of the ministry as a platform, a place to talk from. And they hadn't got the cringe at all, like they would now, because the intellectual calibre of Ormond theological hall and the ministry was perfectly intelligent and respectable.

This radical Christianity was not unique to Scotch. There was less of it officially at Trinity, but there were boys who were asking questions about the state of the world. In many church and government schools there were teachers who had been shaken by the Depression and were becoming alarmed by the rise of fascism in Europe; and the Student Christian Movement at the university was very much concerned with the quality of life on earth for all God's creatures. At MLC the timing was a little different. In 1939 the Rev. John Grove was succeeded as principal by the Rev. Dr A. H. Wood, and in the next twenty-seven years the school was to be more religious and more Methodist than it was at any other time in its history. Dr Wood was the son of Salvation Army officers, and he never lost the commitment to social justice and world peace awakened in his youth. He had an un-Methodist love of church liturgy, but his heart lay with the passionate, democratic spirit of the Bible Christians and the Primitives. At her Sunday School and 'Comrades' girls' club at the South Camberwell Methodist Church *Betty Thomas* was im- bibing 'pure socialism—Christian, of course':

> And that was backed up at MLC by Dr Wood. Not that he ever said that capitalism was a bad thing, but his whole view of the world was of people living in holy poverty. You couldn't get rich really, because you were meant to be looking after the poor, the wretched etc., even though he didn't say that sharing worldly wealth was what it was all about, it was by implication. Look at him—I'm sure he only had two suits, one for Sunday and one for the rest of the week. I'm sure that he felt in his heart that the rich had an extra struggle to see God's vision—it would come naturally to the poor. He had no time for earthly possessions—his eyes were steadfastly fixed upon the Hill.

The schools and chaplains were consciously shaping future citizens as much as young souls and they talked much about 'service'. Yet only in hindsight did *Betty Thomas* understand what was being taught to idealistic young people in their churches and in their schools in the 1930s and early 1940s. She emerged from MLC afire to serve the world:

> So that by the time you entered university, everything pointed in the same direction—that you were not expected to be accruing possessions, you were expected to *serve*. But it wasn't until much later that I realised that the message would be different for boys because the whole feminist theory hadn't hit. Many years later, while reading for my second degree at Monash, I picked up something about middle-class American males.

And American males, according to this writer, had a steep gradient—everything, all satisfactions, including sexual satisfactions, had to be postponed for THE GOAL. Now the goal was not service for suffering humanity—the goal was either becoming head of B.H.P. or Western Mining or the top of a profession. It was individualistic.

She came to see the different roles the church directed men and women to play, and how they complemented each other. The middle-class Christian marriage was a double-act, where the wife's Christian service and charitable works legitimated the husband's pursuit of wealth and prestige in the temporal sphere:

> You get this very strange business growing up in the Methodist Church, and I'm sure in the other Nonconformist churches—the Anglicans and Catholics are free from this because they have to serve all the world. What you get is that the Church is supposed to be the home of the tired man coming back at the end of the day; just as at the end of the day he comes to the family home and expects to find serenity after the stress of the market place. This was always in Methodism—I've got it going back to the 1840s to show how conservative it was. The wife was supposed to provide the vine leaf and the shelter and the shade after all the turmoil. In the same way the Church is supposed to provide the spiritual serenity at the weekend, where he's supposed to get his spiritual recreation in preparation for the week ahead.
>
> But the woman is not getting the double message at all. She's getting one message—to give up, to serve, to 'give and give and give again what God has given me'.

But the social gospel of the radicals, while not new, was gathering apace through the 1930s and blossomed along with the secular left during the war. If it affected only a few, it none the less signalled a dramatic change for Protestant intellectuals. Radical Presbyterians and Methodists were detaching their churches from their intimate relationship with modern capitalism, striking a sharp cleavage between middle-class intellectuals and middle-class moneymakers. And if the Church failed to shape new believers in God and Christ, it continued to provide a moral structure for young secular radicals. If the numbers taking Communion were dwindling, the Christian moral universe survived.

But for boys, 'service' was complicated by 'service to one's country', above all in war.[15] World War I haunted not only some unhappy homes, it hung like a black cloud over the whole society. James Austin was taken every year to watch the Anzac Day march which took three hours to pass; (once he saw men marching: 'but it isn't Anzac Day?' he protested to his mother, 'No, they're the unemployed', and this was his first consciousness

---

[15] *Scotch Collegian*, May 1936, p. 11.

of the Depression). All schools, both state and private, lavished collective grief over the Fallen, and teachers known to be ex-servicemen possessed a particular charisma. In Scotch's Memorial Hall, six stained-glass windows of St Andrew and St Martin, Sir Galahad and King Arthur and St Michael and St George depicted the 'Moral and Spiritual Virtues of Soldiers', and above them doves bore scrolls on which were inscribed the twelve fruits of the Holy Spirit: Faith, Meekness, Patience, Long-suffering, Gentleness, Chastity, Goodness, Temperance, Peace, Modesty, Love, Joy.[16] Frank Shann, emotional at the best of times, was shattered by the forty-four Trinity supreme sacrifices, many of whom he had taught. Anzac Day services in the school were profoundly disturbing to the very young, who scarcely understood what it all meant and where it all had happened: Robert Trumble, for one, found it difficult to reconcile religion with the 'cutting down' of so many 'in their youth and early manhood'.[17] Alan Cohn was another sensitive Trinity boy and the war stories in boys' magazines were 'very vivid—I don't think I would ever have been much good in battle or anything like that'.[18] Each Anzac Day service at Trinity, Frank Shann read a poem by Trinity's war poet, G. F. Adeney:

> These were more beautiful that morning: all
> The glory of all light was theirs, for they
> Loved light and feared not death.
> Feared?   rather say

> Went down to death as to high festival.
> Now they return not to us, though we call,
> Nor stand and talk beside us in the the way;
> Only their names are lifted up today,
> More radiant monument in Valour's hall.

> And here, for all time, is their memory bright,
> A flame across the heavens deepest blue;
> A star to follow; an immortal word.
> About the Cenotaph there falls a light,
> The graven names become the men we knew,
> And in the silence are their voices heard.

Some boys reacted against it. Geoff McKee at Scotch found the emotional rendition of J. D. Burns' 'To England' each Anzac Day 'rather artificial: it seemed like a glorification of war itself—I think I was a bit of a pacifist then—those bugles of England never called for me'. In 1935 G. R. Cochrane, as editor of the *Scotch Collegian*, wrote for the generation which had grown up in the shadow of the war:

---

[16] Nicholson, *First Hundred Years* . . . , p. 185.
[17] Dr Robert Trumble, autobiographical manuscript in possession of the author.
[18] Interview with Alan Cohn, 12 October 1990.

The war was the greatest and most drastic lesson that the world ever had; it is still suffering the after-effects of the cataclysm . . . we see the crippled soldier in the street; we see the man with the ashen face and the brass badge in his button hole . . . during those four years there was born a generation which is now entering upon adult life and is filling the upper forms of our schools, a generation whose nervous tension reflects the stress of the days when it was born.[19]

It was an extraordinary thing to write in 1935 but, as the Spanish Civil war grew more serious, many young men realized that they would have to go to war all over again.[20] James Austin experienced a special fatalism:

I always had this feeling that we had been through the war—my father and my only uncle, who was killed in France in 1917—and in the fullness of time, somehow or other in my twenties or thirties, another war would appear in which I would go—like a pre-ordination. Funny feeling.

And so were boys prepared for the supreme sacrifice and the just taking of human life.

The learning of goodness and the finding of faith pervaded every part of growing up. The Christianity that *Gwenda Holtby* and *Amelia Friend* absorbed in their homes, at MLC and at their respective Malvern Methodist churches, sent them out into the world to serve and to live for others. But it was not exclusive to church and college people: it was in fact the basic ethic of the times. Working-class children were also brought up to live for others, for if they did not help each other, they could not survive. It was the most powerful and morally significant social ethic of Australian society, taught in homes comfortable and poor and in schools religious and secular. And with it came a certain diffidence. *Amelia Friend*:

It was the sort of atmosphere in which we were brought up—you were expected to contribute to the society in which you lived in some way. Not in any showy sort of way—we were discouraged from that sort of thing—you looked down on the people who made a great song and dance about what they did. It was just part of life.

Being a Christian meant caring about people:

It was very important to my parents that you did care about being good. We were never allowed to say anything against people. My parents used to say, 'If you can't speak well of a person, then don't speak at all'. I don't *quite* go along with that. When you're bringing up children they've got to

---

[19] *Scotch Collegian*, December 1935, p. 205.
[20] Ibid., May 1936, p. 11.

learn to make choices. We were never allowed to gossip; we were told to mind our own business and we were not to discuss the family business outside. We learned to be discreet in that way.[21]

Amelia grew up strong and independent and she was caring, not simply because she was told to be: 'I don't think I was as courteous as I was encouraged to be—I was always pretty forthright; I was always arguing with someone—I just wouldn't accept the thing because they said it'. In retrospect *Gwenda Holtby* can see where the ideal of Christian service sometimes went too far for women and girls:

> I think that one of the sad things of the Methodist stress on work and living for others and so on, is this residual feeling of guilt. There's a feeling that nothing is too much to do for other people—there's no limit to the amount of work you can do—there's always something more that you could have done.
>
> I think my childhood was a little too guilt-ridden, but I don't think that very much was talked about guilt and punishment in that period. I think that my parents were almost totally free of any ideas on child development, because there wasn't very much thought about it. They thought that kindness and warmth were quite enough.

Protestants sometimes envied Catholics their confessional. *Marina Graham* did find relief in it, but that only lasted for a few days, so that by the time of the next, she was again stricken with feelings of guilt and inadequacy. However, there was a positive side:

> Every little girl was brought up in those days with the ideal of Mary as the perfect woman. And living in the country as I did, I had the little altar—which really is rather charming—with the statue, the blue and white one. I used to put flowers in the vase every day and we always had a little votive lamp burning there. And even though we lived in the constant danger of fires—bush fires and the house burning down—I always believed Our Lady would never let the house catch on fire; and this burned constantly and was known as '*Marina*'s little altar'. So there was a gentle influence in our lives.

At Genazzano, the ideal of service was different from MLC's. *Elinor Doyle*:

> We had the nuns who presented our idea of service, but since the FCJs were only a teaching order there wasn't—as there might be in other convents—an alternative model of nursing or being a missionary or whatever. So it did seem to me that you were either a nun or a mother;

---

[21] Interview with *Amelia Friend*, 21 November 1990.

and the third thing—doing something else—was something you did while waiting to be a wife and mother. Certainly the ideas of charity and unselfishness were there, but the way religious studies was taught, one would think more of sending money to the missions, helping a particular Catholic charity. I think it would have been different from MLC because of the models of women we had as teachers.

Mary Geoghegan, however, did not come away from the refined—if too quiet—charm of Genazzano, expecting to lead a life of continuing elegance and ease:

I got a great message that in life we were going to get a cross to bear and the sooner you took it up the better. You were going to have a hard life and that was all the better. I read about one fellow who went into the Jesuits and took to wearing a hair shirt. If you give yourself pain, it was a good thing, whereas now we'd say that was quite ridiculous—there's quite enough bad things that happen to you without searching for them.

The experience of religious faith and commitment in adolescence was complicated by the emotional turbulence of sexual and intellectual maturation. In those churches which encouraged conversion experiences, adolescence was regarded as the optimal age for religious intensity, but not all adolescents welcomed such experiences. Betty Jackson was alarmed by it in her Methodist congregation at Camberwell: 'You had all these people who were converted and you felt inferior because you couldn't be converted. It was my only fear of religion—I think it was a sort of feeling that there was something out of control'. 'Fire and brimstone' and the terrors of Hell were now being shut away in the closet by embarrassed Protestants who preferred a more rational religion; but the Catholic Church still employed the full Christian repertoire of Eternal Damnation. The missions of the Redemptorist Fathers are now fondly remembered as splendid entertainment by *Maeve O'Hara*: 'Oh they were great fun, walking up and down with their berettas on, shouting about mixed marriages'.[22] But if the highly imaginative young suffered morbid guilt over trifles, far more important was the success with which the nuns at Genazzano taught their pupils how to have a spiritual life. *Maeve O'Hara* was given a religious structure to her daily life that was to last a lifetime. The FCJs, silent, concentrated on prayer and meditation, were simply very good at teaching their girls how to practise their faith. Catholicism demanded extraordinary self-discipline—it was a faith that had to be lived every minute of the day if it was to be lived properly. And there was no question that God was not of this world and that this world

---

[22] Interview with *Maeve O'Hara*, 3 December 1990.

was full of sin, so that, as Thomas à Kempis taught, it was always a fear-some struggle between living for God and enduring this mortal coil:

> This life is so replete with temptations, pains and miseries, that it becomes insupportable to a soul that loves God, and is afraid of offending Him. How shall I live, does it exclaim, and not sin? yet how shall I sin and still live? to be ever falling and then rising again; ever resisting my passions, and fighting against the regular desires of my heart—is this life? It is continual death. But let us not grow weary of repressing, of fighting, and conquering our predominant passions, for in this consists the merit of supernatural life, of a life conducing to eternal happiness.[23]

The task to imitate Christ or to follow the Lord was learnt in many ways. Lawrence Cohn cannot remember ever consciously thinking about the question of personal goodness, for 'it was all around me'. His faith came gradually, 'there was no blinding light', and in retrospect he thinks it is easier to become a Christian when you are in a minority: 'the conversion to Christianity is something that most people who say they're Christian don't experience in a country like this'. For *May Featherstone*, the witness and example of other Christians made more impression on her than any ministers. The biggest influence on her was Ruth Flockart, the senior singing mistress at MLC, 'because she *lived* as a Christian—she wasn't frightened to speak about it—she was so committed; and in the way, in the singing, that she interpreted the words of the hymns'. Winsome Walklate can never remember a time when God was not close and that she was not 'aware of His love'. And then came the vocations. If John Jamieson knew that he would be a Presbyterian minister from the age of eight, Sister Anthony Buckley knew she would be an FCJ nun from the age of twelve: 'In the first year I was here as a boarder, John Burke gave the Retreat—three days of silence in Holy Week; and he said,'Who's going to be number four?'—there had been three FCJs from the start of the school in 1889—and I can remember sitting there and saying to myself, '*I'm* going to be the fourth'. Sister Dolores Kirby was likewise drawn to the spirituality of the FCJs when she was a boarder.[24] And *Helen Browne*, 'a rough girl from the country' ambitious to go to the university and do medicine, came to board at Genazzano for the final two years of her schooling: 'I think my poor parents didn't know what had come over me—all the ambitions to become a doctor or do journalism, all gone. All I wanted was this convent. My parents must have been out of

---

[23] Thomas à Kempis, *The Imitation of Christ*, p. 224. *Marjorie O'Donoghue*: 'We were called at 6 a.m. with the bell and prayer—'Praise be to Jesus'—'time to get up girls'. 'Today wear summer uniforms—no cardigans'. Mass in the chapel at seven—then in our silent ranks to the Refectory for breakfast—Mother would every morning read an excerpt from *The Imitation of Christ*. Only after that would our silence—since waking—be broken—and then it was French throughout breakfast'.

[24] Interview with Sister Dolores Kirby FCJ, 1 September 1989.

their mind, but they never discussed it with me'. In his last year at Scotch, Alan Reid was also poised to do medicine when:

> I'd always gone to church because my parents went. It was expected, and in the early teen years it was the place where you had your social life. And then the guy who had the most influence on me at that point was Colin Gilray. He was just brilliant when he dealt with the Prophets—I can always remember the things he said about Amos. That was the turning point. And it was followed (and psychologically one could obviously explain it away) by becoming quite convinced that somehow God was saying, 'You're not going to be a doctor, you are going to be a minister'. I went home and told my parents and they were not very happy. It took my mother a very long time to accept it; my father was a very quiet Scot and he went along with it much quicker than my mother did. And in some ways it was also Colin Gilray who helped them come to terms with it. I had to go back and do a second year matric and he was tremendously helpful to me. There was that twofold social-prophetic gospel that was opened up to us by Colin Gilray, and the psychological experience, the insertion of certainty in what you were going to do.

The Centenary of Victoria in 1934 inspired the Churches to celebrate their own centenaries with mass displays of devotion and solidarity. The Catholics' National Eucharistic Congress was magnificently staged and Protestants were either impressed or appalled by the massive crowds at the open-air Masses and parades through the city. The Congress officially brought Catholic Action to Australia, and Father Martindale's sermon on 'Men's Night', before an immense crowd holding votive candles in the Showground, made an intoxicating call to the laity: 'Every Catholic, then, is called to regard it as his duty to work in co-ordination with the Hierarchy, and under their guidance, at something that is meant to change the world. You are not only to receive, you are to give; and you are to give not only to your fellow Catholics, but to every human soul your influence can reach'. The true Catholic now had to combat the 'evil of the Moneymakers'. But Catholic Action started with personal reform—a new commitment to living a Catholic life in every respect, 'the Christianizing of yourselves' and at the heart of the matter for men would be 'chastity and honesty'. Thus the future of the Church lay ultimately in the hands of Catholic women, with their 'innate spirituality', as the guardians of Christian virtue.[25] The Methodists published a history, rehearsed their legends and indulged in a lot of massed singing. In 1937 the Presbyterians celebrated their centenary with a pageant which proceeded straight from Moses and the Burning Bush to the Scottish Covenanters, excluding rather a lot of Christian witness and history in

---

[25] Murphy and Moynihan, eds, *The National Eucharistic Congress*, pp. 53, 70–1. The crowd is claimed to have been 150 000—perhaps this is something of an exaggeration.

between.[26] But as the Catholics flexed their muscles, the Protestant churches were uneasy over the back-sliding, even in strong middle-class congregations. Enrolments at Sunday schools were falling off and many blamed the polio epidemic, except that the children never came back. And while there were hosts of young people committing themselves to the church, others quietly left once they were old enough to evade or withstand parental authority. None of Oswald Barnett's children shared his religious beliefs, no matter how much they loved and admired him. June Barnett on Sundays was 'always dying for Mondays so I could go back to school', and took pride in coming bottom of the class in Scripture at MLC. It was Betty who had been 'the trail blazer—I had lots of terrible fights, and I used to beg Mother to allow June to play golf and not to send Le to Sunday school'. But by the time it was Le's turn: 'I can remember saying to Dad, "I don't want to be taken into the Church—I haven't got any religious convictions". And he said, "That's all right darling—as far as I'm concerned, you live your life as a Christian" '.[27] Middle-class Australians remained morally and psychically shaped by organized religion, and most believed that they believed. They certainly believed that life had to be lived 'by the golden rule'. Christianity taught them how to be good, but not all who endeavoured to live Christian lives believed that one did so in order to save one's soul.

Minds and Schools

The only truly indelible marks of being middle-class were mental, not monetary. To sustain life as a middle-class person, a man or woman had to be able to earn a middle-class income; and to do that, they needed particular intellectual skills. Whether it was among the bullockies and bush workers of Joseph Furphy's world, or among the urban hordes, the true mark of being 'middle-class' was being educated. When middle-class people went out into the world, they were expected to be able to perform specific tasks and to be able to exercise a certain authority. And in the making of middle-class people, schools did much to equip them with the intellectual skills, the language, the style and the confidence for them to exact deference to their gentility.[1]

A common defence of the right to private schooling has always been that it produces higher academic standards, but in fact little attention has

[26] Adams, *Memories of Darling Road*, p. 21; Mac-Ormiston, *A Pageant: A Hundred Years of Presbyterianism*, pp. 3–4.

[27] Interview with June and Le Barnett, 17 July 1990.

[1] See A. F. Davies, *Skills, Outlooks and Passions: a Psychoanalytic Contribution to the Study of Politics*, pp. 5–6, for a discussion of the 'urge to exact deference' in the formation of a political leader. But this insight can be applied generally to the psychological processes in the impressing of one's caste status on others.

been paid by historians as to what actually happened in classrooms and what were the educational results. The matter is also complicated by the history of the educational infrastructure. The Australian élite as listed in *Who's Who in Australia, 1988* reveals Melbourne and Sydney to be quite different societies: that in Melbourne the products of private schools predominate, and in Sydney the products of the old selective government schools predominate.[2] A staggering 81 per cent of the Victorian-educated male élite came from a mass of private schools and just one and a half government schools.[3] But from the beginning, the assumption had been in Victoria that secondary education was properly the preserve of the private schools, and Graeme Davison locates this in the strength of voluntarism in nineteenth-century Melbourne.[4] The campaign for the government to provide full secondary schooling encountered bitter opposition from the private schools in Victoria. Scholarships were sufficient to give the poor but clever their chance; anything more, opined the Rev. Dr W. H. Fitchett, was 'simply socialism'. And what this meant was that secondary education maketh the middle-class man or woman, and if such education were to be made free and universal, the existing middle class would be swamped with *parvenus*, and the social structure would collapse. Therefore the Melbourne High School had to open under the guise of being a training school for teachers only; except that the teachers at once set about the task of preparing students for matriculation to the university. University High School followed, and by the end of World War I the two institutions were bulging. Victoria's then director of Education, Frank Tate, was determined that secondary education continue to be extended to the country, so in the early 1920s the fateful decision was made to build more new high schools only in those parts of the metropolis not serviced by private establishments. Either by default or by design, the entire eastern and southern suburbs of Melbourne were left to the private schools, and, not until the mid-1950s, when Box Hill Boys' High and Camberwell High started their first matriculation classes, was there anywhere east of the inner city for a state-schooler to qualify for the university.

---

[2] From Peel and McCalman, *Who Went Where in Who's Who 1988: the Schooling of the Australian Elite*, p. 25: Type of School attended by Profession, Victoria and N.S.W.:

Profession	Number	Protestant Victoria% (NSW %)	Catholic Victoria% (NSW %)	State Victoria% (NSW %)
Medicine	176	59.7 (37.9)	14.2 (18.6)	26.1 (42.8)
Academic	318	51.9 (20.6)	10.7 (8.8)	37.1 (70.6)
Judiciary	109	50.5 (33.8)	37.6 (19.0)	11.9 (45.8)
Business	400	63.0 (36.3)	10.0 (11.5)	25.0 (50.7)
Public Service	157	33.2 (14.6)	21.0 (17.9)	46.6 (64.2)
Law	102	54.9 (29.3)	20.6 (32.0)	22.5 (38.7)
TOTAL	2066	51.9 (29.3)	14.4 (14.8)	31.8 (54.8)

[3] See Appendix III, table 1.

[4] From a seminar discussion in 1992.

The distinctive feature since the 1880s of the middle-class Protestants' use of private schooling had been that it was for 'finishing'. Only the rich, the upper middle and upper class sent their children to private schools throughout, and the clientele of Melbourne and Geelong Grammars distinguished themselves from that of Scotch and Wesley Colleges by their greater use of private preparatory schools. Not that Scotch did not have a flourishing Junior School, but the overwhelming majority of Scotch boys in the 1930s had received most of their education in state schools.[5] Eighty per cent of the 1934 Senior School intake at Scotch were to be at the school for no more than four years, and half of those just one or two. The schools were not pleased at being so used and both Wesley and Scotch, by the end of the 1930s when enrolments were stronger, endeavoured to prevent boys over fourteen from coming to the schools. At Trinity, numbers were too low to give Frank Shann the courage to refuse older boys admission, but he exhorted parents again and again to send their sons sooner rather than later, so that the baleful effects of state-schooling could be minimized. And he unashamedly reminded them that the school's prefects were almost exclusively pure-Trinity boys.[6]

The Protestant middle class was as much, if not mostly, a product of the state system; for Catholics it was obviously different (although country children like Sister Dolores Kirby often started in a bush school before going to the city to board). Sister Anthony Buckley, being the only girl, was sent to live with her grandmother in Yarram so that she could attend the new convent. Some of these country Catholic schools were nasty, and others simply depressing. *Veronica Keogh* was sent to board at the FCJ convent in Benalla: 'I can't say I enjoyed it at all—we used to go for walks on Sunday in black stockings through the cemetery'. Some city girls started at local schools before going to Genazzano: *Margaret Power* went first to a Brigidine school, Lyndale (now Kilmaire), and 'loved it':

> I could read a bit before starting school. My first recollection of letters is of my father drawing them in crumbs on the bread board at breakfast. Lyndale was a very good school, and with another lass we were always first or second throughout primary school days. I was good at my work because I enjoyed it. I didn't have a lot of other distractions. We lived a long way from the school and there weren't many school playmates around, so I just got on with it and enjoyed it. My parents were very proud of me and you're pleased to see them proud of you and pleased with your success.

Happiness at primary school had everything to do with academic success and academic success had everything to do with learning to read.

---

[5] See chapter one, footnote 19.
[6] Geoffrey Blainey *et al.*, *Wesley College: the First Hundred Years*, pp. 177–80; Trinity Grammar School Annual Report, 1932, *Mitre*, May 1933; Annual Report 1933, *Mitre*, 1934.

And learning to read the English language is difficult. Recollections of the educational standards of the past are among the most treacherous for the oral historian. Memories of the accurate spelling, speedy arithmetic, sound grammar, legible handwriting, and, of course, the firm discipline 'in *my* day' have to be treated with caution. Moreover, the expectations of the syllabus were very different from what they are today: as recently as 1956 all that was expected by the end of grade three in Victorian primary schools was that each child should know to start a sentence with a capital letter, and to end it with a full-stop.[7] The syllabus demanded that children acquire basic skills in language and mathematics, and memorize, by rote, slabs of knowledge. Those who found it easy to sit still and concentrate, and who had a naturally retentive memory, did well. Classes were large, and could be up to ninety in working-class schools, but teachers were usually well in control. The syllabus was rigid, but there were many teachers of genuine intellectual distinction in the primary division— people who in a later age would have had the chance to go to university. The 'E' forms of the metropolitan central schools, which prepared the abler students for the junior government or private school scholarships which could take them further, were formidable. Betty Blay is one of many grateful graduates of Spring Road Central School, Malvern:

> If there were any extra values added to what I got at home, then I got them at Spring Road—I didn't get them at MLC—there they were only reinforced, they reinforced the work ethic. But I think the thing I got from Spring Road was a love of learning, because we had such good teachers, with such a good general knowledge.

The teachers were nearly all female, single and Catholic. Boys and girls were treated differently in that boys were strapped and girls were not but the teachers appreciated clever girls and 'I never got the impression that I was inferior at school—never, at any time'. Betty wanted to learn: she could read by the age of four, she 'devoured books' and she wept when she made mistakes:

> Miss Morrison, my grade six teacher once told my mother, 'She was sitting up the back crying her eyes out, and when I came up she said, 'I can't find where you got that naught from?' And she was right—I had put an extra naught on the board but no one else noticed it.

There were few children like Betty. In the big classes there were many who passed through unnoticed: there were some who could not see clearly, but no one noticed; and there were some who could not hear

---

[7] Reminiscences of teaching at George Street Primary School, Fitzroy, from David Hornsby, principal of Ringwood Heights Primary School.

properly, but no one noticed; and there were many who appeared to have learnt to read and do sums, but they weren't very good at it and had learnt only by rote. And there are many who remember that the biggest lesson they learnt at school was that they were not much good at lessons. They remember too the covert cruelties of frustrated and distressed teachers. Betty Jackson commenced school at Camberwell Primary School, and loved it, except for one year:

> I remember grade three with horror. The teacher decided that I couldn't add up, and every morning we had a sum and every morning I was practically sick. I wasn't put up because I couldn't add up. I can't remember that second year at all. Perhaps I was too young, because after that I wasn't old for my class. But the fact was that later I enjoyed maths and did physics at university. I can't understand it. And I can remember weeping and weeping because one man teacher said I was frivolous and I didn't know what frivolous meant. But otherwise I wasn't conscious of being happy or unhappy—it was just a fact of life.

And there were the overt cruelties of bullies. Ken Tolhurst's father was an Anglican vicar who was moved so often that Ken went through ten schools and was happy only at Trinity. The roughest schools were Deepdene State School—'my brother and I had to start with our backs to the wall every day'— and Eltham State—where there were many state wards who would 'come to school in the bitterest weather in bare feet— they used to jump up and down in the mud and shout "cheddar cheese" and we were always having fingernail inspections'.[8] Hugh Stretton found Beaumaris Primary School a 'rough, stinking place—nothing awful happened to me, yet I took against it'. He was rescued and sent to C. C. Thorold's Mentone Grammar School of thirty-nine students: 'he was a gorgeous teacher—the best English teacher I ever came across'.

Yet despite the crowding and the rigidity of the state and Catholic primary schools, it seemed that children were learning enough to satisfy the teachers and to placate the inspectors. But the syllabus was so limited that children who were naturally neat and had quick memories and were born readers forged ahead and were accelerated. The teachers were pleased, the parents were proud, but the children eventually suffered. *Stella Davies*:

> I started school on my fourth birthday—both Mum and Dad and the headmaster thought I was ready for school. And at the state school I was always first or second in the class, and Mum got very uptight once when I came third. Then I had one year at the Higher Elementary School and I began to slip back—we took on board French, algebra and geometry.

---

[8] Interview with Ken Tolhurst, 16 November 1990.

Mum said, 'Just as well you're to MLC next year, that will get you back'. But it didn't. I got worse and worse. I was too young—I was eighteen months younger than a lot, and eighteen months at that stage is critical. I don't recollect ever failing anything, but I went from the top of the tree down to the top of the next third. And Mum couldn't understand this and there was a lot of talk about taking me away from MLC and sending me to Stratherne which was smaller, but it wasn't that—I was just too young.[9]

It was all very haphazard. *Mary Geoghegan* and *Marina Graham*, having been accelerated at other schools, both arrived at Genazzano far too young for the class. *Elinor Doyle*, one of the school's best scholars in its long history, had to repeat third grade because of bad handwriting, even though she had been reading with ease since the age of three. The nuns boasted of her fluency—but she still had to produce 'neat work' in her copy book, in the approved Genazzano handwriting. She had also missed many months of school due to severe childhood asthma. In retrospect she is grateful for having been kept with her own age group: she was in a class full of creative talent, in music, painting, drama—she was never bored.

Memories of the private preparatory schools are mixed. Many were very happy, but there are stories of the same places which disagree. George Morcom loved the Misses Wymonds' 'Clarence'; James Murray was shattered by it.[10] But one of these private schools, St Andrews, was a world unto itself, and in charge of the primary grades was a Miss Margaret Lyttle.[11] Jean Cane and Winsome Walklate both went there before they came to MLC. Winsome:

I didn't go to school until I was six—Mother didn't believe in children going to school too early—they should be taught at home. I remember my first reading lesson and I seemed to read within a week or so—so I must have been taught partly how to read before I went to school.

The school was founded on Christian principles. It was unusual in that the headmaster was a Presbyterian minister, and he had an open door and the children would come up and talk to him at lunchtime. And if you had any quarrels, you joined the queue and went and told Mr Lawton. We had school meetings—it was run on very democratic principles, for all the school came to the meetings to do with the running of the school. It seems quite extraordinary, but that's how it was.

And I was introduced to the Greek myths and legends sitting under a blazing blue sky and a red gum tree in bloom. We carried our little chairs outside, and we heard the story of the Golden Fleece and Perseus from Miss Lyttle. It was lovely. We had no prizes, no exams, long lunchtimes when we

[9] Interview with *Stella Davies*, 12 December 1990.
[10] Interview with George Morcom, 17 September 1990; Murray, *The Paradise Tree*, p. 77.
[11] She soon after founded Melbourne's most successful private 'alternative' school, Preshil.

played on swings. And they still had cows for the dairy, so you could observe the natural functions of a cow with much interest. It was a boarding school as well, and we had lunch with the boarders, and I used to sit near the headmaster who had intelligent conversations with the teachers. And I remember one saying, 'Well, I've only read the headlines' and I thought— How strange. Does anyone read beyond the headlines in the newspaper?

For a rejected child like Jean Cane, St Andrew's was 'sheer joy'; and it had an enduring effect in that it showed her that bad things could be changed, that the world could be made to work differently. It made her a radical: 'I've *always* felt it, but I couldn't practise being a radical at MLC, except through my writing perhaps—I've always written copiously'. In 1932 she had a poem in *Silver and Green*, and it was one of the very few pieces in the school magazine set in an Australia that a child could actually observe; it was full of longing for vivid life, and prophetic of her later career:

> Bourke Street, Bourke Street, biting cold or summer,
> Strange faces peering from the left and from the right,
> Wherever I should be, it would be the same for me,
> The same old, dirty, crowded street, alive with life and light.

When Winsome Walklate moved to MLC, however, things started to go wrong. Not that she was unhappy at MLC—she loved the school (it was her mother's old school) and she loves it still. She made wonderful friends who have lasted a lifetime; she behaved herself, but she was often away sick. Her perpetual respiratory infections and distress were maturing into severe asthma, and the clever girl who had learnt to read in a week at St Andrews began to fail her examinations. She lost her confidence; she missed so many weeks of school that her maths fell irretrievably behind. Everyone was kind, but she was a failure. Not a lot of fuss was made about that, because most girls at MLC in her year likewise failed. Of the 284 girls born in 1919–20, who proceeded at MLC beyond the Merit Certificate (year 8), no fewer than two thirds of them left the school without being able to pass the Intermediate Certificate (year 10); and half of those failed dismally before the Intermediate year. Often the teachers wrote 'hopeless' on their record cards and quietly despaired: the slow, like the poor, will always be with us. And while it is commonly believed that girls then had lower aspirations than boys, and that their parents were similarly expecting less of them, almost three quarters of the MLC and Genazzano Survey women reported that their fathers did not consider their education less important than that of their brothers.[12] In fact of the 175 girls who left MLC without the Intermediate, only five had marks which suggested that

---

[12] Survey: 'Did your father believe that girls' education was less important than boys'?': Yes: MLC, 22%; Genazzano, 28%; 'Did your mother believe that girls' education was less important than boys'?' Yes: MLC, 18%; Genazzano, 21%.

they could have passed the Intermediate had they attempted it. Overall, merely 10 per cent of the whole cohort could be said to have left school prematurely—that is, they appear to have underachieved—and some of those may have gone on to other schools. Sadly, the vast majority of girls who left MLC below the Leaving Certificate (year 11) did not go further because they could not pass. And of the full cohort of 284 girls, 55 per cent have to be classified as very 'weak students'—unable to read fast enough, unable to write adequate English prose, unable to do basic mathematics, unable to commit facts to memory, unable to cope with school. By present-day standards it looks a dreadful performance.[13]

Yet, for its time, MLC was a good school. Among the private girls' schools it was second to the venerated PLC in academic standing. But even PLC's scholastic reputation, according to its historian, Kathleen Fitzpatrick, paled when she analysed the failure rates within the school.[14] The boys did better, but still not all that well. Of the private schools, Scotch did best with 39 per cent of the boys who entered Senior School in 1934 leaving the school without the Intermediate; but of the 84 boys who did not—or could not—attempt it, two thirds failed year 9. Overall, of the 267 boys who started their secondary education on that first day of term in 1934 nearly a quarter could be judged as 'hopeless'. And at Trinity, of the 88 boys who were born in 1919–20 and who proceeded to the Senior School, 43 per cent left without an Intermediate Certificate.[15]

How did these leading private schools compare with the government schools? All high schools were Class A schools, but the Melbourne high schools felt the depression keenly. All but Melbourne Boys, MacRobertson Girls' and University High schools lost their Leaving Honours (year 12) classes, and tuition fees were introduced. It would cost a school teacher £12 to put his daughter through Leaving Honours at MacRobertson Girls' High ('MacRob') and twelve guineas at MLC where teachers' and ministers' daughters were charged half fees. Retention rates fell in government schools and rose slightly at Scotch during the Depression, although the immediate effect of the economic slump was a massive increase in the numbers attempting the public examinations as those soon to join the job market sought to improve their chances. The three leading high schools were not academically selective during the 1930s in the way they were to be later, but they were informally selective in that they educated those just out of financial range of private schooling but anxious for education and social improvement. Few who knew they were unlikely to pass bothered to enter a high school.[16] And at MacRob

[13] See Appendix I, table 5.
[14] Fitzpatrick, PLC—the First Century, pp. 237–8.
[15] See Appendix I, tables 3 and 6.
[16] Victorian Government Printer, Education in Victoria, p. 57; L. J. Blake, Vision and Realisation, vol. 1, pp. 498–505.

the girls did much better than at MLC: of the 509 girls born 1919–20, 51 per cent left without the Intermediate, but 13.5 per cent left after passing year 9 because they needed to enter the workforce, so the comparable performance with MLC is a 'failure rate' of 37.5 per cent, and comparable with Scotch. At Melbourne Boys' High the results were similar, with 35 per cent of the 322 boys who entered the school in 1934 below year 11 leaving school without the Intermediate. It was not a good performance. Just under a quarter of those 322 boys were 'hopeless' and out of the school by the end of year 9, and another 32 per cent failed the Intermediate or passed with an average under 60 per cent. Finally, at the co-educational Essendon High School, 36 per cent of the boys and 52 per cent of the girls left without the Intermediate.[17]

The Class A schools prided themselves on teaching and marking to a higher standard than that of the public examinations sat for by the Class B schools. Often a student who had performed poorly was advised to sit externally, so the Class A schools' official failure rates were low. Most Class A schools awarded the Intermediate or the Leaving certificates on the basis of a whole year's work—term examinations and weekly testing constituting a form of continuous assessment. At Trinity Grammar Class A status was newly won in 1933 and greatly prized; yet as ever there were doubters and Frank Shann was quick to reassure parents:

> I am most anxious that you should join me in an affirmation of the fact that the system is *fully safeguarded* as far as the maintenance of standards is concerned. It is not an easy way to pass an examination. Indeed I want to emphasize the point with all my might that it was not a question of 'passing an examination' at all, but it is rather a method of reaching a standard on the part of the boys and of certifying to that fact on the part of the staff . . . Judgement of boys is going on throughout their course.[18]

The Intermediate class at Trinity in 1935 contained thirty-nine boys, and for many it was a desperate struggle to 'meet the standard'. In May the class average was below 50 in history, Latin, arithmetic and algebra—subjects in which the cleverest boy scored 70 (fourth place), 95 (first place) and 96 (first place). By August the class average had crept up to 56, but still most boys flunked Latin, French and arithmetic (the dux scored 100 for arithmetic). By the end of the year the class had conquered arithmetic, but Latin and French were lost causes to the end and robbed boys of the language they needed for a full Intermediate pass.[19] *Dick Wallace* was one who failed French:

---

[17] 'MacRob 1919–20 Cohort': records of the 509 girls at the school born in 1919 or 1920; 'M.H.B.S. 1934 Cohort': records of the 322 boys who entered the school in 1934 below the level of Leaving Honours: 'EHS 1919–20 Cohort': records of the 141 boys and girls at the school born in 1919 or 1920.

[18] *Mitre*, May 1934, p. 10.

[19] School reports of Lawrence Cohn, kindly lent to the author.

I went to Trinity on a half scholarship from Mont Albert Central—we had this cramming form, the E form. All my family—my sister at PLC, my brother at University High—went on full or half scholarships. I was there from 1933 to 1935 and I got a job half-way into 1936.

In those days, as you turned sixteen, you were looking for a job—hopefully you had your Intermediate. I didn't have it *technically*—I got the right number of subjects, but not the right ones. But I overcame that. Whenever I applied for a job they'd ask, 'Have you got your Intermediate?' and I'd say, 'Six subjects'. That's not lying—but I should have got French and history and I didn't. But they never seemed to ask for any forms, so that seemed all right.

At least the boys at Trinity Grammar were doing better than their social superiors at Melbourne Grammar, where 57 per cent of the 168 boys who entered the Senior School in 1934 left school without at least the Intermediate.[20] And Melbourne Grammar, like all but six Protestant schools and all Catholic schools, was a Class B school, where students sat the easier public examinations. Despite this, the Melbourne Grammar boys found the Intermediate a fearsome academic hurdle: in 1930, 39 per cent of them passed in their first attempt in December, and in 1931 only 34 per cent did. But the performance of the boys from Geelong Grammar was truly appalling: in 1930, 19 per cent passed the December examinations, and in 1932, 22 per cent were successful. Intensive and expensive private coaching during the January holidays usually pushed another 15 per cent through in the February supplementary examinations, and with that, Melbourne Grammar enjoyed an Intermediate pass-rate which was close to the state average.[21] This too was improving in the 1930s: in 1921, 65.9 per cent of the 3891 Victorian candidates failed the Intermediate, but ten years later, at the height of the Depression, a record 7805 sat, and only 56.3 per cent failed. By 1935 the time-consuming February supplementaries were abandoned and, for the first time in Victorian educational history, the pass-marks were lowered to 40 per cent for two out of the minimum six subjects needed to pass. The 'rot had set in' and in 1935 only 43.4 per cent failed.[22]

It needs to be remembered at this point that the bulk of these candidates came from white-collar families. Moreover, the Class A

---

[20] *Liber Melburniensis*: records of the 168 boys who entered Senior School in 1934. Melbourne Grammar seems to have been divided down the middle between the sportsmen, who came for the old school tie, and the scholars, because its performance in the Leaving and Leaving Honours was respectable. Of the 1934 Cohort, 57 per cent left with nothing, 11 per cent left with the Intermediate, and 32 per cent with Leaving or Leaving Honours. This cohort won three Senior Government Scholarships and one University Free Place.

[21] Geelong Grammar School Archives: Headmaster's Correspondence: R. P. Franklin to J. R. Darling, 15 June 1933; notes made by Darling during the correspondence. I am endebted to Dr Peter Gronn for finding this material. See also Weston Bate, *Light Blue Down Under: the History of Geelong Grammar School*, p. 205.

[22] Victorian Government Printer, *Education in Victoria*, p. 57.

schools' results were amalgamated with the Class B schools' results and, since the Class A schools culled their candidates, their official failure rates were very low. Therefore, there must have been many private Class B schools, both Catholic and Protestant, with failure rates for the Intermediate of over 70 per cent. Genazzano was a Class B school and, because it was so intimate, the nuns did not need to keep detailed records, but if *Margaret Power's* memories of Genazzano are of the excitement of the teaching, especially in languages, *Veronica Keogh* remembers being in an Intermediate class where only two of the fifteen girls passed.

So how difficult were these examinations and why did so many fail? I have consulted a group of retired senior teachers who were themselves at secondary school in the 1930s and early 1940s.[23] Some of them experienced difficulties as secondary students and all became remarkable teachers. Collectively they have been part of every reform of the Victorian public examination system since 1944. I asked them to evaluate the papers set for the external Intermediate, Leaving and Leaving Honours papers for 1935, and to compare them with the intellectual demands of the recently superseded Higher School Certificate. The consensus was that the examiners' expectations were very different in the importance accorded clean and accurate work. Misspellings and grammatical flaws lost marks in all subjects which required essay writing, including science. In mathematics, an arithmetical slip lost you 3 out of 10, and a mistake in method, 7 out of 10, so it was easy to score 0. These were black and white days; things were either right or they were wrong. The student with the naturally retentive memory was truly fortunate, for even by Leaving Honours, the rote memorization of texts, bare facts, esoteric vocabularies and rare grammatical constructions mattered far more than conceptual grasp or insight. A student of the 1980s would have been utterly defeated by the French and German papers of the 1930s but, in most of the other humanities, the intellectual demands of the 1930s papers were lower than would be acceptable by the 1960s. The Leaving Honours European history paper, for instance, was taken only by candidates who had already matriculated for the university, and yet a year 11 of the 1980s could have managed it comfortably. As for irony, it had yet to be invented: the examiners for the Honours English Literature paper scolded those candidates who had dared to think that the motto on the brooch of Chaucer's prioress—'Amor Vincit Omnia'—could be a reference to 'anything but divine love'.[24]

---

[23] In late 1989 I asked them to assess the examination papers and to discuss them at a joint meeting. They doubled up for most subjects and the English and history papers had four assessors. Their comments come from their written notes and from the taped record of that discussion. My thanks go to Betty Mackay, Betty Malone, Betty Jackson, Ursula Gottschalk, Barbara Sutton, Dorothea Cerutty and *Peter Robertson*. Also present for the discussion were Joy Parnaby, Brenda Niall, Philippa Ryan, Frances O'Neill and Ailsa Zainu'ddin.

[24] University of Melbourne Schools and University Examinations Board, *Examiners' Reports, 1935–36*, p. 353.

The histories were among the subjects to have changed most from that day to this, and the performance of both teachers and pupils was poor. Examiners of the 1930s were determined that Australian children should know all about Wellington, Nelson and Clive of India and very little else. One history teacher at MLC in the 1930s was dubbed 'underliner', because like so many around the state, she taught entirely by calling out the lines in the text book that the girls had to underline and memorize.[25] The author of a number of these textbooks, renowned for their dryness, was R. H. 'Forty-five' Clayton of Scotch College. His classes were only partly like that, as Hugh Stretton gratefully remembers:

> A marvellous history teacher, who was a curious phenomenon in himself. A strict Plymouth Brother, a man of utterly liberal mind in the classroom and unspeakable anywhere else. Clayton was a selfish teacher—other teachers would say—he taught all the A classes and made everyone else teach the rest. He did some dreadful things. He wrote his own textbooks, which were very banal, ordinary—digested out of somebody else's I'm sure. And every class was the same: he made you sit and get through the textbook, and he made you underline the right bits and mark them 1,2,3,4, in the margin, so that you had a visual memory of the structure of facts. And then in the nineteenth minute of the class, we would mercifully manage to divert him. And we were in our final year when the penny finally dropped that it had *always* been in the nineteenth minute of the class: that in the Intermediate year we had diverted him into arguing trams versus buses; in the Leaving year we had diverted him into talking about Australian income tax policies; and in the Honours year it had been about the League of Nations and international affairs. So he was doing an exact fifty-fifty mix of belting in memory of necessary things by crude methods, and making people write, talk and think. I've met no better teaching prescription anywhere ever since—perhaps not always done in quite that manner.

MLC also had some exciting teachers, and Joyce Thorpe so hated to miss a minute of Miss Ellen Christensen's English classes that she once asked her to 'please get on with the lesson' while Miss Christensen was chatting to a couple of her favourite pupils: 'And she was furious with me—she absolutely demolished me; and several of the girls came afterwards and said, "How could you do that?" So that seemed to be a terrible, shameful thing I did at MLC'. Miss Christensen's English and history classes awakened intellectual excitement in many; for those older, like Betty Blay, there were Mrs Landen and Mr Philip Le Couteur. At Genazzano the quality of history teaching was mixed, as Mary Thompson recalls it. The nun teaching Australian history was an underliner *par excellence*, who 'made it so boring that it took me years to get around to it'; far more ex-

---

[25] Betty Malone and Dorothea Cerutty, Examinations discussion.

citing was Denys Jackson, the darling of the Campion Society and on loan from Xavier College: 'We used to sit outside in the garden and I had him all to myself. I read later what he wrote, but I never saw him again'. As for the brilliant Mother Philomena Beck, she was at the other end of the spectrum from the underliners:

> Mother Philomena was fabulous. I didn't pass, but I knew all the interesting bits. There were long bookshelves right along the room and she'd say, 'I'm not quite sure—look up on that top shelf, about three books to the left—you'll find it on page seventy-five'. She had a photographic memory. But she knew all the scandals of Europe—she made it so interesting.

The examiners found fault with everyone but themselves. The Leaving European History paper they believed to be interesting and they were prepared to credit 'any element of correctness, even in partial answers', but they found they could only pass 41 per cent: 'too many [had] but a vague, scrappy and inaccurate knowledge of what they [had to] write about'. Above all, the candidates could not write:

> The majority of answers of any length were continuous passages without paragraphs, marginal or other headings, and without any attempt at logical arrangement. Still the worse fault is that candidates do not answer the question set, either from an inability to interpret it, or, lacking the knowledge, from an attempt to side-track the examiner by writing something akin to it.[26]

Complaints about literacy and comprehension dominate every history and English examiner's report from the Intermediate, right through to Leaving Honours: spelling, grammar, punctuation, structure and logic— all were too often 'deplorable', and these were the students who were failed. But there was also regret at how little these young Australians were learning from their underliners:

> A doubt as to whether the subject is fulfilling its function as a humane study must visit the examiner confronted with such statements as that the French are a 'nation composed chiefly of cowards', and that the gold rushes brought to Victoria 'Japanese, Italians, Americans and other undesirable races' and that the Armada was defeated 'owing to the superiority of English courage' or even more sweepingly, because 'the English race was much superior to the Spanish'.[27]

What these examiners' reports suggest, as do all the detailed school records I have analysed, is that many students had real problems with

---

[26] *Examiners' Reports, 1935–36*, p. 355.
[27] Ibid., p. 322.

reading and writing. Given a basic literacy test, they would have all passed and entered the historical record as literate but, as they progressed up the educational ladder, the literacy demanded of them became more complex. Once past the Merit Certificate at year 8, they had to write more individually-composed answers, and could no longer rely on the rote memorization of pithy blocks of information copied from textbooks or the blackboard. Many were also likely to have been slow readers, and slow readers not only could not keep up the pace, they also had poor comprehension and found the task of ordering facts and thoughts on paper very difficult. In the 1950s slow readers were singled out among the students at the University of Melbourne as a major cause of the unacceptably high failure rates in many faculties.[28] The frightening question is, how many Australians of all social backgrounds were similarly handicapped? To what extent were low retention rates aggravated by the fact that a large proportion of children were seen to 'fail' at school before the compulsory leaving age? For how many Australian men and women was the conviction that they were as 'dumb as anything' and 'no good at school' simply the most significant thing they learnt there? This window into the classroom provided by the student records of these middle-class and lower-middle-class schools enables us to glimpse the monumental task it has been—and remains—to bring about mass literacy. Compulsory schooling had been in effect for two generations by the time this generation was at school in the 1930s but, as every teacher knows, just sitting in a classroom does not guarantee that a child will learn to read, let alone quickly and acutely. This tale of human waste and frustration provides some historical background to the findings of Rosie Wickert's chilling survey of Australian adult literacy, where only around a third of the population 'possesses analytical thinking skills when it comes to the understanding of prose text', and the older they are, the worse they are.[29]

What happened with numeracy and higher mathematics in the 1930s? Intermediate arithmetic has acquired almost legendary notoriety. The number of talented, even eminent, adults who struggled to pass is remarkable. Graham McInnes was one who utterly failed to thrive under the tuition of the brilliant A. E. ('Stonk') Ross at Scotch: 'I failed my . . . intermediate . . . in algebra and arithmetic, never having been able to master either simple proportion or a simple equation . . . In the final exam in algebra I received zero per cent. I attempted every question but got none of them or any part right'.[30] Dorothea Cerutty had her University Free Place, her Moran Bursary and her honours, and was ready to go except that she had failed to pass an Intermediate mathematics subject: 'Dorrie couldn't do maths, so Dorrie was sent out to the garden for the

---

[28] W. H. Frederick, 'Components of Failure', pp. 18–20.
[29] Rosie Wickert, *No Single Measure: A Survey of Australian Adult Literacy*, pp. 20–1.
[30] Graham McInnes, *Goodbye Melbourne Town*, p. 97.

lesson—it took six exams and three years for me to pass'. Intermediate arithmetic was a very practical subject. There were additions of large sums of pounds, shillings and pence, the calculation of compound interest at 2 $^1/_2$ per cent, a square root sum, some long division and multiplication, some logarithms, some simple stocks and shares, and a number of those calculations about work done, pipes laid, goods sold, and houses bought by Smith and Brown. The examiners were not pleased: 46 per cent of the candidates in 1935 scored under 50 (40 was a 'lower pass') and for that the examiners blamed the teachers.[31] Too few teachers, it seems, cared about those doomed to fail. Margaret Bickford remembers of MLC in the late 1930s that there was no actual teaching of skills: 'You were just to do things if you thought you could do them'.[32] In other words, if the student could not master the work, then that was the student's problem, not the teacher's.

The morality of teachers was different. Many, especially in the private Class A schools, took pride in failing students in droves because that showed they were upholding standards. The principle was not 'what can we develop in this student?' but 'is this student worthy of passing here?' Education was a ladder of achievement where the unable were progressively 'weeded out', until only the truly brilliant were left to glitter in splendid isolation. *Peter Robertson* was an admiring former student of 'Stonk' Ross, and went on to teach senior mathematics for many years. To his eyes the Leaving Honours mathematics papers of 1935 were too hard for most then, and would be impossible today. But in the 1930s the examiners were not interested in producing a 'clever country', they were looking for the gifted: 'they must have passed people on little scraps of answers, and usually just to get 5 out of 10 right was enough to get a first class honour:

> I think that until quite recently in internal exams, teachers would take pride in setting clever questions, trick questions. And it's only now that teachers have learned that nothing is gained by setting hard papers. We tend now to be much more straightforward, more down to essential concepts.[33]

There were teachers who saw their role differently. *Neil Ewart* remembers one at Scotch in the 1930s 'who used to have a saying at exam time that he was there to find out what you *did* know, not what you didn't know— and that separated him from all the other teachers'.[34] Schools tended to assign their best teachers to the best students, and those who were struggling were condemned to suffer the often appalling attentions of the

---

[31] *Examiners' Reports, 1935–36*, p. 27.
[32] Interview with Margaret Bickford, 22 October 1990.
[33] Interview with *Peter Robertson*, 13 February 1990.
[34] Interview with *Neil Ewart*, 11 December 1990.

worst. Teaching has always been stressful and frequently thankless, and the plight of the near-impoverished spinster was particularly unpleasant: at MLC by the end of World War II senior teachers earned less than the male gardener.[35] It is not surprising therefore that the oral record of school days hints of injustices and mental cruelties perpetrated both consciously and unconsciously by angry and frustrated teachers. The student records too have their nasty moments: 'cries about school—needs strict form mistress'; 'likes boys—self-satisfied'; 'neat but dull'; 'no background'.[36]

'No background' was of course a euphemism for 'common' and, though an offensive judgement, it was partially an accurate one. A major reason for children then (and now) finding difficulty with analytical reading and writing was that so many came from homes where there were few books, and where adults rarely, if ever, discussed ideas, religion, politics or even just life itself. The constraints of Christian charity and emotional repression rendered many adults pathologically afraid of conflict. Discussion was dangerous, because discussion might swell into debate, and debate might escalate into disagreement, and disagreement might explode into anger. Some remember inter-war middle-class life, especially among Nonconformists, for its dread of 'unpleasantness' above all else. In Sadie Copeland's loving Baptist family, even personal family matters were not discussed: 'Mother and father didn't tell me terribly much about things that went on, and it was quite rude to ask questions— I still find it difficult to say, "Well what do you do?" '[37] Perhaps even more important was the fact that many Scotch, Trinity and MLC mothers and fathers of the 1920s and 1930s had little confidence in their own intellectual skills. Those who replied to the Survey from the four schools are not representative of their own generations academically: less than 10 per cent of the MLC and Scotch respondents, and around 13 per cent of the Trinity and Genazzano respondents, left school without the Intermediate.[38] Yet even among this academically select sample of the schools, a third of the MLC fathers, a quarter of the Scotch fathers, and almost 40 per cent of the Trinity fathers had left school at fourteen or younger—and these figures are likely to be optimistic guesses.[39] As for literacy and the habit of books in the home, only 55 per cent of the fathers and slightly more of the mothers were frequent readers.[40] And in each of the schools those whose parents were new middle class did worst and those whose parents were well educated did best: in the Scotch 1934 Cohort, not

[35] Zainu'ddin, *They Dreamt of a School*, pp. 268–9.
[36] MLC 1919–20 Cohort.
[37] Interview with Sadie Copeland, 21 November 1990.
[38] See Appendix II, tables 2a, 2b, 3 and 6a.
[39] See Appendix II, tables 1a and 2a.
[40] Survey: 'Did your father read a lot?' Yes: Scotch, 61%; Trinity, 51%; MLC, 59%; Genazzano, 59%.
    'Did your mother read a lot?' Yes: Scotch, 64%; Trinity, 60%; MLC, 57%; Genazzano, 69%.

one of the fifty-two sons of 'business' attemped Leaving Honours and merely 15 per cent of the professional men's sons left without the Intermediate.[41]

With little help from home, however well-meaning their parents, children easily lost confidence, especially in a big and famous school where so much was lavished on the talented at the top. Boys who did poorly and who also were ordinary at sport, suffered, but girls were more subtly vulnerable. Of the Survey women, 60 per cent from MLC reported that they had adequate self-confidence while at school, but at Genazzano, borne down by the Catholic cult of feminine humility, fewer were confident as schoolgirls.[42] Mother Bernadette resented *Monica O'Farrell*'s 'forwardness': ' "Cast your eyes downwards when you speak to me"— but I never did, I would look straight at her'. And Sister Anthony Buckley remembers: 'If you ever had any ideas about yourself, you were soon reduced to nothing'. Problems with confidence were more important than girls' low academic aspirations in these two schools at least: most took their schoolwork seriously, and of those who did not, only a handful are still unrepentant.[43] Just under half were not frightened by examinations.[44] Neither were their parents expecting too little of them, for only the Genazzano fathers—28 per cent of them at least—significantly believed that girls' education was less important than boys'. The most important reason why MLC had so many girls who left without the Intermediate was that these girls were being allowed by their parents to stay on longer at school, even though they appeared to be 'hopeless at lessons'. MLC, unlike PLC, always saw itself as a comprehensive school and provided generously for non-academic girls with its highly regarded business school and its 'accomplishments' subjects for those in what they called 'Special'. In other words, still at MLC, and therefore represented in their records, were many pupils who were usually culled out by the age of fourteen. The failing girls at MLC reflect the educational standards of the wider population now lost to the historical record; they do not reflect on the quality of MLC itself.

Boys did poorly also. James Austin was too dreamy and never mastered mathematics, so he left before the Intermediate examinations when a job as an office boy came his way. *Walters Rhodes* also did not try, but like James he belonged to a category which often suffered

---

[41] See Appendix I: table 2 for the full figures. In summary, 48% of the fatherless boys, 15% of the professionals' boys, 35% of the 'Commerce' boys, 56% of the 'Business' boys, 78% of the 'Commercial employees' boys, and 46% of the farmers' and graziers' boys left Scotch without the Intermediate.

[42] Survey: 'Did you have adequate self-confidence at school?' Yes: MLC, 60%; Genazzano, 40%.

[43] Survey: 'Did you work hard at your schoolwork?' No: MLC, 17.3%; Genazzano, 29.2%. 'If not, do you regret that now?' No: MLC, 21%; Genazzano, 29.8%.

[44] Survey: 'Did you find examinations frightening?' No: MLC, 47%; Genazzano, 45%.

academically—those without fathers at home.[45] But for *Walters* there was a double blow in that when he was sixteen, he also lost his mother:

> I suppose a lot of people have said the same thing—if you knew what you know now, you would possibly have taken a different course. I don't say it would have changed my life, because my life changed when my mother died. And then the war on top of that. But I don't think people realized in those days the benefits of study like they do today. I regret one thing—that I never learnt languages. My maths—that's been all right. I'm not brilliant.[46]

Tom Beenie was not a keen scholar—'I used to do what was set and that was it'; anyway, he lived for sport.[47] Elaine Corran had 'a wonderful time at MLC' and often did well in assignments. Yet she did poorly in examinations: she couldn't understand it and neither could the headmistress, Mrs Landen. 'But I had my successes. I came second in the class in algebra, but since everyone in the class failed and I got 21 and the top girl got 23. Some just got nothing that year—they just didn't understand it.' There was another reason why Elaine was having difficulties learning, but it was not until she was in her early forties and the mother of three sons did she discover that she was very deaf. Why hadn't she noticed her deafness years earlier? 'I suppose it was because I was a compulsive talker.'

Schools could be cruel places, and those buffeted by the storms of adolescence or bearing heavy emotional loads found little sympathy. Mrs Landen at MLC often did extend kindness and understanding to those who were troubled: when Dorothea Cerutty was senior prefect, her mother was desperately ill and often on cold mornings the headmistress would make her a cup of warm cocoa to start the day. But the puritanism of the times so infected schools that there was little sympathy for human weakness and difficulty. Jean Cane was a clever girl, but even she suffered dreadfully for a time at MLC:

> You take a decent well-behaved kid like I was. I was so nervous and I think it was because I was so awfully put down at home. And when I was asked to stand up and read something, my voice would just go. It would be down in my boots and I couldn't read. And they regarded that as a shocking weakness; nobody ever tried to find out why. Probably it lasted for about two years, and then gradually I pulled out of it. I even captained a debating team when I was in Leaving and I didn't do too badly at it. But there was no kindness there—anything but.

Lurline Keck was another who failed her Intermediate and she is still visited by anxiety when she is reminded of MLC. Betty Jackson

---

[45] This was noticeable in all the schools studied.
[46] Interview with *Walters Rhodes*, 27 September 1990.
[47] Interview with Tom Beenie, 11 July 1990.

remembers well the feeling of entrapment and inadequacy that was the lot of so many school children of the period:

> I didn't enjoy the learning at MLC. When I was at the state school I can remember absolutely loving history and geometry, but when I went to MLC, I was quite convinced that I couldn't do any of the work. I was always doing wrong. I had to do Latin and most of the form had had two years Latin. And in the first few weeks I hadn't learnt my Latin vocab.—I just didn't know I had to learn it. And being given a detention and then not knowing what a detention was—so I said blithely to the teacher, 'I haven't been to detention yet' and she doubled it. And the next lesson I said to my neighbour, 'I've got two detentions' and the teacher gave me a detention for speaking. So I ended up the morning with three detentions. And in my first six weeks I got something like thirteen detentions. I was a law-abiding girl—I just felt bewildered.

Such experiences were to make her later a singular teacher at MLC.

Dr Max Kemp has devoted his teaching and research career to the plight of the child who fails at school. He went to Trinity in 1940 as a St Paul's Chorister. His parents were working-class and during the Depression his father was unemployed until he found a job as a labourer with the Camberwell City Council. By 1940 the family's fortunes had improved: both sons were at Trinity, and their father had become a masseur, and was in the Army medical corps. But things went wrong for Max once he got to Trinity:

> My feelings about Trinity as a school remain affected by the long years of hopelessness I experienced scholastically. Trinity was graced by some first-rate scholars. During my first year at the school, when aged nine, and having come from a government school which taught me to read and write, I was in a class of eight boys. That should have been an ideal condition for learning. It was not. We were taught by a later-revered, delightful woman who was still in training at the private teacher education establishment, Mercer House. At that time she was not remarkably *au fait* with the basics of management, planning or teaching. I can sense even now the steady draining of my self-confidence, which was daily pitched against a small team of bright kids who could run their own show without a teacher's help, and especially from one who was quite ineffectual at that time. Her successor in 1941 was worse and whereas other boys seemed to learn in spite of the awfulness of the teaching, I could not. The war years affected the quality of staff, of course, and Trinity was plagued throughout the period to 1945–6 by some remarkably inept teachers, appointed, it seemed, only because they were male, upright and breathing.
>
> The pattern having been set in 1940–1, the remaining years until I was seventeen became a succession of ever-deepening failures as more bright

boys successively enrolled and pressed a batch of us into a widening, and thickening, bottom layer of the scholastic pile. I managed to be 'kept back' twice during secondary school. On one occasion, during my absence, my class friends were told by a teacher that I should have been in a school for the mentally retarded. My friends thought this was terribly funny, thank goodness, and were bursting to tell me. I was shocked. The scar still itches. I had thought I was simple, dumb and lazy: mental retardation had not been one of the options. The scar never really healed despite the compensations of becoming a good school footballer, and enjoying the plaudits of those with brains but different goals. Perhaps these experiences were important in the shaping of my later decision, as an adult, to acquire qualifications, even if I could never feel that, in the process, I became more than half-educated.[48]

Those who passed at Trinity did better than at many other schools. During the 1930s Frank Shann worked hard to make the school more academic and to motivate boys to aim for the university, so that while 43 per cent of the Trinity Cohort left school without the Intermediate, 25 per cent left with it and another 32 per cent went on to the Leaving and passed. Of those who passed Leaving, just over half attempted some honours. Shann pleaded with parents to allow boys to take two years over the honours course as a better preparation for the university, but only a third of the honours boys—five in all—did go: two to do medicine, one law, one theology and one agricultural science. And of the boys who did only Leaving Pass, four went to university without the extra years at school.[49] Money rather than academic ability was the real impediment: in the Trinity survey, which included many younger men who matriculated after the war when scholarships were more numerous, just 23 per cent of the respondents reported that their parents could have afforded to put them through university without financial assistance.[50]

The Depression bore down on the Scotch Cohort of 267 boys who entered Senior School in 1934. After the 39 per cent who left with nothing, 21 per cent left with only the Intermediate and 31 per cent left with only the Leaving. Of the original 267, just twenty-one— or less than 8 per cent—completed year 12 successfully. This was still vastly better than the equivalent retention rate in the government schools which I have calculated to have been less than 2 per

---

[48] Letter to author, 21 September 1990.
[49] See Appendix I, table 6.
[50] Survey: 'Could your family afford to pay your way through university without scholarships?' Yes: Scotch, 41%; Trinity, 24%; MLC, 41%; Genazzano, 47%.

cent.[51] At MLC retention rates were low also, with just seventeen out of the original 284 girls attempting honours, and, during the 1930s, the girls at the co-educational University High School did better than the girls of MLC in the winning of Senior Government Scholarships.[52]

But schools were changing in the 1930s. New extra-curricular activities began to expand the mental horizons of solid young citizens from unsophisticated homes where little was known of the arts. 'The general attitude of the times was that only "poofs" and "dills" did arty subjects', remembers one old Scotch boy who now is a keen theatre and concert-goer.[53] Hugh Stretton is grateful to Scotch for the new worlds it opened to him:

> I got to Scotch in May 1936, aged eleven, which must have been quite soon after Gilray did. He emptied the hall of whatever dreary old pictures had been there, bought the Carnegie Collection of Modern Art prints, and hung that around. When I got there the music consisted of the French teacher who could bang the goanna for a hymn in assembly, so Gilray hired John Bishop who made a most extraordinary tense arrival at the school—in morning assembly with a thousand philistine boys, the headmaster introduced him and said we had a new music master and he was going to say a few words. And Bishop came forward looking like the most laughable cartoon intellectual, with hair all over and a Byron tie and things you didn't wear then, and flung both hands in the air and said, 'Music is a WONDERFUL THING'. I don't know why nobody hooted, but five minutes later he had them in the palm of his hand. All sorts of good things followed. Gilray hired Francis Roy Thompson and Oscar Helms, who were quite respectable painters and linocutters.

---

[51] See Appendix I, table 2. The reports of the Ministry of Public Instruction in the 1930s gave the numbers enrolled in registered schools over the age of fourteen, but no further breakdowns into age groups or school types (i.e. Catholic or Protestant). The government schools' enrolments were broken down into ages and level of instruction; however there are no figures for the size of primary school cohorts. Therefore, just as an estimate, I have divided the number of children in all state schools between the ages of six and fourteen by eight, which gives an approximate cohort, averaged over the years 1934–36 and rounded out, of 26 000. In year 9 in 1934 there were 5335 pupils or 20.5 per cent of the original cohort; by Intermediate, that figure had dropped to 2488 or 9.6 per cent; by Leaving it was down to 926 or 3.6 per cent; and by Leaving Honours it was down to 301 or 1.6 per cent. It is impossible to know how much of this state school brain drain was from students transferring to private schools for their final years. See *Reports of the Ministry of Public Instruction*, 1932–37.

[52] See Appendix I, table 5. A crude guide to the relative academic standing of the Melbourne schools in the 1930s is the number of Senior Government Scholarships won. For the years 1932–39 the numbers were: Scotch College 44, Melbourne Boys' High 42, Melbourne Grammar 33, MacRoberston Girls' High 26, University High 25 (12 went to girls), Wesley College 23, PLC 19, St Kevin's CBC 16, MLC 10, Xavier College 7, Geelong Grammar and Geelong College 5 each, Trinity Grammar, Presentation Convent and Melbourne Girls' Grammar 4 each. Caulfield Grammar won only one, in 1939, when Peter Karmel topped the state.

[53] Survey No. 739.

So we stopped drawing plaster casts of the Greek foot and did more
interesting things. Above all he hired a man called Arthur Davies—
a small, intense, singular man, a marvellous Shakespearian producer
and we played Shakespeare in real circumstances in a three-decker
theatre that still existed in town. Without even trying to learn
it, I knew two plays by heart, just from playing minor parts
in them.

At Genazzano, extra-curricular life was quite different. There was music
and art and literature, but always under the direction of adults—nuns and
teachers; and when school magazines made a sporadic appearance, they
were not edited and written by the girls. Trinity and MLC both came
alive in the 1930s with clubs and societies, music and literature, and the
three Protestant schools supported impressive school magazines, edited by
students under the eye of teachers. At Scotch a small group launched a
school newspaper *Satura*, which was entirely independent, and which set
one boy on a career path that would see him become the editor of one of
Australia's leading daily newspapers. Scotch had the most to offer, but
Trinity and MLC were not far behind. There were school tours, groups
listening to symphonies on seventy-eight gramophones and a select band
at Scotch fascinated by 'hot rhythm' from America. As the academically
successful moved up in the school, teachers looked for those who showed
the promise of seeking a serious life—the boys and girls who stood aside
from the rough and tumble, whose eyes were fixed on finer things. And
in those years a small group of men and women who would exert much
influence on their nation was being prepared. The outside world began to
call them, as it also tantalized most with the promise of adventure and new
experiences. At MLC the girls' creative writing in *Silver and Green*
revealed unconscious yearnings for lives of excitement and deep feeling,
which, it seemed, could not be found in the avenues of Camberwell or
the expanses of Caulfield. Romance—general, not sexual—happened to
other people in other places. Then in 1936 it happened to 'twenty-three
excited MLC schoolgirls' when they set off under the control of Miss
Olga Hay, to explore Central Australia. June Barnett was one of the lucky
twenty-three and she reported for *Silver and Green* that the 'trip was a
thrill from beginning to end'.[54] These suburban girls camped out under
the stars, rode camels and played football with Aboriginal boys. They visited a colony for the unemployed and witnessed an Aboriginal funeral.
What June could not record in the school magazine was: 'Olga Hay was a
very lively character, and when the Ghan would stop from time to time,
she had a gun—I can't think why—and we'd line up beer bottles and
shoot them'.

---

[54] *Silver and Green*, December 1936, p. 22.

Manners and Society

When Graham McInnes was a lad at Scotch College, his stepfather had a memorable confrontation with a local policeman in Malvern by name of Kelly. In these early days of motoring, George Thirkell drove a Chrysler with panache and utter disregard for the road laws. Taking Graham to Scotch one morning, he committed a string of crimes: 'Fifty on a main commercial thoroughfare . . . failed to stop on whistle . . . cut across traffic lane . . . ignored silent policeman' wrote Constable Kelly on the ticket. George Thirkell ignored it, 'Tom Blamey's not going to like this . . . when he hears of it'. General Blamey was Melbourne's new Chief Commissioner of Police and Thirkell had served in his brigade at Flanders. Constable Kelly had to admit that he had only been on 'special duty' in German New Guinea because of his 'chronic ticker'—' "we can't all be heroes" he added nastily'.

> Dad said, 'That's right'.
> There was a long, long pause. Then the cop began to fold the ticket lengthwise, then crosswise, then in accordion pleats until it was really quite small.
> 'You really know Tom Blamey well?' he asked finally.
> Dad said, 'Not all that well, but we're both members of the Naval and Military Club'.
> The cop nodded slowly and put the ticket into his pocket.
> 'All right', he said, 'drive carefully'.[1]

It was an important lesson for the young middle-class trainee. For normal, mischievous boys, the local police—Messrs Chase and Kelly—had been spoilsports who ticked them off for riding on footpaths and playing in stormwater drains. But part of a middle-class boy's growing up was to realize that the police were his protectors, even his servants; and that middle-class crimes were peccadilloes, while working-class peccadilloes were crimes.

All children had to be taught their station in life. The most powerful mental mark of being working-class was not proletarian class solidarity, but believing—or fearing—yourself to be inferior. At the same time, respectable working-class parents were vigilant lest their children ever 'got big-headed' with 'ideas about themselves', because that broke the code of basic equality and 'living for others' within their community. Respectability itself was a salve to the stigma of social inferiority: 'they can do what they like to me, but at least I've got my self respect' and many parents laboured hard to teach their children not to be intimidated by

---

[1] Graham McInnes, *Goodbye Melbourne Town*, pp. 86–7.

their social betters: 'Now listen here, you kids are as good as anyone and don't you ever forget that. You've nothing to be ashamed of. You look them straight in the eye, and speak up. Don't let anyone put you down, d'you hear'. But it was hard, as Constable Kelly of Malvern knew only too well.

Middle-class children had to learn how to 'exact deference', and they also had to come to terms with the fact that, while they were superior to the working class, they were inferior to the rich. But whereas the respectable working class endeavoured to convince themselves and the watching world that they were 'as good as' their social betters, the middle class placed themselves as the centre—they were the backbone of the nation; those 'with a stake in the country'; the shoulders upon which responsibility for the well-being of society actually fell. The moral middle class was a deserving middle class, who had got where they had got, not by silver spoons, but by hard work and good character. As Sir Robert Menzies said on behalf of his 'Forgotten People': '. . . to say that the industrious and intelligent son of self-sacrificing and saving and forward-looking parents has the same social deserts and even material needs as the dull offspring of stupid and improvident parents is absurd'. Judith Brett's brilliant reading of that speech and of Menzies' personal and political psychology has provided the most intellectually powerful understanding yet of Australian conservatism and of the particular pressures and constraints of middle-class life before the 1970s. She has identified the distinctive grievance of a class who believed themselves to be bearing the full responsibility of running the nation while the working class were lazy and the rich were self-indulgent.[2] The quality of its middle class, in Frank Shann's eyes, determined the civility and moral well-being of a society and the place upon which all that depended was the private school:

> Life is in Victoria, I believe, more pleasant that it is in New South Wales, people have better manners and speech, political thought is saner, business is more honourably conducted, and the financial position of the community is sounder, largely because of the peculiar services rendered by the Public Schools of this State, where secondary education is less the concern of government than in New South Wales.[3]

The private school did more than educate—it *made* you middle-class, it gave you lifelong, indestructible membership of the caste, not for anything actually learnt at the school, but just by the fact of 'being there'. At the crudest level, an old school tie enabled you to feel superior without having to achieve anything else at all—a fact that made the more sensitive uncomfortable: privilege should be earned and then never abused and the

---

[2] Judith Brett, *Robert Menzies' Forgotten People*, pp. 59–73.
[3] *Mitre*, May 1932, p. 8.

most noble conceived that 'from those to whom much is given, much will be required'. Mere money did not entitle you to consider yourself 'better' but you could be such an improved human being that you did have a special responsibility of leadership. As the editor of the *Scotch Collegian* reminded his fellows in 1935:

> . . . once more many of us must face again the prospect of leaving Scotch College and of entering upon life alone . . . As members of a public school, we should bear with us into life ideals and standards above the average, and should make our influence felt wherever we may go. It is in this way alone that we shall bring honour to Scotch College and make the public school an institution of ever-increasing value to the social organization of today.[4]

The manufacture of the young middle-class person concentrated both on the inner self and the outer presentation. Voice and language were more difficult to change than clothes as emblems of class membership and they therefore received a great deal of attention from family and school. A broad Australian accent, poor grammar, limited vocabulary and rough colloquial speech all marked you as lower class or 'common'. Even so, Scotch boys did pass through a phase in the 1930s of affecting a broad Australian style, and 'followed the example of the boarders amongst whom the accent and racy idiom of the Australian country town was pretty well *de rigueur*', remembered the school historian, Harvey Nicholson.[5] The style was rural and racy, not urban and proletarian (which was too close to home for comfort); but there is no question that the differences in speech were nowhere near as acute as in England. Many middle-class men served in the lower ranks during the wars without revealing their genteel origins; the old Etonian, George Orwell, however willing, found he could not in *The Road to Wigan Pier*.

Just the same, parents and teachers, most of all mothers, took great care in teaching children the verbal marks of being middle-class—or as they would have expressed it—'polite' and not 'common'. Certain words were definitely common like the indigenous 'lolly' instead of the safely English 'sweet'. 'Pardon' was inexcusable and no well-bred person declared on being introduced that they were 'pleased to meet you'. The 'lady in the lolly shop' was the 'woman in the sweet shop', for women could only be ladies when they were entitled to be. Polite people never relieved themselves in the toilet—usually they simply left the room, but if pressed they were going to the lavatory. Australian polite people clipped their speech, hoping that it sounded English; common people took rests in inte-REST-ing, expanded their umBARellas, had FOURheads, ofTen went to the fiLLUMs, had misCHIEVIous children, sometimes

---

[4] *Scotch Collegian*, December 1935, p. 206.
[5] Nicholson, *First Hundred Years . . .*, p. 246.

contracted ath-E-lete's foot, did drawRing and sent their offspring to schools which had aSHFElt playgrounds. Even more socially damaging were grammatical errors like 'I come home' and 'I done that'. 'Youse' was unforgivable, as was SAIZ for 'says'. 'Haitch' at Genazzano spelt utter disaster, being the ultimate Irish–Catholic solecism; at MLC Mrs Landen betrayed her lower-class origins by persisting in calling thrIppence thrUppence.

The common were not only uncouth, they had nasty habits. For one thing, they smelt. And this was true, as George Orwell again had the courage to make plain in *The Road to Wigan Pier*, but the polite divided into those who believed the poor were dirty because they were lazy and those who believed they were dirty because they had inadequate washing facilities and insufficient income to buy changes of clothes. In 1950 the Student Christian Movement held an industrial camp in Fitzroy under the leadership of the Rev. Steve Yarnold: 'Forgive us, O God', they prayed, 'for the women who bend their backs over primitive wash-tubs in filthy yards, for we have not given them a chance to know the joy of cleanliness'.[6] They smelt and they were rough. State schools had bullies, and Harvey Nicholson praised Scotch for its protectiveness towards small boys compared to 'the state schools at which the majority of Scotch boys had spent their earlier years'.[7] State school boys were fair game, however. At Carey Baptist Grammar School, *Albert White* remembers the boys chasing state school kids up Barkers Road and, at Scotch, where he finished his schooling:

> One lunchtime the word got round that kids were swimming in the raw down in Gardiner's Creek. I went down to take an interest in the fun that was going on. Then Colin Gilray came striding across the oval, heading down that way with a rather forbidding expression on his face and I headed off in another direction altogether.
>
> Next morning in assembly—'An unfortunate incident. Some children from the local state school chose to go for a swim in Gardiner's Creek', he said. 'Of course I don't admire their taste.' (Gardiner's Creek used to smell like the gas works.) What our naughty Scotch boys had done was pelt them with rocks, lumps of earth and everything, and really attacked them every time they went near their clothes. And some had spare periods and kept them there until afternoon play, unable to get their clothes. Then Colin Gilray went down and caught them.[8]

Scotch in fact had its share of bullies. *Albert* was bright, quiet, and dogged. He was also small, and there was a trio at Scotch who had been bailing

---

[6] Australian Student Christian Movement, University of Melbourne, *Report of the Industrial Service Camp*, p. 41.

[7] Nicholson, loc. cit.

[8] Interview with *Albert White*, 2 July 1990.

him up. One Friday afternoon, while the chemistry teacher was at a meeting, the boys were meant to be doing their chemistry practical work, without supervision. *Albert*'s persecutors went for him, and the other boys, to make it fair, restrained two of them so that it was one-to-one:

> It finished up that I had the bunsen burner on a rubber tube and I'm swinging it round, whacking him, and he was throwing dishes and things at me. By the end we were sweeping armfuls of bottles of reagents off the shelves at each other—broken glass everywhere. It was fighting ammonia. It finished up with the two of us jammed into a rubbish bin and he had a stranglehold on me and I had a toehold on him—neither of us would give way and the bell had gone. Why someone wasn't seriously damaged in the eyes, I don't know.

Albert not only survived Scotch, he enjoyed it—there was so much to do—but he was always an original. He liked to cross class lines for instance: 'I always was a great one for talking to tradesmen, council workers—I'd chat away with them; I was a good conversationalist for a little kid—I was always for getting to know and understand people'. Valerie East was another who dared to make friends with local working-class children, finding companionship as well as unexpected complications of class and gender that led to battles; but for most there were always barriers. Slum children played on the street, even in the gutter, and stayed out late on hot summer nights. Respectable children were careful about where they played and who they played with. Geoff Tolson did play with local state school boys in his street: 'there was no unpleasant void, but I don't recall our parents talking to each other'. State school children who transferred to private schools had to decide between keeping their old local friends and starting afresh, but unless there were close ties through the local church, going to a private school usually necessitated the building of a new social network—you had entered a new world.

The erection of class barriers between the common and the polite, the rough and the respectable, was complicated by sectarianism. Even though Presbyterians and Evangelical Anglicans did their bit for bigotry, Methodists and Catholics were particular antagonists. Drink was an obvious divider and Presbyterians and Anglicans were somewhat compromised by the habits of many of their co-religionists. The Methodists had their black sheep also and most Methodist extended families have at least one ancestor who is *believed* to have drunk to excess. Of course, temperance made sense, because drink *was* a curse to the poor and aspiring. In the 1920s, as the battle over Local Option in the eastern suburbs saw Nonconformists succeed in bringing prohibition to the cities of Camberwell and Box Hill, Catholics and Nonconformists knew their enemies. *Elinor Doyle*, from an abstemious family, none the less used a ruler at Genazzano, stamped with the campaign slogan of J. J. Liston's

Licensed Victuallers' Association. Many young Methodist ladies were taught that the 'Irish had a particular fondness for drink', the majority from MLC remember hearing adults express 'fierce disapproval of Archbishop Mannix', and around half absorbed the belief that the 'Labor Party was dominated by Catholics'.[9] Even at Genazzano, the most affluent and educated of the four school communities, there is a sense of Catholic grievance and three-quarters still believe that it has been more difficult for Catholics to enter the élite, whereas just a quarter from MLC agree with them.[10] This is a telling difference in perceptions, yet the Methodists are closer to the mark, for by the 1930s, Methodists and Catholics were probably level-pegging in their distribution in the middle and upper classes. Oliver MacDonagh has analysed the New South Wales Census of 1933 and found Catholics only a little behind the Protestants in their representation in incomes over £300 a year—a better result for Catholic social rising than Catholic legend would generally allow.[11]

There was no doubt, however, about the stigma of being Irish and Catholic—as one MLC informant said in an unguarded moment: 'it's not a very good heritage to have is it?' It is not surprising, therefore, that there is a certain ambivalence at Genazzano over Irishness, and while those with a European heritage mostly treasure it, only half of those with an Irish heritage do.[12] Only a minority from both Genazzano and MLC believe that the top Catholic schools enjoyed the same prestige as the top Protestant schools.[13] *Elinor Doyle*:

> My parents did to some extent see colleagues in the medical world who purposely set out to make non-Catholic friends as being social climbers. They really didn't do it. My mother was rather shy anyway, and didn't particularly want to go anywhere and that was an excuse for not going.
>
> I think the upwardly-mobile lot felt there was a social disability in being Catholic. Therefore anybody who felt impatient with that or wanted to go to Government House garden parties or join the Melbourne Club, or whatever, would feel that the Catholic labels would pull them back.

---

[9] Survey: of the MLC Survey, 60% were Methodist, 15% Anglican and 12% Presbyterian. Only 37% of the MLC parents were not teetotallers, however. Q. 'Were you brought up to believe that the Labor Party was dominated by Catholics?' Yes, 56%; N/A, 6%. 'Can you remember Protestants expressing fierce disapproval of Archbishop Mannix?' Yes, 80%; N/A, 6%. 'Were you brought up to believe that the Irish had a particular fondness for drink?' Yes, 44%, N/A, 6%.

[10] Survey: 'Has it been, until recent times, more difficult for Catholics to achieve prominence in society?' Yes: MLC, 23%; Genazzano, 73%; N/A: MLC 28%; Genazzano, 7%.

[11] Jackson, *Churches and People*, p. 43.

[12] Survey: Genazzano: 'Does your family have any European heritage?' Yes: 53%; N/A, 12%. 'If so, is this important to you?' Yes: 72%; N/A, 2%. 'Does your family have any Irish heritage?' Yes: 85%; N/A, 2%. 'If so, is this important to you?' Yes: 53%; N/A, 8%.

[13] Survey: 'Did the top Catholic schools enjoy the same social prestige as the same Protestant schools?' MLC: Yes, 37%; N/A, 23%. Genazzano: Yes, 38%; N/A, 35%.

My father had put a lot of energy into making St Vincent's as good as any other hospital—to raise the professional standard and to build up the Clinical School, which was then relatively new. I think this influenced his thinking quite a lot. He'd done his own training at the Royal Melbourne, and had friends there, but he was committed to St Vincent's. When 'our' hospital had equal standing with 'theirs' that would be time enough for border crossing.

The *Doyles* were part of a quiet social circle in Kew of Catholic professionals and intellectuals—people who liked books and enjoyed talking about them, who met to play tennis or who dropped in for a cup of tea after Mass. Their children were the centre of their life, their religion a support and an identity, their politics, despite their material comfort, sympathetic to Labor. It was an enclosed, self-sufficient social world.

Catholic rejection by the Protestant ascendancy was very real. Mary Thompson remembers being on a train in the Western District with her parents when one of the squattocracy joined them: 'it was a funny thing— the men mixed with the squattocracy so Dad and he were talking away and he looked straight through my mother'. Hence much attention was given in Catholic schools—both select and systemic—to teaching clear and confident speech, deportment and perfect manners. The FCJ nuns took particular care at all their schools with deportment and also took a close interest in what their old girls wore when out in society or back visiting the convent, so that the Genazzano girls entered the world 'able to go anywhere'. (A high standard of dress and elegance still exists in the Genazzano world, while many MLC old collegians remain comfortable with Nonconformist dowdiness.) Even so, puritanical Protestants made even highly intelligent Catholics nervous. For Mary Thompson, the 'absolute epitome of respectability was a Presbyterian elder. Then one of my friends married one, and I was so terrified that I used to get vulgarer and vulgarer every time I opened my mouth. And he used to say, "Mary's such a nice girl—why does she say such terrible things?" We eventually became really good friends'.

The wonderful thing about the private school was that its conferring of superiority was unambiguous. For the rest of his life, the lucky old boy need say no more than, 'I was at Scotch' or 'knew him at Grammar' (the most brazen added an 'of course' which sealed that sense of belonging to the only caste that mattered). But in a more serious and interesting way, the private school—especially those regarded as 'good schools'—actually legitimized social superiority and thereby banished guilt. And they did this in a number of ways. First, those who succeeded in getting to a private school *deserved* to be there—they were there because their parents had worked hard for it, and men in particular still are conscious of the sacrifices made by their parents.[14] That consciousness was heightened by the Depression but was there in good times also. There was no need for guilt about privileges and, if society had to tolerate the misbehaviour and demands on the public purse of the undeserving poor, it should also respect the just rewards of the deserving. And one of those rewards was to give one's children a 'better start' by sending them to a good school.

Second, private schools were better at training minds and society needed trained minds to guide and rule it. Those with a fuller academic training were entitled to their superior position in society. This, of course, had a moral nobility: the life of the mind, the banishment of ignorance and the pursuit of knowledge were human endeavours upon which the health of civilization depended entirely. Knowledge was more important than material wealth: *Doug Gordon* grew up surrounded by the 'Scottish ethos' where 'education was worth starving yourself for, so if you did nothing else, you educated your kids'. Ken Tolhurst's mother 'had a very strong belief that education was the secret to being a complete person'. The schoolboy mind, being immature, comprehended this a little differently: the 1934 editor of the *Scotch Collegian* argued that public school boys started out in life with two advantages: 'We have been guided to think, not merely promiscuously and at random, but with definite logical aim, and in accordance with a perspective on life which has been acquired by our Public School system through centuries'.[15] (As we have seen, many pupils left good schools scarcely educated.) Third, the private school gave you culture. The editor of the *Scotch Collegian* for the following year insisted:

> In times when the classes which remained untaught at the bottom of the social scale are now taking the advantages without acquiring its cultural refinements, it is important more than ever before that poetry should not be forgotten or discouraged. All but the basest natures have poetic feelings . . . and every human being has need of art.[16]

Being introduced to high culture was very important for a number of Scotch boys in the 1930s and 1940s, and Harvey Nicholson has written of the ex-state school boys who were won over to serious music by John Bishop's 'sparkling personality'.[17] (Despite this, only a third of the Scotch Survey acknowledged that the school had fostered in them a love of the arts; the three other schools fared somewhat better.)[18]

---

[14] Survey: 'Did your parents have to sacrifice to send you to a good school?' Scotch: Yes, 77%; N/A, 3%. Trinity: Yes, 78%; N/A, 2%. MLC: Yes, 63%; N/A, 1%; Genazzano: Yes, 56%; N/A, 4%.

[15] *Scotch Collegian*, December 1934, pp. 204–5.

[16] Ibid., December 1935, p. 203.

[17] Nicholson, *The First Hundred Years*, pp. 281–2.

[18] Survey: 'Did your time at a church school foster a love of the arts?' Yes: Scotch, 33%; Trinity, 44%; MLC, 65%; Genazzano, 62%.

Most important of all, private schooling produced a finer moral being. This was a complex set of notions, drawing long on the public school culture transported from England intermeshed with religion; and if it defined and proclaimed superiority, it was perceived always as a superiority tempered with service and responsibility. In 1923, at the unveiling of his newly painted portrait at Scotch, Dr W. S. Littlejohn said:

> One of the most remarkable developments of recent times is the growth of the Public School spirit. Public School boys . . . are realizing a solemn trust has been committed to them to hand on to those that come after the highest ideals of service and sacrifice. From those who have gone before they have received a flaming torch; theirs to see that it is neither dimmed nor trailed in the dust, but passed on with the sacred flame burning more brightly than ever. The name of Public School must never be dishonoured.[19]

This new intensity, redolent of Arthurian romance of 'knightly virtue proved', was a legacy of the war; eleven years later Colin Gilray, taking over the school just as the Depression eased, expressed it differently for a different time:

> Great problems await the boys of the present generation and on the spirit in which they face them, be it craven-hearted or courageous, prejudiced or self-regarding, or open-minded and unselfish, depends the woe and weal of our people. I hope that working together with a full sense of the issues involved, we may be able to send out year by year from Scotch College a goodly proportion of young men with high ideals and sufficient courage to bring them to bear on the political problems of life.[20]

Again the boys receptive to such a call interpreted it a little more crudely. The *Scotch Collegian*:

> In any community there is, of course, a class possessed of higher intelligence, or more highly trained for the purpose, which is capable of filling responsible, executive positions, and a class of less education or intelligence which is more fitted for manual or simpler tasks . . . The fact . . . remains that as members of a Public School, as the future university graduates, as leaders of future thought, we have certain standards to maintain . . . Public School spirit which incorporates ideals of fair play, of good taste, of gentlemanly conduct, must not suffer, and it is our bounden duty to do our utmost to carry with us into after life the ideals and spirit of the Public School.[21]

---

[19] Nicholson, *The First Hundred Years* . . ., p. 158.
[20] Ibid., p. 207.
[21] *Scotch Collegian*, August 1935, pp. 115–17.

It was a confusing mixture of messages sent out to young people in these church schools: they were being trained for adult life as more intellectually and morally refined beings. They were surrounded with teachers and parents and preachers who told them that much was expected of them—that they were different, privileged, fortunate and therefore burdened with a special duty of service. At the same time Christianity taught that the poor shall inherit the earth, that all were equal, rich and poor, in God's eyes and that there was a very real conflict between Christian humility and secular ambition. As one Genazzano woman noted on her questionnaire, 'I was not taught class distinction either by my parents or school'.[22] Within your own social group, standards of consideration for others were high; and on the playing field the victorious were expected to be discreet and modest, to protect the self-esteem of the vanquished and to keep the joys of victory in proportion. It was poor form to boast and to glory in success. And because life should be lived first for others, your own needs had to come second— it was proper to be disinterested and diffidence was very much a virtue. Among the best writing on this sense of service is Warren Osmond's biography of Frederic Eggleston as an intellectual in Australian politics. Eggleston's great-great-grandfather had been converted by direct contact with John Wesley himself and, if the colonial descendant had lost belief in a personal Christ, he remained a secular Methodist, disdaining the accumulation of material wealth but committed to service, of 'throwing himself out of himself'. Even so, he was far from oblivious of the conflict between living for others and the legitimate needs of the self: 'A central issue in his life was how to define and submit to the common good, the "universal social order" without betraying his own integrity or identity'.[23]

Much of this conflict between the needs of the common good and those of the self depended on personality; but diffidence and humility and disinterestedness were seen as virtues, deeply embedded in the moral code. It did not necessarily make for an easier life. Geoff Serle:

> I always had a strong code of some kind, and I suppose, without making too much of it, what some people saw as unselfishness. But looking at it from another point of view, it's a difficulty in looking after one's own interests, or feeling that one's own interests were ever-paramount. And it took me a long time to recognize in the world how self-centred and thrusting and ambitious most people are in their various relationships. It was the same for my father, Percival Serle: he was not very good at looking after his own interests and had difficulty in putting himself

[22] Survey No. 78: Genazzano.
[23] Osmond, *Frederic Eggleston*, p. 3.

forward. And it's not so much an admirable moral trait as a personality thing. In my own case, home, church and school coincided in training, but personality may have been the most important.

Ailsa Thomson similarly learnt from her Methodist parents a diffidence and a modesty about her own cause: 'Mum and Dad would never have *put themselves forward*', but the difficulty for girls, and for women, was to see where kindly diffidence was quite different from low self-esteem, where 'in that typically feminine way one thinks that one is not worthy of office or honour'. Important too was the constructive discussion of problems and conflicts. Ailsa never saw her parents display any conflict in front of the children—'I hate debates'—and in later life, this preference for discussion became an important part of her feminism:

> In our History of the Education of Girls Group at Monash University, it's 'let's get together and talk about things in a way that's *constructive*'. I've seen so many academic debates that are sheer destructiveness, and that sort of thing has perhaps unconsciously thrown me back to seeing other ways of doing it.

Archie Crow was an idealistic boy at Scotch, a leader, and even though he realized that the boys were being trained 'to play a responsible part in the community' and that some would become 'captains of industry', he cannot remember boys talking about making money. And yet making money—not necessarily a fortune, but enough to sustain a middle-class family—was the most important gender role conditioning that boys received. The prospect of living life as an independent gentleman of private means was scarcely an option for any Scotch or Trinity boy of the 1930s. Instead, if they were to do nothing else, their first responsibility was to earn a living, to provide; and, if they married, to earn enough so that their wives did not need to leave the family home to work. Each boy had to be able to stand in later life as an independent economic unit. This was, of course, all taken for granted, but the burden to provide was still a burden and it was intrinsic to the concept of masculinity. It was possible for men to dislike violence and rough sports, it was possible for men to like ballet and decorative arts; but it was not possible for men to refuse to provide. The male economic role was as powerful as procreation, for if men refused to accept that responsibility, society would collapse. And the middle-class boy was expected to find work that befitted his membership of the public school caste. Status signs were keenly watched and there was little mercy. John Leckie's family owned the oldest and best-known grocery shop in the City of Melbourne: 'we had a colossal business—we looked after all the private schools and many of the Toorak families'. Even so, his father had great difficulty in getting John's sisters into St Margaret's School, Berwick; but, at Scotch, John was but one of the many sons of 'trade'. After three years and armed with a partial Leaving Certificate, he joined the family business and began studying for his Master Grocer's Certificate, which was examined from London:

> One thing that happened to me at the Palais de Danse when I began to realize how snobbish people can be. I served behind the fresh food counter and I was covered with cheese and fish, and by the end of the day, it went right through you. So I used to go home, have a shower and get changed. Two or three girls used to come into the shop on their way home from work on a Friday night—it would be about seven o'clock—and I'd look after them. This night I went home, got changed into my dickie suit and down we went to the Palais. And guess who was in the party—these two girls, and they wouldn't even speak to me until somebody said, 'He's the boss's son' and suddenly I was acceptable. That's always stuck in my mind.[24]

From the age of around sixteen many young people joined the private school social set: dancing lessons from Miss Lascelles at St George's Hall, next to the Malvern Town Hall; tennis lessons from Leo Guiney in the city. At seaside resorts like Lorne (the Presbyterian playground) and Ocean Grove (the Methodist resort), Mornington, Sorrento and for the wealthy, Portsea, the private school set created a microcosm of their metropolitan society. They played cricket and tennis, they danced and they flirted—making friends from other schools, widening their associations and possible marriage partners. For most that social network fulfilled a social rather than an economic purpose of providing jobs and contacts—it was an act of caste solidarity which cemented one's place in the caste for life. When Geoff Tolson's father encouraged him to leave Scotch after the Intermediate so that he could study electrical engineering at the Melbourne Technical College, he found being cut off from these networks disorienting. Despite the sectarianism of their elders, there was considerable tolerance between Catholics and Protestants in the social whirl, and the more sophisticated Genazzano girls—once they were old enough to go dancing—often mixed with Scotch and Grammar boys. And, of course, at the Head of the River the six 'public schools' made a great display of their separateness and superiority.

There were products of private schools who were not socialites and who found the smart life foreign and distasteful. *Betty Thomas* recalls clearly how she learnt her place in the class structure in the 1930s and during the war:

---

[24] Interview with John Leckie, 5 June 1990.

I never felt inferior at MLC. I don't think we had too many Toorak types at MLC, or if they were, they didn't talk about it. I had the feeling I was one of the majority—everybody was short of money during the war. Scotch was thought to be above MLC and some of the naughty girls used to talk to Scotch boys—and they used to talk to Xavier boys too. We felt Scotch was very posh. I never had any particular brief for Wesley—I never felt they were as good as us. I had the feeling that they went there because it was the 'socially-up' thing to do. I was so absorbed in this women's world that boys were of no particular concern. As for getting involved in *boat races*—how *stupid*. I was a terrible prig.

The working class was different and unfamiliar. Aged fourteen and a girl guide, *Betty* went on a camp in the Christmas Hills with working-class girls from Collingwood:

I had no experience of what to do with inner-suburban kids. We got on all right—my idea was to take them out hiking all day and bring them back exhausted because that for me was just the most marvellous thing to do, and I guess I had the push to carry the day. We did Bible study as well, but for me the great delight was taking these kids hiking. Then as a duty I went to visit them afterwards, and immediately realized I was on foreign territory. I'd never seen houses where the doors just opened out on to the street. And there was a smell about them.

Few middle-class young people got that smell of poverty in their nostrils, even though some of their teachers, headmasters and clergy believed that they should. The classes led segregated existences, and Richmond and Collingwood were places you peered at from the safety of the train, or passed through swiftly in the family car. The poor were unfortunate and one should care for them, but they were not your friends nor possible marriage partners. Considering how many of the inter-war middle class were new, the degree of social isolation was extraordinary. Even Oswald Barnett, who by the late 1930s was at full stride in his slum abolition campaign, had been shocked by the first slums he had visited in the 1920s.[25] Despite his social origins, the culture of working-class respectability had shielded him from the worst of Australian poverty. Barbara Falk and the late Kathleen Fitzpatrick were two of many young Australian intellectuals who did not *see* the slums and poverty until they went to London. They returned to see Melbourne very differently.[26]

And yet many of the young people in the private schools of the 1930s were becoming aware that there was something wrong with the world. As they grew and matured, increasingly the outside world acted

---

[25] Howe, *New Houses for Old*, p. 23.
[26] Barbara Falk, *No Other Home*, p. 135; Fitzpatrick, *Solid Bluestone Foundations*, pp. 185–6.

upon their developing understanding of themselves and society: for this was a Depression generation. John Leckie sometimes went on the delivery run for his family's grocery, even before he left school: 'One time we were finishing near midnight in Caulfield on Christmas Eve, and we got to this house in Booran Road. I knocked on the door with a parcel— the Stevedoring Commission used to make up parcels for people—and this woman opened the door and I told her who I was and she burst into tears. She said, 'That's the only food we've got in the house'. Alan and Lawrence Cohn's mother was often in tears also during the Depression, as their father's dental practice wound down—people still had to go to the doctor but the dentist was a 'luxury'. The brothers knew that they had to come top of their classes at Trinity, or else their scholarships would lapse and their schooling would end. The middle-class story of the Depression is a hidden one; and the help was often kept secret. *Margaret Power*'s father was an estate agent and for her the Depression is 'rows and rows and rows of keys in my father's office for empty houses':

> I think my father must have been a remarkable person. I know he paid a great many rents to keep people in their houses. I think that nobody will ever know what my father did, but we survived. I can remember people all the time talking about how hard-up they were; and I can remember occasions when we'd all be packed into the car and we'd go off and deliver parcels to people. But we were never told what was going on. There was a degree of pride because some of these people were relatives— protecting other people's pride; also of not trumpeting your good deeds and protecting the children. One year our toys were disappearing—it was only afterwards that we realized that they'd been given to somebody else because our parents knew we were getting new ones at Christmas.

Among the hardest pressed in the middle class were the clergy. Many ministers' stipends could not be paid in full; in the case of the Rev. George Cerutty, the vicar of the inner suburb of Newport, his parishioners had little to spare:

> For most of the six years my father worked for nothing except for a fund from the diocese which is called the Clergy Provident Fund which came in as a sort of dole. And on Friday nights the delicatessen shop down the street at Newport sold at a cheap rate anything that was left. We would join a long queue, and then Dad would come along and find a pregnant woman or an old woman or a child, and he'd move Mum and myself further and further down the queue, so that the doors would shut and Friday night after Friday night we went home with nothing. And when there was nothing else she could do, Mother would bake what she called Eccles cakes—flour and water, lightly spiced with a few currants. And we were actually hungry—hungry with the people to whom Dad ministered in those awful years.

But life remained worth living:

> It didn't matter if you were hungry, it didn't matter if you were
> poor—there was always loveliness. I can remember Mother—hungry,
> poorly clad—grabbing my hand (and I was a university student on a
> scholarship in those days) and running down North Road, Newport,
> because the *Joseph Conrad* in full sail was coming up the river. And there
> was *beauty*—beauty in the sails. And there was nothing else—a drizzly old
> bay with the shipping and the chimneys belching smoke. And on the day
> of the Tall Ships for the Bicentenary, I sat here in this chair and I cried
> because I remember Mother seeing loveliness in a four-masted ship. And
> that was the way I was brought up at home and at MLC: you didn't have
> anything, you didn't own much, but there was the glory of living in a
> very, very beautiful world. I was taught that it didn't matter what you
> owned—you owned the earth and you were master of all you surveyed.

The Depression none the less took a terrible toll on her father's health,
and by 1944, aged just sixty-one, he died: 'he came down with pneumonia and the death certificate said he died with a lack of blood to the
brain'.

It is difficult enough to measure the effects of the Depression on the
working class with the limitations of official statistics; it is even more so in
the case of the middle class: but if we use the private schools as a
barometer, then the 1930s were less of a disaster than the 1890s. At Scotch
the total enrolment fell by only fifty between 1930 and 1931 and the
school historian paid tribute to the 'Scottish spirit of the school' in that
'the majority of parents were prepared to make the sacrifices needed to
continue to send their sons to the school'. The boarding house was
affected more, and Scotch had a heavy back-log of unpaid fees by 1934—
£7164 10s 6d. The school was able to cope: most paid later and the fees of
promising boys were paid by generous old boys. MLC entered the
Depression in poorer financial health: in his decline, Dr Fitchett had lost
his grip on the finances and an inquiry in 1929 found that the school was
in debt with merely 32 per cent paying the full fees, so extensive were the
concessions for ministers' and teachers' daughters and brothers at Wesley.
Even so, the decline in enrolments was minor, as it was at PLC. In fact it
was the small schools like Trinity which suffered and Frank Shann's efforts
to keep the school going were nothing less than heroic. Some of the more
select schools survived by not paying their bills (which damaged the early
educational publishing ventures of F. W. Cheshire, for instance, and
bankrupted at least one Malvern grocer). At Trinity thirty-one boys
gained their Intermediate in 1930 and but thirteen the following year.
Shann was careful not to push parents too hard financially—but he did
plead for boys to stay on for as long as possible. The Depression in fact
made parents take education more seriously, so that once the crisis eased,

enrolments rose in most good schools. Boys often stayed until they found
a job and sudden mid-year departures became common. Shann worked
hard to find his school leavers jobs as office boys and trainees. He had
contacts in insurance and city businesses, and his efforts on behalf of a
dreamy, unsuccessful boy like James Austin were just as vigorous as they
were on behalf of the clever. And he was justifiably proud to be able
announce in his annual report for 1933 that every Trinity boy who left at
the end of 1932 had found a job by the end of 1933. This was the old
school tie at work.[27]

The effects of the Depression on the middle class were subtle. People
economized and one of the economies was 'church'. Between 1927 and
1940 the Hawthorn Presbyterians steadily lost members—two hundred
from a peak membership of over six hundred.[28] More telling are the
private stories, but there is a problem in how people perceive the effects of
such an event on their lives. Asked in 1990 whether their families had a
difficult time in the Depression, 77 per cent of the Trinity men said 'yes',
followed by 65 per cent from Genazzano. Scotch and MLC were further
behind with 56 per cent. The Trinity figure fits the social composition of
the school, the Genazzano figure does not, and a key to the disparity lies
with MLC. Many MLC women answered 'no' because they considered
their family's plight as trivial compared to that of the unemployed. There
were more Genazzano families on the land, but the Genazzano figure is
perhaps a little inflated by Catholic social grievance, while the MLC figure
is reduced by Methodist diffidence. Asked why they left school when they
did, not many left for financial reasons. *Dick Wallace* keeps it in perspective:

> I grew up right through the Depression, but we were a bit privileged.
> OK—I went to a minor public school; my father had a car—it was an
> office car, but it was a car. We even had holidays twice a year. At Easter
> we used to go down to Mornington—to two old ladies called Miss
> Jenkins—and we'd hire two or three bedrooms in their house. At
> September the family would go for one or two weeks at a boarding house
> in Healesville. It was good fun and we had enough money to do that
> apparently.
>
> You didn't go round the whole time saying—oh dear, isn't the
> Depression awful. I don't think anyone told me there was a depression. I
> didn't know there was one. You didn't have much pocket money or
> anything. Money was counted by the one shillings and the two shillings.
> I've often thought that it must have been an effort for my family to keep
> me at Trinity—you had to have cricket creams and act the part a bit,
> which really wasn't necessary.

[27] C. E. W. Bean, *Here My Son*, p. 90; Blainey, *et al.*, *Wesley College*, pp. 162, 179; Zainu'ddin, *They Dreamt of a School*, pp. 197–8; Nicholson, *First Hundred Years*, pp. 187, 195, 210; F. W. Cheshire, *Bookseller, Publisher, Friend*, p. 60; *Mitre*, May 1932, p. 7, May 1930, p. 15, May 1934, p. 10.
[28] Bradshaw, *Rural Village to Urban Surge*, pp. 98–9.

As for many working-class people, the stringencies of the Depression were only 'worse than normal' and reinforced the virtues of thrift. *Doug Gordon*:

> Father's attitude, which he tried to instil in us, was that you set an example in order to influence the whole family. When the Depression was on, to be wasteful was iniquitous. Now, he smoked, so during the Depression he rolled his own. And leaving food on your plate was definitely Non-U—you'd overestimated your capacity. It was just frugal. He'd been brought up that way by his parents. They had to be—the number in the family and they shifted around a bit. There wasn't much to spare there, but I've always thought that Father overdid it a bit.

Some did well out of the Depression: the *Ewart* family's breakfast food business flourished and *Neil's* father was able to build a large house in Toorak. Businesses which took advantage of the particular needs of the crisis—like Repco with automotive parts—flourished. If people could not afford new cars, they would buy spare parts and repair them; and if people could not afford detached houses, they could make do with a villa pair or a flat. Those with the cash to spend on property in the 1930s made a killing later, and many property owners greatly increased their equity in the following decade. Colin McCathie's father, however, was a true Depression victim:

> My father was a surveyor who specialized in land subdivision, and come the Depression, no one was subdividing land—the firms just bolted. For some years things were very tough. I didn't go to Scotch until after eight years at state school. In my first year there my five cousins paid for me, the next year my godmother did. That got me to Intermediate standard and there I finished.
>
> Father's problem started in 1928 and went on for some years. I don't know much about it—he didn't like to talk about it. He got dressed in his suit and collar and tie and went to the city each day—all those years he wasn't working. Except that he was secretary of the Victorian Amateur Sports Association and a few things like that. In earlier life he had been a surveyor at the Water Commission and in 1934 he got a job again there and that involved him being away from home, up in the Goulburn Valley.
>
> He was very quiet, but he was by nature a quiet person. Mum was more upset than he was—she battled on. They stayed in the same home that they had bought in 1924. I remember three cottages in Hawthorn being sold to pay for the house instead of being passed on to we three boys. I don't know what they lived on, except that Dad got occasional jobs. Apart from that, they must have lived on savings.
>
> My father died in 1939—he had cancer. My mother lived on until 1960.[29]

---

[29] Interview with Colin McCathie, 4 December 1990.

John Blanch's father had been a victim as a youth of the 1890s depression, forced to leave school early and to start working. But he was 'always a very enterprising fellow'—he dabbled in land, had served with distinction in the war and was a manager of the Malvern Presbyterian Church when the value of his properties collapsed in the 1930s catastrophe. He was determined not to go bankrupt. Their Caulfield house was sold, along with many possessions, including John's violin, and his wife and children moved into a flat opposite Scotch while he went to South Africa, taking with him some agencies so that he could make enough to pay all his debts. It took him five years but he did it. Ralph Coyne's father was a New York Jew who had met his Australian wife in Yokohama. In 1923 they settled in Australia, bought a grazing property and were doing well until the Depression struck: 'it knocked my father seriously' and by 1935, he had died. Ralph was just fifteen: 'It made such an impression on me that I felt I had no right to be at a school like Scotch when my older brothers had been pulled away'. His mother persuaded him to at least complete his Leaving.[30] It was an end to the good times for many. Winsome Walklate's father's income as a commercial traveller 'fell by hundreds' and family life never quite recovered the security and ease of her 1920s childhood. And *Veronica Keogh*'s father used to 'sweat in bed' with worry over his carrying business during the 1930s and, like many, she is astonished that he managed to send his five children to university. For others, the Depression was second-hand, but no less affecting. Joyce Thorpe's mother never forgot her roots:

> I knew a lot about the Depression because all Mother's brothers were out
> of work. We used to get people coming to the door and I can remember
> being very impressed when my mother—who was very careful about
> money and who would never give away anything—gave two men who
> came to the door a meal of bacon and eggs out on the veranda. It amazed
> me that my mother did that, knowing how she felt about money.

The Barnetts, too, were 'terribly aware of it—we were constantly being told we had to care for poor old so-and-so, who couldn't get a job and they were working on the road around the Yarra'. For *Philip Hardwicke*'s father the Depression brought unemployment and broke his heart. Deaf from childhood, he was always isolated but, even as a young boy, *Philip* tried to bring him into family conversation:

> Most of the discussion was political because my father enjoyed laying
> down the law. Labor was in the wilderness and the Depression made him
> depressed. He was an idealist—he had this vision of what society should
> be, and it annoyed him that people were narrow-minded and selfish and

---

[30] Interview with Ralph Coyne, 22 June 1990.

ignorant, and just didn't have this broader vision. It really worried him.
He didn't quote Marx, but he had Marx in his library until my mother
threw him out. I remember her telling me once that he'd come home to
find she'd thrown all the controversial books out of his library, so I think
he had a bit to put up with. I remember one evening Dad walking up
from the railway station with a neighbour and when he got in he said.
'Look, I told him all about it, I explained the situation from A to Z, but it
didn't sink in'.

Thus the private school world encompassed a wide range of
experience and destinies, yet was linked by a common membership of the
caste. And that caste could not always protect you: Colin McCathie's
father was himself an Old Scotch boy, but the dour internalizing of his
anguish could well have shortened his life. If, at the time, the Depression
seemed hardest on mothers and it was the women who were pitied, it was
more often the men who died. They could not cry, they could not drink,
they could not go bush. Everything depended on the male burden to
provide—the home, the food, the clothes, the doctors and the school fees.
And if a marriage soured, an honourable man with a sense of duty could
not leave—he had to see it through to the end.[31] Those who could not, or
who died too soon, or who lost their capacity to provide, had 'failed' their
dependants, and the significance of such masculine 'failure' can be sensed
from the diminished academic performance of those without fathers.[32]
And since most of these absent fathers were so because they had died
rather than because the marriage had fallen apart, unresolved grief and
emotional isolation affected their children profoundly. *Walters Rhodes* lost
his father when he was six, and his mother ten years later. School work
was impossible. 'I took off for Queensland for two years I was
shattered'. *Betty Thomas*' father died of a heart attack in the sea after
rescuing his wife from drowning:

> Suddenly I was plunged into adulthood, as it were, within an hour. Mum
> hardly spoke during that year that followed. Her way of coping with
> shock and grief was to go inward. I used to think she was angry with me
> over something I said, but I realise now that it was that.

Her mother had to go to work, first standing up in a dry-cleaning factory
in Richmond until she learned to type. Her husband's friends quietly
dropped her as the family's circumstances were reduced and being
an attractive, but unattached woman, she was *de trop*. Even in her
local Methodist Church, as a working woman, she felt herself to be

---

[31] Survey: 'Did your parents ever separate or divorce?' Yes: Scotch, 7%; Trinity, 5%; MLC, 2%;
Genazzano, 4%.
[32] See Appendix I, table 2.

unacceptable. Dr *Frank Doyle* died at only fifty-three, with three children still at school, the youngest being only six. The big house was sold but there was still enough to educate the children. Many widows, once the grief became manageable, blossomed with responsibility; but others faced a relentless grind of lifelong frugality. Betty Blay had come to MLC on a scholarship and had been 'jumping to get into class', but she already knew in her honours year that there would be no money for university so, despite excellent results, she began pupil teaching. Then her father died. He had been a gambler and left unexpected debts. They had just bought a new house in Armadale, so the only thing to do was to take in boarders and for Betty to go to a better paid office job in the Australian Paper Mills:

> I went there as a clerk and I stayed sixteen years. I not only worked at a job I did not like, I came home each night to eight boarders. My twenties were an absolute—not a waste, because they probably made me a nicer person—but as far as frivolous twenties, they weren't worth having. I was stoical. As soon as Dad died I remember thinking—'this is it' and I just accepted it. I wasn't angry but I was very sad. There'd be times when I used to think, as I said to Auntie Ginny one day, 'Life isn't sweet' and she said, 'No it isn't, but you shouldn't feel that at your time of life'.

For Ken Tolhurst 'late adolescence was a very bad period' of his life. A beloved teacher at Trinity, Fred Lavender, had died tragically while on his honeymoon. And the Tolhursts, as an Anglican clerical family in the bush and on the outskirts of Melbourne, lived in genuine poverty. He was under great pressure to enter the church but, even though the only way he could have gone to university was on a theological scholarship, he was too confused to have a vocation. His father had had a bad war and 'was always visibly affected' by it, and his mother had seen the worst of it in London. They had brought up their children as Christian pacifists, yet

> by this time it was absolutely clear to me that we were going to go to war. It was clear to Frank Shann, who made a statement about it in the Anglican Synod. And when the pressure really came on and Chamberlain came back from Munich, my father turned round and said, 'We're going to have to fight the bastards again'. So where does that leave an eighteen-year-old? I was terribly confused.

In 1937 Ken was editor of the *Mitre* and he editorialized:

> The embittered and cynical post-war generation is slowly passing away and soon will be replaced by another. This rising generation is a thoughtful and serious one, with no fixed ideas but a hatred of war, and it is the bounden duty of our schools to seize on this fact, and utilise it to the best advantage. A good school can always fire its members with fine ideals, and indeed

must do so if a general conflagration, culminating in the destruction of our wonderful civilization is to be avoided. The youth of today must be given wider knowledge and better understanding of international affairs, including some insight into the habits, customs and mode of life of every other race, and a true understanding of their point of view on every subject of common interest. Only when a sense of the brotherhood of nations is alive and vital to all will 'nations learn war no more', and they shall beat their swords into ploughshares and their spears into pruning hooks.[33]

This was already happening in the schools by 1935. The Depression, the rise of Fascism, the Spanish Civil War all combined to convince the serious-minded among the young that war was inevitable. The 1930s saw the emergence for the first time in Australia of a dissident intelligentsia, and into the schools, both state and private, came a new breed of young teacher who talked to their charges about controversial things and who encouraged them to read dangerous books.[34] At Scotch an older teacher like R. H. Clayton did not shrink from the alarming course of world events either, as Geoff Serle gratefully remembers:

> We had a form library and subscribed to the Left Book Club and the Right Book Club. We read books of the day like Stephen Roberts' *The House that Hitler Built*. We certainly talked about Germany and Italy, Nazism and Fascism. And he made us talk. I was very reticent and didn't talk much, but he made us and it was a great benefit.

In the early 1930s, those disturbed by the Depression yet fearful of Communism had looked to Fascism's apparently good record of providing jobs and rebuilding society.[35] At Genazzano, politics was far from the nuns' concerns, but Catholic Action, inspired by the National Eucharistic Congress of 1934, took hold with the encouragement of the nuns. Two discussion groups were formed among the Old Genazzano Association which bubbled with enthusiasm at this new opportunity for the laity to discuss doctrine and liturgy; but less than a third of the Genazzano Survey women were ever to become involved in Catholic Action.[36] Students of the time remember watching newsreels about Spain and being told, 'Now girls, you must all clap for General Franco'. At MLC Sadie Copeland often walked up Glenferrie Road with her favourite teacher who had spent some years in Germany, 'and she used to tell me how lovely the German people were and how Hitler had done so much for the poor and that was the way he had won the masses'. Such sentiments were far from unusual. Fred Archer, working at Menzies Hotel

[33] *Mitre*, May 1937, p. 3.
[34] Geoffrey Serle, *From Deserts the Prophets Come*, p. 154.
[35] Frederick Howard, *Kent Hughes, a Biography*, pp. 57–66.
[36] *Old Genazzano Review*, 1939, pp. 6–7.

in the 1930s, eavesdropped on the clientele: 'A most bitterly condemned man was President Roosevelt. "Class traitor" was the accusation. I heard Hitler praised because when referring to priests and clergy, he said "We'll be putting those lusty gentlemen to work". Mussolini had admirers because he said, "I'll make my life a masterpiece" '.[37]

By the end of the 1930s the temper had moved to the left. In many schools branches of the League of Nations Union had been formed, and certainly at MLC it overtook the S.C.M. in membership. Nettie Palmer came twice to the school to speak about the Spanish Civil War and Oswald Barnett came often to talk about slums and poverty.[38] At Trinity and Scotch the grief-stricken Anzac Day commemorations had not raised a generation who saw glory in war, and in 1938 the editor of the *Mitre*, J. D. ('Dave') Levick, son of the vicar of St Barnabas', Balwyn, agonized over the pacifist's dilemma:

> Europe today is seething with wars and rumours of wars. Small boys drill with importance, carrying their guns over their shoulders—not just toy guns, but messengers of death. Little children who are not yet old enough to bear arms, play with their toy soldiers, lining them up in order of battle. Everyone is saturated with the idea of the glory of battle, although this is veiled under the less direct title of Patriotism.
>
> We, in Australia, although not altogether receiving limitless encouragement to put into practice pacifist principles, at least are not taught about the so-called nobility of warfare; the children in the schools are taught to realise its uselessness and tragic horror. These idealisms unfortunately cannot prevail against the methods used on the other side . . . Even the most faithful among pacifists cannot help experiencing an occasional patriotic aggressive sensation. This is just another instinct he has to fight, and while nationality remains so clearly defined, he will always have to struggle with it.[39]

Almost exactly four years later, Dave Levick died in the last half hour of the fall of Singapore—struck down by a shell while going to help a wounded comrade.

---

[37] Fred Archer, *The Treasure House*, p. 29.
[38] *Silver and Green*, December 1937, pp. 6 and 9; December 1938, pp.13–14.
[39] *Mitre*, December 1938, p. 3.

4

Coming of Age
1939–1945

Coming of Age
1939–1945

Becoming a Man

The six years of war were twenty years of change. I often think that the war had a bigger effect on me and my age group than anything else. I was nineteen. I went in the day it started and I came out seven years later. So I went in as a very raw kid—and nineteen in those days was far more innocent and lacking in worldly knowledge than now. We were babies. As for the bees and the flowers, we didn't even know what the bees looked like

Dick Wallace

It was a cruel coming of age. At school during the Depression these young men had just set out on their paths to adulthood only to have their youth consumed by war. The two world wars have been the great engine houses of social and political change in our century, and few citizens of the combatant nations evaded the transformations that total war brought to their society. In Australia World War II was even more intrusive on private life than had been World War I. It was a true total war in that there was effective conscription: all able-bodied men whose skills were not needed by war industry were required to serve. Male and female civilians were 'manpowered' and directed to work in industry; food, clothing and petrol were rationed; citizens were prevented from moving around their own country freely; studies, careers, businesses, ambitions, passions and loves had to be suspended, some to be lost for ever, others to be replaced by new opportunities. The war changed destinies both for better and for worse. It dragged young Australians from city, town and countryside far away from the familiarities of home and community into a shared enter-

159

prise of life and death. Above all, it took away personal freedom and private life—the individual had to surrender independence and autonomy to the collective needs of the nation. It was a supreme test of mettle and maturity.

The rites of passage from youth to manhood did not depend on being blooded in battle—rather it was again that 'recognition of necessity'. Maturity entailed the acceptance of responsibility, the delaying of gratification, the enduring of fear, tedium and frustration, because if a man was to eat and keep a roof over his head, to provide for a family and to live in a style that befitted the expectations of his family and his friends, then he had to acquire self-discipline and he needed to recognize and accept necessity. As one Trinity man noted as his greatest life satisfactions:

> Good health—inherited wisdom. Psychological outlook towards being prepared for the unknown! My father's wisdom passed on to me—avoid excesses, follow the straight and narrow path in all things. Avoid making an enemy. Your word is your bond.[1]

The middle-class man could not relent in his public performance of propriety and efficiency. If he was seen going too often to pubs or to bookmakers, questions would be asked about his morals. And if he was to be secure in his middle-class occupation and income, he needed to be liked—or at least respected. He needed also to know how and when to be humble, and how to earn his place. Most middle-class men of the 1930s obtained their living by employing skills and expertise that had been 'learned on the job'. They did not have portable qualifications—only reputations; and their sons likewise had to start from the bottom and work their way up.

If the plight of these college boys was less serious than the *Struggletowners*, they were still a Depression generation. The old school tie helped some in finding that first job as office boys and trainees in the 1930s, but who your family knew was even more significant. Fatherless boys and those whose fathers were themselves victims of the Depression found it harder than those whose fathers were 'on the inside instead of the outside/always looking in'. Colin McCathie left Scotch in 1934 wanting to go into engineering, but 'couldn't get a job anywhere' for eighteen months until he chanced on a position as a pharmacist's delivery boy. Eighteen months later the pharmacist asked Colin if he would like to be his next apprentice. The dreams of engineering were abandoned, his salary dropped to fifteen shillings a week and his godmother paid the £100 premium. He attended the Pharmacy College part-time for three years until the war began and he entered the army. He was not to qualify until

---

[1] Survey No. 1054: Trinity.

1948, by which time he was a married man needing a house for his growing family; then came school fees and he was never to acculumate the
capital to buy his own shop. James Austin and *David Miller* both had to
leave Trinity early before their academic potential could be discerned
amidst the dreaminess and restlessness of boyhood; Tom Beenie would
have preferred to stay longer at Scotch, especially for the sport, but he
went to a business school cum agency, and succeeded in obtaining one of
the two jobs they suggested. Despite this more select form of job searching, he also had to start at the bottom, wearing his school suit, and being
paid 13s 4d a week for 'just licking stamps'. James Austin likewise jumped
at the chance of an office boy's job in the brush trade: it was lonely and
tedious, he was 'dead scared' that his girlfriend might see him as he did the
boss's menial tasks, 'but it was good in the sense that I learned about
something—to this day, give me a week's notice and I'd go back and do
the same job', and thus the boy who was hopeless at mathematics began to
acquire commercial skills.

Many of these school leavers were very innocent. When *Albert White*
went for his first job interview at the State Electricity Commission, he
walked in the door of the office but the Chief Engineer said nothing—no
'hello' or 'please be seated'—just silence. *Albert* had been brought up to
speak only when spoken to, and he stood there, frozen, for five minutes
before saying, 'It looks as though we're not getting anywhere' and walking out. *Philip Hardwicke* had grown up oblivious of the real world:

> My mother said to me, 'You should get a job'. But I didn't know
> anything about starting work. We had a neighbour whose brother had a
> top administrative job in an insurance company, so Mum said 'Why don't
> you go round and ask them'. I did and they gave me a reference. I was
> interviewed by this man at the insurance office and 'Oh yes, we'll give
> you a position—start in a week's time'. I was an office boy on 19s 6d a
> week.

Deep inside himself *Philip* knew what he wanted to do:

> I remember as a small child being entranced by the movement of trees
> and going outside on a windy day and dancing with the movement of the
> trees. Then I saw a children's ballet in a pantomime and in musicals that
> we used to go to. Not that we went to anything very often—we didn't
> frown on it or think it was unChristian—it was that we couldn't spend a
> lot of money on that sort of thing because you had church things to
> support.

But such dreams were impossible in the Melbourne suburbs of the 1930s:
'I lasted at the insurance company for five years. The office was very

interesting—the point I remember from death claims was, no matter what anybody died of, it was usually 'as well as arterio-sclerosis'.

Insurance jobs were keenly sought, even as salesmen, because one of the effects of the Depression was to drive able and personable men into sales, thereby raising the quality and status of the field.[2] *Dick Wallace*'s first job was as an office boy in insurance, and he too went off into manhood in his school suit, topped by a huge hat with a three inch brim: 'I looked like a mushroom—you used to hold up the brim to see who was underneath'. And he was soon aware that in his particular insurance company there were only boys from minor Protestant schools like Trinity—no Scotch or Grammar boys, no high school boys, and certainly no Catholics. Yet this was not entirely the old school tie at work. The networks the middle class used were more intimate than that of a big school like Scotch, where only the particularly deserving boys were singled out for Old-Scotch patronage. Your local church was often a better source of 'contacts'. Trinity, being smaller, was more active on behalf of its jobless old boys and Frank Shann used his connections in insurance and city businesses well: 'You've got a job, that's more important than exams', he told James Austin; 'Mr Phillips has promised that if you are suitable, he'll look after you and pay you £5 a week at the age of twenty-one'.

It was of course different for the successful scholars, but those who entered the university were the fortunate. In the 1930s the majority of Scotch and Trinity families could not afford to put their sons through university without a scholarship, and even some with scholarships could not afford it either. Lawrence Cohn and Ken Tolhurst were both gifted scholars who could not afford to take up their university Free Places, and for Ken to watch his schoolfriends who had had inferior results go up to the university was a 'bitter disappointment'. Shann recommended that Lawrence Cohn train as an actuary, and for Ken Tolhurst he offered the financial patronage of the Ballarat Diocese if only Ken could find a vocation as a priest:

> Looking back now, the worm was in the apple years before. I was
> sceptical. At no time did I believe in the Virgin Birth—by the time I was
> twelve or thirteen I reckoned that was superstition, so it wasn't going to
> be easy.

He had grown up in the Anglican Church and he was well aware of the career structure it offered the ambitious:

> My mother saw me going through Melbourne University, then Cambridge
> and then coming back to being a bishop at thirty-five. She was no dill.
> She could see all this—that for any bright young man there was a career

---

[2] L. L. Robison, *A Century of Life: the Story of the First One Hundred Years of National Mutual Life*, p. 86.

path that you just had to walk up, and as long as you kept your nose clean, you had to finish up somewhere in the episcopacy. And that actually happened with a couple of very bright young fellows.

The headmaster and the bishop pleaded and promised; Ken insisted he was too bad a risk. The bishop declared he was willing to take that risk— 'I won't let you', said Ken. Instead he found a way into radio and advertising, writing, learning, developing.

Many of the most able and sensitive of these middle-class boys felt a 'call'—not often to the ministry, but commonly to 'a serious life'.[3] Of course, even at Scotch College, only a minority could realistically dream of becoming 'rich and famous', and most young men who had no hopes of university and the professions aspired to a job, as one boy wrote on his enrolment form, 'in a good office'. Traditionally, the learned professions, in particular medicine, offered the most certain chance of prestige and esteem and, for some, riches. Senior doctors and lawyers did make good money, although they too had been pegged back by the Depression. At Scotch medicine had always been the highest secular calling and the school made it plain to promising boys that that was where their future lay, as one remembers:

> By the 1930s the Medical School at Melbourne University drew its intake almost entirely from the six A.P.S. private schools. Their Matric. syllabus was pitched towards medicine (biology and Latin). There were other factors (med. tended to run in families). There were no cut-off marks. No quotas. Scotch was *expected* to provide an appreciable number of first year students. The matric. biology class was seen (in toto) as med. course material. The syllabus was virtually the same as for Zoology I in the med. course. I was actually told—by the biology teacher—that I was to do medicine and to inform my parents so. It was a long expensive course. Everything from fees to microscope to basic library had to be paid for. School days were thus a preliminary to undergrad. days *among the same company,* which went on into professional life. Thus most doctors of my generation were school-day friends. Communication was/is easy. In passing—it was considered the worst possible form to present for any (of the many) oral examinations in medicine wearing a school or Old School tie.[4]

By the late 1930s the University of Melbourne was in a state of transition. In some faculties it was still the leisured preserve of the affluent yet indolent, and students repeated subjects for years without fear of being sent down.[5] Many students started at sixteen and it was not unknown for the precocious to graduate in medicine by the age of twenty-one. The

[3] Russel Ward, *A Radical Life*, p. 93.
[4] Survey No. 761: Scotch.
[5] Ruth Campbell, *A History of the Melbourne Law School, 1857–1973*, p. 157.

dearth of scholarships for any but the brilliant kept the university socially exclusive: the college residents looked down upon the day commuters, and the day commuters looked down upon the part-time evening students, and everyone looked down upon 'the minions of the Teachers' College' for as that great school teacher and literary critic A. A. Phillips admitted, 'teaching was considered almost a noxious trade, only formally to be considered a profession'.[6] Yet, between the wars, the Australian university world was still astonishingly culturally isolated. Vera Jennings remembered of her student days the difficulty of obtaining books, and most of the French texts had to be typed and roneoed. (Even in the 1940s there was a time when the only copy of Yeats' poems was owned by a member of staff.) People were starved of serious music and theatre: Vera Jennings enjoyed opera and singing, 'but we had no music among ourselves, no radio, no records, only an out-of-tune-piano', hence it was a particular pleasure to be invited to spend an evening listening to a gramophone, even though she found these musical encounters embarrassing, 'not knowing when an instrumental piece had really ended, or what to say in appreciation'.[7] This aesthetic starvation underwrote the thrill that the Ballet Russe's season in 1936 gave young theatre-goers in Melbourne, and there were not a few, both male and female, for whom the ballet 'changed their lives'.[8]

Between 1919 and 1939 the number of students almost doubled, and although the number of professors increased by only half, ten new associate professors were appointed. Moreover, nearly all the new appointments of the 1930s were Australians and among them was Max Crawford, appointed to the chair in History. Since his return from Oxford, he had become aware of a new vitality in the intellectual life of Australia which he later wrote about in *An Australian Perspective*. He perceived a 'new level of maturity and professional skill' and pointed to the admission of university graduates to the Commonwealth Public Service, the expansion of the Council for Scientific and Industrial Research and the forming of the Australian Broadcasting Commission. Within the University of Melbourne the appointment of Dr Raymond Priestley as Vice-Chancellor in 1935 initiated 'a great era of experimental reform'. University staff began to enter public life with a new vigour and a sharpened critical sense, yet it was 'an intervention not always welcomed by those persons in the community who believed the universities should be content to produce lawyers, doctors, engineers and teachers of perfect orthodoxy'. Crawford titled his chapter 'Coming of Age'.[9]

---

[6] A. A. Phillips in Hume Dow, ed., *Memories of Melbourne University*, pp. 40–1.
[7] Vera Jennings in ibid., pp. 13 and 21.
[8] *Veronica Keogh* and Mary Thompson.
[9] R. M. Crawford, *An Australian Perspective*, pp. 68–9.

The young men seeking a serious life were poised to inherit, teach, administer, investigate, judge, prosecute and defend, heal and preach to a changed, more complex and yet more open Australia after the war. But, for all the intellectual stirrings by the late 1930s, most remained enclosed in their caste. Laurie Provan found the transition from Scotch to University 'delightful' because 'one advantage of going to a big school was that when you did go to university, you didn't feel lonely'.[10] Hugh Stretton, however, after his inspiring last years at Scotch, took the regulation path to Ormond College only to find 'the most appalling, old-fashioned, sheep-station bastardization initiations. Terrible—the exact opposite of Scotch'. Even if they wanted to, it was difficult to join the outside world. The Old-Scotch tie linked old boys and saved many of them from venturing into new social networks both in the university and out in the world of work. John Leckie is still perfectly frank about it:

> I think there's a bit of vanity in all of us. In the pre-1939 days, the mere fact that I could wear an Old-Scotch tie—I thought I was a cut above other people, for sure. And if you met someone from school, you gravitated to them. I used to walk down Collins Street in my little pork-pie hat and my Old-Scotch tie. But the war changed everything—I went into a new social world.

Geoff McKee was in the billiard room at Ormond College when the announcement came over the radio that Britain was at war with Germany:

> My thoughts were—What's going to happen? Are we all going to be bombed out of existence? Will I have to go off to war and be shot somewhere? The enthusiasm of the World War I diggers was never in my mind. I think I was a born coward—I could see the possibility of being bombed, shot or gassed. And one wondered when it was going to end? By the time my engineering course was over and I went into the army, it was the bad days at the end of the 1941, when Britain was standing on its own and things looked really bad. It was just disaster after disaster, and it continued with Malaya and Singapore.

Dick Wallace also remembers vividly 3 September 1939, the day the war started. He was in the militia, the Victorian Scottish Regiment:

> We all had to go down to the Drill Hall in South Melbourne and we sang around—sang German songs, anything we could think of. It was just a bunch of silly kids. We'd all had fathers and uncles who'd gone to the war and they were heroes. The image we had of the First War was heroic and there was very little that was written criticising the war. The horrors

---

[10] Interview with Laurie Provan, 4 April 1990.

of war were not written of that I can remember—it was all 'over the top boys' and comradeship. I don't think that it was until our war began to get a bit nasty that they started to talk about the First War.

As with the conspiracy of silence that older women create to protect the young from the fear of childbirth, so had the veterans of the First War not told the whole truth. They had, of course, returned to a society which scarcely understood what they had been through, and their code of mas-culine endurance had inhibited them from unburdening themselves of their memories. (The late Fred Farrall, despite his radical and pacifist associations in the Communist Party of the 1930s, could not talk of his experiences on the Somme until his doctor prised it out of him in 1942, and thereby cured him of a host of psychosomatic ills.)[11] The responses of the 1939 generation ranged wide. John Blanch was just a year out of Scotch when war came, but he was in every way prepared to enter the army and serve. As an idealistic young man, who had been honoured with the captaincy of the school, he knew leadership and resourcefulness were expected of him and he rose to that challenge. He had been a cadet 'for years', was now in the militia and 'I knew my drill book backwards and could shoot and all the rest of it'. The army was 'thirsty for people with that sort of knowledge' and by the age of just twenty he was a captain. He divides the men in the forces into three categories: 'one—those who tried to dodge it; two—those who went into the militia, but who didn't be-lieve the war was serious and yet who volunteered to go to Egypt or somewhere; and three—those who volunteered right from the start and said, "We're part of the British Empire and we'll get into it and do what we can" '. There were many like John Blanch, who committed them-selves without reserve; but there were others whose emotions and moti-vations were more troubled.

There was no question that the top brass of the three armed services looked to the private schools to provide the officer caste. C. E. W. Bean was not only the historian of the Anzac legend, he was also the historian of the private or 'corporate schools', and in writing their collective history just after World War II, he traced their emergence as worthy successors of the Arnoldian tradition to 'the growth of corporate spirit among those re-turning servicemen [in the 1920s] who were old boys of good private schools'.[12] Scotch's official history marked the school's emergence as one of the great schools of the British Empire by the 1920s, because it was by then 'hallowed by a renown, a tradition and a unity won by the valour and discipline of its sons in the ordeal of war, in the "test of conflict and of battle flame" '.[13] The British had complained just before World War I that

---

[11] Interviews with Fred Farrall, 1986, tapes in possession of author and ABC Radio.
[12] Bean, *Here My Son*, p. 87.
[13] Nicholson, *Scotch, the First Hundred Years . . .* , p. 112.

the Australian officer corps was deficient in 'public school values', and had called for the new military college at Duntroon to be a school rather than a traditional military academy. But while permanent army and militia officers dominated the officer corps in the first years of the war, promotion through the ranks became characteristic of the First A.I.F.[14] By the 1930s Duntroon was finding it difficult to recruit boys from private schools and those educated in the 'Arnoldian tradition' were 'conspicuous by their rarity'. (Duntroon's tradition of bastardization must take some of the blame for deterring entrants—one graduate 'believed that he suffered more in his Duntroon bastardization than he did as a prisoner of war of Japan'.)[15] World War II was different again. This war now required an educated officer corps, able to perform more complex mathematical calculations and to understand a more advanced technology and nowhere was the need for a numerate serviceman greater than in the Air Force. The Air Force quickly became the most exciting and prestigious arm of the three services and the most desired recruits were those from private schools. On 20 February 1940 J. V. Fairbairn, an old Geelong Grammarian and the Minister for Air in the Menzies government, wrote to J. R. Darling, headmaster of his old school:

> . . . I am particularly pleased to hear what you have to say about the number of application forms for the R.A.A.F. which you have had to sign on behalf of the Old Boys, as I got the information a couple of days ago from the officer in charge of the Recruiting Depot in Melbourne, that the Melbourne Technical School had sent more applicants for training as air crews than the six Public Schools put together, which made my blood run cold.[16]

It was deeply worrying, because around half the pilot observers would receive commissions, and there were not enough boys from private schools who could meet the minimum educational qualifications of passes in Intermediate mathematics and physics. Darling provided educational testimonials for his old boys who were *sans* Intermediate, but he felt uncomfortable about it.[17] And the Air Force soon realized that it would have to complete the work left undone by the schools and provide basic courses in mathematics to reservists awaiting call-up.[18] *David Miller* from Trinity was one such. He had missed many months of school because of

[14] Lewis, *Our War*, p. 62.

[15] C. D. Coulthard-Clark, *Duntroon: the Royal Military College of Australia, 1911–1986*, pp. 12–14, 123 and 125–6.

[16] Geelong Grammar School Archives, Headmaster's Correspondence 1940, A–F, I am indebted to Peter Gronn for this material from Geelong Grammar School.

[17] J. V. Fairbairn to J. R. Darling, 19 March 1940, and J. R. Darling to J. V. Fairbairn, 14 March 1940, ibid.

[18] John McCarthy, *A Last Call of Empire*, pp. 36–7.

the polio epidemic and an accident. He was good at English but weak at mathematics, and he was forced to leave with only the Intermediate when his father's business again ran into difficulties. His old school tie and his energy got him into the Air Force and he demanded to be a navigator: 'But your marks aren't good enough?' 'Since when have school marks been a test of ability?' He became a navigator and so it was only during the war that he realized that he 'had got a brain, could work and see things conceptually'. At twenty-one he was discharged with the D.F.C.

Few questioned the assumption that while government schools were good at teaching mathematics, they could not inculcate the qualities of manly leadership. As C. E. W. Bean said when he summed up the private schools' contribution to World War II:

> But, highly unjust as it must have been to some splendid high school boys, whose training today is strongly in the Arnold tradition, it is not unnatural that leaders looking to the morale of their cherished unit should choose boys from the schools which admittedly fostered that tradition in Australia and still necessarily give Arnold's methods their fullest scope.[19]

Bean's conception of the Anzac ideal unconsciously reveals much about Australian and British class assumptions during both world wars. His ideal Digger was a bush lad and his ideal officer a product of a 'Public School', even though he acknowledged that many fine officers were not. He sensibly pointed out that while many schools claimed to have had the best war record, his 'guess' was that 'at the top of the list would be found some small bush State school with nearly every available pupil in each world war enlisted'.[20] Never, it seems, could such a school be in *Struggletown*. The urban working-class male might have a larrikin's courage, but he was also dangerous—he was sharp, disrespectful, sometimes criminal and more than likely to be a member of a trade union as well as a Catholic. The rural poor, by contrast, could be relied upon to be politically conservative and to know their place. 'Jo' Gullett's typologies of his comrades in arms in Bardia included only a handful of Australian proletarians, who, while colourful, lacked the moral straightforwardness of the country lads and public school boys who crowded his fond memories.[21] And Lieutenant H. A. Engel wrote back to the *Scotch Collegian* 1943 of his pleasure in his artillery battery, in which 'the public schools are well-represented . . . and I need hardly say that "orderly rooms" are infrequent'.[22] Questioned fifty years later, this generation from Trinity and Scotch continues to believe overwhelmingly that church schools provide a better moral education

---

[19] Bean, *Here My Son*, pp. 203.
[20] Ibid., p. 199.
[21] Henry ('Jo') Gullett, *Not as a Duty Only: An Infantryman's War*, pp. 1–12.
[22] *Scotch Collegian*, 1943, p. 93.

than government schools and that they have a special duty to prepare young people for leadership in society.[23]

The actual performance of the Trinity and Scotch men did not quite fulfil these expectations. Just over three thousand Scotch men served in the war and three hundred and twenty-seven of them died; from Trinity four hundred and thirty served and fifty-two lost their lives—in each case a death-rate much the same as for the wider Australian forces which served overseas. Where they were different from the average was in the proportion of commissions and in their distribution between the three services. The Air Force (which included those who served with the R.A.F. in the European theatre) comprised 20 per cent of the Australian armed forces, but a third or more from Scotch, Trinity and a matched cohort from Melbourne Grammar joined the R.A.A.F. or R.A.F. And for each school the percentage in the Navy was higher than the national average of 5 per cent: at Melbourne Grammar 13 per cent were in the Navy and 65 per cent were officers. In the three services the proportion with commissions ran at 46 per cent for Melbourne Grammar, just over 40 per cent for Scotch and only 25 per cent for Trinity (although Trinity's record-keeping was not as careful as for the other two schools). As it stood, however, a Trinity man was still two and a half times more likely to become an officer than was the average serviceman.[24]

Of the 267 boys who entered the Scotch College senior school on that first day of term in 1934, the war records of 171 could be traced. Twenty-eight of them died, eleven became prisoners of war, and fourteen were decorated; fifty-nine were officers and thirty-nine were N.C.O.s, so that 43 per cent achieved no position of authority in their war service. The break-down of the war record in each of the three services reveals the distinctive experience of these middle-class young men. Just twenty-one served in the Navy, but thirteen of them became officers, one died and one became a POW. Two won the D.S.O. Fifty-one, or 30 per cent, were in the Air Force: almost half were officers and sixteen—or a horrific 31 per cent—lost their lives. Three won the D.F.C., one the A.F.C., one the D.F.M., and only one was taken prisoner. Finally there was the Army. Ninety-nine served in the Army but only 21 per cent were officers. Eleven died, nine were POWs, two were awarded the Military Cross and

---

[23] Survey: 'Do church schools give a better moral education than state schools?' Yes: Scotch, 81%; Trinity, 83%; N/A, Scotch, 7%; Trinity, 8%.
'Do church schools have a special role in preparing young people for future leadership in society?'

	Scotch	Trinity	MLC	Genazzano
Yes %	75.2	65.7	79.4	79.2
Yes, qualified %	6.8	6.0	3.3	5.0
No %	12.0	17.5	11.7	10.
Not answered %	6.0	10.8	5.6	5.8

[24] See Appendix I, table 7: War Record of Scotch, Trinity and Melbourne Grammar Men.

four were mentioned in despatches. Two former POWs did not survive the war long.[25] These boys of 1934 were of military age when the war started and many went in on that first day. They had all left school, almost 40 per cent of them without the Intermediate, but one of those rose to be a Squadron Leader in the Air Force. They were among those in the Army who went to the Middle East and they were among those who were taken prisoner at the fall of Singapore; they were among those who fought in the Battle of Britain and were Pathfinders; they were among those who fought in New Guinea, East Timor and through the islands; they were among those who patrolled the North Sea in submarines; above all they were among those who had a grindingly long war, endured in extremes of climate and terrain.

Many of these private school boys brought into the forces some very real skills in leadership, but their strong representation in the officer corps was partly due to the manner in which the Army was formed in the first two years of the war. Many serious young men had been convinced that a world war was imminent and had joined the militia in readiness. There was not to be a 'Public Schools Company' as there had been in the First War, but certain divisions of the militia, such as the Victorian Scottish Regiment and the Melbourne University Rifles, were more 'social'. Their prior training in school cadet corps also brought into the A.I.F. a number of ready-trained officers, whose efficiency and commitment were impressive, and the Sixth Division thus became the point of origin for a high proportion of officers for the whole Army.[26] James Austin, for instance, was no longer the dreamy youth who had been hopeless at examinations—by the age of twenty, he was tall, with considerable physical presence and a couple of years experience in the militia behind him. An acting sergeant, he found himself up for officer selection for a new unit:

> We got wheeled in, one after the other, and I looked at those three
> fellows—one bloke I didn't know, one bloke I wasn't certain about,
> and one bloke—I *knew* that one. And they asked me questions—'Where
> did you go to school?' 'Trinity Grammar School', and I saw two of
> them look at each other. Then the questions became a bit detailed.
> 'We'll offer you Surveyor No. I—the maths expert at battery command
> post'. And I knew my maths inability and I begged, 'I think that might
> be beyond me—I want to stay with the guns'. 'All right, you can
> become gun sergeant of number one gun'. When I came to my senses,
> I asked who those fellows on the board were. Two of them were old
> Trinity Grammarians.

---

[25] Ibid., Scotch 1934 Cohort.
[26] F. W. Speed, *Esprit de Corps: The History of the Victorian Scottish Regiment, passim*; John Barrett, *We Were There: Australian Soldiers of World War II*, pp. 86, 276–7.

He was soon selected for officer training and 'got through all right', even if 'it was a bit difficult'. A year later Tom Beenie volunteered for the A.I.F. rather than be drafted, and from then on, the destinies of James Austin, Tom Beenie and John Blanch intersected.

Once John Blanch had transferred from the militia, he was drafted to the Eighth Division H.Q. and sent quickly to Singapore, with an advance party of seven officers, to make arrangements for the first brigade of the Eighth Division A.I.F. to be sent to Malaya:

> In Malaya I did the first experiment up there of living in the jungle. We were attached to the British Army and at Mess formal luncheon one day at Singapore Fortress—only seven of us there, including our General, Gordon Bennett, and I was the most junior officer as a captain, sitting at the end of the mess table. There were a number of senior people from the British Command and they said to Gordon Bennett, 'Bennett—you know a white man can only survive three days in the jungle', and Bennett, looking his fiery, red-headed self, looked down the table, caught my eye and said, 'Blanch, I think you'd better go out into the jungle for three weeks', which upset some of the Brits, but I think it was quite justified.

The British had not come to terms with the need for jungle warfare, relying on their ability to hold the advancing Japanese at Singapore. James Austin was in a training camp in Malaya when the war with Japan broke out, and three weeks before the end he wrote to his mother, 'Don't worry, Singapore will hold'. But when he eventually got on to the island, he saw that it was hopeless: 'There was not a single concrete fortification on the north of the island—there were huge guns pointing the wrong way, and even if they fired, they were no damned good because those guns were sited to fire on ships at sea'. John Blanch:

> We knew what the Japanese had done in China—we'd studied that; we knew they were quite well-trained troops, but I don't think that the Australians have been given enough credit. The first three contacts were ambushes on bridges, where they blew up a bridge with at least five hundred Japanese in each case.

But it was a long coastline to defend, and exhaustion and illness took their toll. John Blanch was suddenly stricken with meningitis and was among the last to be invalided out, on a perilously overloaded boat which managed to reach Batavia (Jakarta): 'I hated to be invalided out—I felt I was leaving my own troops'. He brought with him, however, his expertise and trained thousands in the arts of jungle warfare before serving at Bougainville. He also did much to defend his general, Gordon Bennett, against charges that he should have stayed with his troops in prison camp rather than bring his knowledge and skills back to Australia.

As the Japanese closed on Singapore Island, James Austin was released from H.Q. duties so that he could join the 2/15 Field Regiment
and fight in the battle for Singapore:

> I was lucky in a sense that the 2/15 Field Regiment—my four gun
> troop—was led by a man of forty who didn't give a damn for anybody.
> He was quite determined he was going to die—a Swede, named Captain
> Mark Lindgren. The troops just called him 'Uncle Mark'. Absolutely
> unflappable. And his next in line was a good bloke (a young bloke) and I
> was next. And we only lost one man killed. We didn't lose a gun—we
> were there. And we fired thousands of rounds and it was just a wonderful
> feeling of 'What the Hell'. Absolutely no fear. No one gave a hoot. But
> we were lucky—we were surrounded by panic-stricken troops and we
> held.

Also in a strange way, James Austin was prepared for the worst: his grandfather had been accidentally killed while still a young man, his father had
been buried alive and lost his senses, and James fully expected that destiny
held for him a life cut short by war. Tom Beenie and his fellow troops,
however, came to Singapore tragically unprepared for anything:

> My cousin and I joined in October 1941—we were sort of semi-trained.
> We went across in the *Aquitania* and the people were taught more on the
> trip going to Singapore than they ever learnt in the army before. Many of
> the blokes had to be shown how to load a rifle for a start. I think we got
> there on 21 January and we were P.O.W.s on 15 February, but we never
> operated as a unit because nobody wanted us when we got there. We
> went across the causeway to Jahore and they said, 'We don't want you
> here—shoot back'.

The fighting was fierce and in six weeks two thousand were killed, but
with the surrender the worst was yet to come.

James Austin knew the Japanese to be 'well-blooded troops', 'but we
didn't realise that they were bastards' until the news came that Japanese
guards had massacred Australian wounded, including men from his own
unit. And he had to learn to live with being a captive:

> You got a routine going. We all had to work—all the officers had to do
> something—you either took charge of working parties or you worked
> with the men. We were all together in that sense and we all worked in
> the gardens. I spent six months in hospital with dysentery and so forth,
> which of course helped me avoid (though I didn't know it at the time)
> certain work parties. It was a matter of luck. We took the view that
> Singapore was a dead loss—it couldn't feed itself and we tumbled to the
> idea that your best hope lay in being in a place which fed itself, where

you were surrounded by rice fields and preferably away from anything strategic. The world was going to hit Singapore at some stage. Unbeknown to us, there was enough food in Singapore for five years. The Singaporeans had a rough deal—mostly Chinese. The first job our unit had—thank God I wasn't detailed—two officers and twenty men were told that they were wanted down on the beach the day after we'd marched out fourteen miles to the Changi area. When they arrived there were a hundred Chinese bodies, who'd just been machine-gunned by the Japanese. 'Go and get them buried.' That woke us up a bit.

Tom Beenie was reasonably well when, after three months confinement in the Changi area, the Japanese came and rounded up large work parties. 'We were told we were going to a holiday camp', but it was to be three and a half years slave labour on the Burma–Thai railway. A quiet man, he coped by withdrawing into himself and living strictly by his gentlemanly code:

> Naturally the prisoners were all very good to one another. There was no animosity between them. But through illness and moving on to camps so quickly, you never formed a relationship—we were sent from the fifteen kilometre to the twenty kilometre, but if you were sick and stayed behind, you were changing people all the time. Generally they were all very helpful to each other, especially the sick. And I didn't know whether to call some of the people stupid, brave or greedy—there were hundreds of them that did it—they'd risk their lives and go out of the camp at night and go down to the Burmese villages and trade with watches from sick men or anything, come back, keep a bit themselves and pay you. They were terribly brave and many of them were caught. And the improvisation people did   I helped a professional shave down his stick, making a golf club for himself. Another person collected every bit of tin he could find and he used to make billies to boil coffee. They'd get the rice and burn it until it was black, then they'd put it in the bottom of a four gallon drum, put water on it and boil it and that was our coffee. There was very little stealing.

James Austin remembers the hunger pangs in Changi: 'You were always in a state of anticipation. You adopted certain tricks of spinning things out, that if you had a plateful, you deliberately ate the less palatable first, so that your hunger was partly assuaged when you came to the more affluent part of the meal—the meat'. He is a big man, who in his twenties weighed eleven and a half stone, but at his worst with dysentery he weighed less than eight. Tom Beenie was of medium build and lithe, but on his release he was a skeletal seven stone. James' intestinal system has never recovered its equilibrium; Tom's heart was mortally weakened by his being forced to work while sick. He died in 1991.

The mental effects were more complex. Tom Beenie kept his war to himself, and James Austin did also until the last ten years. James remembers the Burma railway men coming back to Changi: 'It was terrible—we were absolutely shattered. They came back in trucks, standing up, holding each other and we were helping them off the trucks—it took them about three months to recover their poise'. Their emaciation was all the more horrifying because they had been the physically fittest when the original work parties were chosen. For James his years as a POW influenced him 'more than any other event—I still think every day of something that happened. I occasionally have dreams of fellows with me—I can still hear their voices even though they're four-fifths gone'. And after the war, even though they had passed the severest test of character and humanity, there was a sense of failure:

> You felt that everyone else—they talked about Alamein, Shaggy Ridge—Oh gosh, all these fellows you talk to, they're in the Navy and they're shooting up this, and they're in the Air Force and they're bombing that, and they're in the Army and talking about foxholes in Kokoda. Ours seemed to be so . . . it wasn't guilt exactly, but then it is. You wanted to be out. I remember being amazed, meeting a fellow officer in town one day, 'What are you doing, you're still in uniform?' 'Yes', he said, 'I've signed up for another twelve months'. 'God', I said, 'United Nations and all that—there won't be any war—no future in that game'. How wrong I was.

Those who enlisted early in the A.I.F. and went to the Middle East, survived and returned to serve in New Guinea and the islands, endured a long war, fought in vastly different but equally trying terrains. *Richard Stanton* was one who served from the Middle East to New Guinea to Borneo: 'the war wasn't kind', is all he says, and he was later to pay for it. Jungle warfare had its particular horrors—the unseen enemy, the enervating humidity, the perpetual wetness, the tropical diseases and pests. Corpses decomposed rapidly, and the Australians stumbled on the remains of comrades who had been tortured and sadistically slain. Given the number of atrocities committed by the Japanese, the rate of retaliation in kind by the Allied troops was commendably low. But almost as many died of disease as died in action against the Japanese, and the field hospitals were often too full of wounded to tend to the sick as well: John Leckie had dysentery and dengue fever at the same time: 'which is a bit difficult because one makes you want to sit down and the other makes you want to stand up—you battled on with it'. It was not easy for good young men, raised in church-going homes, to take a human life, even for a soldier as fine as John Blanch:

It's a severe shock to see someone killed or to have to kill someone. But when it's you or him, desperation means that you try and make it him rather than you—you don't have time to think about it very much. You don't know how you're going to react until you get into a situation and survival is a very important thing. You want to survive rather than be killed, so you naturally act accordingly. It sounds awfully animal-like, but it is that.

War also elicits unsuspected courage and commitment. Ralph Coyne was a gentle man with old-world manners. His time at Scotch had been cut short by his father's death and he had never been drawn to the Scotch cadet corps. But seeing the war coming and alerted to the dangers of Nazism by his Jewish heritage he had joined the militia. In the A.I.F. he went into Signals and was set to go off with the Seventh Division when a major came round recruiting for a special unit which would fight behind enemy lines. He volunteered and served as a commando in East Timor, Borneo and New Guinea:

It's been a very privileged war-time experience—if very scary. We did not expect to see our homeland again. Those who came through were very lucky fellows, because the odds were usually against one, particularly in East Timor, where we were only 250 men and the Japanese built up their strength to 20 000 because of our activities. So there was a lot of chasing—hit and run and so on. We only lost five men. Our training led us to a peak of endurance, certainly better than the average infantryman.

The story of the Australian commando units on East Timor is one of the most heroic of the entire war:

Our lives were entirely dependent on the loyalty of the Timor natives because we lived with them in their villages. We could not move outside a village without people for miles along knowing because they had a strange yodelling system which echoed down the mountain valleys till it carried on. You could hear it being picked up, so whether it was Japanese movement or Australian, it was being communicated.

Our role there was to keep Australia informed of the Japanese build-up of forces, and guerrilla warfare. We were only there for four months. A sister unit had been caught there when the Japanese landed, were driven into the mountains and given up as lost, until some months later a radio signal was heard in Darwin which purported to be this sister unit of ours. And it was only by asking challenging personal questions about family members of the men on Timor that the authenticity of the radio call was confirmed. I don't think that they lost more than a dozen men out of the 250. They had made their radio out of parts stolen from the Japanese and with the help of the Portuguese, and gradually, bit by bit, building it into a kerosene tin, they made a radio which brought them back to life. Our job was to go over and relieve them. We were helped by native boys of eight to eleven—they would come along and ask if they could carry your pack. We had jettisoned everything that we could, even razors and toothbrushes, mirrors—things of that nature—because it's a very mountainous island—up to 10 000 feet—and it was terribly exhausting. We could not afford to move around the roads—they were very poor in any case—so we had to use native tracks. And so the very nature of our work was hit-and-run—let a force of Japanese come into very close range and we were heavily armed with sub-machine guns, machine-guns and rifles—so we'd have a tremendous kill-rate, then run for our lives. These Timorese boys were so very wonderful.

As important as the rigours of combat was the impact of the personalities of one's fellow troops. *Dick Wallace*, making the transition from the Victorian Scottish Regiment, which was full of chaps he already knew, was apprehensive: 'I thought—there'll be all these big tough blokes and I wondered if I was tough enough to stand up to it. But then I found that a lot were little blokes like me'. Ralph Coyne entered another world in the Commandos—'a marvellous education in human nature', and for Geoffrey Serle the war years were simply the most important of his education:

Not only did one carry out a variety of tasks, many of them menial—peeling spuds, and sweeping and cleaning, latrine fatigue, mechanical things, how to operate guns. And physically developed in various ways. But also, coming from a relatively sheltered background, then knocking around with all kinds and conditions of men—no women at all. (There were glorious days later in the war when I came out of hospital and reported back to Cipher and found myself put in a Sydney office with twenty-four beautiful women. That only lasted a week or so because I was due for discharge.) This was an extraordinary education, an education in vice and virtue essentially—there were criminals and no-hopers and there were men of great beauty of character. I strongly believe that this and later experiences of knocking around were the most important parts of my education in being an historian, which most academics have not had the fortune to have had. I certainly did emerge with a great regard for the virtues of the common man—perhaps a bit sentimental.

I think my personality changed greatly too, in that for many years I could talk to anybody in an outgoing kind of way. I changed back again because I became a relative recluse as a scholar—as I got older I lapsed into my natural personality, as it were.

If the celebrators of 'public school values' were gratified by the number who obtained commissions, it needs to be emphasized how well so many blended into the common herd and took on the mantle of being ordinary blokes.

Another consequence of war service for this generation was the way it perpetuated the separation of males from females that had existed since their early school days. *Dick Wallace* now marvels at the 'complete cutting off from women' and 'for a year of my life, I don't think I saw a woman— I certainly didn't touch one. Occasionally you'd see a nursing sister somewhere in New Guinea, and you'd say—there's one, there's one of *them*'. The Second A.I.F. appears to have been more chaste than their fathers had been in the First A.I.F., if the incidence of venereal disease is an indicator. There was less opportunity in the Pacific war compared to the Middle East, and it was home leave that brought the highest risk of infection, both from prostitutes and 'amateurs'.[27] Preventive measures were difficult to implement and many servicemen refused to use condoms, despite the risk, but a large proportion of the men simply suspended their sexual lives for years on end. *Dick* again:

> The majority of blokes coming out of the Army aged twenty-six to twenty-seven were virgins. I was at twenty-six and boy, you wouldn't strike that now. We'd talk about how you should treat women and did you want your sister to be a virgin and the majority of them would say— yeah, yeah, that seems pretty right. Again—'doing the right thing'. I think I had the idea that sex was a rather naughty thing to do. You didn't 'do it', particularly with somebody you liked and you wouldn't 'do it' with somebody you didn't like. I'm sure of that. A lot of my mates were as puzzled at the end of the war as they were before it started. As a teenager, the schools were segregated; even at Mont Albert Central the girls all went up the front of the room and the boys at the back. And apart from your sister, you'd go for months without talking to a girl. They were different. They were *them*.

But if they stayed virgins, they still learnt more about life than they would have at home. When Alan Cohn was nineteen, he would occasionally go out at night and his mother would lie awake until he came home; but in the Navy, he was thrown into the world of the forward mess deck and 'a bunch of torpedo men who used the most lurid language I'd ever heard and it soon gave me the feeling that there were other people in the world than the sheltered people I'd been accustomed to'. Tom McCaw's father had married late in life, and at home it was 'a bit like an on-going Forsyte Saga—I don't know what I would have been like if I'd continued living with my parents—the war made me a lot more positive'. Thus there were deep psychological changes and superficial cultural ones,

---

[27] Allan S. Walker, *Clinical Problems of War*, pp. 268–9.

there were political and religious changes and there were regressions and disgraces. Few who went through either active service overseas or the mind-numbing boredom of service within Australia did not experience a sudden personal growth in maturity.[28] But perhaps for Australian society one of the greatest benefits was the mixing up of men and women from all social strata, from east, west, north and south, from suburb and bush town, from slums and villas. Few have made the point more tellingly than Russel Ward, recalling his first night camped on the Sydney Showground:

> That night I shared a pen in the pig pavilion with an Irish Catholic rookie of about my own age. Never before had I been so close to a person of the old religion. He was a decent, earnest chap who knelt down, or rather up, on the prickly straw palliasse to say his prayers: an act which surprised his lapsed Protestant companion who had somewhere acquired the notion that Catholics left communication with the Divinity exclusively to the priest-hood.[29]

The experience in the ranks taught tolerance and enabled both the aspir-ant lower class and the receptive middle and upper class to cross class lines. As one very successful Old Scotch man testified: 'I soon realized that there were just as many marvellous people amongst those who did not have the privilege of my education and that every group in society had its share of stinkers. Religion and politics were subjects constantly debated and I be-lieve we all finished up much better people, with a broad view of life in general and racially tolerant'.[30] The war was more than a leveller—it was a unifier, which brought young white Australians closer together than they had ever been before.

But not for all. *Philip Hardwicke* was doing very well in the offices of the insurance company until the war became serious:

> The minister at our church had introduced the young men of the congregation to a pacifist periodical. I got involved in that and they used to have public meetings at the Friends' Meeting House at the bottom of

---

[28] Survey: 'Did your war service significantly affect the course of your life?'

	Scotch	Trinity
Number who served in W.W.II	67	112
No	33%	30%
Yes	67%	70%
For the better	58%	71%
For the worse	29%	17%
Both	2%	3%
Not answered	11%	10%

[29] Ward, *A Radical Life*, p. 147.
[30] Survey No. 783, Scotch.

Russell Street in the city, so I felt it was my bounden duty not to co-operate with the military. The outcome was that I had to report to the area officer and state my position. I had the medical exam and then they threatened me with further action.

There were three of us brought up for trial. There had been one in Essendon prior to that, but this was the first one near home. One of us was a Jehovah's Witness and the other was the son of a conscientious objector from London in World War I. I was the first to go into the dock. First of all, the people in charge, because it was new to them, were setting up procedures and carrying on with a lot of how-do-you-do, and I was standing in the dock there for I don't know how long. Eventually I was questioned by the area officer who was acting for the military, and he asked me some questions which I didn't think were altogether relevant, so I turned to the magistrate to ask him if it was necessary for me to reply to those questions and the next thing I found myself sitting on a seat outside the Court House, with my head between my knees—I'd fainted.

We were exempted from combatant service, but we were still required for non-combatant, which I refused to do. After that the management at work got aware of it and they said, 'We don't want our firm's name coming up in connection with this', so I was dismissed. I then took a job looking after a young man who was mentally unaware, and I lived with the people and I was an attendant for both day and night.

Philip was fully prepared to 'take the consequences' and go to gaol, but he also had a vocation to serve. He was inspired by the work of the Brotherhood of St Laurence and of Oswald Barnett, but his mother said he would need qualifications and suggested that he should train for the ministry. Thus he fulfilled a call to the cloth which, like John Jamieson, he had first articulated at the age of eight. *Albert White*'s moral response to the war was also outside the mainstream. He had always been one for asking awkward questions and after leaving Scotch he went to Swinburne Technical College to study engineering. During a students' guided tour of the Ford works at Geelong he became suspicious of the management's behaviour, so he slipped away to the factory floor where the workers told him a different story. He made new friends and started reading widely, but before the war 'it was more of a game really':

> I was reading all sorts of books—Leninism and Stalinism. And when the Communist Party was made illegal, some of my friends had good libraries and didn't want to get caught with them, so I got landed with all these books, because I reckoned I was not likely to be discovered. Bob Menzies would have had me in gaol.

He was in a reserved occupation, but was critical of the war until the Soviet Union came into it: 'I realized that once it was on to that extent, you didn't have much alternative'. He worked in munitions, ten-hour night shifts for two weeks, then two weeks day shift, including Saturday and

Sunday: 'I probably did more for the war than I ever would have done in the army'.

Dissident voices were growing in this generation, and even though they were less dangerous than the Communist Party, radical Christians joined in the determination to use the upheavals of the war to build a better world. John Jamieson was studying for the Presbyterian ministry at Ormond, an intellectual and spiritual powerhouse during the early 1940s. Teaching Old Testament was the Rev. Professor Hector Maclean, a socialist, and teaching theology was the Rev. Professor Norman Macleish, a 'Tory'. The ministers who trained in these years rarely wavered in their faith in later life, for the intellectual buttress implanted by Ormond withstood almost anything: 'Also there is a sense of Presbyterian stubbornness— you've committed yourself to this thing—you mightn't know what He's up to, but by God you're not going to allow Him to get away with it—it's a very Jewish thing in a way; it's an argumentative sort of relationship with God'. The power of Maclean's and Macleish's teaching was in 'the onlyness of God' and 'at one stage I wasn't sure whether I should become a Jew'. Politics were tightly intertwined, and it was while at university that John came under the political influence of the Rev. Stephen Yarnold and his Christian Commonwealth movement: 'He sought a Christian revolutionary social order and the way that Christians could be the agents of such an order—it was an attempt to find a way of true democratic participation in the new order which we all believed must follow the end of the war'.[31]

Within the armed forces there were men and women who were being changed in their ideas, and one of the great achievements of the Army was its education service. Geoffrey Serle, placing its contribution within the context of the wider cultural history of Australia, discerned 'a quickening, an alertness, a revival of utopian hope', and after the shock of the fall of Singapore, 'a marked growth of self-confidence and a sense of independence which reflected military and industrial achievement'.[32] The most significant and numerous of those who benefited from the books and records, who found a voice in the Army's magazine *Salt,* were those for whom such things were new. For the receptive working-class serviceman, the war offered the first chance of achievement, self-confidence and intellectual expansion. And it was so also for those middle-class boys who had been 'no good' at school. James Austin was another who discovered during the war that he had a good mind:

> We all formed groups in Changi. There was one group—'Towards a New Order'— and who were the main protagonists? Alex Downer, the pure Oxford man, true liberal in a way, with a conservative slant; and a

---

[31] Letter to author, 28 March 1991.
[32] Serle, *From Deserts the Prophets Come,* p. 177.

fellow named Mick Keen from Adelaide, who was Irish and strict Labor. But they drew very small crowds indeed—far fewer than a lecture on the future of chicken farming, which grabbed the English officers, don't ask me why.

Those middle-class men with commissions—and there were not many who had become officers from *Struggletown*—entered a closed world of deeply conservative values. If there were radicals emerging in the armed forces, there remained in the officer corps many who distrusted Labor governments and who detested trade unions. Older members of the officer corps often had family links with the White Army of the 1930s and drew deeply on long resistance to organized labour.[33] The trade union movement and the Australian Labor Party had ended the Depression defeated and demoralized, but war industry brought a sharper industrial consciousness to the struggles over wages and conditions. Once the Soviet Union entered the war and at Stalingrad withstood the German advance for the first time, the left basked in the Red Army Barrackers who flocked to raise funds for 'Sheepskins for Russia' and who marvelled at the Soviet Brave New World. There was genuine admiration for the Red Army within the officer corps of the armed forces also, but civilian radicals were anathema. James Austin was 'not a political animal at all' during the war, and cast his first vote at the age of twenty-six for Menzies: 'the troops, especially the officer group, were very critical of the Labor government'. And when John Barrett made his superb survey of returned men, he found only 16 per cent were 'completely favorable' to trade unionists, 28 per cent did not answer, and the rest were hostile.[34] These men of World War II were different from their fathers, who had come back from the battlefields and wanted only for the world to be as it was before it all went mad. The second war had been for Australians a true total war—no one had escaped the dislocations, the new social possibilities, the new ideas. Sir James Barrett, a shrewd observer of the young, wrote at the end of his autobiographical review of *Eighty Eventful Years*:

> The only aspect of modern life which tempers my pessimism in this regard is the intelligent interest in politics, both national and international, being displayed by the younger generation of today. Impulsive and prone to visualise a world made angelic by a few simple socialistic laws as they are, in these young people, in their early interest in the way the world is governed, there is a tremendous force for good. They are unhampered by the memory of good times we older folk have known and, consciously or unconsciously, attempt to revive.[35]

---

[33] Michael Cathcart, *Defending the National Tuckshop, Australia's Secret Army Intrigue of 1931, passim;* Coulthard-Clark, *Duntroon*, p.113; Robert Coleman, *Above Renown, the Biography of Sir Henry Winneke*, p. 113.

[34] Barrett, *We Were There*, pp. 321–2.

[35] Sir James Barrett, *Eighty Eventful Years*, p. 118.

Becoming a Woman

I can remember Reverend Mother in my last year saying to a group of us,'Whatever you do, don't be old maids. If you're not going to be a nun'—obviously number one was to be a nun—'for heavens sake, get married'. I remember going to chapel once, and I used to pray a fair bit (I was pretty good on the praying—mainly for something I wanted) and thinking, 'I hope I won't be like Auntie *Jennie,* an old maid', and yet feeling that I would be.

If it seemed to the girls of Genazzano that destiny offered Catholic women only two choices—that you were either a nun or a mother—it was not really so different at MLC. While it was not explicit, to pursue a lifelong career was assumed to require celibacy. A woman could not divide herself between professional work and the care of children and husband; and a woman could not openly pursue sexual fulfilment outside marriage. If a state school teacher married, she had to resign at once because the Public Service assumed that a married woman was unfit for work and likely to fall pregnant at any tick of the clock. There was no provision in either regulation or custom for women who might not bear children or who might find care for their children while working. Only widows were exempt. Officially there was little flexibility—you were either one or the other and that was that.

There were women who lived or thought differently and offered the young alternative role models: Alan and Lawrence Cohn's aunt was a radiologist and was regarded as 'very forward': 'she did all sorts of naughty things—she smoked, she drank alcohol, she had a career, she had a car, she went overseas and she actually went up in an aeroplane. We were frightened of her originally—later we found there was no need and we had a very good rapport with her'. There were discreet feminists among mothers and grandmothers, aunts and family friends, who taught girls to prize a certain independence, both material and mental.[1] Winsome Walklate's grandmother always believed that 'a woman needed a room of her own' and left her estate to her three granddaughters so that they could enjoy an independent income. Such mothers had often had incomes or careers of their own. Ailsa Thomson's mother was a university graduate and had been a teacher, and there was no question that if you had the ability you went to the university and found a career, so that Ailsa left MLC fully determined to return to teach there once she was qualified. Betty Jackson's mother had also been a teacher:

---

[1] Norris, *Champions of the Impossible*, pp. 48–9.

Mother's attitude was unusual for the time—it was that you didn't have to get married at all costs. Whereas my aunt, who also had a family, I remember once saying to me when one of my friends stopped coming around, 'What happened to so-and-so?' 'Oh, I find him boring.' And she said, 'You mustn't be too particular'.

My mother's attitude was that a lot of people were just interested in their work, and lots of mothers would have been ashamed, but there was nothing like that about her. She was also quite definite that it was important that I should have an ample supply of money because I must be independent and it was easier for the boys—one was in medicine and one had a good job in a bank, so they were obviously going to be quite comfortably off. She stressed that she had seen too many women having to move out of the family home and not have enough. So I've never felt aggressive about women being put upon, *except* that I felt that the teachers at MLC were put upon, but I don't know that I thought that in the context of men. Even if I was accepting that a woman's place was in the home, I didn't feel timid inside myself, and I always had the feeling that if I wanted to exert myself, I would. And I think my mother had that.

The proper role of woman was a source of a certain hypocrisy in the middle class: hypocrisy because while the ideal was to be a kept woman—first by one's father and later by one's husband—the reality was that the majority of both mothers and daughters worked for their living at some stage in their lives. And, ironically, it is at Genazzano, where the conditioning was strongest and the social expectations the highest, that this generation's mothers had had the highest rate of participation in the workforce.[2] As for their daughters, only half leaving Genazzano in the 1930s and 1940s expected to have to earn their own living, whereas almost three quarters from MLC did. Few mothers were as frank as Joyce Thorpe's, however:

> She married quite young because she believed quite firmly in marriage. She looked upon a man as a meal ticket, I have to be honest. And this is one of my big feminist things: I was brought up with 'the thing to do is to get married' and you married as suitable a man as you could find. And she told me that you didn't really have to love a man. My mother was quite devoted to my father, but you always felt that the great love was from my father towards my mother—which is the reverse of what happens in most marriages. Most young girls fell madly in love—I did—but my mother didn't—she was looking for a nice man who would look after her.

Parents wanted their children to marry happily, but there was no question that a woman's economic destiny was determined by her choice

---

[2] See Appendix II, tables 5a and 5b.

of husband. And, for the middle class, that choice depended not just on emotional and sexual attraction, but also on status and projected income—it was a risk to marry too far 'down'. Yet looking back, only a quarter of the MLC women remember their mothers as being anxious that they 'married well', and at the more social Genazzano the figure rises only to 39 per cent—which is still less than half.[3] There was an unspoken expectation that women should marry men who were at least potentially their social equals, but in retrospect too there were interesting hopes for the future: only half from both schools wanted to get married and have children 'more than anything else' when they were young; and of those who didn't, 20 per cent wanted to become 'an independent woman'.[4] Three-quarters of the MLC women expected to have to earn their own living; fully 42 per cent from Genazzano did not.[5] Life did not turn out like this, however. By the age of nineteen already half the Genazzano women were self-supporting, in the next ten years another 22.5 per cent joined them and 8 per cent became self-supporting after the age of thirty. In their full life-span only 20 per cent achieved the genteel security of being kept women all their lives. At MLC the expectations of having to work were much higher, and their participation in the workforce was higher, so that merely 11 per cent have never worked.[6] It was not the fact of having to go to work that mattered so much as the nature of that work and the degree of commitment to it. There was a double-think, for while training to be a teacher was a good vocation for a girl, it could not be a lifetime commitment without at least the appearances of celibacy. You were either a 'nun' or a mother.

When these young middle-class women entered the workforce, they did better than their mothers, leaving behind the manual and unskilled occupations which had sustained almost a third of the MLC mothers and 15 per cent of the Genazzano ones when young. As ever, upward social mobility within families took place in generational steps: the manual occupations were replaced with clerical ones, the clerical workers' daughters

---

[3] Survey: 'Was your mother particularly concerned that you "marry well"?' Yes: MLC, 24% (N/A, 9%); Genazzano, 39% (N/A, 12.5%).

[4] Survey: 'When you were young, did you want to get married and have children more than anything else?' Yes: MLC, 54% (N/A, 3%); Genazzano, 53% (N/A, 7%). 'Or did you desire to become an independent woman?' (Number of answers: MLC, 126; Genazzano, 70) Yes: MLC, 21%; Genazzano, 19%.

[5] Survey: 'Did you expect to have to work for a living?' Yes: MLC, 74% (N/A 2%); Genazzano, Yes, 56% (N/A, 3%).

[6] Survey: Age when first worked for living:

Age range (%)		MLC	Genazzano
	15–19	59.3	50.0
	20–29	26.6	22.5
	30–39	0.9	4.2
	40–49	1.4	1.7
	50–59	0.5	1.7
	NEVER WORKED:	11.2	20.0

entered the lower professions, the lower professionals' offspring entered the learned professions and the intelligentsia. The proportion from MLC in clerical occupations halved between the generations and in the professions almost doubled; at Genazzano the proportion in office work fell to a quarter and those in the professions almost doubled. Where the two schools differed most was in teaching and nursing: at MLC teaching was the largest profession and nursing was for those who were not bright enough for medicine or whose parents could not afford it; at Genazzano, fully a quarter were in nursing and only 6 per cent became teachers.[7] Teaching was a problem for Genazzano girls—nearly all their teachers were nuns, therefore teaching meant a training and a career in government or Protestant schools. Even though she had been an outstanding teacher in the Tasmanian Education Department, *Marina Graham*'s mother was dismayed at her daughter's ambition to teach.

Yet however serious a young woman's desire to enter the world of work, few questioned that they should take on careers that were extensions of the feminine mission to nurture and to civilize.[8] From the 1920s the expanding helping professions attracted middle-class females with a sense of vocation—perhaps as much a secularization of the missionary spirit.[9] Even clerical work was a form of service to male authority figures, and by contrast, only 2 per cent of these middle-class women were ever to own their own business.[10] The most daunting of the helping professions was medicine, and many of these women wanted to become doctors but were thwarted by the low level of science teaching at school. Dorothea Cerutty longed to do medicine but once she accepted that her mathematics were beyond hope she felt only relief: 'I'd been struggling in a world where I had no place—the whole of my bent is romantic and ridiculous and imaginative'. The few who did make it were only to be admired, and some feared that marriage might not come their way. The medical student world was cruelly sexist: the women students kept to themselves in the dissecting room; only the massage or physiotherapy students who were 'usually much better looking' (according to the late Professor Sir Douglas Wright) attracted any male attention.[11]

---

[7] See Appendix II, table 8a: Women's Occupations in their Twenties.
[8] Genazzano: Destinations of School Leavers: 1946–48: from *Fidelis*.
  Novitiate: 2
  University: 15 (MBBS 1, Law 2, Arts/Law 1, Science 2, Arts 5, Music 2, Phys. Ed 1, ? 1)
  Professional: pharmacy 1, physiotherapy 1, teaching 3, kindergarten teaching 3.
  Nursing: 11, dental nursing 1.
  Emily McPherson College, 12 (2 girls waiting for nursing), Mothercraft 1, Invergowrie 1, office work 9, lab assistant 1, 'work at St Vincent's' 1, *Advocate* office, 'work after holiday' 1, hairdressing 2, dress designing 1, hat designing 1, florist 1.
  'keeping up music and singing' 1, 'home duties at present' 13.   TOTAL: 82 girls.
[9] Kerreen M. Reiger, *The Disenchantment of the Home*, p. 151.
[10] See Appendix II, table 8b.
[11] R. Douglas Wright, in Hume Dow, ed., *Memories of Melbourne University*, p. 69.

Veronica Keogh was for a while a massage student and, as a captain of Genazzano, she felt under some pressure to enter the order:

> In my last year at school I was given privileges and I could go off and study by myself somewhere and on Saturday night I'd look at all the lights of the city sparkling. And I'd been used to being barefooted and spending all summer holidays in bathers. It was that idea more than anything else that I couldn't tolerate—being fully dressed all the time. I don't think it was any other aspect that concerned me. It certainly wasn't the lack of marriage—I don't think that crossed my mind.

So she went to the university. She sensed that she had a gift for art, but a family friend warned that 'commercial art would not provide security in another depression', so she had to do something vocational and, since her brothers were doing medicine, physiotherapy seemed sensible:

> I didn't know anything about it—it went over my head. Also—talk about a shock—we went straight into the Anatomy School for dissection. You were supposed to have a second-year girl helping you and mine was often absent and in love (she married him and didn't finish) and I was supposed to dissect the arm and remove it. And the kids who were doing the chest were sick of me being too slow because this other student never came, so one day I went in quietly and got a saw and sawed it off rather than dissect it.

Diving off Frankston pier in the holidays, *Veronica* broke her hand and thus she and Massage parted company and she entered Arts. In the 1930s Melbourne University was still very social: there were serious students, but there were also a lot of girls from private schools more interested in social life than study (enrolled in B.A. Matrimony). Jean Cane was a serious student and became the first to graduate in both Arts and Social Work but, like many from MLC, she had little social confidence:

> When first I went to the university I was scared of the men, because I suppose so much had been made of my brother, who was the clever one, so all the boys must be clever. I was soon disabused of that—a lot of them were anything but clever, and I found that some of my essays were topping the class. But confidence came very, very slowly and I was very shy. I was too shy, to begin with, to join in the social life of the young people of the church. It was only later that I did and that's how I met Alan—we played tennis, belting each other off the court. I went off and did a course in ballroom dancing and I had an affinity with dancing; but after I'd been at the university for a while I got over that. The Student Christian Movement helped a tremendous lot—although they did say it was a matrimonial bureau. There were a lot of people like myself who were there and we'd have stimulating conversations. And for us a well-organised world was a Christian aim.

In reminiscences of the university in the 1930s and the 1940s, the Labour Club has loomed large, but for most young people from private schools the religious societies were more significant in student life, and their focus was on Christian action in the world. Jean again:

> When I started voting, I was uncomfortable with the idea of voting conservative because I didn't believe in it, but nobody in our family had ever voted for anything else but conservative. I belonged to an S.C.M. group who were very keen on co-operatives—we could see this as an alternative to Communism and conservatism, and in 1939, the year I started my Social Work course, we had a big group and I was the secretary. We started off a student housing project and we got a grant from the National Union of Students to conduct a survey. Then during the holidays I did the Social Work field work, and then Political Institutions with Ian Milner and Economic and Social History with Joe Burton—I loved that. So my radicalism all developed out of that, and I joined the Labour Club for the year that Joe Burton was there.
>
> I went to a Labour Club weekend (I had to tell my parents it was just a university weekend—Mother would have felt betrayed, I think). There were a number of avowed Communists in the Labour Club and the thing that bothered me when they discussed things was that I realized that they were not really interested in the advancement of the working classes as far as conditions were concerned. And they told me quite flatly that social workers were anathema because they helped people to be satisfied with their lot, and they wanted them to be dissatisfied so that there could be a revolution. I didn't believe in revolution. I believed in socialism—I believed in peaceful means towards it. And after a lot of heart-searching and after a very nasty session, when they voted Joe Burton out, I resigned. Not only that—I felt I wasn't a strong enough person to take a position myself—it sounds cowardly. They were very fierce.
>
> The Communist Party was élitist and made sure that it remained so, especially in countries where it was in power. It hurt me in 1990–91 to see the baby thrown out with the bath water in Eastern Europe— socialism being thrown out with Communism—it really hurt me, because in those countries socialism's got so much more to give them.

It was also prudent to leave the Labour Club. The war had started and the Communist Party was proscribed: 'Witch hunts were on and there was a danger of being flung out of university and I couldn't afford that. But my parents remained in blissful ignorance that I had ever been in the Labour Club'.

Yet however committed to her career a young woman may have been, there was no question that her place in the world of work was seen differently by men and was rewarded differently. Women's professional salaries were disgraceful: in 1941 the principal's salary at the Yooralla school for handicapped children was *raised* to £260 a year and a young

teacher with a good honours degree and a Dip.Ed. started at MLC on
£195—less than the male basic wage.[12] Betty Jackson:

> When the Assistant Mistresses Association started the demand for increases
> in salaries and so forth, MLC was one school which was against it. It was
> *being genteel*. Money was a dirty word. And I think that the independent
> schools played on the women's feelings by the implication that if they got
> an increase, the schools couldn't survive. And I remember someone
> getting annoyed with me when I said—we're really subsidizing the
> parents who have higher salaries than we have. But something was
> instilled into us—it was Service. Now whether that was because we were
> women, I don't know.

Legend hath it that one staff meeting when the teachers were told 'From
those to whom much is given, much will be required', Betty Jackson ven-
tured 'But not very much is given to us'. Women teachers in government schools earned a 'living wage' which enabled them to live
independently; only those whose families partially supported them could
afford to teach in private schools.

If teaching was hard work, nursing bordered on slavery, yet the
young ladies turned out by Genazzano rose to the challenge and displayed
an awesome dedication to their profession. After losing her first boyfriend
in the battle of Bardia, Mary Thompson went nursing and found the
world of St Vincent's Hospital was of coarser cloth than Genazzano:

> Oh there were some frightful women there and it was very embarrassing
> for a Catholic to have them there with Protestants, particularly some
> residents—well-behaved, sophisticated people. The nuns were really
> aristocratic in my day at Gen., but at St Vincent's some were real bog
> Irish—they were hard and common and so completely different. There
> were three or four nice ones, but one nun hated to give you linen to
> change the beds, and of course, that was hard during the war. I was at a
> party the other day and I said, 'Did I dream it, or did I really on night
> duty, climb along that ledge in Victoria Parade to get into the linen press
> the night that Sister Thais wouldn't give fresh linen?' And another
> woman said, 'Yes you did'. I finished my training in 1945, and much to
> my surprise, I was asked to stay on.

The war intruded on young women's lives, as it did on young men's,
although few joined the armed forces and middle-class girls were not as
vulnerable to Manpower directives as were working-class girls already in
factory work. What the war really affected was the pursuit of marriage. As
young women went out to the world of work or study, at the back of

---

[12] Letter from Barbara Sutton in possession of the author; Norman Marshall, *The Yooralla Story*, p. 59.

their minds were the exigencies of finding a husband and, for those who were not natural social butterflies, the years of waiting and hoping could be difficult. The pretty and the chatty who danced and flirted with ease seemed to take it all in their stride; the shy and the serious-minded found it hard. Boys did not make passes at girls who wore glasses and gentlemen were widely believed to prefer blondes; intelligent girls were 'sexless blue stockings' and no chap could marry a girl smarter than himself. The prejudices abounded. The only salvation of the shy and the serious was the community of the church, where equally serious or just-as-shy young men could be met over a tennis net or at a brother's birthday party or at a school friend's home. (Most of the boys were just as shy themselves.)[13] There was a wide social gulf between the social and the churchy and it was awkward for those who found themselves in, or who aspired to, the wrong social scene. Only children often found the group sociability of social life a strain. *Gwenda Holtby*:

> I think it's a very poor beginning to social life. We had a great yarn at
> one S.C.M. conference in a group of only children, and they decided that
> they never quite knew when other people wanted them to stay in a
> group or were tired of them. And kids who'd grown up in a large family
> were used to being told to get lost or something, so they had a social
> ability by the age of five that only children get perhaps by the time
> they're fifty.

The Genazzano girls often had social confidence—certainly in knowing the formalities, they 'could go anywhere', and even though the Catholic Church encouraged temperance, alcohol did lubricate the cogs of the social machinery. Making a formal debut at the Genazzano Ball was popular until the war, whereas at MLC many thought 'coming out' was 'corny'.[14] Some Genazzano girls joined the sophisticated social scene and patronized Melbourne's handful of night clubs, sampling cocktails and dancing partners. Eleonore Bibron's father ran Old Admiralty House, where patrons always wore evening dress and could have alcohol if they brought their bottles in during the day and left them with their name on. New Year's Eve, Melbourne Cup Night and Boat Race Night were the 'three big nights of the year; and you had to get a special permit to have liquor and they clamped down on Boat Race Night because one young man was taken home on a stretcher and his father was a judge'. The Brenan sisters had The Embassy and *Veronica Keogh* was able to persuade her parents to allow her to have her twenty-first there because she was

---

[13] Survey: 'Were you shy with girls when you were a young man?' Yes: Scotch, 68% (N/A, 4%); Trinity, 68% (N/A, 1%). 'If so, did going to a boys' school aggravate your shyness?' Yes: Scotch, 44%; Trinity, 44%.

[14] Survey Q. 'Did you make a formal debut?' 'Yes: Genazzano, 48%; MLC, 24%.'

'mad on dancing'. The night for the sophisticates at the Palais was Friday, its 'dress up' night, but there was always something on. Skiing was also 'very important' to *Veronica* and her sister, and they went to Mount Hotham:

> It was special too that hardly anyone went around 1939 and it was very difficult to get up there. You'd go by train—which was part of the fun— and get on a bus for Harrietville. Stay the night at the hotel there and then get on these little horses for as far as they could manage the snow, and then you'd take your skis off the horses, and with frozen fingers try and fasten on the skis. I had football boots and funny little old skis and all my clothes on my back for a fortnight. Not that I was terribly aware of it at the time, but it was a very small group, very socially élite—the Brockhoffs and the Winter-Irvings—that mob.

Back in town the Italian restaurants were popular and Mary Thompson treasured her friendship from Genazzano with the daughter of a leading Italian restaurateur. Nurses from St Vincent's went in search of good food on their few nights off, but many had little energy for social life: 'You have to be interesting to be asked out', says *Frances Costelloe,* 'you can't be yawning your head off and asking if it's time to go home'. In reaction to the death of her boyfriend Mary Thompson had the nervous energy to burn the candle at both ends: 'On your day off, you'd sleep all day and be terribly heavy when you woke up, especially if you had a cold, so you'd go down to the New Treasury dining room—I never drank much, but there they had trays with big glasses—Oh it was wonderful—the beer cleared your head'.

Such pleasures were not for Methodists, unless they were rebellious. Lurline Keck:

> The first year I started work there was a little Christmas party (I'd have been close to eighteen) and I remember coming home to my mother and telling her I'd had my first taste of sin. She looked very startled and I think it was a relief to find it was a glass of sherry. She did give me a little talking to, reminding me of the dangers of drink. It felt very daring.

Drink was a touchstone of Methodism and therefore a powerful symbol of rejection of the church and its culture. In the Barnett family June was quick to cast it aside: 'I can tell you when I had my first drink: when I went to Western Australia and on my eighteenth birthday they gave me a white lady and I haven't looked back'. But her sister Le, also a non-believer, has never liked alcohol and has remained an abstainer. Ailsa Thomson gradually ceased attending the Methodist Church after her marriage, but has also remained a teetotaller. Around a third of the MLC women are still teetotallers, compared to 10 per cent from Genazzano, and half the MLC women were still not drinking alcohol by the age of thirty.[15] Cocktails and Italian restaurants were not for Methodists: *Gwenda Holtby*'s parents never went to a restaurant 'for the whole of their life', but 'I can remember when I was a student being absolutely thrilled to go to the Society Restaurant—an Italian restaurant that was manned by Italians and to eat Italian food—we thought that was very advanced and radical'. But Methodists had lots of fun. The Church was in fact ambivalent about dancing: no dances could be held in church premises, but many good Methodists did ballroom dancing or danced at home. There were still circuits of 'surprise parties' in the suburbs, where a group descended on a friend's house on a Saturday night, bringing a plate, and the carpets were rolled back for dancing. There was a lot of social sport—tennis and badminton were for mixed company—and there was bushwalking and camping—all organized from the church. It was very wholesome.

Joyce Thorpe is now grateful for her Methodist upbringing: 'I didn't touch alcohol until I left the university, [and] discovering after marriage that I was a very sexual being, I am sure that, had I not been a teetotaller during my adolescence, I would soon have become pregnant and married'.[16] Woman's true destiny was sexual, and yet respectable young women were expected to make the right choice on the basis of chaste ignorance. There was no equivocation in the churches' standards: sexual intercourse was only moral within marriage and, while a blessed expression of physical love between a man and a woman, its grander purpose was procreation. At the same time many people had an insistent libido which chafed at the prospect of years of continence before marriage and years of regular restraint after it. We will never know how many among the respectable broke the rules—or bent them, although there were certainly men and women who did, especially on the fringe of respectability, in the arts or left-wing politics, (although the Communist Party was conspicuous for its puritanism); but few, even in bohemian circles, could get away with promiscuity. Much of the problem was that mechanical contraceptives were unreliable: condoms broke, caps did not fit or pessaries did not work. Extramarital sex carried a very real danger of unwanted pregnancy and an unwanted pregnancy brought a very real danger of either lifelong shame and grief, or damage—even death—from a backyard

---

[15] Survey: 'Do you drink alcohol?: Yes: MLC, 68%; Genazzano, 88%. 'At what age did you begin to drink alcohol?'

	MLC	Genazzano
Teens (%)	21.4	39.6
Twenties (%)	52.4	42.5
Thirties (%)	15.2	5.7
Forties (%)	6.9	2.8
Fifties (%)	2.1	0
Sixties (%)	0.7	0
Not answered (%)	1.4	9.4

[16] Joyce Nicholson in Patricia Grimshaw and Lynne Strahan, eds, *The Half-open Door*, p. 136.

abortion. The proportion of first births conceived outside marriage in Australia has remained significant throughout the twentieth century, and certainly in closed communities rapid arithmetic accompanied the birth of first babies. (It could be embarrassing to conceive on your wedding night and then deliver prematurely.) But more important than any knowledge of what could go wrong was the lack of any sexual knowledge at all and the very real fear religious young people had of committing a mortal sin.

The Catholic Church was quite explicit in its teachings:

> You would hear from the pulpit very direct directions as to how to lead your life. They used to have Missions and they'd have a visiting priest come into the parish to give a Mission and if you participated you'd be up there every night for a 7 o'clock lecture and you'd be there every morning for 7 o'clock Mass for about ten days. People used to love to listen to the Redemptorists—all fire and brimstone. And I can remember one priest saying, 'And some people do "it" every night' and I was vaguely puzzled as to what was wrong with "it"—and I suppose I wasn't quite sure what they were doing every night. And there was this very strong proscription against marrying non-Catholics—it was forbidden to marry outside the church. Also you would almost feel unable to go back to visit the Gen. nuns.

Human sexuality was portrayed as a burden of potential sinfulness, but it also tantalized—it was 'forbidden fruit':

> I was really very innocent—this is getting a bit close to the bone—but as regards our faith, there was a very strong [thing] against sex. I can remember a priest saying from the pulpit that it's a mortal sin not only to take part in illicit sex (I don't think he used the word 'illicit'—he probably just said 'sex'), but it was also a mortal sin to *think* about it. So we got into the way of closing our minds a bit to it.

The attractive and socially confident could go through escort after escort with scarcely a kiss, let alone a 'feel'. Many young people were astonishingly chaste and their chastity was easy because their sexual desires were so contained by fear, ignorance and convention. Moira Lambert's frank recollections of her life as a young middle-class Catholic woman during the war reveal a social whirl of compulsive dating and virtually no sexual passion. She was considered a great beauty and went out with scores of young men, but she was known as 'the girl who didn't kiss' until one fatal night in 1944 upon a remote beach when a 'casual peck' from an accomplished lover sent her 'off into the stratosphere' (writing more than forty years later, she still lacks a vocabulary for sexual passion). When her sexuality awoke, she was a sophisticated twenty-six-year-old.[17]

---

[17] Lambert, *A Suburban Girl*, pp. 146–8.

Such libidinal anaesthesia was not uncommon, but neither was it frigidity. Lurline Keck:

> No one knew anything about sex at school. I can remember a few
> whispered, furtive conversations with much sniggering, but no one knew
> very much about it. When girls started their periods they used to tell their
> best friends that it had started, and those who were a bit later were always
> disappointed at being 'out of the club'. I think we were kept fairly
> sexually ignorant, and even when I left school, sexual experience just
> wasn't part of your expectations. I know that it was a different
> environment—there wasn't the pill and so on. I mentioned this to some
> friends and we all agreed that everyone realized that it was out of reach—
> there were exceptions. So you found your enjoyment in other ways—
> you played tennis and went on hikes and had musical evenings. There'd
> be some kisses goodnight at the end, but not much else. But that was
> probably security. But I don't remember thinking much about it and
> I would have to say that I wasn't very sexually aware until I was
> first married.

This anaesthesia was created by the simple means of ignoring sex. Probably the Catholic Church was more explicit and girls were taught that they were 'responsible for men's passions' and 'for tempting them to fall into mortal sin'. Protestants tended to say virtually nothing at all. Everyone *knew* of course, but if sex was ignored, it might just go away. *Betty Thomas:*

> This 'boy thing'—my parents were not inclined to push me into the
> company of boys—that was not their scene at all. There was a wowser
> element there, and also 'we want to control the company our daughter
> goes into'. I was not aware of this, but being at a girls' school provided a
> channel for all those emotional needs that growing girls have. There was
> everything—there was a whole world there to be loved. I do think that
> MLC girls probably came a cropper afterwards. I was just lucky that I met
> a bloke who suited me and we stuck together. Neither of us really met
> anybody else, we've in a sense been together all our adult lives; but it
> sheltered me from the worst pitfalls. There were stories of eminent
> Methodist ministers' daughters going mad once they went to uni, but it
> never happened to me because I met up with this bloke who was busy
> saving the world. And we trotted around doing it together. We were
> collecting for European Relief and he was so busy organizing this relief
> programme which he built up himself to save German children (as a
> Jewish boy—and I think that's why I liked him) that he really skimped on
> his studies, yet he ended up with first class honours. And I suppose being
> a snob that impressed me—and he could play the violin beautifully.

Three-quarters of the MLC parents and 80 per cent of the Genazzano parents ignored sex to the extent that they neglected to give their daughters an adequate sex education. The men fared no better, although fewer experienced sexual difficulties because of their ignorance than did the women.[18] But what young people did not know, perhaps they might not miss. Accidents did happen and Elaine Corran can remember many good Methodist girls who had to marry in a hurry, but the disgrace was appalling. (The Rev. Francis Morton, while vicar of Dunolly in the late 1930s, officiated at a shot-gun wedding where the bride's unforgiving grandfather forced her to wear black.)[19] But there were others who were eager for knowledge: Winsome Walklate worked as a medical secretary in a doctor's rooms where she avidly read Havelock Ellis and all the books she could find on sex: 'and I do believe that the Victorians had a whale of a time sexually—they just didn't say so'. It was still very difficult, however, to obtain a clear understanding of the 'mechanics of sex'. Joyce Thorpe's first opportunity came at university in a lecture by Dr Raynor Johnson:

> He was Master of Queen's College and a very great man. And I went to an S.C.M. conference and he gave us lectures on sex and you could have heard a pin drop—obviously, even to the boys a lot of this was new. It was a very fine lecture he gave us, but we still didn't learn the mechanics of sex. I was married without really knowing the mechanics of sex, and there are a lot of women I've talked to who didn't know the mechanics of sex when they were married. They didn't know about an erection—a most extraordinary thing—I knew nothing about an erection. But he did teach us a lot. Then we had groups where we discussed—I don't know what we discussed when we didn't know the mechanics of sex, but we learnt something. And when I got home and I told my mother this, she was absolutely shocked. And she said, 'That's terrible—you didn't talk to boys about those things', and I said 'Yes'. Then she said—and this is a classic feminist story—'No nice boy would marry a girl that talked about things like that'. She was quite hung-up about sex.

It was all very confusing. One young Genazzano woman, when she went to confession after having 'a bit of a flutter' which she admitted she had 'enjoyed', was surprised and relieved when the priest only said, 'It sounds as though you had a good time'. Most young people negotiated the straits of premarital sexual life without mishap and young men really did respect young women.[20] Mary Thompson:

---

[18] Survey: 'Did your parents give you an adequate sex education?'

	Scotch	Trinity	MLC	Genazzano
Yes (%)	21	18	25	20
No (%)	76	78	73.5	78
Not answered (%)	3	4	1.5	2
'If not, did this create difficulties?'				
Yes (%)	28	32	40	33
Not answered (%)	4	2	3	2

Nearly all reported that any such difficulties were overcome in time.
[19] Francis H. Morton, *My Guardian Angel*, p. 56.
[20] Survey: 'Did men respect women more when you were young?' Yes: Scotch, 79%; Trinity, 77%.

Looking back I often think how lucky we were. One fellow I was very keen about—there's a porch at St Vincent's near the Outpatients, and one night he'd hung his raincoat over that and we were canoodling away and he said, 'I'd like to sleep with you' and I said, 'Yes, I'd like to sleep with you. Isn't it a pity we're so well brought up'. It never occurred to me to have any other reaction to it. But I went out with an awful lot of boys and I never had to fight for my virtue—*never*. And they weren't Catholics a lot of them. One of the boys at Newman College said they were told it was better to get drunk than to have sex and that's why so many of them got to the passing-out stage.

The war changed much in private life, and for many the dislocation was worse than the anxieties of the Depression had been. The war cut at people's emotional core, separating loved ones, bringing death and dis-ablement, grief and lasting distress. The war also thrust sheltered young people into the wider world, and young people met and married partners who hailed far from their home communities, both geographically and socially. But the war brought changes *to* women—far fewer were dragged away by the war to new worlds and experiences. June Barnett and *Veronica Keogh* were among the few who enlisted in the women's services and private-school girls found themselves even more likely to receive commissions than were their brothers.[21] *Veronica*'s first reaction when she heard of the outbreak of war had been 'a feeling almost of adventure', but, once commissioned, her reputation as a former captain of a convent school thrust upon her the responsibility of 'upholding morals'. The luxuries of the officers' mess astonished her: 'It was like a beautiful hotel—we were waited on by the ranks', and the new friends she made challenged and extended her. She learnt much about herself and her deficiencies, but the war taught a girl with only Intermediate arithmetic how to be in charge of operation communications and plotting, and it took a convent girl into a world of freedom and independence.

But the lot of most women was to stay at home and wait; and as they did so, they had to assume new responsibilities. *Monica O'Farrell* was still a schoolgirl during the war:

> My father lost a lot of authority in the family. I really know that now.
> Mum became the dominant person—she developed her own successful
> business. That was very fulfilling. Dad was away for nearly five years, and
> even though he was a Lieutenant Commander in the Navy, at the end of
> the war, somehow or other, he wasn't as dominant. I think that was true
> of a lot of men who came back—the women had found their feet.

Valerie Golding's family had had a bad time in the Depression and her fa-ther had been reduced to selling insurance door-to-door, so when he went off to the war, her mother decided to complete her qualifications as

---

[21] Only 10 from MLC and 5 from Genazzano served in World War II; see also Lorna Ollif, *Women in Khaki*, pp. 32–66.

a pharmacist. They lived above a pharmacy in Richmond—'it was noisy and you always had drunks on the corner coming to the door', but it was a new beginning which brought security and comfort once the war was over. Many young people were deliberately sheltered from the anxieties of the war: Ailsa Thomson's parents rarely talked about war news and politics 'because they were protecting us from the full horrors of it', although her mother was able to return to teaching for the first time since her marriage. Ailsa went on to university in 1945, a strangely quiet and feminine Melbourne University with so many young men away, and apart from those who had loved ones in the services, the war was somehow remote: 'I was a fresher and I was at an age when I believed that deadlines were deadlines and I sat up all night to write an essay, then because it was V.P. day, we were all given an extension of time. I can remember the end of the war quite vividly because we all went down to the city from college with the college gong secreted under somebody's gown'. Some very daring girls went out with Americans, but of those who lapped up the Hollywood charm and the nylon stockings, it was the already married and the already sexually experienced who played the most dangerously.

For those already in love, or who fell in love during the war, the anxieties cut deep. Some lost their young husbands, others their young fiancés; and children lost fathers they barely knew. In John Barrett's survey of returned men, 16 per cent went to war leaving behind wives and children, and fully half of those reported that their children suffered psychological damage as a result.[22] In 1935 Thelma Squire's father had been one of the first European warders at the new Changi gaol in Singapore, and on New Year's Day 1942 he was on leave in Melbourne. They knew the Japanese were in Kuala Lumpur and that Singapore would soon fall, and that day a telegram arrived recalling her father to duty. Thelma's mother got the telegram and hid it, but her sister persuaded her to give it to him because 'he could never live with himself if he ever found out'. When he got it, he booked a flight at once:

> My mother took to her bed with a migraine attack and I can remember the day my father had to go on the flight. I cooked him a boiled egg and we sat in the kitchen. My mother was absolutely distraught and prostrate. And I sat there in tears and I was saying, 'Daddy—do you have to go?' And he broke down and said, 'Yes I do'. We finished our boiled egg and we caught the tram along Riversdale Road, and we saw him off. And we didn't hear from him for three and a half years. My mother got a job at a warehouse in Flinders Lane. I was still at school and things were very unsettled because we didn't know if he was alive or dead. Singapore had been bombed and we hadn't heard anything. My mother really went through a torrid time. She said that her saving grace was when she would come up to Gen. She'd walk through that gate and the peace would just

---

[22] Barrett, *We Were There*, p. 371.

descend on her. And I came home one day and said to her that I'd like to become a Catholic—'That's all right'. Afterwards I asked her why she hadn't had to discuss it with Dad and she said that he had the foresight to say before he went back, 'She's in that atmosphere, she's going to be influenced by it and I've no objection if that's her wish'.

Her father survived the war but not for long—his heart had been fatally weakened by malnutrition.

Sadie Copeland was another who sat at home and waited. She had met her Frank on a cruise and in 1939 they became engaged, bought a block of land in North Kew and planned a three-year engagement. Then in September war broke out and Frank, who had had three years in the Royal Australian Engineers, decided that he would join the A.I.F. They discussed marriage plans: 'Supposing something happened to me, or I was missing, it wouldn't be fair if I tied you down'. 'No—I'd rather be married to you and send you off knowing you had your other half back home waiting.' They had a small wedding at the Collins Street Baptist Church:

> Then we went up to Marysville for four days. Frank was determined to be married as a civilian, so when we came home he entered the Army. They kept on saying he was officer material and they sent him to do a course at Melbourne University, and in that three weeks we had three whole weeks of a flat on our own—he coming home for his evening meal and things were just sort of normal—or fairly normal. Our baby was five months on the way by the time he was put in the 2/22 Battalion and he was sent to Rabaul. Suzanne was born in the August and the first to know was the Army officer who censored my letter. When she was five months old, the Japanese struck and all communications were cut. Sue became very sick and what had actually happened was that I was breastfeeding her and I had begun to worry—I was so amazed that all that had had such a physical effect. From then on, there was no contact. We got news of Japanese attacks, our men were outnumbered fifteen to one. It was just human sacrifice—the government knew they were just a façade, a token force. The officers decided that the best thing was to try to escape—after putting up a tremendous battle. I was quite sure that Frank would try to escape—he had a lot to live for and he wouldn't see the sense of just giving himself up. A lot of conflicting stories went on, and I just could not understand when the other men got back, why he wasn't with them. They kept on saying to me, 'Look I saw Frank—only a few days ago—he's on his way'. So I searched the Heidelberg Repatriation Hospital, asking chaps over there who'd got back, and one man told me, 'He told me he'd go back—he had a wife and child to think of and he tore up his diary'. That didn't seem to me to be like Frank—he was a battler, always; but there again, I did not know what may have motivated him. Another story was that they had a little motor boat and they were half way down the coast and they were having breakfast on the shore and the natives told the Japanese, so the Japanese sat down and had breakfast

with them. There were so many stories that I gave up believing any of them—I didn't know what to think. Two hundred out of a thousand escaped through the jungle back to Australia.

However, a very strange thing happened. In March the Japanese, in a raiding mission over Port Moresby, dropped two bags of mail from the prisoners of war and one of them was for me—and for Sue—always Sue was in it. (He'd managed, just before Christmas, to send her a tiny Chinese needle-worked blouse, and one for me too—that was the last boat that got out of Rabaul.) Eventually, after a long silence, there was a letter for me. And this was a most wonderful letter—full of courage, full of hope. It was only written in pencil, but he tried to help me to feel he was getting on very well. He said that he'd made himself comfortable with a copra bag as a hammock. There was just one part where I felt that he wasn't getting enough to eat: 'We're reasonably well fed, though I can't say we're getting fat'.

He was held in Rabaul—of course there'd been massacres. They'd massacred the whole of the Salvation Army there. There were some pretty terrible stories coming through. I felt quite certain that he was all right and that he'd come back. And also I had to be very positive because I had a little girl who'd never met him, and I wanted her to be confident that she did have a daddy. I felt that faith would be the main thing, however somebody said to me at one stage, 'It mightn't be God's will that he'll come back'. Well, I hadn't thought God would act *that* way—but however. I realized later that I would have to trust Him, whatever happened. We were allowed to write about twelve words a month, and as I heard a lady saying on the television the other night, you felt you were writing to the man in the moon, because you got no answer at all. And of course, they were gone—we didn't know. The amazing thing was—the government was paying me a living soldier's wage for three and a half years after he died, because they didn't know. They did ask some war widows to pay it back—fortunately they didn't ask me—I was just so grateful for that.

After the war finished, after Hiroshima, the news came over the air that the Japanese had admitted that they had the names of the men who were on a Japanese boat called the *Montevideo Maru* and that it had been torpedoed by an American submarine. They didn't ask any questions—as far as they could see it was just an old cargo boat. It happened on 22 June, our second wedding anniversary, that the 2/22 Battalion was lost. But one thing I'm grateful for is that he died early—he didn't have to suffer. I never ever gave up hope. I just felt so strongly—especially getting that letter. There was an experience I had at a musical concert—we used to go to concerts, Frank and I—all of a sudden there was this feeling that he was free—I could feel him very close and very free. He was not restricted any more. And I didn't know whether this meant he was free from captivity or he was free from life.

With the coming of peace it was time to rebuild—both private lives and the world.

5

The Trials of
Experience
1946–1966

The Trials of Experience
1946–1966

Perfect Homes

Neil Ewart: There was the question of reaction to the war. The recent Gulf war further highlighted apparently significant differences between the 1930s youth and the post–World War II generations, differences which leave those of my particular era bemused. Conflicts such as Korea and Vietnam, whilst sometimes brutal and always dangerous, were small-scale for Western societies in comparison with World War II—casualties were minor, tours of duty were short, back-up facilities of food, communication, medical attention, were vastly superior. Yet the resultant trauma induced in personnel, even their families, has been such that considerable debriefing, skilled counselling and visible approbation have apparently become necessary requirements to enable reasonable rehabilitation. How can it be that around 1945 some millions of boys, having endured greater hardships over much longer periods of time, went home and readjusted themselves as best they could with, I believe, no less success. I remember being demobilized in a dusty wooden-floored office at the Melbourne Cricket Ground. After four years away I hazily signed some papers in the silence and as I walked towards the door a corporal looked up from his desk, smiled and said, 'So long Sarge'. And after four years, that was it. The smile though, said it all, knew it all. That is probably why some of the boys of that time still get together in their funny clubs where, with all their differences, there is the smile that 'knows'.

I got on a tram and went home to a young wife who had her own readjustments to come to terms with, which she did with patience. I believe that we were pretty typical of the era. That corporal would probably have made a good counsellor. Attitudes to war and disaster have not changed. Reactions certainly have.[1]

---

[1] Letter to author, 8 March 1991.

Not all found the return to peace and private life as manageable as did *Neil Ewart* and his wife; and for those who had need of counselling, there wasn't much. Even the POWs received little more than physical care: 'I think the main thing they wanted', recalled Tom Beenie, 'was to get us gradually back on to decent feed and not be skinny wrecks when we came home'. Some did return to civilian life, exhausted and traumatized, only to break down once there was time and space for it. Men of all social conditions had become habituated to using alcohol to cope with stress and, while most regained control of their drinking, it sometimes lay dormant only to reappear in middle age as other stresses became intolerable.[2] The sheer volume of young human beings caught up in the dislocations of war damaged, often for ever, the local networks of neighbourhood, church and school. Those who had not been in the services often fared worse than those who had, for at least the R.S.L. and unit organizations quickly kept those who wanted it within the bonds of intimacy created by the war.[3] Tom McCaw rejoined the C.M.F. after the war: 'mainly through a shortage of friends, so I took it up again and I stayed twenty-two years'. And he was never to recover his old-school links: 'I've largely lost contact with Scotch people; and even if you meet someone in the shops or something, you find yourself groping for some common ground. I've never been drawn to Old Boy reunions'. *Ron Pearson* returned to his old job in a bank which had been reserved for him, but the world still seemed turned upside down: 'You came back to a world which was quite different because so many women had taken men's jobs that they had to adapt to that. That was one of the more difficult aspects'.

Perhaps the strangest adjustment of all was in resuming control of one's life. Even for officers, service life had provided a total world where all decisions about the spending of each day were in effect made for you from above and by the structure. Some found civilian life back home dispiriting after the excitements of service overseas.[4] Those who had been officers had to rejoin the ranks of ordinary civilians. John Blanch went from commanding an infantry battalion to being a cadet journalist: 'it was quite a step—I enjoyed it immensely. I was suddenly learning about civilian life. The chief of staff put me on all the different rounds like the Courts, the Parliament and what we called the city round, the western round and the shipping round. And you learn a lot writing about things—you've got to look up a lot of references and ask a lot of questions'. That very freedom of mind and action after the securities of life in the services could be difficult to handle, however, and some felt unsettled. Young middle-class ex-servicemen did have more choice about what they could do with their lives than their working-class comrades, but there were

---

[2] Kate Darian-Smith, *On the Home Front: Melbourne in War-time, 1939–1946*, pp. 142–4.

[3] Interviews with Walter Stone and Geoff Tolson.

[4] McCarthy, *A Last Call of Empire*, pp. 129–31.

contending needs. The Australian government was offering retraining and financial assistance for university and professional study, but many of these young men were equally anxious to get on with married life. *Richard Stanton*, after a long and arduous war, threw himself into building his career and starting a family:

> There was a very genuine attempt by the government to rehabilitate us blokes, so that straight after the war, when I went back to the office, I was determined I was going to get on and on and on. I started studying immediately under the Rehabilitation Scheme: they gave you all the written material you wanted, the books etc., and we just studied at home. I used to study every night of the week—I relaxed on Saturday night and I'd go to bed early on Sunday, but most of the weekend I'd study, and every week night. So I qualified as a Chartered Accountant in two and a half years of night study, which was phenomenal really. The benefits were that we could do the examinations every six months instead of every year. It was very onerous and my health at the end of the qualification had already started to run down.

John Barrett's survey for *We Were There* revealed that three-quarters of the respondents resumed the occupations they had had before the war, and furthermore most remained in those occupations for the rest of their working lives.[5] In their twenties, these men from Scotch College and Trinity Grammar, and the future husbands of the MLC and Genazzano women, had a similar range of occupations. Between 24 and 30 per cent were professional or semi-professional men, although, apart from the Genazzano husbands, the number in the learned professions was under 7 per cent. At the other end of the scale, the proportion in low status occupations such as trades and petty clerical and sales, ranged from 36 per cent from Trinity to 27 per cent from MLC. It was in this group that the most upward mobility could be expected in later life, for it included the office boys, junior bank and insurance officers and the young salesmen who were undergoing their unofficial apprenticeship for commercial careers.[6] But even among this sample of middle-class men, the Commonwealth Reconstruction and Training Scheme offered many the chance to change career. Just over a third of the Old Scotch Collegians undertook further study under the scheme and exactly half the ex-Trinity men did.[7] Many used the CRTS to complete or commence studies they had planned before the war, but the financial support also enabled people who had had no hope of university studies in the 1930s to obtain a tertiary education. It

---

[5] Barrett, *We Were There*, pp. 376–7.
[6] See Appendix II, table 7a.
[7] Survey: 'Did you undertake any further education under the Post-war Reconstruction Scheme?' Yes: Scotch, 36%, Trinity, 50%.

was a difficult decision and some men still debate whether they made the right choice. *David Miller* had left Trinity with only the Intermediate; demobbed after outstanding service, he now had to find a career which matched his capacities:

> It was a funny transition. I was dropped out of the sky, so to speak, on 14 September 1945 and all my cobbers were still overseas coming home, and I was in a suit. I went back to the engineering industry to a firm where no one had served in the Services other than I. Melbourne was a funny place—it was quiet, like a Sunday. There was an uncertain feeling. I remember my pay—in the Air Force I had been getting 27s 6d a day and I now got £5 2s 6d a week—life was real and earnest.
>
> I had considered taking up full-time academic studies and, rightly or wrongly, I decided not to. My reason at the time—though that might have been an excuse—was that my parents were not in a position to fund anything, and therefore I went back to part-time studies. I have regretted that ever since. I would love to have done engineering or law and commerce.
>
> I came back at twenty-one and we married in 1948 and we were immediately sent by the company to Western Australia. The years straight after the war were strange years. They were like something out of a movie of the 'thirties—like nothing moved forward.

Then suddenly he found his *métier:* 'what I call the *in*-securities industry— I just clicked with it straight away. I found it just fascinating'. It was the beginning of a marvellous career.

The C.R.T.S. enabled Alan Cohn to go to university while his brother Lawrence preferred to continue as an actuary. James Austin decided on teaching and within a couple of years found himself in the history school at the University of Melbourne, and poised to make a career in tertiary education. Jean Cane's husband took on engineering under the C.R.T.S., but Jean was not permitted to support him as a working wife, because as soon as she married she lost her job as a social worker with the Victorian Government (a position she had pioneered) and they commenced married life and parenthood in genuine poverty. War experiences had changed interests: Archie Crow had enrolled in medicine before the war; when he returned, having learnt Indonesian during his war service, he did Arts, majoring in languages. And yet time had also stood still. *Doug Gordon* remembers waiting outside the old Zo-ology lecture theatre for his first lecture in first-year Medicine in 1946. Some faces were familiar and they realized that they had waited in just that place for their first lecture six years before. They went inside and there was the same lecturer. The lecturer started, they took notes, but they need not have bothered for the lecture also was exactly the same.

Those who returned to study or to occupations which had been held for them at least had their lives defined for them over the next few years;

those who wanted to venture out on their own in business stepped out into the unknown. Ralph Coyne:

> I was demobbed from the Commandos in December 1945. During the war I had been reading, mainly through the Army news publication *Salt*. It had some stimulating articles, and I felt that there was going to be a very big opportunity to help develop export of Australian merchandise. That appealed to me and I decided to become an exporter. I found it tremendous fun—challenging, stimulating, meeting interesting people and writing to countries I'd never heard of. I had deferred pay, and the Australian Department of Trade would let anyone have inquiries they were receiving from different countries and you took it from there. And so I was exporting all kinds of things, from billiard tables to food, agricultural equipment—anything that was asked for. It was like putting your finger in a pond and seeing if a fish was going to nibble at it. Business people were warning me, saying, 'You're not adding enough profit'. And I thought, I'm making enough to live pleasantly, why be greedy? But then I met Bobbie and we fell in love and I learnt very soon that I should have heeded the advice of these more experienced people in business that I was not making enough money to marry, so I quit it.

Neil Ewart had a family business to return to and, with energy and imagination, he commenced a most successful business career, moving the family interests into new areas of investment in food and agriculture. Tom Beenie found himself invited into the family tanning firm, breaking the company's rule of only taking in relatives who had already proved themselves elsewhere. Poor John Leckie, however, returned after a nasty war to find the family business sold and the money gone:

> The war was a shattering part of my life. From the age of nineteen to twenty-six—I lost that social life and I came back and we'd lost the business. Things were totally different. I was in Heidelberg Repatriation Hospital for a short period. I think a lot of blokes had a really tough time—plenty out at Heidelberg suffered very badly. The little quiet blokes, they're pretty tough. Usually the ones with lots to say didn't do much.

Four months after he was discharged, he was in an accident and broke both legs and went straight back to hospital for a year. When he was finally a free man he was grateful to find a job as a salesman in a car business owned by a Scotch College family. Kep Henty-Wilson did get some financial help from his father to start a business, but it wasn't enough and his work history over the next twenty years was common: after a rigorous war flying Lancaster bombers, he came back without any idea of what he wanted to do. He tried a mail-order catalogue business, then after he had

married, his father lent him enough to buy a women's wear shop in
Toorak Road, South Yarra, which he managed with his wife; that is,
until she became pregnant, which 'made an entire difference to the cost
structure of the business'. He started accountancy, which he did not finish
until 1956, eleven years after the war. It was too long, but he had three
young children and it was hard, after putting in a day's work at the office,
to settle down to effective study as well as be a good husband and father.
He had to buy a house, but the amount he needed exceeded the finance
available as a War Service Loan, so he had to borrow from a bank and it
became necessary to take a second job, lecturing in Accountancy at a
commercial college. By now there were school fees to pay and his
unsettled career had limited his retirement benefits, so it was clear that he
needed to qualify for something better. He did the Chartered Secretaries
course by correspondence, attained top place in the final examinations
and in 1965 became a company secretary. He moved into senior
management: 'so I finally used to good advantage the qualifications I'd
struggled to get'.[8]

These young men were able to benefit from the expansion of the
Australian economy in the 1950s and 1960s as Australia partook of the
world-wide growth in demand.[9] And with that economic growth came
an increase in the public service as well as in administrative jobs in
business. Education emerged as a major source of employment, not only
in the schools servicing the growing families of the 1950s, but also in the
universities. Geoffrey Serle saw himself before the war obtaining perhaps
a second-class honours degree and entering the Education Department:
'one didn't dream of becoming an academic—there were just no jobs before the war'. *Albert White*, although in a reserved occupation during the
war, was one who was drawn to teaching after it. There was a twelve
months crash course and when *Albert* started his first teaching round, it
was the first time in his life that he had been inside a state primary school:
'I was taken into a grade two of forty children in a crowded room on a hot
February day, and the first thing that hit me was the smell of little children'. But he loved teaching.

The learned professions, especially the Law, had languished during
the war and the Stock Exchange had found the dislocations of the war
more damaging than even those of the Depression, but the immediate
post-war years saw a rapid growth in legal work, with traffic accidents and
workers' compensation keeping the courts busy.[10] There was a rush of
young people into Medicine and, in 1946, the Melbourne Medical

[8] Interview with Keppel Henty-Wilson, 29 October 1990.
[9] W. A. Sinclair, 'Capital Formation' in Foster, ed., *Australian Economic Development in the Twentieth Century*, pp. 12–14.
[10] F. Maxwell Bradshaw, *Selborne Chambers*, pp. 28–9; Arthur Dean, *A Multitude of Counsellors*, pp. 235–8; R. N. Hughes-Jones, *Wm Noall and Son*, pp. 58–66.

School introduced quotas for the first time: fully half of those who started that year were ex-servicemen. The university was forced by the explosion of numbers in all faculties to open a branch in Mildura and for three years all first-year medical students enjoyed the 'collegiate atmosphere' of the rural campus.[11] As the young doctors, lawyers and engineers graduated, there was no shortage of work, although few started professional life with any money behind them. The ex-servicemen among them were either in or approaching their thirties, so that further study for fellowships and postgraduate qualifications entailed a fearsome sacrifice by their wives and new families. General practice was still rich and fulfilling, offering a wide range of work from obstetrics to surgery, so that many able young medical graduates found great satisfaction working in the new suburbs as family doctors. *Doug Gordon* was one:

> I think general practice was tremendous. I enjoyed it. I was fortunate—I did a lot of surgery and I did my own obstetrics and gynaecology. I did like looking after children, not babies—couldn't stand babies—I made a paediatrician look after babies until they were six months old. But kids, yes. But if you're going to do that in general practice, you've got to live in the city and on the periphery. When I started practice in 1955 the kids were like seeds in a caraway seed cake—you had to be careful you didn't run over them every time you turned a corner.

Doug Gordon brought to the sharing of a group practice the same practicality and fairness that had made him an outstanding officer in the war:

> I was under pressure. When you're in an eight-man practice you're under pressure to perform. It was one of the few group practices to stay together and one of the oldest group practices in Australia. And the only reason it stayed together was that all down the line, from way back when it was started, people were compatible. Plus we ran it on a cash basis. At the end of the month we paid the bills or the overheads and then divided up what was left equally and so there was no 'I'm a surgeon or I'm a physician and I should get more'.
> We discussed cases over lunch. We did an unusual thing which I don't think other practices did—but we employed a cook and we sat down to lunch if possible. And that's when you had your bleats, complain about how your partner treated your patient last night.

As the servicemen returned to study and work it was clear that they were already a remarkable generation. For all those left damaged by the war, many more had been matured by the experience, had learned how to

---

[11] K. F. Russell, *The Melbourne Medical School*, pp. 172–3, 180–1.

apply themselves, to work with others as a team, to lead with good humour and to endure hardship and frustration, even boredom. Middle-class boys had acquired new manual skills and a familiarity with the practical tasks of daily living; and they had had some of their snobberies extinguished by life in the ranks. They had also, in the way that men have had to prove themselves from time immemorial, attained manhood by the facing of personal danger. There were, for all, inglorious moments they wished would depart from memory, but at least they had 'been there', had done the job required of them and had survived. In the universities around the country straight after the war, the fresh school leavers were somewhat in awe of these men who had been through so much and who were so capable; and the returned men themselves had no time to waste. When they went out into the world to earn a living, they were often driven men, desperate to catch up financially on the decade or more lost through war and study. If they were accomplished and impressive, they also grieved for their lost youth. 'I grew up a mile', says *David Miller*, 'I saw the world and had some fabulous experiences, but I didn't have a youth'.

The 1950s saw Australians engrossed in private life. It had been a long deprivation because, even before the war, the uncertainties of the Depression and the intimations of war had dampened the joys and expectations of the young. The very nature of war is to invade even the most private areas of experience, destroying people's control over their own lives, clouding their family life and sexual relationships with fear of loss and tragedy. Now, with peace, Australian people of all classes could expect a quiet security for family life such as had not been possible since the mid-1920s. For many in their late twenties and early thirties this was the beginning of their fulfilled sexual life; it had been a long wait. Betty Blay:

> Finding my sweetheart—ah, that was a romance. We were pen friends and we wrote for about three years before we met. Just before the war, I was getting a bit punch drunk. I had had a very swift romance that blew up with a boy at the office, flared up like a rocket, lots of sparks and then there was nothing left. He went off to the war and married someone else without even telling me, so I was a bit sore.
>
> By that time my war work consisted of writing letters—I had about fifteen correspondents, and I think a padre put me on to John. I wrote to him first in Darley, then to the Middle East for two years—he went through El Alamein—came back and we met for about a fortnight. Then he went up north in the middle of the fighting for eighteen months and when he came back, he was seven stone, full of malaria and dengue fever, and that was that.
>
> We lived happily ever after, because although we came from different religions (he was a Catholic), we had the same sort of attitude. We were both tolerant and we had both been through the mill. We were terribly battered when we married. We just fell on each other as if to say 'Thank God we can relax'. He'd had a hard life when he was young.

The pair of us were just exhausted. We didn't have much money but we battled along. Then I had a most fiendish menopause. I thought I was going to breeze through it, but I didn't. I think that possibly I was so tired—I hadn't had any youth. I had two little babies and I had a husband. He was working at Maribyrnong so we were up at a quarter to six each morning. We didn't have any money, we didn't have a car, we didn't have anything. And I think I was just so exhausted that it all came out.

Unlike her sons' generation, she never regretted that her long wait for marriage had enforced celibacy: 'I'm very glad I was a virgin when I got married, and I'm still glad although I can understand people who say—I'd like to live with so-and-so'. She also fulfilled her dreams of a university education, ultimately taking out an M.A. in history and, at the age of fifty, she began her career in secondary teaching.

Until the war, preparation for marriage by an engaged couple entailed two, three or more years of saving for a house before they took the final step. It was a demanding ethic for young men: that they make enough money, in a sense, to earn sexual fulfilment. A young man's ability to make the money demonstrated his fitness for marriage, a fitness which, especially in times of economic depression, was a financial rather than an emotional accomplishment. The war changed this. No longer could couples plan with confidence, no longer could they get to know each other gradually amid the routines of ordinary life. Love now entailed fear, fear of the yellow telegram that announced: 'killed in action' or 'missing'. And so many threw caution to the winds and married quickly during periods of leave, or became engaged after a whirlwind romance so that courtship and the first years of marriage were conducted by letter. One MLC woman who did so, only later to divorce, wonders now at the resilience of those wartime marriages: 'Settling down to civilian life was difficult and financially a struggle and I wonder that so many marriages lasted as long as they did'.[12] Lurline Keck remembers well the 'contagion of marriage' straight after the war:

I wasn't allowed to get married until I was twenty-one, so a week after my birthday I did. We met at the church when I was sixteen and probably drifted into getting married. We were boyfriend and girlfriend, then he went off to the war and we wrote to each other all the time. And a lot of my young friends were being married and getting engaged and it was all very romantic. We were always going to kitchen teas and weddings. Also, it was the only opportunity for sexual experience—you wouldn't die wondering, as the expression used to be. Most of those marriages have survived quite well. I have two girlhood friends whose marriages broke up after about ten years, but most of them have lasted.

[12] Survey No. 363: MLC.

The 1950s and early 1960s were a world gone mad with marriage. Of that generation of Australians only 4 per cent of women and 8 per cent of men were never to marry. And they were, in the actual starting of a family, the most fertile generation in Australian history. They were also either very chaste or very careful before marriage, because the late 1940s and early 1950s saw the lowest rate of illegitimate births and pre-nuptial conceptions for the twentieth century.[13] But for those whose husbands and lovers did not come home from the war, for those who preferred independence, for those who were homosexual and for those who simply never found the right partner, it was an alienating time, and even in suburban church communities, the single found themselves pushed to the margins of society. Unmarried people who taught in schools were often better off because the community of colleagues provided companionship, support and intellectual stimulation. The collective private life of the staff at MLC was rich and sustaining, and the presence of a compelling and inspiring male principal in the Rev. Dr A. H. Wood provided an umbrella of male clerical authority which not a few welcomed. Dorothea Cerutty fondly remembers:

> One day I blew into Dr Wood saying 'This is impossible'. Of course I expected 'With God, all things are possible' and it came. But I was so angry that I said 'Yes, that's all very well Dr Wood—you and God can say what you like, but there's the case of poor me'. And he said 'My dear Dorothea, in the face of the twofold opposition of the Almighty and myself, I don't think you really have much hope, have you'.

Unmarried academics also found themselves welcomed into the social life of married colleagues but, on the whole, single men and women had to forge their own circles of intimates and many found deep satisfaction cultivating the art of friendship. But it was an appalling time to be homosexual:

> After Trinity I went to Melbourne Grammar where I was expelled for a homosexual episode. This affected my self-confidence and has made me rather anti-social. Melbourne in the 1950s was not forgiving, and indeed in the nineties one can still be put down for a sexual preference. Life in the closet as an Anglican priest produces many tensions.[14]

For one MLC woman, among her life satisfactions in her sixties would be: 'Having the confidence to design and build three houses, and to go-it-alone in a society which in the 1950s was conservative about relationships'.[15]

---

[13] Wray Vamplew, *Australians: Historical Statistics*, Sydney, 1987, pp. 42–3, 53.
[14] Survey No. 1101: Trinity.
[15] Survey No. 339: MLC.

In those prosperous times most married early, and for Catholics this entailed a biological destiny of bearing a very large family. Not all young women were confident that they could physically and emotionally cope with six or more children. Those who were ready to marry later found the pool of available men much diminished—bachelors and widowers were rare and divorced men out of the question for Catholics. And there were those for whom peace could not abolish mourning: 'When I was eighteen I had lots of friends, both male and female, and I enjoyed many sporting activities—tennis, basketball, swimming etc. Dancing was a favourite pastime. My twenty-first was in April 1939, then a few months later the war started. The boy I would have married was later reported as "missing" in Malaysia'.[16] For Sadie Copeland, peace meant the start of life as a widow:

> I didn't know quite where to begin. I had started going back to
> Melbourne Tech. to do some further art study and I was teaching craft at
> a school. Sue was four by then. I also had to tell her and I didn't know
> how to suddenly say that Daddy wasn't coming home, but it worked out.
> We were just walking along the street together and she was talking about
> when Daddy was coming home—I mentioned it and she took it very
> well. I don't know the impact on a four-year-old, but she accepted it. By
> then my father had died and Mother was a wonderful support. She and
> Sue and I lived in the home that Mum and Dad had bought for £750
> until Mother was nearly ninety-five.

Sadie built a career as a commercial artist, working for many years in Christian Education and later illustrating children's books; but as a war widow, she was an outsider:

> I don't know why, but the Repatriation and even the people, seemed to
> regard war widows as not quite up to the normal sort of person—they
> were quick to be suspicious of us. People would say to me that they were
> amazed that I'd been faithful all those years—I couldn't help but be. But
> the Repatriation had the right to walk into a war widow's home, go
> through all her drawers, go through all her possessions. And if there'd
> been a rumour that she'd been playing around with anybody, we heard
> that they would stop the pension and could even take the children. And I
> lived in terror of this.[17]

Those who found life partners often found them in new ways. The war had enabled young people from quite different social milieus to meet, mix and marry. There were brides from Newport and Williamstown and

---

[16] Survey No. 385: MLC.

[17] The saviour of the war widows was Jessie Vasey, the widow of General Vasey, and founder of the War Widows' Guild. Sadie: 'We learnt how to weave and embroider fine linen—she really fought for us tooth and nail—she was wonderful'. See also Mavis Thorpe Clark, *No Mean Destiny*, Melbourne, 1986.

Carlton among the marriages in Scotch's Littlejohn Chapel in 1946, but more telling is the schooling of the wives and husbands of those who responded to the survey.[18] Just under a third from Scotch married women who had been to state schools only, as did 42 per cent of the Trinity men. At MLC over half married men who had only been to state schools, and the status and career patterns of the MLC husbands by the time they were in their fifties would be still a bit behind the Scotch and Trinity men. But if these middle-class women married 'down', most of their husbands would be able to realize their class expectations by middle age. With Genazzano it is more complicated: 21 per cent married men who had been to state or Protestant schools, but this does not necessarily indicate that the full 21 per cent married out of the faith, because Catholics still attended Protestant or state schools when Catholic schools were unavailable or considered academically weak.[19] Around half of the Protestant men needed to take out a War Service Home Loan, whereas the Genazzano husbands were somewhat better off.[20] Geoff McKee had started a career as a patent attorney when he built his first home:

> We went without. We never got ourselves into debt other than the mortgage and there we had a War Service Loan and that was one of the few good things that the ex-servicemen did receive—less than 4 per cent interest rate which stayed at that all the time. We had no car. I used public transport to go to the city; I had a bicycle which I used to get to the railway station for a long time. I didn't have a car until I was forty and then only because there was a family car that I could take over. Our house was begun in 1948—it took eighteen months because materials were short and they used to disappear off the block. When we moved in we still had no bath for six months because of the shortages—and an electric copper and the traditional cement troughs. We had one radio and we didn't get TV for quite a while after it arrived. And we got a washing machine in the late 1950s.

Once they had a roof over their head (and often they were camping with parents or renting a place because of the acute shortage of housing) these young couples set about the business of having babies. These were very wanted children. For Lurline Keck it was one of the reasons she got married: 'I was just longing to have a child of my own and I have derived enormous pleasure out of family life'. This was a deeply idealistic generation and they were going to do everything better than had past generations:

---

[18] Marriage books of the Rev. Alec Fraser, Scotch College Archives.
[19] Type of school attended by spouse:

	Scotch	Trinity	MLC
Church (%)	44	39	22.2
State (%)	31	42	67.8
Mix of both (%)	25	17	19.5

Genazzano: (%) Catholic 79, State 10, Protestant 11.
[20] 'Did you or your husband take out a War Service Home Loan?' Yes (%) Scotch, 55; Trinity, 54; MLC, 46; Genazzano 33.

My mother wasn't at all demonstrative—I'm sure she was fond of me, but
I have said to my brothers that I feel that they were much more
important to her than I was. And they told me that I'm wrong, but I'm
sure I'm right. I don't ever remember sitting on her knee and having a
cuddle, whereas I've always shown a lot of affection to my children and
grandchildren. I talk away to them as equals as much as possible. My
mother was very helpful with my children and she would come and stay
if I was in hospital, but she always expected me to be perfect in behaviour
and manner.

Many new wives and mothers were older and had had a long wait: Mary
Thompson was nearly thirty when she started and she wanted a big family: 'so I had to hurry. Peter was born in 1950 and Robert in 1958—five
in eight years. Peanuts!' Mary also was determined to do it differently and
better:

> One of my cousins went to the Mercy and they were very short of staff
> and it was one of those nights when all hell broke loose, and she was just
> shut in a room and left all alone. So I thought to myself 'That's not going
> to happen to me. If I can help myself I will'. So I did Grantly Dick
> Read's natural childbirth, and I'd been relaxing so much through a very
> slow labour that when Sister Fabian, who ran maternity, would come
> with a cup of tea and say 'What are you doing Mary?' I'd say 'Oh that
> was a contraction', and she'd say 'Don't be silly'.
>   Of course when I finally got going I went absolutely mad and yelled
> blue murder. A friend who was in the next room swears to this day that I
> went through hell, but it was like an Indian on the war path—it was just
> sheer exhilaration. I was so excited that the pain didn't worry me. Bill
> had nine nieces and if I'd had a girl I wouldn't have wanted to have any
> more. And I can remember—he was just coming out and I put my hand
> down and he grabbed my finger and I screamed 'It's a little boy, it's a
> little boy, it's a little boy'. I was on cloud nine for about a week. That
> really was one of the most thrilling moments of my life.

Mary Geoghegan was another devotee of Grantly Dick Read:

> You see, native women take a step off the path, squat down and have the
> baby and catch up. There is no such thing as pain in childbirth—it's *natural*,
> and it's only that people fight it and tense up. And so you went into hospital
> and the sister said 'I think you should have an injection'. 'No, no, no—I'm a
> failure.' In the end the doctor said 'You're going to have an injection' and
> you wept and cried and said 'Now see—I've failed'. And you find out later
> that with all these native women—quite a few of them die as they step into
> the bushes and the babies are stuck and they have labours of three and four
> days. That man has a lot to answer for.

There are a number of men who have a lot to answer for in the advice they peddled in the twentieth century on the bearing and raising of children. This generation was caught between two fashions of child care which were antithetical: the cold rigidities of the schedule feeders *versus* the romantic permissiveness of Dr Benjamin Spock. Those trapped by family wisdom and the cultural lag in the infant welfare centres into schedule feeding and the virtues of prolonged crying in the small baby suffered along with their wailing babies.[21] Middle-class mothers, literate and fearful of moral flabbiness, had always been more susceptible to the preachings of the reformers. Middle-class mothers sometimes tried too hard, read too many books and paid too much deference to male professional expertise. In reaction to the systematizers, the psychoanalytically-based theories of Dr Benjamin Spock offered liberation from the fears and repressions that had clouded the affective and sexual lives of the parents and grandparents of these young marrieds. Marriage and parenthood had to be made better—more loving and tolerant, joyful and free, human and just plain normal. The work of Ilg and Gesell inspired a new spirit in the care and education of the very young, a new sensitivity to the innate rhythms of childhood. Some young parents navigated these perilous waters with common sense, often because of the practical and humane advice of their doctors: Winsome Walklate's Dr Winifred Kennan said 'with a smile' that feeding the baby 'an hour either way will do'. Even more important, she told her 'to feed the baby if it cried in the night or you'll lose your milk'. One of the disastrous consequences of the male expert was the loss of the art of breastfeeding, and the boom babies were conspicuously big, fat and bottle fed. Those who did manage to breastfeed rarely got further than three months, and once second, third or fourth babies came, mothers were too tired and too constricted by the family's routines for breastfeeding to endure. Women were still shy of the intimacy of breastfeeding, but they were different from their mothers in that they did expect and want to enjoy sex. In this the world had changed a lot since World War I. Marie Stopes' *Married Love* had helped many a marriage since the 1920s and Van de Velde's *Perfect Marriage* had been published (and on the Papal Index) since 1926. If people found sex difficult to talk about, they still wanted it to be good and fulfilling, and so with the assistance of enthusiasm, patience, books and occasional wise professional advice they got there.

They were also different from their parents in that even though they were struggling to buy homes and catch up on the equity they had lost because of the war, they enjoyed the luxury of being able to have lots of children. Whereas for the Protestants between the wars the most popular family size had been two or three, there were more families with three

---

[21] Joyce Nicholson, *The Heartache of Motherhood*.

and four children in the 1950s. For the Catholics, very big families returned, with over a half of the Genazzano women having five or more.[22]
Frances Costelloe, who had been sent to board at Genazzano at the age of
six, married a Gippsland dairy farmer and had ten children:

> Oh well, we liked them. They're fairly close, I had them in sixteen years. I
> was very happy. I didn't find it burdensome, tiresome or anything like that.
> We enjoyed it and *Jack* worked hard. I lived in a house when I had the first
> two where we had porous tiles on the house and the tiles had to fill before
> we got any water—with two babies. But never mind, we got through that.
>
> At night they went to bed. They were good sleepers. When they were
> small, we had mid-day dinner—it suited *Jack* too—so those children had
> their dinner and their baths before he came in at night. They all helped
> and they all had jobs to do. Some had to collect the chips, some had to
> feed the chooks—so they were all occupied, there was no time to be
> bored. They were happy—there were no tears or grizzling. You had a
> few bullies at times and you had to put them in their place. *Jack* was very
> good—he would take them for a drive on Sunday if he had the time.
>
> I would never have liked to have had children in Melbourne—I
> suppose you had a bit of law and order in the country. There's not that
> distraction. You made the rules to suit the house and suit the family. It's
> not like this day and age where you're running them to basketball one
> night and netball another—couldn't have done that.

Nancy Naughton had nine children in the city, but hers were well spread
out: 'The last one left home only five years ago and we've been married
fifty years and I had a child within the first twelve months'. Her first five
came in six years, but then she suffered a couple of miscarriages. 'Then I
had a sixth child. I've got great faith in prayer—as we were living down in
a small place in Hampton and I earnestly prayed that we'd get a bigger
place'. They found a bigger home and then she prayed, 'Please God, if
you can get us a house, I wouldn't mind having another baby. I did and
he's now thirty-six'. Her husband, Kevin, was busy running Naughton's
Parkville hotel, but he still helped in the home and the children all had
their chores: 'For instance, I had a checklist on the back door: have you
made your bed? Cut your lunch? Whatever they needed each day'.

This was the ideal of Catholic motherhood, but not all women were
blessed with the physical stamina and not all husbands were able to help.
This generation of Catholic women was the last to have large families:
Mary Geoghegan had seven, six of them by the age of thirty. *Monica
O'Farrell* had nine pregnancies in twelve years:

> Two miscarriages, seven live babies, so I really was pregnant most of the
> time. And I used to know by the next day—I'd feel slightly off colour
> and think 'Oh No—I can't be pregnant again. I look now at myself and

---

[22] See Appendix II, table 9: Family sizes over three generations.

I'm amazed. When I see a pregnant girl I think, Oh you poor darling—I hope you can manage. I don't know how I did it. I'd finished having those children by the age of thirty-two. I was very fit and athletic—I'm carrying more weight now than when I went into the labour ward to have my sixth child.

It was their Church's ideal of Catholic family life which marked them as different. *Marjorie O'Donoghue* can remember thinking of Protestant friends who could do things not allowed Catholics: 'We can't do the things that they can because of our upbringing and standards—but that probably was the only time that I ever noticed a *burden*. But I think the comfort [of faith] has far outweighed that'.

Joyce Thorpe in later life wrote an angry book about the heartache of motherhood in her generation, for which she attracted both criticism and gratitude. She loves her children dearly, but has had the courage to admit that she could only cope with two instead of the four that post-war fashion dictated.[23] Being a middle-class mother involved rather more than being a loving and nurturing parent: it demanded a complex performance of housekeeping, educating, transporting, and entertaining. And the more successful the father of the house, the more demanding became the mother's role. Those who lived quiet lives in the suburbs, whose social life revolved around the church, who did not own beach houses, whose children walked to the local state or parish primary school and played in the street after school—these were less pressured families. Yet out in the new streets of North Balwyn it mattered to be able to send your children to a private school because if you could not, that constituted a loss of caste. The new suburbs were somewhat democratic. Next door there might be working people, tradesmen, people who had been born in suburbs like Richmond and Collingwood. The state schools of suburbs like Box Hill and the growing Blackburn had working-class children and middle-class children all mixed in. Only at grade six would their different destinies become apparent: the workers going off to the technical school, the lower middle class enrolling in the new high schools, the future middle class entering private schools for their secondary years. Within this Survey generation, less than a third of the Protestants were able to send their children to a church school for their entire education.[24] And it is this

---

[23] Nicholson, *The Heartache of Motherhood*, p. 32.
[24] 'Did you send your children to a church school?'

	Scotch	Trinity	MLC
No (%)	16	27	15
Secondary only (%)	54	46	49
All through (%)	30	26	31
N/A (%)	0	1	5

'Did you send your children to a Catholic school?' Genazzano (%): No, 7; secondary only, 11; all through, 82.

vital third which marks off the upper middle class. Even though school fees were comparatively modest in the 1950s, it still meant that a man had to generate a lot of income very quickly after getting married and starting a family. And that financial imperative translated into long hours at work and little time at home. Of course many hardworking fathers did all they could: *Marjorie O'Donoghue* and her husband divided the comforting of night-waking children between them: he would get up to the older children and she would see to the baby. (And if she slept on her good ear, she wouldn't hear the baby either and her husband would get up.) Some of the young professional men could afford to pay for domestic assistance for their wives, but many more were struggling to keep up, and there was no extra cash. The middle-class patriarch's burden remained: the family's income and control over its destiny depended on his ability to bring in the money. If he failed, then they all failed. It was stressful and unrelenting and it was predicated on a strict division of roles. Joyce Thorpe: 'If you study the private lives of our great achievers in work or sport, you will find, particularly with sport, that it almost always involves long absences from home and to the woman is left the sole task of rearing the children. It is not only a very lonely task, but also a very worrying one and, when things go wrong, the woman not only blames herself, but is blamed by society'.[25] The men too, had their needs. Their working hours were long and they wanted more from marriage than a bed and bills, but their wives were often exhausted, even depressed: 'There was an awful lot of guilt— that you had to be good wives and good mothers', confesses one. 'I remember a solicitor who was married to one, saying to me once, "Genazzano girls—they make magnificent mothers and rotten wives". I don't know—we *tried*'. Winsome Walklate's mother had educated her daughters in the arts of marriage: 'Mother said, "A soft answer turneth away wrath" and my father adored her. And she had perfect freedom and so do I'. And Winsome still feels for men, working their lives away for their families: 'They've worked so hard. And I often think when I hear the traffic going by on Doncaster Road—I think of all those people, mostly men, going off to earn their living. And when they're coming home, I pray for them and I pray that their wives have a nice dinner for them, because I think they deserve it'.

Most people were too busy to notice, but in some households tensions were building. All kinds and conditions of men and women were being forced into identical moulds. Women wanted their children, but some found early motherhood isolating and suffocating. A woman doctor from MLC admitted: 'I had several years of feeling isolated and unsupported as a "100 per cent mum" when my five children were small and our then home was in an area without kindergartens etc. I would not have

---

[25] Nicholson, *The Heartache of Motherhood*, p. 42.

expected this at the age of eighteen. Sadly, I did not enjoy my children's growing years as much as I would have liked'.[26] But while the children were small, it was also still a time of innocence, and the young parents fully expected their children to enter adolescence and adulthood with the values and expectations they were teaching them. There was so much to do in the meantime and, caught up in the rush to provide and to remake the world, life flashed past too quickly. *Neil Ewart*:

> I tried to be a more democratic parent and would have liked to have been very much more so. I don't know how common this would be, but I very much admire the parents of today—my daughters' generation. Looking back, I thought I was being a great parent. We stampeded after the war, with all the change that was taking place.
> We were conscious that we'd broken clear of the Victorian generation and that was gone and would never return. And it was an open book, as far as our kids were concerned, to show them what life *should* be about. Our kids were all going to have the greatest education—we were really going to boom ahead and we went crazy for it. I suppose I always worked seventy to eighty hours a week—for donkey's years—which meant you sacrificed your family. Then your business: I travelled a lot and was away from home—a lot of things I regret, because looking back I could have been a much better parent.

Winsome Walklate would also one day have regrets, not about her own children, but about her generation as parents:

> It was always feeding the baby and if the baby cried, you fed it, and if the baby was uncomfortable, you made it comfortable—at some cost to yourself sometimes. But everything was done to please the baby—you sacrificed to educate them, and honestly I think we indulged them.
>   We did it because it was after the war and we wanted to give them the very best. Europe had been through tremendous hardship, and it's difficult to imagine what it's like when everybody's in uniform and the whole world's gone mad—they're all killing each other. And when peace came, you aimed to please your children. That was one reason. And the other reason was that we wanted to make a good new generation. That to me was one of the biggest changes and we did it ourselves.

Perfect Worlds

The century was not yet half over and already there had been a world war 'to end all wars' and a collapse of the global economy which had brought another. If young parents were determined to 'make a good new genera-

---

[26] Survey No. 310: MLC.

tion', many people on the threshold of their civilian careers were dedicated to making a better, safer world. The hope for a safer world was widely shared, but the form that better world should take was bitterly contested. And the conflict between those contending visions quickly plunged the world into danger again, and poisoned the political and intellectual life of Australia for the next four decades. The battle was between those who wanted to restore the securities and habits of the past, and those, who, with all the rational clarity of the young and unencumbered, wanted to change the world utterly.

For the most militant, it all seemed plain enough in the closing months of 1945. Around 23 000 Australians had by then placed their hopes in revolution and joined the Australian Communist Party. The world was in tatters and the historical moment had come for capitalism and imperialism to be brought down by their internal contradictions. And so while the Australian people sank into relief that peace had come at last, senior cadres within the Communist Party saw a glimmer of hope that the laws of history were at last taking effect. Little was known of life and politics within the Soviet Union, and many of the books from the Left Book Club which reported on the great experiment were silent on secret police and spy trials. Instead they showed how the Soviet people were remaking their world and remaking history, and guiding them were intellectuals and artists who under Communism were properly recognized for their usefulness to society. Marxism, as an intellectual system was deeply satisfying both in its completeness and in its capacity to reduce social analysis to cast-iron principles. For earnest young people raised on Bible study, it provided dense texts whose wisdom could be extracted under the guidance of teachers in a Marx School. It even held many of its meetings and activities on Sundays, a conflict of interests that deterred an idealistic *Betty Thomas* from joining while still a school girl at MLC. Betty Barnett had been 'terribly religious' until the age of eighteen, when: 'I read a book which had been given to father called *Red Bread*. I still have it, I love it so much, written by a Russian-born American who went back to Russia—Maurice Hindus—and that made me a complete Communist. I joined in 1939 and my first child was born in 1941 and I resigned within a month because I couldn't do what the Party demanded of me. But my husband stayed on as a Party member until Hungary, when he resigned'. Her sister June joined while she was an officer in the Air Force, and Ken Tolhurst was one of many in the armed forces who decided that but for the Russians, the war would have been lost. Twenty million men, women and children of the Soviet Union had given their lives in the war, and their heroism and endurance had awed the rest of the world. For a generation that had known only depression and war, Marxism provided both explanations and solutions. It provided a plan for living, not just for society but also for the party member. It gave many the radiance and utter conviction of religious faith, and it seductively offered intellectuals and artists influence and esteem. There was a purity of purpose for those who craved action, and it offered action immediately, the chance to make history. Above all, it spoke to people of high moral purpose, desperate to see an end to poverty, ignorance and war.

Ken Tolhurst joined the Communist Party just before he left the army in 1945. He became a 'floating member', directed to work under cover among ex-servicemen. He joined the R.S.L. and was soon elected to the Caulfield District Board: 'and then I got terribly pissed off with it and I just couldn't stand it, even as a loyal comrade'. He devoted himself to work within the university and became editor of the student paper *Farrago* for a year, then in 1948, with his wife Moira, he went as the Australian delegate from the National Union of Students to the International Union of Students in Prague. They stayed two years and he was directed to establish the Press and Information Department of the I.U.S. He travelled all over Europe, including the Eastern states; he was in Italy during the agricultural labourers' strike and 'that was very frightening'; his bureau was the first to receive reliable news of the Vietnamese insurrection against the French, 'brought by two boys who walked from Vietnam'; and in Prague he worked daily with the Russians:

> I would never accept the attempts by the Soviet comrades to run the place, and I was the only comrade there that took that attitude. We had a very fine young man who was in my department called Yuri Mamriken—he was the Russian editor. He spoke English as well as us— we used to discuss Shakespeare and Galsworthy. He was the sort of person that Lenin would have said of: 'that is what I want for the future'. Of the others, there were one or two real fleas and one or two real bastards, but by and large they were good young men. They'd had a bad time during the war—Yuri had fought at Leningrad.

Now inside the Communist system, he could see for himself what was really going on: 'a lot of very bad things began to happen':

> Yuri started to go around playing commissars with my staff and I pulled him up one day and said, 'Yuri, you are not to do that. You are not to play commissars in this department. I am running this department and if you want to do that sort of thing, we will have everyone here and discuss it. We'll do it democratically, but we'll not have a Russian comrade go through and do what you're doing'.
> And he said, 'Do you not trust me?'
> 'Yes, I do trust you, but I want to remind you of something—to remind you of Comrade Malinowski'. (He was a Tzarist spy, one of Lenin's most trusted people.)

Yuri went off his brain: 'You can't say that'.

'I've said it and that's the way it is. I will trust people according to how they behave and what they do'.

I had no further difficulties with them and this seemed to change their whole attitude to me. I was no longer regarded as somebody who could be pushed around.

It was a quite terrible business. I began to understand exactly what I was involved in. I was in Hungary and Bulgaria between August and October 1949, and in Hungary I was in charge of all media for the World University Games and suffered repeated midnight arrests of my Hungarian staff. Then in Sofia the Jugoslav delegates to the I.U.S. Council were arrested and deported after iron-clad assurances that this would not happen. By the end of 1949 I was quite convinced that this was no place for me and I had the problem of extricating myself—which is never easy—because by this time I knew too much. I was privy to real secrets.

With the assistance of the British National Union of Students he got away safely, and returned to finish his Commerce degree at the University of Melbourne. On completion he went into private enterprise, having decided that this phase of his life should be devoted to his growing family. He has had a highly successful career in market research and consultancy. As for politics:

I was mentally out of the Communist Party before 1952 and completely out by 1953. I just withdrew steadily and carefully because I knew what sort of things they'd do. It's legendary what they did to Ian Turner—they put around stories that he was homosexual. But my biggest worry was that the party would 'out' me with my employers and I had a family to protect.

That phase of my life I'm still quite proud of—I'm proud of what I did. I had ideals and I had ideas and I did my best to carry them out. The fact that it didn't work is another question. In fact I haven't really changed what I think—that remains very much with me. I'm not sure that socialism's failed yet—that's just a version of it. I've worked ever since for world peace.

Young radical Christians also were fired with a moral passion that was alarming to many of their fellow parishoners. *Amelia Friend*'s Labor sympathies were part of her changed vision of the modern church in the world:

I'd gone to Europe in 1937 with my parents. They stayed six months and I stayed for two years. I taught for a year in a wealthy school, then I worked in the slums of London for a year. Each summer I went to international conferences—the World Student Christian Federation and I was one of the four Australian delegates to the W.S.C.F. General Committee. I also went to the first World Conference of Christian Youth, just six weeks before war broke out. That changed our lives; it was the most marvellous ecumenical experience and I became an *Ecumaniac* and have remained so ever since.

She was changed and the government of her native country also perceived her as changed:

When I came back from Europe, war had been declared and I joined the staff of the Melbourne Y.W.C.A. Some months went by, and then the executive director said one Friday afternoon, 'Could you be in on Monday at 11 o'clock because someone is coming to see you'. 'Who?' 'I haven't time to tell you now, but come in at half past 10 and I'll tell you all about it'.

So I went in and she said, 'There's a detective coming to talk to you'. 'What for?'

She said, 'Well—I don't want you to be worried about this because we're standing behind you, but someone has reported that you are a Communist'.

So the first question he asked me was: 'Is it true that you won't sing *God Save the King?*'

'No', I said; 'but I sing it as a prayer not as a jingo'.

I just couldn't believe this. It was 1940.

For *Betty Thomas*, still at school during the war, there was no question that she was learning her socialism from her geography teacher at MLC, from the Sunday School lessons of Girlie Leigh in the South Camberwell Methodist Church and from the Bible classes run by the Rev. Cliff Wright: 'we were going to save the world through Christian socialism, we were going to re-create Heaven on earth, even though now you might laugh and say what a hopeless lot that was, but the Communist Party was born in Scotch and Wesley as much as in the techs'.

If changing your political beliefs and disagreeing with your elders is common and unremarkable for the young today, for the young men and women of the 1930s and 1940s it was a new and often painful process. Fewer than 16 per cent of the Survey men and women reported that they had rebelled against their parents' political beliefs, and the proportion who had rebelled against their parents' religion was even smaller.[1] With Geoffrey Serle it was not so much a rebellion against his parents, as a breaking free of the middle-class mind-set:

---

[1] 'Did you rebel against your parents' political beliefs?' Yes: Scotch, 13%; Trinity, 14%; MLC, 15%; Genazzano, 13%. 'Did you rebel against your parents' religious beliefs?' Yes: Scotch, 8%; Trinity, 11%; MLC, 9%; Genazzano, 5%.

The extraordinary thing in the end was how much it took to break my mould. I think I was fairly incurious, had a fairly closed mind. Indeed in my last years at Scotch, I was not prominent among the more adventurous senior officers of the school who were trying to initiate reform. Just as I think that my academic qualities were having a retentive memory and being good at figures, rather than beginning to play with ideas in any sense—and that was enough to give you a pretty good academic performance. And Steve Yarnold and the influence he had on us and the group around him—I'm sure I was dragged along. But the net influence of Steve and Clayton on opening up your mind—they were hammering away for years and it didn't have much impact on me for some time after.

But I went into the army and suddenly it was all there. And of course one craved to read, to get the privacy to read, and one craved like minds to talk to. And within no time at all I was a socialist of a sort. An evangelical tract which captured me was by Sir Richard Acland—a founder of the Commonwealth movement which stood socialist candidates at English by-elections late in the war. Just as later on, after the war, I still had vestiges of a Christian approach. With Arthur Burns, my room-mate in Ormond, I used to see a lot of the Rev. Professor Hector Maclean—a great old man of a Christian Socialist kind. I began to read Harold Laski and in first year had read Tawney's *Religion and the Rise of Capitalism*—that *great* book, whose prose had such a striking effect on us. Tawney meant more to me than anyone else; and I fell under the slightly not so respectable sway of Laski and his voluminous writings. And I read some of the Marxist stuff. But I'm on record in my letters home in 1943 making a pretty reputable statement of why I would never join the Communist Party. This is a pretty standard happening among my generation.

There was another intellectual journey that went side by side with the move to the left—the discovery of being Australian:

At the same time I got completely engrossed in the problem of being an Australian. I think the war and Australia's part in it—what we were doing wherever we were—just forced our minds on the whole nature of the country and its place in the empire. And the great revelation for which I was fully ripe was reading Hartley Grattan's *Introducing Australia* in 1942. I've put into print that great moment when Stephen Murray-Smith and I ran into each other at Port Moresby—we spent twenty-four hours talking to each other flat out, and I lent him *Introducing Australia* and said, 'You must read this—pity it had to be written by a Yank'.

After being seriously wounded in New Guinea, Geoff spent eight months in hospital, eight months in which he read 'practically the whole corpus of Australian history, such as it was', Australian fiction and a bit of poetry. It was the beginning of a personal exploration which was to make him one of our most distinguished historians.

The fascinating dilemma of the Melbourne middle-class left of the 1950s and 1960s was how middle-class and Protestant and private-school it remained. There were still too few among the intelligentsia who had working-class origins (although Commonwealth and State Education Department scholarships were beginning to open the university doors for state schoolers and more Catholics). However well-intentioned, middle-class intellectuals found it somewhat difficult to engage with urban working-class Australians—just as had the inventors of the Australian Legend of the 1890s (as Graeme Davison has so amply demonstrated); and as had C. E. W. Bean in locating the cradle of the Anzac Tradition in the bush school not the urban slums.[2] The missionary and charity model bedevilled the British and Australian left, because working-class people did not want to be saved: they wanted secure jobs with decent pay and to be left alone to manage their own affairs.[3] Many left intellectuals could not in conscience join the Labor Party, for party membership implied endorsement of the White Australia Policy. And disappointed in the reluctance of Liberal governments to reform state education, the middle-class left enrolled their own children in their old private schools. But there were other sources of alienation. For all the peacefulness of life in the suburbs, as the ex-servicemen got down to the serious business of 'making a good new generation' and the Australian economy began to blossom, the public and religious life of the 1950s and 1960s was full of hate. And the catalyst of all that hate was Communism.

No sooner had the war ended than the ideological cold war began. Many in the free world, who had wanted very badly to believe in the Soviet Union, had to come to terms with the agonizing realization that its brutalities matched those of Nazi Germany. The cold war was also a propaganda war, so it was possible to deceive oneself that the 'bad things' being reported of Stalinist repression were all lies. This was one manifestation of the tyranny of distance, perhaps, that the left was able to deceive itself for longer than could its comrades in the United Kingdom. But as the Communist Party faltered and the disillusioned resigned in their thousands after 1948, the non-Communist left settled into centre stage; except that many, who had always seen the dangers of fanatical Communism, found themselves tarred with the same brush by the conservative majority and the security forces. Blameless scholars knew that ASIO had a file on them; others, guilty of youthful Marxist indiscretions, feared being exposed and losing their jobs. The middle-class left intelligentsia began re-thinking a social democratic programme for a new Australia and, with that, a critique of suburban culture; at the same time they

---

[2] Graeme Davison, 'Sydney and the Bush: an Urban Context for the Australian Legend', *Australian Historical Studies*, no. 71, October 1978.

[3] See McCalman, *Struggletown*.

could not help feeling embattled and marginalized.[4] The universities became a refuge, even though savage conflicts erupted there between left and right, especially between lapsed Protestant left and devout Catholic right: for while Australian society became ever more secular, sectarianism remained as pervasive as ever. Geoffrey Serle:

> Our hearts were in the right place, but it's shameful to look back now to when I was an undergraduate and see how narrow the influences on us were and how unchallenged. Ours became the orthodox, dominant, intellectual viewpoint. We were so bigoted: we couldn't have anything to do with Catholics who thought themselves good Labor people. Or some of us wouldn't—I don't think I was particularly guilty of that.

The difficult thing for the Left to empathize with was that the Catholic Church's opposition to Communism was religious more than political. (This was not exclusive to Catholics: Winsome Walklate's opposition to Communism has always been that it is 'against religion'.) Communism was materialist, it was an enemy of the Church, it persecuted, tortured and murdered priests, it reviled religion as an opiate: 'Now away with all your superstitions/Servile masses arise, arise'. Catholic social thought, however, was not necessarily anti-socialist and, in the Catholic Rural Movement, celebrated a romantic Catholic communalism; and within the Australian Labor Party, Catholics were comfortable with the 'socialization objective'—the project of 'civilizing capitalism'. On the other hand, their church forbade collaboration with Communists and refused known Communists admission to the sacraments.[5] Catholics as a community wanted state aid for their schools and certain Catholics had come to the realization that the 'White Australia' Policy was deeply offensive. The savage conflict within the Labor Movement which culminated in the Split of 1955 and the founding of the Democratic Labor Party had little to do with the middle-class Catholic world of Genazzano, but they were none the less drawn—often unwillingly—into the political and sectarian turbulence of the 1950s.

It was an exciting and challenging time to be a Catholic. In many ways young Catholics were even more caught up in the great yearning for idealism engendered by the Depression and the war; and the crusade against Communism was represented as a life-and-death struggle, every bit as vital as the world war itself had been. It was also an exciting time intellectually to be a Catholic, and for those who were fortunate enough to go to university, the Newman Society, under the guidance of the

---

[4] Alan Gilbert, 'The Roots of Australian Anti-Suburbanism' in S. L. Goldberg and F. B. Smith, eds, *Australian Cultural History*, pp. 33–49.

[5] B. A. Santamaria, *Against the Tide*, pp. 219–20.

Jesuits, wove the young Catholic men and women into a self-contained spiritual and intellectual community. By the end of the 1950s there had appeared for the first time a highly educated laity, trained in critical thinking and, as Father Roger Pryke observed in 1959, these young Catholic intellectuals had their own ideas to contribute as the Church faced the post-war challenges of its role in industry and politics, education, immigration and liturgical reform.[6] The Catholic Church was wary of the secular university and the dangers it posed to the faith and chastity of its young; and it was a fear not without foundation. The university was still a very Protestant institution, disdainful of superstition and romantic piety. Behind their backs Catholics were pitied for 'believing all that mumbo jumbo' and allowing themselves to be 'brainwashed'. Teachers and other students were often quick to assume that Catholics came to the university ill-prepared for independent thought and in urgent need of demystification; and one internal investigation singled out their religion and alleged high incidence of neuroticism in the analysis of academic failure rates.[7] *Mary Geoghegan* was a gifted student, but she almost failed her first year:

> It was a very difficult transition. We really had been spoon-fed and we learnt great hunks of *Paradise Lost* and stacks of Shakespeare. We were really *told* almost what the preferred reaction you should have to a certain thing, whereas now they ask you. So that was all given to you, whereas the girls from PLC had actually gone to the Public Library and studied on their own. And I *just* got through first year and I got such a shock that I did an honours course after that and I worked hard.

For *Marina Graham* the late 1940s and early 1950s were 'great days' at Melbourne University and she remembers with gratitude Professors Ian Maxwell, Boyce Gibson and Joseph Burke; and among the younger men Max Charlesworth and Vin Buckley. Even so . . .

> We were still a very conservative lot. Father Jeremiah Murphy apparently used to remonstrate with Prof. Maxwell and say—look, be gentle with our little girls coming from the convents and don't give them all those racy eighteenth-century novels. That was actually our introduction to sex education, come to think of it, having to read *Moll Flanders* and *Tom Jones*.

But the intellectual ferment of the Campion Society and the Newman Society was really for men only—women were welcome but merely as handmaidens; and much of the real intellectual excitement was found in passionate arguments in pubs. 'It was a very male thing', recalls *Elinor*

---

[6] Quoted in Campion, *Rockchoppers*, p. 170.
[7] H. H. Hohne, "Success and Failure in Scientific Faculties of the University of Melbourne', pp. 110–13.

Doyle. 'Let's all go down to Naughtons or Jimmy Watson's—and girls didn't go to pubs in my time; you just weren't asked and you did feel left out.' There was plenty of work for women to do, especially in the Industrial Groups which were fighting Communism within the trade unions, but women were rarely seen or heard or read as intellectual leaders.

At the university the Catholic societies were spiritual communities as well, and the maturation of one's faith was nourished and enriched by the life of the society. The Newman Society said the Rosary every afternoon at five past one in a classroom in the Old Arts building, and although she sometimes wished that they would cancel it, *Marina Graham* always went, 'and I can honestly say that I didn't have any ulterior motives because some of them did go along to meet their current fancy, but I can remember doing it because I was that sort of person—I had a lot of religious scruples and I felt I should do it'. For *Marina*, her faith was strengthened at university:

> A lot of people predicted it wouldn't be, but it was and it became then on a more intellectual level. We moved out of the rather childish world of pious customs and special devotions and all that sort of thing. And I began to find elements of my religion in Fine Arts and in literature.

There was no question that the Catholic Church expected its university representatives to remain apart from the rest of the world. 'Because of the training at school, we were almost programmed to seek out Catholic friends and that was a great limitation', remembers *Elinor Doyle*. She might have a cup of coffee with other students, but then retreated to her 'own safe, known group':

> I don't really think that I made non-Catholic friends until I went to the A.N.U. in the early 1960s. I had a few accidentally, I suppose—there was one who strayed into the Catholic group—but it really was an exciting event to meet somebody who'd *not* gone to Xavier or St Pat's. And I felt a bit unconfident with them—not exactly that there was any hostility, but that they wouldn't really want to mix with Catholics.
> There had been vague plans of my going to Oxford, then my father died just after I did Finals—but if I'd gone then, I guess it would have been quite different. As it was, my university friends were nearly all people I'd gone to school with, or my brothers had been to school with, or who lived nearby. I had a very sheltered, limited life, and looking back I think my time at Melbourne University was rather wasted—at least it could have been a lot better if I hadn't felt that the Newman Society was the only place to be. (And I wasn't crazy about the Newman Society either.)

In the world of Genazzano, political choices and beliefs had as much to do with class as they had with religion. Upward social mobility had weakened the sentimental attachment to Ireland and the Catholic politics of rebellion: asked in 1990 about their reaction to the historic closeness between the Catholic community and the Labor Party, only 7.5 per cent replied that it was one of pride, 28 per cent that it was one of irritation, and the remainder felt only 'indifference'.[8] (One Labor voter replied that her reactions over the years had been 'all three'.)[9] Eighty-five per cent have an Irish heritage, but only half of these reported that it is of importance to them; whereas almost three-quarters of those with a European heritage still treasure it.   In one Genazzano family their voting history encapsulates the changes through generations and the impact of upward mobility and education:

> I think my mother's family were always Labor supporters, being the Irish policeman and all that sort of thing. My mother, who went to Genazzano, never voted Labor—she always voted Liberal. My sister, brother and I all vote Liberal—no DLP support at all. And my daughters—both of whom are in the professions—have voted Australian Democrat, Labor and Liberal.

The explosion of Catholic politics in the 1950s came as something of an intrusion into the established Catholic middle and upper class, and quite a number who felt obliged to vote DLP out of loyalty to the Church were in fact Liberal voters. *Frances Costelloe*'s dairy-farmer husband was deeply interested in politics and history; and there was an important personal connection with Genazzano: 'We followed the Split because Bob Santamaria's wife went to school with us and she was a friend of the family and we were naturally interested. A terrible time for her, I would think'. It was the Country Party in 'Black Jack McEwen's' day which 'used to be good': and *Frances* admired Henry Bolte: 'Who wouldn't eh? He was honest. There are some good Labor people, but you've got to be very careful. Chifley—he worked hard, he was a good man. And Menzies was good in his day'. Thus it was Curtin and Chifley, Bolte and, above all, Menzies who were the most admired among the political leaders of the 1940s and 1950s. Seventy-nine per cent of the Genazzano women admired Menzies and merely 44 per cent Bob Santamaria; Menzies even did better than Archbishop Mannix on 61 per cent.[10] Margaret Mary Martin represented an important strand in the middle-class DLP constituency:

> I was born in 1932, the third and last child of an Irish father and a mother descended from Irish immigrants (or convicts). My father was always anti-English, pro-Irish, pro-Labor and pro-education. [He was a senior

---

'What has been your reaction over the years to the historic closeness between the Catholic community and the Labor Party?' Indifference: 52.5%; Irritation, 28%; Pride, 7.5%; N/A, 11%.

Survey No. 38: Genazzano.

[10] See Appendix II, table 12.

Commonwealth public servant.] My two older brothers went to St John's primary school in Hawthorn and then to the Jesuit St Patrick's College in East Melbourne. (We lived in a Jesuit parish, Immaculate Conception.) I went to the Brigidine School Lyndale (now Kilmaire) from Preparatory to year eight, but because I did well at school and because it was considered a better school educationally and socially, I was transferred to Genazzano for my last four years of schooling. I felt inferior there at first, particularly so-cially, but this feeling I received from my fellow pupils, not the nuns or teachers.

My family were always Labor voters but anti-Communist, but at univer-sity I joined the DLP, although there was some slight conflict between the Newman Society, whose chaplain was Father Golden SJ, and the Santamaria-led faction. I had an uncle by marriage, also of Irish descent, who was a state Labor M.P. and I had many heated and acrimonious argu-ments with him about politics and religion. I felt that he should have 'crossed the floor' in the debate, but he said it was better to 'stay in the La-bor party and change it from within'. My husband, who was also educated at St Pat's East Melbourne, and I were both DLP voters and subscribers to *News Weekly*. We both did International Relations at Melbourne University, where the lecturer, Professor Macmahon Ball was considered pink, but we balanced this by being in discussion groups or go-ing to talks organized by the Jesuit Institute of Social Order in Kew.[11]

There was both in the DLP and the Catholic left (represented by the *Catholic Worker*) a powerful idealism that was driven by a vision of a better world; and there was agreement too that a better world was one which was shaped by Christian principles. They were opposed, however, as to the means of achieving that better world and on the reality of the Com-munist threat. The whole Catholic Action movement since the 1930s had offered the laity the chance to do God's work in the world and there were many sensitive young men and women who were aflame with a political missionary zeal. By the 1950s the accumulated work of the Young Christian Workers Associations, the Campion and Newman Societies, the Industrial Groups and the Movement had produced a generation of young zealots, particularly among the men. With prosperity there came a new romanticization of traditional Catholic family life, and one group, under the leadership of an inspiring Melbourne solicitor, Ray Triado, conducted an experiment in Christian community living at Whitlands, near Wangaratta. *Marjorie O'Donoghue*:

It was an idealistic community, not a religious community, though it was pretty close to it. They were married couples on the whole and they went away to live a purely spiritual and Catholic life. They were a separate thing from the Catholic Rural Movement—they were an

---

[11] Letter to author, 28 October 1990.

idealistic group who turned their back on the world and thought they could make a go of it together. And I think it all worked out quite well until they got their children up to education times and they found that they couldn't live away from the world and give their children all that they were entitled to.

Pauline Grutzner spent time at Whitlands before she came to the realization that the community seemed to negate a good deal of what was important to her. At the time, it appeared 'authoritarian, anti-humanist and false in the sense that they lived poorly at other people's expense'. Later she became a missionary nun.[12] Another spiritual movement which attracted young women from Genazzano was The Grail, a lay religious group which gave women the chance to deepen their religious life. They took vows and were required to leave on marriage, and their activities in Melbourne were centred on the historic Hawthorn house Tay Creggan which had been given to them by Archbishop Mannix.[13] Critics found the ladies of the Grail somewhat precious and the movement dematerialized after Vatican II. Young men could be just as idealistic, such as those who spoke on street corners for Catholic Evidence: 'they were well-educated, they knew what they were talking about—full of faith and so on', remembers *Helen Browne*. And it was in this atmosphere of vivid Catholic lay witness that the middle-class Catholic birth-rate rose so dramatically in the 1950s, often at the insistence of zealous young husbands who glowed with pride at Mass at their perpetually pregnant wives and crocodiles of children. Appearances were sometimes deceiving, for not all such Catholic marriages were joyful: if for some it was an exhilarating time to be a Catholic, for others, especially women, it was becoming very difficult. And the Church, in drawing the laity into its active leadership, however much that was meant to be under the leadership of religious, was at the same time fostering a laity which was capable of thinking for itself. If Catholic Action invigorated the Church, it also opened the floodgates of individual conscience.

As ever, those drawn out of their daily lives to become involved in politics and religious activism were a minority. Judging by their reading of the Catholic press since the 1930s, just 20 per cent of the Genazzano women read *News Weekly* and a tiny 4 per cent the Left's *Catholic Worker*.[14] Overall only 30 per cent of the Genazzano women ever became involved in some branch of Catholic Action, few of them for long.[15]

---

[12] Letter to author, 7 December, 1992.

[13] See Sally Kennedy, *Faith and Feminism, Catholic Women's Struggles for Self-Expression*, pp. 164–9.

[14] 'Which, if any, of the following publications have come into your home regualarly at various stages in your life?' None 27%, *The Advocate* only 52%, *Advocate* and *News Weekly* 11%, *News Weekly* only 6%, *Catholic Worker* and *Advocate* 1.7%, All three 3%.

[15] Survey: 'Have you ever been a member of a Catholic Action group?' Yes, 30%; No, 67.5%; N/A, 2.5%.

Neither was Catholic political activism monolithic. Catholic critics of the DLP and the Movement discerned a cabalistic deviousness that revealed them both to have much in common psychologically with the Communist Party: here too was a glowing mission to save the world; here too was a ruthless enemy; here, too, the rules could be bent because the end justified the means. *Monica O'Farrell* had come under the influence of the Catholic Left from a family friend and kept her own counsel on how she voted: 'The Church had no right to direct people's votes'. If the middle class as a whole felt somewhat remote from the Split, it still set alight a Catholic institution like St Vincent's Hospital: *Maeve O'Hara* remembers 'everyone talking about it' and nearly all were DLP. As for the reaction among her Genazzano friends: 'a lot of people after the crisis said they'd never vote Labor again and voted Liberal'. There were unswerving Labor voters in the Genazzano world: Nancy Naughton's father was a Melbourne City Councillor and a strong Labor man, and to her the DLP were 'splitters':

> His allegiance to the Labor Party was founded on his feelings for 'brother man'. He said that his attitudes were formed on the fact that he was 'friend, philosopher and guide' to so many of his customers. The 'haves and have-nots' were so often quite obvious. And being opposite Melbourne University made him very aware of the privileged and of others, eager to improve their future. Another belief of his was that Australia was a wonderful country and that legitimate tax was a fair and just contribution to live in such a land. I've been deeply influenced by these attitudes of my father's.

And Sister Pauline Grutzner has been a socialist all her life, without finding a political party which coincided with her particular beliefs. The foundation of her socialism was laid by the nuns at Genazzano: 'in the course of classes on Catholic social teaching given by Father Denis Murphy who was the parish priest at Deepdene, in the history lessons of Mother Philomena Beck, and in the introduction to Catholic Action which I received in one of the first Young Christian Students' groups'. But the Catholic Left felt very isolated in the middle-class suburban parishes of the 1950s. If the Split relieved some middle-class Catholics of any lingering obligation they had felt to older loyalties, for many more it was but an unwelcome intrusion.

The perfect worlds of the Left and of the Catholics were but counterpoints to the grand theme of middle-class ideals and politics: the moral community as defined and led by Sir Robert Menzies. He was by far the most admired public figure and politician in the lifetime of this generation.[16] And this admiration was not just for his skill as a politician or

---

[16] See Appendix II, table 12.

his strength as a national leader, it was also because he made Australians feel good about themselves—he had stature and that stature elevated the nation. Above all he understood his true constituency: he penetrated and comprehended the soul of the middle class in a way no other Australian politician has then or since, and he reshaped conservative politics in this country so that it was perfectly adapted to the aspirations and ideals of post-war suburbia. He is remembered with deep feeling rather with than approval or gratitude for actual policies he implemented. It was not what he *did* that lives in the memory, but what he *was*. Hein Altman was 'an unashamed admirer of Menzies—he was a father figure', and since his going, 'conservative politics—politics generally—have undergone a steady decline'. Tom Beenie married Le Barnett and they agreed to differ on politics: 'I'm completely Liberal—there's a difference in this house' and for Tom, Sir Robert Menzies was our finest leader—'most definitely', whereas 'the later ones I hadn't much time for'. For Robert Trumble 'Sir Robert Menzies steered this country through probably its best times—before inflation became rampant and I think he was a very skilful and good prime minister. I think he gave great service to this country, the proper recognition for which is now long overdue'. Winsome Walklate grieves for Menzies' reputation:

> I've always been interested in politics and I liked Sir Robert Menzies, so much. And it's sad to see the image of a great man being desecrated. I'll tell you why I liked him. Mrs Grist, who was our help for so many years had grown up in Jeparit and she'd known Robert Menzies' father. Sir Robert and Dame Pattie Menzies were known to my parents—Dame Pattie Menzies was a friend of my mother's—and when Mr Menzies (as he was then) spoke in our electorate, because it was Kooyong, he used to open our Methodist Church fêtes. And Mrs Grist would always come to our fête—she was as fat as she was square and of an Irish background—and she always went up to Bob and had a talk with him and he was friendly to her. There was nothing snobbish, and I thought that he was a great man because he could stay friends and talk about Jeparit days.

Like many who went through the war, John Leckie thinks highly of John Curtin and Ben Chifley: 'My politics are more Liberal, but they were in a day when a bloke was worth more than a present-day politician—I think they were genuine in their attitude'. But it was Menzies he most admired and longs for still: 'I think he did a lot for Australia. OK he made some mistakes, but who hasn't? And when I see what's going on today, I wish he was back there—it's only my opinion, but I think we're going down the gurgler, in every way'. Another who has defended Menzies' place in history is the former head and deputy head of the Prime Minister's department, Sir John Bunting. Bunting was a Trinity boy of the 1930s, and along with the headmaster's son Sir Keith ('Mick') Shann, was among the first to enter the Commonwealth Public Service after it was opened to university graduates in 1934.[17] Bunting was one of those closest to Menzies and his relationship was one of undisguised admiration. Both as a man from the world of the 69 tram and of Canberra, he was able to put into words what Menzies meant to the 'Forgotten People':

> On the spiritual side, Menzies, with human vision and care, and directing himself to the individual, set as his goal the freedoms and dignity of man. He defined his freedoms: 'To work, to think, to speak, to choose, to be ambitious, to be independent, to be industrious, to acquire skill, and to seek reward.' These are what he sought, with social and industrial justice added, all for the individual man. His call for support of Australia's middle class—salary earners, shopkeepers, skilled artisans, professional men and women, farmers and so on—has come back into some prominence. He looked to have public policy directed more towards them, and this he achieved, to his great credit, without new social divisions. It was not, as some would demand, restless achievement, with every day a new excitement. His mind was not of that kind. There was no rush to new things, nothing unusually experimental. But there was change and progress, on the basis of thought and proven value. He acted upon mainstream common sense and principle, and observed the truth that practically every political problem is a human one. He produced a coherent Australia. He developed its harmonies. He gave new unity, new stature, new dignity. He gave new international standing. He respected institutions. These were, as I see it, his great distinctions, transcending in worth even the richness of economic development, for as he would himself complain, whatever the material achievements of a nation and their importance, its state of well-being is not to be found without also going behind the material to the spiritual, to the hearts and minds.[18]

Menzies first made plain his bid for the hearts and minds of the Australian middle class in his radio broadcast of 1943, 'The Forgotten People'. Judith Brett's reading of that speech and of Menzies' own heart and mind has explicated post-war conservatism with a new clarity and force. Menzies gave voice to the longings and fears of the Australian people and, with unerring accuracy, he was able to identify the sense of class grievance borne by the middle class.[19] Since the disgraces of the 1890s the Melbourne middle class had seen itself as a deserving class, and yet their moral worth was not always given the recognition it was due—

---

[17] Frank Shann strongly supported Sir James Darling's campaign to open the Public Service to university graduates. Both believed that the entry of promising young men from Protestant private schools would elevate the cultural and moral tone of the political bureaucracy, which had hitherto been too much the preserve of Catholics and state school men. See Peter Gronn, 'Schooling for Ruling: the social composition of admissions to Geelong Grammar School. 1930–1939', pp. 83–7.

[18] Sir John Bunting, R. G. Menzies: a Portrait, pp. 185–6.

[19] Brett, Robert Menzies' Forgotten People, pp. 1–73.

they were becoming forgotten, especially since the Depression and war had placed the issue of working-class suffering on the political agenda. Despite the cold war, the moral barometer had shifted and, to some extent, that shift was effected by changes in the churches. With the growing Left intelligentsia emerged a new generation of more radical ministers and priests. The younger clergy was moving to the left and there were talks in suburban Methodist and Presbyterian churches about Christ being the first communist. Yet even the most tactful and moderate support of the Australian Labor Party enraged conservative congregations as John Jamieson found to his grief as a young minister in his first church, and young radical Presbyterians had difficulty finding congregations to call them. The Rev. Eric Owen was shattered by Menzies' accusation in the parliament that his Convention on Peace and War held in Sydney in 1953 was infiltrated by Communists, and the Rev. Dr A. H. Wood, who had worked with Owen from the beginning, felt forced to resign from the committee lest he injure the school—MLC—of which he was principal: 'As he went from my manse, I felt sorrier for him than for myself . . . I believe that his loneliness was the greater', wrote Owen later. 'His statement in the public press announcing his withdrawal from the movement can have given little comfort to his critics for his last word on the subject was his firm conviction that the movement was sound.'[20] By the 1958 federal election Dr Wood was President-General of the Methodist Church of Australasia: he deplored those churches which attempted to 'dragoon voters' but his own advice on the election, commented the political scientist Don Rawson, 'could only have helped the A.L.P.'[21] The fury of conservatives towards left-wing Christians knew no bounds. Oswald Barnett was asked to resign from his directorship of the City Mutual Life Assurance Company because he was auditor of Australia Soviet House and he nearly lost his accountancy practice.[22] *Amelia Friend* was again investigated by ASIO just days before the Communist Party Dissolution Bill referendum. She had always been scrupulously careful in the Y.W.C.A. not to introduce politics into youth work but, after her second encounter with ASIO: 'my friend and I said—we've got two days left and we're going to use that forty-eight hours to influence as many people as we can. If this is what they're going to do *before* they get the right, what are they going to do afterwards?'

The revolutionary dreams were now dangerous and the consequences grave. After the war June Barnett had decided to enter the diplomatic service, and she resigned from the Communist Party 'because it was imbued in me that in the Public Service, you don't have politics'. She

---

[20] J. E. Owen, *The Road to Peace*, p. 15.
[21] D. W. Rawson, *Australia Votes: the 1958 Federal Election*, p. 125.
[22] Howe, *New Houses for Old*, p. 67.

kept her left-wing friends, including a man called Fred Rose. In mid-1950 he invited her to his home in Canberra to meet someone: 'It was at night—I didn't know his name and I didn't see his face properly—we just walked around. And he asked me if I'd pass on some interesting information from Foreign Affairs. I said that I didn't see the top secret stuff and that I wouldn't if I did. And that's all that happened'. But it led to her appearance before the Petrov Royal Commission in 1954 where she was called as a witness to identify a Walter Clayton as the man who had asked her to pass on secrets. There was some resemblance, but she wasn't sure—it had been in the dark and four years ago, and no matter what pressure she was put under in the witness stand, she could not lie.[23] Her career was impeded for the next six years, but she was finally cleared for good promotions and overseas postings. But Petrov continued to haunt her. In 1965 the Melbourne *Herald* reported the return to Australia of Fred Rose and included a photograph of June captioned 'The Former Spy'. She sued for defamation, but as she didn't want a posting to Geneva interrupted, she settled out of court for 'an inconsiderable sum'.

The crusade against Communism contained a degree of moral panic. Panic because conservatism had lost the central moral ground to the Left, and what Menzies offered the Forgotten People of the Australian middle class was a renewed moral authority. 'The tremendous and urgent truth is that no man deserves either the vote or the name of Democrat unless his heart has had some discipline towards unselfishness, whatever his daily job may be, has been trained to form judgements which proceed from the mind and not from the pocket', he wrote in a foreword to a pamphlet by S. R. Dickinson in 1945.[24] Menzies' conception of citizenship, of each independent householder, making, in free association, a harmonious society which had abolished unpleasantness and conflict, appealed deeply to the young families engrossed in private life in the new suburbs. The Labor Party and the left talked harshly of division and class conflict and reminded people of the pasts they wanted to put behind them. Menzies offered a safer, more civil world, where there was prosperity and hope both for the individual and the nation. And his was an Australia which applauded those who worked hard and 'got on', for he had not made the middle class exclusive. Quite the reverse: Menzies was deeply moved by the processes which plucked the gifted out of obscurity into distinction, and he saw education as the most important ladder of opportunity in society. He loathed left-wing academics but he will be remembered gratefully for what he did for the universities.[25] The middle class he denominated as the

---

[23] Robert Manne, *The Petrov Affair*, pp. 193–4; Nicholas Whitlam and John Stubbs, *Nest of Traitors*, p. 147.

[24] S. R. Dickinson, *The Essential Basis of a New Order for the Education of the Young as Social Units*, I am indebted to a thesis by Andrew Read for bringing this quote to my attention.

[25] Cameron Hazlehurst, 'The Advent of Commercial T.V.', p. 115.

'Forgotten People' were, as Judith Brett has argued, a moral category and thereby open to all aspirants who possessed the appropriate moral qualities. And he explicitly excluded from the moral universe he constructed for the Forgotten People both the idle rich (who could look after themselves) and the faceless working class (who were protected by law and were 'monolithically organized' in the labour movement).[26] In other words there was no need for the middle class to feel inferior to the rich, as there was no need any longer to feel sorry for the poor as a class. He celebrated a responsible individualism, where the welfare of society could be ensured both by general prosperity and the exercise in daily life of Christian charity and personal kindness. Society would be good because it was composed of good individuals.

For Winsome Walklate, rebuilding the world morally would come from the practice and teaching of Christian citizenship:

> The end of the war came and we were starting our lives together and the New Life. We had a block of land in a sea of mud with no sewerage on it, and it took about two years to build on that land. It was just in North Balwyn, behind the little church. And in my heart I thought —I'm going to support that church—I'm dedicating my life to that church, the North Balwyn Methodist Church.
>
> Now I believe that there were a lot of other people like me and we flocked to that church. We were all the same. Our husbands were exservicemen and we came to build peace. We had ideals and we came to bring our children up in the church and it wasn't necessarily to follow Methodism; it was to follow Christianity.
>
> We had a wonderful series of ministers and wonderful youth groups with a hundred in a group. Our church was full of people and children and we had wonderful preaching. Clubs were started—a club was begun for women known as 'Friendship' and we've just celebrated the fortieth anniversary of the club's commencement. It wasn't for raising money originally—it was purely for giving friendship to young wives one night a month. We had good outreach and a wonderful spirit.

In the 1950s Winsome's church was filled to overflowing and worshippers were forced to follow the service from the car park.[27] In all the new middle-class suburbs of the 1950s the churches boomed with the invasion of young marrieds and their children. Being part of the church was still seen as being part of parenthood: church, Sunday school and church social life were 'good for the children' and built community in the new suburbs of the 'Bible Belt'.[28] Neither were these busy Christians stuffy and in-

---

[26] Brett, *Robert Menzies' Forgotten People*, pp. 41–4.

[27] Winsome Matenson, *From Open Fields: A History of the Trinity Uniting Church, 1941–1991*, p. 19.

[28] Rhys Miller, *Calling and Recalling: One Minister's Pilgrimage into the Uniting Church*, pp. 96–101; Trevor Byard, *Merriment of Parsons*, p. 181.

hibited. While Rhys Miller was minister at the Gardenvale Presbyterian Church, satirical reviews enlivened parish life and his daughter will be forever remembered for singing (to the tune of *Oklahoma*'s 'Oh What a Beautiful Morning'):

> O what sudden awakening
> Elders are filled with dismay
> They've got a horrible feeling
> Church union is coming their way.

As her father remembers: 'After drinking solemn toasts to 'poor Calvin' who was dead, and 'poor Wesley', also declared dead, the audience was admonished':

> O the Presys and Methos should be friends
> Presys sometimes drink a lot
> Methos never touch a pot
> But that's no reason why they can't be friends.[29]

Religious revivalism was fuelled by the crusades of the American evangelist, Billy Graham and, for both Protestants and Catholics, it was a time of earnest religiosity.[30] And with that went a keen sense of sectarian differences, differences which affected both political and social debate. There were also ominous signs of coming change. For Methodists by 1964 the possible extension of hotel hours—the abolition of six o'clock closing—dominated the *Spectator*. The church was rocked when the Rev. John Westerman changed sides and supported 10 o'clock closing and with the extension of hotel hours came the demoralising defeat of the teetotal movement which had held such influence over Victorian life since the days of Marvellous Melbourne.[31] Even in the dry suburbs, liquor shops were opening and the Bible Belt shrank. By the early 1960s there were other intimations of a changing Australia. Those churches which served older communities, where there were few young children, were beginning to die. John Jamieson as a minister in the country during the 1950s found it 'tough going' and blames the war for having a 'devastating effect' on religious belief.[32] One man from Scotch testified that his experience as a prisoner of war destroyed his faith: 'So many horrific episodes makes one question why God permits same'.[33] The great Epping Street Methodist Church in East Malvern had begun to empty and, by 1968, would

---

[29] Miller, *Calling and Recalling*, p. 94.
[30] Adams, *Memories of Darling Road Uniting Church*, pp. 156–7.
[31] Betty Feith, 'What are the Spheres open to Women?', p. 13.
[32] Letter to author, 28 February 1991.
[33] Survey No. 709: Scotch.

have but forty-three members and a Sunday school enrolment of thirty-five. There were few young couples moving into the suburb; and those who did were frighteningly different—Greek, and Orthodox in religion. For a fatal instant, the church's in every other way gentlemanly historian revealed the inner fears of middle-class Australian Protestants:

> After a decade of post-war immigration Australia had received thousands of new citizens from Italy, Greece and other mainland European countries, most of whom were nominally Catholic or Orthodox, a minority Protestant and virtually none Methodist. . . Many Australian Methodists of that time looked to British immigration to redress the balance that had swung heavily in favour of the Catholics, both through ten years of immigration and also through a hundred years of natural increase, for the Catholics had long benefited from strict marital laws which ensured that they bred like rabbits! These facts were rarely stated in public, but all Protestants were aware of them and they were undoubtedly a factor in the Methodist Church's 'Bring out a Briton Scheme'.[34]

Beset not just by the Communist menace at home and abroad, but also by the rising tide of Catholicism and foreignness, this was a form of Protestant panic; and grief for the loss of the known, tried and trusted. The perfect world of conservative Protestants, of harmony between church and home, neighbour and fellow parishioner; where kindness and charity could be relied upon in times of trouble, was hard to re-create in an increasingly secular and pluralist Australia. If the churches full of young families were so heartwarming, the emptying of the older churches was truly frightening. The young marrieds were good at working with their neighbours, establishing local kindergartens and schools, and the returned soldiers remained close, not just in the R.S.L. but also in Legacy and in unit organizations. (Ralph Coyne's ex-commando group painted each other's houses until age defeated them.)   But Australian society was changing both in composition and in culture and many of the certainties that this generation had imbibed at home, church and school were becoming less secure. Triumphant victory for the Liberal–Country Party coalition in the federal election of 1966 marked also the end of the great alliance between Sir Robert Menzies and the Forgotten People. His successors faced a changing Australia, and the moral middle class—and their children—would be both agents and victims of that change.

---

[34] Bossence, *Epping Street*, pp. 99–100.

6
Mid-Life Crisis
1967–1975

Mid-Life Crisis
1967–1975

Archie Crow had returned from the war with a distinguished record and a knowledge of Indonesian. He abandoned the medical course he had commenced before the war and took out an Arts degree, majoring in French and Dutch. He then spent a year in industry until a former colleague from the army recruited him to the Department of Defence's Joint Intelligence Bureau. It was a challenging time to be in Defence intelligence: Colonial regimes had toppled, China had just fallen to the Communists and Australian forces were helping to staunch the advance of Communism in Korea. Archie Crow did well. There were too few in the bureaucracy and the universities, let alone the parliament, who knew something of our Asian neighbours, and within eight years he was appointed as the bureau's representative in London. He was earning a good salary, which was just as well because he and his wife now had five children to rear and educate. He was entering his forties and had everything to look forward to, except that he was quietly but inexorably changing. And the place that quickened that change was one which has changed lives for more than a thousand years:

> The turning point in my career . . . was a visit to the tiny island of Iona, off the west coast of Scotland, during my Defence days in London. As an old Highland gardener once remarked, 'Iona iss a very thin place. There's no much between Iona and the Lord'. A power house of the Holy Spirit from the time of St Columba's landing in 563 A.D., Iona was to become one of the three holy places of Christendom—with Jerusalem and Rome. Kings of Scotland, Ireland, France and Norway lie buried in the Ridge of Kings, clan chiefs of Scotland in the Ridge of Chiefs. Viking raiders have harried its shores and massacred its monks. The Reformation reduced its abbey to ruins.
>
> In the centre of the restored abbey today stands a most significant piece of sculpture: a personal inspiration and a portent of things to come. Called the 'Descent of the Spirit', it is sculpted by an Austrian Jew. The Virgin

241

Mary, enclosed within three great folds, held together by the beak of a dove, is being lowered to the waiting earth. On the back are inscribed these words in French, 'I, Jacob Lipchitz, faithful to the religion of my ancestors, have made this virgin for the better understanding of men on earth, that the Spirit may reign'. Three identical bronze statues were made: one stands in the cloisters of Iona Abbey; one in the Cultural Centre of Los Angeles; and one in a beautiful Roman Catholic church high up in the mountains of Haute Savoie, France. Jew and Christian, religious and secular, New World and Old World, all branches of the Christian Church, are being drawn together under the gentle and beneficent influence of the Spirit of God.[1]

It was the beginning of a call to the Presbyterian ministry, but it was another year before he felt compelled to make a decision:

Things that had been germinating in my mind for some time made me say, 'You've just got to make a decision about this'. And when I got into the study programme at the Theological Hall, I really had a great sense of release and relief. I was exploring things I'd felt starved of; because the war dominates your whole existence, you're locked in for a period of years.

It was something I enjoyed very much. And very often I got right to the top of the wall and I could have fallen one way or the other, because I was coming in at a later stage, and I think that one of the things the theological course does is to break down, smash into bits all your preconceptions, and you've got to build up again.

It's a very healthy thing but it's a painful thing—a lot of your conservative upbringing about what's right and wrong you say goodbye to.

And part of that conservative upbringing was politics:

My politics have changed completely, really. My family were solidly Liberal and I was too; but when I began to think for myself, I began to look at politics in terms of people's needs and the whole broad spread of society. Through my church life I thought more and more in terms of the care of people and who was doing the most for the underprivileged, so for about thirty years now I've voted Labor.

If the term 'mid-life crisis' has become a cliché, it still has meaning for most people as they enter middle age. For women the tangible changes of the climacteric mark a biological transition that is both an end and a new beginning. Men are not victim to the same hormonal imperatives, but they are no less prone to finding themselves taking stock as they reach

<hr/>

[1] The Rev. Archie Crow, 'The Triple Farewell': text of speech given on the occasion of his retirement as the chaplain of Scotch College, 15 November 1985.

their forties, confronting their accomplishments and frustrations, ambitions and dissatisfactions. For middle-class breadwinners, on whose personal success hangs so much, it can be a crisis of masculinity just as much as the menopause for some women is a crisis of femininity. Some people do change their lives dramatically, but most are too locked into mortgages, superannuation and school fees to take large risks. (For Archie Crow, to enter the church was financially catastrophic.) It is perhaps at this point in adult life that many are conscious that they are sacrificing something of themselves—a certain freedom and perhaps the last of their youthful romanticism—for the sake of families who must be provided for and social roles which must be lived out. People also take stock of their relationships, even their sexuality: are they content with the expectation that their present sexual partner will most likely be their last? They can be visited by yearnings and dissatisfactions which are both unwelcome and discomforting. Some are forced to take stock by the impact of pains long suppressed which explode into mental illness, for sometimes it is not until middle life that one can afford to let go.

And how are their beliefs, principles and prejudices standing up in a changing world? People may even question whether they are being 'true to themselves'. This was of course not a question that one asked oneself as a young adult in the Depression or during the war; and there was scarcely time to ask it in the 1950s amidst the rush into private life; it was very much a question of the late 1960s, a question asked first by the young and passed on to those of their parents who were susceptible. And if there was a point of enragement in the 1960s between conservative middle-class parents and their rebellious, sometimes stoned, hirsute, sexually promiscuous, radical and expensively-educated offspring, it was over their rejection of duty, delayed gratification, self-control and discipline in the pursuit of self-fulfilment and pleasure. The American sociologist Daniel Bell identified the coming of 'hire purchase' or small credit as the nail in the coffin of the Protestant ethic of delayed gratification—the acceptance of work before pleasure. It was not until the 1960s that suburban families had made up for the deficiencies of personal equity and real income caused by the Depression and the war and, with new forms of personal credit and assurances of perpetual prosperity, could really begin to enjoy themselves and spend money. For middle-class Australians it now became easier to travel overseas, and domestic and intellectual culture was enriched by the experience of travel for both the middle-aged and the young. Between Harold Holt's pledging in 1966 that Australia would 'go all the way with L.B.J.' and the bitter dismissal of the Whitlam Labor Government in 1975 this country underwent a cultural transformation. It was both painful and exhilarating, and while it was very much part of events and influences abroad, it also had indigenous roots. It was unsettling for many Australian people, and it marked a turning point in our national history from which there was no going back. Australia changed profoundly in a mere decade, and changed for ever.

The private was inextricably bound up in the public and most intrusive of all was the Vietnam war. That war brought the turmoils and doubts of the 1960s into every home, rich, comfortable or poor, which had sons of military age. Good-living, patriotic families discovered they had sons who did not want to fight in this particular, or even any, war, and for that they might go to gaol. For conservative Methodists it became a fearsome test, because the Methodist Conference had condemned American involvement in Vietnam and declared the Church's opposition not just to conscription, but to the war itself. The clergy on the Left who had been reviled for their involvement in the peace movement in the 1950s found themselves back in the main stream, but it was deeply distressing for those lay Methodists whose politics were different. *May Featherstone* had never been a political person until her son faced the ballot for conscription to Vietnam: 'He was going to refuse to register and the thing was they were going to be gaoled. Then you've got to reconcile that with the law of the land. He went to quite a few ministers about it and we talked long into the night. In the end he did allow his name to go forward in the ballot, but he wasn't drawn out'. Margaret Bickford's eldest son Philip 'was furious he wasn't called up, because he wanted to fight it through the courts' and she saw the Methodist Church shaken into change in that short time: 'The Vietnam thing certainly stirred up a lot of people and there was no concern for the world until that happened to that age group'. The Methodist clergy had been discreetly moving to the left since the Depression; the Vietnam war impelled young Methodists and gradually more older ones to follow. Winsome Walklate took the same position as the church and opposed the war: 'I joined in the protests against that and I was voting for Jim Cairns then—I didn't think we should be there at all'. The Presbyterian clergy and laity were more conservative and the war split the church along generational lines: 'the majority of younger ministers were in opposition to it and a lot of the older ones couldn't understand what was going on', recalls Alan Reid. But by 1970 a small group from John Jamieson's congregation took part in the Vietnam Moratorium march.

For Lurline Keck middle-life brought a complete reworking of her self, her beliefs and her life, and the Vietnam war was one of a number of catalysts. She was brought up to regard self-pity as a sin: she was afflicted but 'I had to make do with the best equipment and go on from there and I think that's good'. Then suddenly at the age of thirty-three she was widowed, with two young sons to rear and educate:

> Dr Wood wrote to me at once, as he did with everyone. And something that helped were remarks someone made to one of my brothers—that he thought I'd be quite all right because I was strong physically and strong mentally. By that time I was strong physically, but I had had this feeling

of really not being good enough for a long time after I left school, and I hadn't been aware that anyone would think that I had a strong character. I think that probably helped me—that chance remark that was repeated to me, and I thought—well, I *am* going to be able to manage this. It was pretty miserable and lonely for quite a long time, but it worked through.

She went to work in an office and became involved again in the local church, even though she still had no real religious conviction. What she did desire, she found, was more education. She tried adult matriculation and she passed. She tried a year at Monash University and she passed. She completed an arts degree and then just kept going until the girl who had failed Intermediate in 1940 took out a Ph.D. in English. Her studies and her sons' growing up reoriented her completely:

I had always voted Liberal because my parents did and I thought it was the proper thing to do. It never occurred to me to vote any other way. Also I didn't know anyone in working-class circles, until I had a plumber come to the house not long after I was first married. I had to make him a cup of tea and I didn't know how to talk to him—I didn't know what to call him and I realized that I didn't know anyone who was working-class—which is really remarkable I suppose. He was a nice young man too—but I found that quite embarrassing.
I didn't think a lot about politics until I started studying at Monash and I found it very interesting from an historical angle. Then at the time of the Vietnam involvement, my younger son John went through a really unhappy stage. He didn't want to register as a lot of people didn't, and I talked him out of not registering, mainly because I was really horrified at the thought of him going to gaol and being abused or something like that—acting as best I knew at the time, but I think it hurt him a lot, although he's never resented it personally.
    There was also the Ryan hanging in Victoria—Vietnam on the federal level and Ryan on the local—and Bolte was just so arrogant and I was very much against capital punishment. So that was the first time I voted Labor and I haven't voted anything else since.

Lurline was not the only Liberal voter repelled by the hanging of Ronald Ryan in 1967. The premier, Sir Henry Bolte, justified capital punishment with a farmer's matter-of-factness: 'Look, on my farm, if I've got an animal that's no good, I kill it. In society it's the same; with a man who's proved to be no good, you put an end to him'.[2] In Victoria this was a turning point, just as much as was the Vietnam war, and the middle class

---

[2] Quoted in Terrill, *The Australians*, p. 32; see also Barry Muir, *Bolte From Bamganie*, pp. 88–95; Tom Prior, *A Knockabout Priest,: the Story of Father John Brosnan*, pp. 141–59.

divided as the churches condemned capital punishment. But Lurline's religious loyalties also began to crumble:

> At Monash I did a lot of Ancient history and Classical literature, and so many of the Bible stories were similar to the Greek myths and so on, and through going to university I began to understand a lot more about different religions and different people's perspectives. But I kept on going to church for a good while, to take my mother who relied on me for transport, but in the end I decided that I really did reject it. My mother was disappointed in me, but I felt it was an important stand for me to take. She lived until she was ninety-nine and she lived next door for a good while, and though she depended on me a good deal in old age, she was also inclined to be a rather dominant figure if she could.
>
> So that's when I stopped going to church, and the relief at having made that decision and not wavering was great. That's quite a long time ago now—about twenty years—and I would never, ever want to go back.

By 1972 there were sufficient middle-class defectors to bring Labor to power. But it was just not the slow attrition of the Vietnam war which caused so many to desert political loyalties of a lifetime; there was also a growing disenchantment with the moral tone and attitudes of the coalition. Caring conservatives had had their reservations for years, but found the Labor alternative unpalatable. Margaret Bickford remembers having lunch in Collins Street with Dr Jean Littlejohn who despaired: '"Margaret—what alternatives have we got?" That was to Menzies—there was no alternative at that stage. I've voted Labor, and many times I'm tempted to vote informally because there is no choice'. Such concerned conservatives were ripe for Whitlam. *Doug Gordon*:

> My politics have not changed much because I've always been a bit of a socialist, but I've voted Liberal. And because I've always been a bit of a socialist but voted Liberal, I suppose it wouldn't be very difficult for me to vote the other way, and so I've often looked at governments at face value and thought—I'll go along with this one. Now I'm sure Whitlam—given half a chance, not controlled by Caucus, would have done a very good job. For the once and only time in my life I voted Labor, but I'm right down the middle and I think most doctors are.
>
> Most of us have seen pretty ghastly poverty. Our practice went from West Heidelberg to East Ivanhoe. And West Heidelberg came from Camp Pell after the Olympic Games; East Ivanhoe drove around in Mercedes and Rolls Royces. The Camp Pell people couldn't look after the houses they were given—within two years there were no flywires on the windows and the flies went zipping through and the children urinated in the corner and the place reeked. Not all—some. And it took the social worker years to slot all these people into the various areas in West Heidelberg, so that the ones who couldn't look after themselves were all

together, and the ones who wanted to try were together. (There'd be an argument about whether that was the right thing to do.)

And so, when you've looked after people like that, got attached to them, see them die, see them get cancer, see their babies choke on a brooch—Oh God! And you've looked after the wealthy who don't pay their accounts, and down in West Heidelberg they're the best payers of the lot, then I think that's bound to make you go down the middle a bit.

There were many like *Doug Gordon* and from the three Protestant schools almost half have voted Labor at least once in their lives, and from Genazzano, just over a third.[3] Their party identifications by 1990 would be markedly different, however, and many of those Labor votes were temporary protests or youthful indiscretions. For the majority, being conservative was instinctive just as much as being Labor can be for the working class. *Stella Davies*:

What *ever* the others did, I'd still vote for the Liberals—that's the way I was brought up, and certainly now I agree with it. I would never vote Labor in a blue fit, because I don't like a lot of the policies and I don't like a lot of the people. And my grandfather was one of the original people in starting the United Australia Party, so you can imagine the way I was brought up.

What was more difficult to avoid in the 1960s was the cultural and moral turbulence, and scarcely a family with adolescent children was unaffected. *Marina Graham* witnessed the 'youth revolution' intimately and distressingly. She too was suddenly widowed at the age of just thirty, and with three children to rear, she returned to teaching and joined the staff of a very academic suburban high school:

When I went back to teaching we were in our gowns and it was better than any private school I've ever experienced—a joy to teach there. And then around 1967 there were a few stirrings; then the great student revolt in Paris in 1968 and we began to get things filtering back from Monash University as a lot of our students had friends there or were aiming to go there. Monash was *the* place where it was all happening.

At this time I was promoted to another local school where there was very little defiance or disruption because there was such a beautiful staff/student relationship—it was an *extremely* happy place. A lot of the staff were doing B.Ed. courses at Monash and there used to be talk about Albert Langer.

---

[3] 'Have you ever, even if only once, voted Labor?'

	Scotch	Trinity	MLC	Genazzano
Yes:	46%	49%	48%	37%
N/A:	0	1%	1%	3%

Then I went to an outer suburban school on a big promotion and I got the full thrust of it there. Far from lack of respect, it was open onslaught almost on teachers. It was not unusual to have things thrown at you. I once had a chair thrown in my direction and I had to duck quickly to miss it. It was up to you—the force of your personality to try to control them. We had a very permissive headmaster and a way-out senior mistress and they were always on the side of 'the kids'. It was simply appalling—every day in every way we were persecuted. Oh dear it was difficult. And I think there were subversive cells in the staff and they used to put notices up—'Your Rights as a Student—what to do if you're summoned to the principal's office'. It was the era of the *Little Red Schoolbook*. That's why I left the Education Department and went to teach at an independent boys' school. But it's different now.

Graham Little has called it a 'crisis of obedience';[4] A. F. Davies saw oedipal conflict with authoritarian parents projected on to educators and social leaders, God and the government, hence Mao's 'extraordinary appeal to Western middle-class youth' was in the way he 'licensed an indulged generation's resentment of authority'.[5] It was acutely distressing to those parents who had dedicated themselves to 'making a good new generation' for this new generation stopped going to church and broke the rules over sex, alcohol and drugs.[6] Winsome Walklate's grief was a common one:

It nearly broke my heart—our son left home at twenty-two and he was living with a girl he'd grown up in Sunday school with. And they lived together—I didn't know—up in the hills. I went to see them and I opened the wrong wardrobe door to get my coat and there were her clothes and I realized that they shared the bedroom. I was just going off to England and I was very distressed about it and I didn't say anything to him. But I poured my heart out to a priest wandering around one of the cathedrals in England, and he said, 'The main thing for you is to behave as a Christian—whatever his behaviour—that's not your business. *You* must be a Christian and keep the lines open'. So I helped them get a house and last year that marriage came unstuck and they got divorced. Neither he nor his wife went to church, except on Christmas Day, but I know he has the strength of faith. I don't care if people go to church or not—what matters is if they have faith.

Margaret Bickford's five children spanned fourteen years and the world in which her first-born grew up was entirely different from that of her youngest: 'Kaye used to say—Mum, you never let us do those things. It *was* a sudden change and it happened around 1970; even Deane, who's

---

[4]   Graham Little, 'Whitlamism and the Whitlam Years'.
[5]   A. F. Davies, *The Human Element*, p. 39.
[6]   Miller, *Calling and Recalling*, pp. 105–9.

eight years younger than Kaye, did entirely different things from the older ones. The older ones had more of a work ethic—they worked and didn't have much social life at all when they were at school, but the young ones went off on camps and rode bikes'. Many families adjusted, but much of the adjustment had to come from parents rather than from their children. Winsome Walklate remains unhappy at the changes in private morality:

> They threw out sex inhibitions and there wasn't much to fight against. As youth we had *real* things to fight against like Nazi Germany and the treatment of the Jewish people—those were real things to fight. All they could do was throw out our standards, our rules and try a few different ones and see how they got on.
>
> It was partly the effect of birth control and if you didn't have different sets of standards, everybody could be living in so-called sin if they wanted to. But the other way seems to me to be much more commonsense, more clean.

Marjorie O'Donoghue now believes that she completely misunderstood what her oldest daughter was going through as a teenager in the late 1960s because, with a busy husband and five other children to care for, she was oblivious of the rapid changes taking place in the outside world. Archie Crow observed it both as a parent and as a school chaplain, because as soon as he finished his ministerial training, he was invited back to Scotch:

> The boys were very different when I went back and I realized that World War II was a watershed, and that those who were born into the years that followed really couldn't be expected to understand what the war was about and what it cost in suffering. Nor could they appreciate the Depression before that—it belonged to before their time and it just didn't equate with the world they found themselves in. They were born into a scientific, a technical, computerized world, so they were—for a time—a lost generation. They were coming to grips with totally new concepts, and they were being obliged to disengage from that world the other side of the divide, and from its images and expectations. The tasks that they were being asked to take on were just so demanding, that if they tried to conform to those older norms, they would never have been able to cope effectively with the new ones. Sterling qualities from the past, though, became masked in the process.
>
> It became a far more difficult time for parents. You had that generation gap which has always existed, but it was never wider than in the period following the war. Parents were saying—that's no way to behave, I know what to do. But any parents who could say—could you fill me in, you explain to me how you see things today, then I'll understand and then maybe with some of my experience, I can help you reach your objectives. But not ask them to conform to something that no longer really existed.

It was not only the young who went into revolt because they were dissatisfied. There were some among their parents who listened to the call for self-realization, for sexual freedom, for social as well as political change. Part of the revolt of the young *was* that they sensed that their parents were subtly unhappy, that they were imprisoned in class and gender roles which rendered them 'inauthentic'. Some were rejecting the yellow brick road to middle-class worldly success and conspicuous respectability because they had seen it make people—their own families—unhappy and unfulfilled. The perfect homes which had raised the baby boomers were seen to have flaws, and things began, quietly but inexorably, to fall apart. It was not really until the 1960s that the media became aware of terms like 'housewife's neurosis' (the male 'mid-life crisis' was still twenty years off). Psychiatric illness had no place in perfect homes—depression and anxiety for people on a good income, with three lovely children at 'good schools', a car, television and holidays away, suggested moral weakness, even ingratitude. And yet there were middle-class men and women who were sick and it was in middle life, with their perfect homes well under way, that they most often broke down. For *Richard Stanton*, the bad bits of his war and the punishing regimen of work he had taken on to provide for his family finally caught up with him. He broke down physically and mentally and he was never to return to normal working life. It was not just the pain of illness that hurt: just as bad was the stigma:

> The psychiatric treatment was useless, but on top of that the
> understanding of the word 'psychiatry' is confused to the last degree. No
> sense in the average person you dealt with—none of them would have
> the faintest idea of what was wrong. I never went round telling
> everybody, but any of them that knew that I had this long medical history
> would not understand it in any way whatsoever. I don't think I got much
> success out of the psychiatric help. A lot of it, as I got older, I began to
> reason out for myself and work things out better.

The best thing that happened to him was turning sixty:

> And this is important. From that day on I would seek places where I
> would be going to things that I normally wouldn't because I was scared
> of it. And they'd say, 'What's your occupation?' 'Retired chartered
> accountant', and everybody saying 'God, you're lucky, being retired at
> sixty. Lovely. And good luck to you—you've probably worked terribly
> hard'. And that was the incredible basis of our life from then on because I
> had nothing to explain.

He is not an unhappy man and considers himself blessed in the devotion of his wife and children: 'They have really suffered and they've been absolutely marvellous—terribly affectionate with me, so life's been good. I feel terribly guilty—my wife won't have a bar of it—but I can think of a thousand things I could have done better'. And *Philip Hardwicke* had settled into an interesting parish and his first child was six months old, when he suffered a nervous collapse from which he has never really recovered. He has not lost his faith, but he no longer feels fit to attend church because he believes he cannot contribute anything. If he had his time over again, he would have trained for the classical ballet and been a choreographer. To borrow Geoffrey Serle's phrase, he is a man of great beauty of character.

According to journalists and pundits, by the early 1970s the average Australian suburban family was in trouble. It was the decline of the supportive extended family and the isolation of the suburban nuclear family, argued some.[7] It was the straitjacket of gender roles and their utility to consumer capitalism, insisted the American feminist Betty Friedan in *The Feminine Mystique*. Messages were coming from America about the pitfalls of the repressed emotional styles derived from Puritan culture which had been secularized as the bourgeois ideal of emotional restraint and rationality. Encounter groups set out to teach people how to reach each other with an emotional freedom which eluded them in real life. So much of the 1960s revolution was about inhibited people desperate to live life with excitement and passion, and 'working all that through' in a relentlessly rational way, applying new rules to replace old ones. There were people, both young and middle-aged, who believed that they did not know how to live and were seeking a new path. What few noticed was that the great weakness of the suburban ideal of the 1950s was its desperate perfectionism. It was a perfectionism born of idealism, and of idealizations. The generation which plunged into building perfect homes came of awareness in the Depression and of age in the war. The good times of security and peace they remembered were of childhood in the 1920s, childhoods which were utterly protected, where everyone you knew went to church and all children went to Sunday school; childhoods which were later idealized: the time when Mother and Father had no worries, when the bills were paid and there was plenty left over; when grandparents were still hale and active and sometimes your best friends and when holidays at the beach were long and golden. Such childhoods were of necessity perfect and *that* was happiness and how life should be. Alan Cohn:

There are times when I look back and I say to myself—and it may be due to the pure ignorance of little boys—that the only time in my life when I've felt that the Australian community and Australian civilization were more or less settled and unaffected by 'troubles', was when I was quite young and just before the Depression. Once the Depression was over, Hitler came on the scene and there was no more security. When the war was over there was the Cold War, there was Vietnam. Even in recent

---

[7] Patrick Tennison, *The Marriage Wilderness*, pp. 204–22; Byard, *Merriment of Parsons*, pp. 156–7.

times the world has seemed to me to be a wild and unfriendly place. I think I'm fairly conservative in nature and that's probably why I don't read modern novels. But on the other hand, I think that I'm fairly progressive in my view of what life should be about and what politics should be about and what the influence of the Christian Church might be.

This was the birth of the particular perfectionism which pervaded middle-class private life in the 1950s and early 1960s, and one of the basic emancipations from the restrictions of the past was to permit oneself and one's family to have imperfections. Judith Brett remembers acutely that struggle with her ingrained perfectionism as she reached adulthood.

For Joyce Thorpe, her escape from domestic perfectionism has become one of the classics of Australian feminism.[8] She married up—out of the world of MLC and into the world of Scotch. Once she became a Presbyterian she was able to do all sorts of things which Methodists could not, like dance, drink alcohol and smoke cigarettes. She sent her daughters to Lauriston, not MLC, because it had more social prestige. A high standard of housekeeping and entertaining was now expected: Methodists did not expect their wives to be social; Melbourne Grammar husbands provided their wives with servants; Scotch husbands required that their wives do it all themselves:

I set up housekeeping in reaction to my mother. I kept a very tidy house. One of my faults during my whole married life was that the house always had to be tidy, and I think I sacrificed the children to that, and I'm always telling young mothers to let the house go. All my close friends (they weren't my friends—they were my husband's friends' wives) were terrific housekeepers and cooks and entertainers. And my children would go to their place and come back and say,'We've had this marvellous meal' and I used to slave away cooking what I thought were adequate meals. And I got a real inferiority complex about my role as a wife and mother, and I was made to feel guilty even because I wrote books—you wouldn't think it possible! I didn't go out to work but I was made to feel guilty—not by my husband but by these Scotch wives. I probably imagined it all—they'd probably say they thought I was wonderful.

These Presbyterian women just leave me breathless. They did the garden as well as everything else and they had big houses and seaside houses—just like me—and yet they managed to prepare better meals and do more entertaining than I did. I blame this on the Presbyterian male attitude. I think a lot of Presbyterian men were very hard on their wives. I reckon we all worked about eighty hours a week because we worked at night. It took ages to clean the house but I'd do it quickly—I'm still finding it hard to do things slowly.

---

[8]   Grimshaw and Strahan, eds, *The Half-Open Door*, pp. 134-53.

As she has written with such feeling: 'I loved my children but I hated the role'.[9] Joyce's salvation was feminism, and she underwent an authentic conversion experience:

> I couldn't believe it. I just felt a new person—my whole life was explained to me. I read *The Female Eunuch,* and the whole sex role conditioning was explained to me—it was like a burden rolling off my back. My book, *What Society Does to Girls* starts by saying 'When I read *The Female Eunuch* I couldn't sleep for three nights'. I just walked around the house in amazement—there was a whole new freedom I had to myself. It was after I started working in the business—I was being a success at work and that was wonderful because I not only found I was good at it, but I enjoyed doing it and I was being paid for it. But I still had this vague sense of guilt.
>
> It was just the most amazing thing that ever happened to me and from then on I went on from strength to strength and I began to assert myself in all different areas. People who meet me now just can't believe the person I was before I became a feminist.

The end of her marriage became inevitable, but the world she entered as a separated woman was far kinder and more tolerant than it had been in the 1950s. Even so, it was the first time in her life that Joyce had lived alone, and the friends of her married life retreated and their place taken by new ones. Her professional and private life blossomed with independence: 'I was a very good child and a good wife and a good mother; and now I'm very naughty—I do exactly what I want to do'.

One of the social transformations of the 1960s was the legitimation of the right to self-development. *Gwenda Holtby*:

> 'Service to others' can make life difficult if you keep arguing—am I doing this for my personal self-development or am I serving? Can I rationalize it, that for my personal development, it is essential that I serve better? That's the feminine martyrdom complex—going on and on for others without the balance of self-development. I don't know how many housewives manage any self-development—the routine of feeding people in large numbers every day, getting and spending.

And yet the women of the survey are not now stricken with guilt about the quality of their contributions to the family, their workplace or the community. In fact the results were significantly similar between men and

---

[9] Ibid., p. 144.

women[10]. Men and women were also more alike in their confession that just over a third of them had ever 'worried much about being a good person'.[11]   And when directly asked whether they ever felt that they were given standards of personal behaviour and selflessness that were in fact too difficult to live up to only 17 per cent replied that they had.[12] This does not mean that the feminist moral victories of the late 1960s and 1970s were not welcomed by many women: 31 per cent of the survey women described themselves as feminists, and not a few, like Lurline Keck, returned to study and remade their intellectual and vocational lives.[13] Some of their achievements as mature-age students were outstanding:

> My parents never recovered financially after my father lost his job in the Depression. My father drank heavily which imposed enormous financial and emotional strains on the family. I don't ever remember wishing we had more money, but I wished with all my heart for an end to the arguments, unhappiness and embarrassment. The important stabilising factors in my life were the church and our extended family. Because my husband and I have not maintained similar strong links with the church, and we moved away from Melbourne, our children have had neither of these 'props'.
>
> I won a Junior Government Scholarship when I was twelve. Four students at my school did. The other three were boys and they all went on to illustrious academic careers, and I do wonder if more interest would have been taken in my career if I had been a boy.
>
> I first went back to work to help with heavy commitments we had—school fees and a mortgage. I was lucky that the Public Service gave me the opportunity to study again. I took out a B.A. in mathematics in 1985 and for the past thirteen years I have been pursuing a challenging and satisfying career as a systems analyst and programmer.[14]

The return to work to help pay school fees and mortgages was common and often the beginning of personal change, and the economic imperative for women to provide a second income must not be

---

[10] 'During your adult life, have you suffered from guilt feelings about the quality of your contribution to the family, to your workplace or to the community?'

	Scotch	Trinity	MLC	Genazzano
Yes	37%	26%	26%	31%
N/A	3%	4%	3%	5%

[11] 'Do you worry much about being a good person?'

	Scotch	Trinity	MLC	Genazzano
Yes	34%	35%	36%	38%
N/A	6%	11%	6%	7%

[12] 'Have you ever felt that you were given standards of personal behaviour and of selflessness that in fact are too difficult to live up to?'   MLC: Yes 17%, (N/A, 3%); Genazzano: Yes 17% (N/A, 5%).

[13] Labels:

	Scotch	Trinity	MLC	Genazzano
feminist	13%	8%	30%	32%
anti-feminist	5%	4%	9%	11%

[14] Survey No. 484: MLC.

underestimated as an agent for the second wave of feminism. Fully 60 per cent of the Scotch and Trinity Survey men's wives have worked since marriage, those with professional qualifications being the most likely to do so.[15] And of the Survey women, 49 per cent from MLC and 38 per cent from Genazzano women were working for their living after the age of forty.[16] Yet there were some who already had the qualifications but for whom the resumption of a career remained difficult. *Mary Geoghegan* had an honours degree in law and wanted to return to practice once her seven children were all at school, but she was out of touch:

> You try to keep up but you're told, 'What do you know?' And I went through a very depressed stage—where if you're put down a lot, you really put yourself down. People were finding it hard to get articles and they set up this course at the Leo Cussen Institute, and even though I was admitted to the Bar, I got in to the course and I was on the Geelong train to Melbourne the next morning. I think that was the happiest year of my life. They weren't all young—there were some people who'd wanted to do law and some school teachers who'd done it part time—it was a fantastic lot. They didn't put you down at all and gave you a lot of confidence in yourself. After that I did things at Deakin until my husband retired.

Feminism was not just for women out in the world; it was also for those at home. Nancy Naughton believes in equal rights for all women.

> . . . because I have a daughter, Michelle Kosky, who heads the AIDS Council in Western Australia and she's always been a radical, and always believed 'I can do as well as a male—I can do it too'. And she'd often encourage me and say, 'You should be running the hotel, or you should be doing this.
>
> I didn't have equality growing up at all. I lived in a very male-oriented family. They could send me to a good school and that would fit me for life, but life for them represented me being married, having children and carrying on with the Catholic tradition. But they never envisaged that I would want to pursue a career, and there was always a put-down from the point of view of intellect: my brothers were the ones who had the right to the newspapers and knowledge—rights to this, rights to that, while I did the errands. I was not aware of it then, but I've questioned it since. And more particularly at this age—I don't resent, I *regret* that I was not

---

[15] 'Has your wife worked since your marriage?'   Scotch: Yes, 59%; Trinity: Yes, 61%; See Appendix II, table 8b.

[16] Respondents' age when last worked for their living:

	MLC	Genazzano
40–49	2.8%	3.3%
50–59	14.5%	17.5%
60–69	29.4%	17.7%
70–79	1.9%	—

given the opportunity of learning to do something—be it a nurse, I don't care what it was—because it's now—I'm still a well person and I'm still an active person—but I haven't got a particular focus. I'm just wafting through.

You're a mother and wife and then you're yourself, and the 'mother and wife' took over with me and I have absolutely no regrets about what I've done. I'm very thrilled to have all our children and they've all turned out terrifically, but I am sorry now that I haven't got something that I can do from now on because it's my thing.

If the decade brought change into many people's lives, it brought a spiritual revolution into the lives of Catholics. In every aspect of Catholic life, there was a 'breaking out'. *Marina Graham*:

> It was like an epidemic. It was inevitable, following on from Vatican II, when suddenly after everything had been so circumscribed and repressed for hundreds of years, that when the floodgates were opened, so many things were swept away. It seems to me to be falling back into place again, but it was, after all, a revolution.

The liturgical reforms were disconcerting at first: a friend of *Maeve O'Hara*'s remembered that 'one Friday you could be burnt in Hell for eating steak and the next week it was all right and that he found destructive of his faith'. And *Maeve* herself took a long time to adjust:

> The loss of the Latin Mass I found very, very difficult. I suppose it came gradually, but they should have kept it. We spent so much time at school learning it—as the priest said the Latin, you would be saying the English. I've been to Brompton Oratory in London, where they're having a Latin Mass, lots of incense and priests with their back to the congregation and packed. Marvellous—and a beautiful choir.

Most, now, have adjusted to the liturgical changes.[17] Yet Catholicism had been a religion of such crystal clear rules and absolute beliefs that the softening of Vatican II produced almost a state of *anomie* for Eleonore Bibron:

> In the old days you knew that you didn't eat meat on Friday, you knew you went to Mass on Sunday—you knew this, you knew that and you did it. But when they opened it out, you didn't know what the hell to do next. I know girls that I was at school with, and when we go back on the reunion days, we have Mass and then have lunch. And girls who are divorced and remarried go to communion. In the old days they couldn't —now they leave it to your conscience evidently.

---

[17] Survey: Genazzano: 'Are you comfortable with the post-Vatican II liturgy?' Yes, 66.7%; Yes qualified, 5.8%; No, 15.8%; No qualified, 2.5%; N/A, 9.2%.

More momentous than the liturgical changes were the theological: God was redefined and for many, like Kate Morgan, it has been wonderful:

> In those early days it was really taught that God was a fearsome God. You were afraid of Him. The Vatican Council changed that. He's not—He's a caring, loving God. I can remember the Redemptorist Fathers—it would be fire and brimstone from the pulpit. You were damned—you were going to Hell no matter what. That was the frightening, fearsome God. That has changed.

For *Monica O'Farrell* the old church was one of fearsome self-discipline: 'You had to improve yourself all the time and I am tremendously self-disciplined and I'm sure it's because of those days'. Now she sees the church as one of loving service to others: but before Vatican II '"caring" wasn't a word I'd ever heard—what you had to do was to work on yourself'.

Monica O'Farrell has needed that immense self-discipline because when she was forty-two and with four of her seven children still at school, her marriage broke down and she went out to work. The perfect Catholic family of the 1950s was also under immense strain by the 1960s. 'We were taught that we were responsible for men's passions, for their falling into a state of sin. And I think that stayed with me in my married life: that if we did something that was against the church's teaching, it was wrong, and that was really the reason that we didn't use contraception'. She found comfort in the nuns at Genazzano:

> I was terribly emotional. I remember the first time I went back to the chapel after my husband left home, and I really was a mess for about six months. I practically faded away and I just wept and wept and wept by myself for the sadness I felt. And I had nothing but love from the nuns.

Hers was not the only Genazzano marriage to collapse under the strain of wanting a modern marriage with at least a breathing space between each pregnancy. *Cecilia Coleman* has written in an unpublished autobiography:

> Was I to continue producing children, why did my duty to my husband and my religion compete with my duty to my own health and my ability to care for my existing family? . . . Our generation, better educated and informed than our elders, in particular the women, were beginning inevitably to question 'God's holy will'. This was the stock answer given to queries adressed to the old-style hierarchy. And I witnessed the stresses, serious medical problems and sometimes loss of life which pervaded our own small practice. I also perceived the hypocrisy, perhaps ignorance is the term which should be used, but for me, what was the difference between condoms and coitus interruptus, or even the accepted 'rhythm method'? It all resulted in a conscious decision to avoid pregnancy.

The argument that one should practise self-control would have been valid were we all able to afford another bed and another room! But to share a bed with someone whom you love, where you retire to relax and forget the day's stresses and toils, two people with different strengths of feelings, desires and passions—it is one thing to practise your own self-control, but must you or your partner be responsible for the other's self-control?

After five children and 'with great trepidation' she sought the advice of a 'theologian in one of our highly respected orders' and a new dimension emerged: 'I did indeed have a conscience and an obligation to use it to best advantage, not necessarily to keep up a productive womb'. And so with 'his blessing' she went home to tell her husband that she could use the Pill. To her despair, she was 'defeated at home'—the one person whom I felt would agree and co-operate could not acquiesce in his conscience'—accelerating the breakdown of an already troubled marriage.[18] The pressure to keep having babies came often from husbands, men who feared for their soul but who at the same time were unprepared to lead a celibate life.

Of course most marriages survived and the divorce rate among the Genazzano Survey women is close to that of the Protestant schools, all of which are under 10 per cent.[19] But with the safety of anonymity in the survey, there were more expressions of marital unhappiness from Genazzano than from any other school, and there is a marked crescendo of discontent and conflict with the church from those born after 1921, reaching its peak with those who were childbearing in the 1960s. Only half of the Genazzano women felt that the Church had provided them with 'sufficient moral guidance' on issues such as contraception, the Right to Life and I.V.F.[20] This generation's reproductive life was a bridge from the old world to the new and, for many, years of anguish and guilt have finally given way to reconciliation. *Mary Geoghegan*:

> People stopped going to confession. It was never a pleasant thing to do—our belief was that you went and promised to do your best never to do it again. So, if you believed that taking the Pill was wrong, you couldn't go along and say 'I'm not going to do it again' when you already had next month's supply. So I think that most of the women who did it stopped going to confession. We didn't say we'd stopped being Catholics, but we stopped going to communion. It was very much before 'God loves you'—it was a sterner God around then and you didn't get the whole

---

[18] Unpublished manuscript in possession of the author, pp. 54 and 57.

[19]

Broken marriages	Scotch	Trinity	MLC	Genazzano
Separated	0.8%	0.6%	0.9%	0
Divorced, not remarried	3%	3.6%	5.1%	5%
Divorced and remarried	3.8%	4.8%	2.3%	1.7%

[20] Genazzano: 'Does the Church give *not enough/sufficient/too much* guidance on moral issues such as contraception, the right to life and I.V.F.?' Not enough, 28%; Sufficient, 48%; Too Much, 15%; N/A, 9%.

church going to communion, particularly if you went to 11 o'clock
Masses. And there was still a feeling that you should fast—it was
preferable, so it wasn't as noticeable as you would think. Anyhow, after a
while you might find a good priest and you might go once a year to
confession and he'd say—look, it's between you and your Maker. And
then it got so that things were not so judgemental. God became a God of
love rather than sitting up there and saying 'hey—watch out'. And
nowadays just about everyone goes to communion.

The Genazzano women on whom Vatican II thrust the greatest up-
heaval were of course the nuns. The religious rule that Kath Buckley,
Mary Kirby and *Helen Browne* had embraced in the 1930s was swept away.
The Faithful Companions of Jesus had been at their strictest in the 1940s
and 1950s, because the order felt isolated in Australia and the determination 'to keep the spirit' caused it to tighten up: 'the superiors were very
careful', remembers Sister Anthony Buckley. The liturgical and theological reforms were not difficult for the religious to cope with, because they
had had a fuller preparation; it was the transformation of religious life
which was shattering for *Helen Browne*:

> I was at the Benalla convent at the time and the superior had come back
> from overseas and she told us all these new things. We had it at night then
> we went to prayers and up to bed. We got our first inklings of what was
> going to happen, that all the old restrictions were gone. I can still remember
> it so distinctly—I felt as though I'd been thrown into the ocean and I was
> treading water. Where do we go from here? I can't tread water for ever. I
> can remember the kind of hushed silence as we all went up, all deep in our
> own thoughts. A whole new concept—not what we'd entered for, but a
> totally new concept and we had to somehow digest that.
>
> First of all we were to get out of our veils. It might seem little, but it was
> frightening. A priest came—he'd been specially brought from America—
> how they were getting their hair permed—you've got to be prepared for
> that—don't be afraid. God—my hair permed! I remember visiting my sister
> and she said, 'Put a bit of lippy on and see what you look like'. I put it on
> and I was like a child, you know, and she said, 'You don't look too bad with
> a bit of lippy on'. Anything like that quite shocked me.

Many of their students and former students were shocked also as the nuns
abandoned their habits, and with them much of their charisma: 'They looked
so terrible in baggy cardigans'. But what was more revolutionary was the
transformation of the nuns' personalities. They had entered an order, which
despite being a teaching one, lived by a rule of silence. The nuns had a pastoral
and educational relationship with their pupils, but they had no free human
relationships. They lived and worked in community, but their relationship
was with God and not with each other. They rarely saw their families and
none of them had been home since they entered the convent. They now had

to learn to talk to each other freely, and live as a communicating religious community; they now could have close friends and their vocation had to be lived out in relationship to people. For many it was a spiritual rebirth; for others it exposed them to a world they feared. Helen again:

> While it was all old-fashioned, I used to like the retreat stages, where it was quiet and you had eight days to sit and live in your own world. I think I might have been happy had I stayed in a contemplative order—I might have persevered in that.
>
> What they were doing was having open days and I got that way that talking to parents and children—you're a nun and you've got to have this image coming across, teaching their children, making conversation and be something that you're not. I was trying to be something I wasn't—all the time—trying to be a good religious. I never said or did anything, but I'm sure I must have given myself away because I felt a total hypocrite, talking to these parents, a holy religious teaching their children.

Her vocation was also under attack intellectually:

> The Catholic Church usen't to hand out Bibles—they didn't read the Bible. And then, when I was teaching religion, I used to teach from Schuster's Bible—it was annotated and selected and it interested me and I thought—Gee, I must get a Bible. I want to look up more deeply what I am teaching. And I remember when I was up at Benalla, asking the Superior if I could have a Bible and she was quite shocked. And she said 'Bible?', looking at me as though I was some sort of strange creature and I didn't think there was anything wrong with it—I hadn't actually heard that Catholics didn't use a Bible. Finally they discovered a Bible.
>
> Well—I got fascinated. It was the first time I had read the Bible—a wonderful story, it intrigued me beyond words. I continued with that so that when I went to Frankston, they made me the Biblical Studies teacher. I loved it. I went into the Protestant shop to buy maps and had a field day. And the kids used to love it, and when I was in the playground they used to treat me like God because they never heard me talk about anything other than God and the Bible. As long as I kept on talking, it was all right because my faith was pretty good. But as I went on teaching it, I began to see holes in it. And I remember the Easter Sunday, I was making my meditation on the Resurrection—I've forgotten which Gospel it's from—and I saw something in it that I'd never seen before: 'They did not go and report it because he had already gone from the tomb'—something like that. And I thought, 'That's true' and I'd never noticed because they'd cut that bit out. I think my faith did a down trot then—He hadn't been resurrected—He'd risen and gone away.

And so, after thirty-seven years in religious life—of striving to sustain a vocation she had doubted within the first six months of her postulancy—*Helen Browne* rejoined the outside world.

7

Age of Wisdom
1976–1990

When I was eighteen I was going to take the world by storm—be the best nursing sister; and then I wanted to meet and marry a man and have lots of lovely children. I did not meet my husband until I was forty-two years old. Anyway one compromises in life. We are very happy. I feel that I have contributed to the community by being honest and doing a good job as a nurse. At all times I have paid my way and have lived a quiet, respectable life. (Virtue is its own reward.)

Age of Wisdom
1976–1990

Achievements and Disappointments

By the end of the 1970s this generation had reached the peak of their careers and public life, just in time to partake of some of the fruits of the decade of greed. The 1980s, under the stewardship of Labor governments all around the continent, saw a boom of borrowed, fantasy wealth and of ostentatious consumption such as this country had not seen since the 1880s. In Melbourne it took a full century for the Land Boom to return—for the values of residential land in the garden suburbs to match those of that 'insane miraculous year' of 1888. But the boosters and boasters of the 1980s were the children of this generation, and while the parents too bought flash cars and took trips overseas, they were, at the same time, appalled by the reckless greed of their descendants. For a generation shaped by the Depression and the war, the intoxicating fantasies of wealth without work spelt only danger. Raised on the virtues of thrift, modesty and solvency, the contagion of borrowing terrified them. It is ironic, but no less telling, that it took another clutch of boosters and boasters to have the nerve to borrow the cash to restore into private homes the mansions of Hawthorn, Kew and South Yarra that had been built in the 1880s. With their heritage hues and gold-plated taps they stand again as ostentatious relics of human folly.

Few of this generation were believers in the new rush to be rich, but most have reached retirement age feeling that they have done well enough. Some, like *Hein Altman*, have been blessed with success. He had been too young for the war and when he began in practice, lawyers were in short supply: 'Professionally it's been terrific—it's provided more material things than my wife and I could ever have dreamed of—not that we're rich, but we're comfortable and we tell ourselves all the time how lucky we are'. But room at the top is limited and the aspirants in the middle class numerous. In the post-war world Scotch College has supplied more men to the élite recorded in *Who's Who in Australia* than any other Australian school: in 1980 there were still more Old Scotch collegians in *Who's Who* than there were Victorian Catholics, although eight years later the Catholics had begun to catch up on the Protestants in areas outside the Law. By 1988, however, products of the five 'Greater Protestants'—the Melbourne and Geelong Grammars, Scotch and Geelong Colleges and the Methodists' Wesley College—made up 41 per cent of the Victorians. If you added in Xavier College, the Catholic 'Public School', the 'great six' had 48 per cent of the Victorian-educated élite. Adding in St Kevin's College, De La Salle and the Jesuits' old St Patrick's College in East Melbourne (completing the 'Greater Catholics') and then including the remaining (or Lesser) Protestants, and 60 per cent of the élite was accounted for. Finally, adding in the 'Lesser Catholics' and the two selective high schools—Melbourne Boys' and the co-educational University High School—and 81 per cent of the male Victorian élite was seen to have been educated in a mass of private schools and one and a half government schools. Victoria's distinctiveness was even more clear when you compare it to New South Wales, where selective high schools assumed the central place in supplying the élite and the Protestant schools have, until very recent times, languished.[1]

Scotch College's contribution to the élite has not only been large, it has also been unusual. While the school has always educated a broad representation of men who achieved prominence in private enterprise, its domination comes more from its scientists, intellectuals and leading medical practitioners. Medicine had always been the highest secular calling for Presbyterians, but steadily through the post-war world, the Scotch medical élite has been shrinking to be replaced by the Scotch academic élite, especially of the generation at the school in the time of Colin Gilray. They have been far from uniformly conservative—in fact notable for their idealism and sense of community service. At the same time, many of these men are grateful to their old school, and have sent their sons to Scotch or to similar schools, confident that a private education does not doom the young to Toryism and selfishness. The Scotch élite is different from the Geelong and Melbourne Grammar élites—it is less wealthy and better educated to a small degree. It is better represented in the public service, and in some respects closer to the élite produced by Melbourne Boys'

---

[1] See Appendix III; also Mark Peel and Janet McCalman, *Who Went Where in Who's Who 1988.*

High than it is to those from the 'Light Blue Down Under' at Corio.[2] But even with Scotch College, those who find themselves in *Who's Who* constitute but a fraction of the men who emerged from the school in the 1930s. Of the 267 boys who started in the senior school in 1934 ten had found their way into *Who's Who* by 1980. Eight of the ten came from well-established families in business or the professions; only two appear to have been markedly better off in their fifties than their fathers were at the same age. In other words, their time at Scotch, while important, was not nearly as significant as their family origins—although this is not to diminish each man's achievements. Trinity Grammar also does well in the national *Who's Who* stakes, having four representatives of the 118 boys born 1919–20 and 38 in total: two were public servants, one a company director and the final one, Lawrence Cohn, has been recognized for his distinguished work in insurance.[3]

For middle-class men it was vital that they succeed out in the world. Being good citizens was also important, but if they could not earn enough money to maintain their class position, then the consequences would be both uncomfortable and humiliating. Few had family capital to fall back on if they became unable to provide. Most hoped to match or even exceed the level of material comfort enjoyed by their parents at the age of fifty, and most accomplished that. It is significant that the men surveyed from Scotch and Trinity, and the husbands of the women surveyed from MLC, were in roughly the same social position by the 1980s. Genazzano had retained its distinctiveness but, within the four school communities, there was little that could could not have been predicted from their career paths as young men. The new group to emerge in their fifties were the senior business executives—the lucky and the talented who had risen from their apprenticeship in clerical and accounting occupations. By their fifties they were owners of large or medium-sized businesses, merchants and exporters, company directors and secretaries, senior managers, consultants, accountants and actuaries. They can be loosely described as 'bourgeois' and they fit the stereotype of the successful product of the private school. But the most significant growth of all had been in the professions and sub-professions, at the expense of 'trade' and small business. The middle class had become even more a salaried class, dependent on intellectual capital and the bounty of the public sector. Yet despite the alleged advantages of the old school tie and the economic growth of the post-war years, a significant 15 per cent from Scotch remained locked into low status occupations of petty white collar work and trades. Comparing themselves with their fathers at the same stage in life, 54 per cent of the Scotch

---

[2] Ibid., pp. 29–30.
[3] Scotch 1934 Cohort; Trinity 1919–20-born Cohort.

men considered themselves better off financially and socially, 31 per cent were 'much the same' and 11 per cent were 'worse off'.[4]

From Trinity there had been more upward mobility, but that was because they had started further behind Scotch. Sixty-four per cent of the Trinity men reported that they were better off than their fathers had been, 28 per cent were 'much the same' and only 6 per cent were in a worse position. In all spheres the Trinity men had caught up on the Scotch men, as had the MLC husbands (half of whom had to get on despite the lack of an 'old-school tie'). Only 7.5 per cent from MLC considered themselves worse off than their parents had been in their fifties, a third were 'much the same' and an even 50 per cent were better off. (Fully 9 per cent felt unable or were unwilling to answer the question.) Genazzano husbands were the most distinguished in the learned professions, with a massive 19 per cent within the wider professional group of 30 per cent. Moreover, the Genazzano women have many more medical practitioners and lawyers in their extended families than do any of the Protestant schools.[5] They also had the most in the Public Service with 9 per cent, their nearest rival being Scotch with 6.8 per cent: yet all Scotch's public servants were middle rank or higher, whereas the Catholics had only one senior public servant, five in the middle ranks and five in the petty grades. Significantly different too was the number of Genazzano husbands at the top in business—a modest 13 per cent—which supports the analysis of *Who's Who in 1988*, where Catholic men, while improving, have not been able to penetrate the business élite to the extent they should have.[6]

The level of contentment with the financial rewards each had received during their working lives was remarkably similar across the four school communities, with just under three-quarters considering that they had been adequately rewarded financially 'for the effort [they] had put in during their working lives'.[7] (A minister's wife with admirable honesty

---

[4] See Appendix II: Tables 4b, 7a and 7b. Survey: 'Comparing your financial and social position by the time you were in your fifties, were you *better off/much the same/worse off* than your parents were at the same age?'

	Scotch	Trinity	MLC	Genazzano
Better off	54%	64%	50%	39%
Much the same	31%	28%	33%	38%
Worse off	11%	6%	8%	17%
N/A	4%	2%	9%	6%

[5] Survey: 'Do you have any medical practitioners or lawyers in your extended family?'

	Scotch	Trinity	MLC	Genazzano
No medical practitioners	65%	73%	60%	46%
No lawyers	72%	74%	70%	38%

[6] Peel and McCalman, op. cit., p. 30.

[7] Survey: 'Do you believe that you/and or your spouse have been adequately rewarded financially for the effort you have put in during your working life?'

	Scotch	Trinity	MLC	Genazzano
Yes	74%	74%	74%	73%
N/A	8%	4%	8%	13%

noted: 'Me?—teaching—yes, fairly adequately; spouse?—the ministry is a vocation, so financial reward *shouldn't* enter into it, but *No* would have to be the answer'.)[8] If we take the ability to send children to a private school for their entire education, then about a third are 'well off ', even though there are many exceptions to this particular indicator.[9] But not so many expressed strong feelings of achievement and satisfaction in their work. This was a Depression generation, and many found themselves in jobs for life which were not their choosing. One Trinity man was sent to school 'to learn to be a clerk and get a pension': his father being 'possessed that a white collar and a pension were more important than doing your own thing; [therefore in school exams] I failed myself '. Only his parents' death gave him the capital to start a small business and 'do his own thing'.[10] But among those who were very successful in business or the professions there was a high degree of pleasure in their work and attainments. One Scotch doctor recorded as one of his deep satisfactions in life:

> A moderately successful career as a general practitioner at a time when the work required of a G.P. was indeed general and not restricted as it tends to be nowadays to so-called 'family medicine'. In a career spanning forty-three years I have been able to deliver 976 babies and to perform a great deal of major surgery. In fact major surgery and orthopaedics have been my prime medical interests within the scope of general practice.

But an even greater satisfaction in his life has been 'an enduring loving marriage and the joyful rearing of a family of five children, all of whom have done well and are, I believe, making a worthwhile contribution to society'.[11] Another Scotch doctor listed as his life satisfactions:

1 The practice of medicine, notably obstetrics,
2 Travel in Italy,
3 Dining and wining with friends,
4 Listening to good jazz,
5 Watching first class tennis,

---

[8] Survey No. 497: MLC.

[9] See chapter five: Perfect Homes, footnote 24.
Survey: 'What were your reasons for not sending children to a church school?' Figures in brackets are the actual numbers.

	Scotch	Trinity	MLC	Genazzano
Financial	(8)40%	(21)50%	(17)61%	(1)14%
Philosophical	20%	21%	7%	(4)57%
Both	20%	19%	14%	14%

[10] Survey No. 1065: Trinity.
[11] Survey No. 787: Scotch.

6 Driving an Alfa Romeo,
7 Growing tomatoes,
8 Observing confusion in the Liberal Party.[12]

An important group who expressed great pleasure in their careers were school teachers. For one, it was not an early vocation: 'I was not at all sure what career I wanted when I was eighteen. In fact I spent several years "in the wilderness" before arriving at schoolmastering, and I count myself very fortunate to have been most happy and fulfilled in my chosen profession ever since'.[13] And for a research scientist, the great rewards have been 'having one's work approved by one's peers and having the work published as a permanent record'.[14] There were also unexpected careers, such as happened to one MLC woman: 'I don't know what I expected at eighteen, but I don't think I expected to teach and do research at a university, because I was not a particularly good student; or to occupy senior office-bearer positions, because I did not see myself as a leader'. She has no doubt that her family background made a great deal of difference in her life: 'I have had a fortunate life, being born in to a family of which my father was a minister in the public eye in Melbourne, which gave me an understanding of a cross-section of people and an ability to relate to other people'.[15]

It is perhaps these unexpected successes which have given the greatest satisfaction. One banker from Trinity reported: 'I reached greater heights than I could reasonably have expected—I have been an earnest conscientious employee and a successful and considerate employer—have made more people happy than I have made sad'. Summing up: 'It's been a good life . . . I suppose I'm a fatalist—get great joy from the world—the elements—the beauty and drama of its component parts'.[16] Such delight in success often comes more from rising from humble beginnings rather than from actually reaching the élite. One Scotch merchant banker was the son of a railway clerk and he describes himself emphatically as 'much better off'. Like many who rise substantially, he was an only child and the family's limited resources were devoted entirely to his education, but he listed as his life satisfactions:

---

[12] Survey No. 761: Scotch.

[13] Survey No. 756: Scotch. He listed among his favourite books, *Goodbye Mr Chips* and *To Serve Them all My Days*.

[14] Survey No. 727: Scotch.

[15] Survey No. 483: MLC.

[16] Survey No. 1002.

A long and happy marriage.
Watching the children's personalities developing.
Helping a number of people who got into scrapes.
Becoming slightly financially secure.
Playing cricket at a reasonable level until 57 years of age.[17]

Another outstandingly successful man from Scotch was the only child of a crane driver, and rose to hold a university chair in law:

> My family background had not prepared me for the possibility of achieving the further education I undertook, and the opportunities that opened up for attaining positions in Australia and overseas. Satisfactions? Being author or joint-author of seven books on Australian law and history, with the accompanying opportunities to attempt in some small way to work towards the development of an Australian identity, separate from the influences of the United Kingdom.
> And to be able to demonstrate that a person of working-class background could be sufficiently enabled by educational opportunities to become the first in five generations in this country to move into a significantly different role in this communiy. To be able to provide far wider opportunities for my children compared to those of my family in previous generations.[18]

Among the most moving of the stories of success were those from men and women who had failed at school, and there are many of them. There are quite a few women who took the opportunity in the Whitlam years to attend the university but, if men did not take the chance straight after the war, they have had to wait for retirement. More common are the cases where men forged ahead in their careers, despite their lack of qualifications. One company secretary left Scotch at the age of sixteen, with only the Merit certificate. His father was a state school–educated boot and shoe salesman who later had his own real estate business. The son left school 'to gain employment to save the expense of my education and to contribute at home'. He rose to become the executive officer for two major non-profit community organizations. In retirement, he tutors at the University of the Third Age:

> I've achieved so much more than I thought I would when eighteen. I feel I've been very fortunate in doing many things in the 'university of life'. No formal qualifications from established universities, but experience in many facets of my activities have enabled me to cope and 'hold my own' in a number of fields.[19]

---

[17] Survey No. 829: Scotch.

[18] Survey No. 735: Scotch.

[19] Survey No. 753: Scotch.

His favourite reading reveals a man fascinated with science and technology but, if his movement into middle-class education was frustrating and demoralizing, his children have fared better and proceeded to tertiary education: a family history which demonstrates how it has taken at least two generations for people who rise into the middle class to master its educational culture.

From the St Paul's Cathedral Choristers at Trinity Grammar come some of the most dramatic changes in destiny. The Kemp brothers both rose to senior positions in education, although for Dr Max Kemp it was despite the school. With others there was not just intellectual potential, but also musical talent. One was the son of a carpenter and the dominant satisfaction in his life has been:

> The realization of the love of my (elderly) parents, through their sacrifice, particularly in the Depression decade (1930s).
> And with the Church which afforded me and my brother a full scholarship—as Choristers of St Paul's Cathedral.
> And for me to lead a most satisfying career in music broadcasting.
> A growing optimism for life and a better world.[20]

Another is John Winstanley. The son of a musician, he was always drawn to a career in music, but as a St Paul's Chorister his schoolwork at Trinity suffered from the long hours of rehearsal, performance and travel and he remains critical of the school for its lack of understanding and support. The musical training in the choir under Dr A. E. Floyd was a different matter:

> While always wanting to be a musician, the thought of a future career as a teacher had never occurred to me—my ambitions lay in the field of Church music, having been a chorister from the age of ten, and in my last years at school being Assistant Organist to Dr A. E. Floyd. He was also responsible for my tuition in voice production, and in Theory, Harmony and Composition of music. It was the excellence of Dr Floyd's training which enabled me to 'get by' as a Warrant Officer Music and later to gain the diplomas in London and ultimately the degree in music at the University of Adelaide, which I could not have done without such a firm basis.
>
> In turn, it was as a result of my appointment as W.O. Music in the Army Education Service—requiring the organization of basic courses and the formation of singing groups amongst the troops—which led to my appointment at St Peter's College, Adelaide, where the duties of Director of Music entailed the combining of class music, choirs and orchestras, with daily services in the school chapel.

---

[20] Survey No. 1128: Trinity.

He went on to become Director of Music at Harrow School in England and to hold senior tertiary teaching positions in Australia. The high points of his career have all been musical: 'I never cease to be grateful for the "gift of music" which I inherited, and for the opportunities which life has given me to develop and express those talents—to be able to experience the great joy as well as the tragedy of music, such as Bach has given us in the St Matthew Passion—and to be able to share this with my family, the choirs and orchestras involved and with the listeners who are also absorbed into the power of music'.[21]

For women, success in careers in this generation has not been the preserve of the unmarried, as it was largely represented to them in their youth. An MLC doctor listed as the unexpected outcomes in her life: 'Originally I did not expect to marry, but had a wonderful marriage. I did not expect to live in the country, but I did and enjoyed it. I did not expect to have my own Australian art collection, but I have. I did not expect to become crippled with arthritis or have diabetic problems, but I have. But I still enjoy life'.[22] Another MLC doctor switched to university teaching so that she could give more time to her children than private practice would allow. Her family has given her the greatest satisfaction in life— 'and they still do'—but she is very conscious of her good fortune:

> I think I have been very privileged to have had parents who were so encouraging and who just assumed that their daughter would have equal chance with their son. To me, therefore, the feminist movement was largely irrelevant, though I acknowledge its importance to those not as lucky as I was. I also feel that I had the best of both worlds as I was able to pursue what interested me in my work without the burden of being the 'sole breadwinner'. The difference I see in many of the students today is that they regard their further education as a right rather than as a privilege. I'm still a believer in the Protestant work ethic. No-one is owed a living.[23]

The medical graduate among the Genazzano women has succeeded in combining private practice with having a family of five and cryptically replied to the questions on her youthful expectations: 'Only ever lived one day at a time'.[24] Genazzano has had its share of medical graduates, but it has an even larger number of women who would have done medicine

---

[21] Survey No. 1157: Trinity.

[22] Survey No. 494: MLC.

[23] Survey No. 509: MLC.

[24] Survey No. 11: Genazzano.

had their families approved or had the school been better at teaching science and mathematics. One whose family forbade medicine compensated by taking out a Ph.D. at Cambridge.[25]

There are also many women who insist that being a wife and mother is a career and that they have found their domestic role entirely fulfilling. Some are quite militant; most have taken deep pleasure in the rearing of their families. For a Genazzano mother of eight, her greatest satisfaction in life has been 'my large family and their achievements'.[26] Another who recorded that materially she was worse off than her parents had been, still had no doubt that 'God has smiled on us'.[27] And there were women from both schools whose lives had been as helpmates to eminent husbands. Only the childless wife of one such regrets now that she 'did not pursue [her] own field of interest'.[28] Perhaps the happy have less to say—'all happy families are alike'—but the simple statements of contentment that pervade the survey attest to the fact that the majority are, in their age of wisdom, happy with their lot, even if there have been regrets, disappointments and tragedies.

There are exceptions. Under the protection of anonymity, some vented their disappointment and despair: one Genazzano respondent complained that she 'married someone who wasn't as ambitious as me' and that 'men are hopeless',[29] but the heartache came more from men than from women, and a handful of men expressed the pain of masculine failure—or *perceived* masculine failure. A mercantile broker confessed that he 'did not attain the heights I aspired to, which was disappointing',[30] and a newsagent that he 'didn't try hard enough'.[31] A college lecturer was hard on himself, if fatalistic: 'Realizing my limited ability, critical attitude and mediocre personality (together with inevitable snubs), I have dismissed any aspirations [to community service]'. Moreover 'I do not believe (as some assert) that you can achieve any goal if you apply yourself assiduously toward it'.[32] A retired bank manager wrote bluntly:

---

[25] Survey No. 69: Genazzano.

[26] Survey No. 40: Genazzano.

[27] Survey No. 34: Genazzano.

[28] Survey No. 111: Genazzano.

[29] Survey No. 32: Genazzano.

[30] Survey No. 783: Scotch.

[31] Survey No. 790: Scotch.

[32] Survey No. 1000: Trinity.

My life apart from my marriage and the company of my children has been boring. The lack of integrity and absolute corruption by business and bureaucrats disgusts me. I have been plagued by serious illnesses and have received very little assistance from the medical profession, most of whom I despise.[33]

The son of a distinguished doctor who also went to Scotch, he lists one of his life's satisfactions as 'being my father's son'. He was unable to afford to send his own sons to his old school. Another son of an Old Collegian also suffered from feelings of frustration and inadequacy, despite doing well in his profession and being recognized by his peers: '[at eighteen] I imagined that I could do as well as grandfather who did very well as an immigrant from Scotland— but no such luck'. His only satisfaction has been 'raising an intelligent family' and his complaint was an anguished: 'I have lived the wrong life and it is too late to advance any further—I don't mean wrong-doing—just failed to utilize the available potential'.[34] The children of high achievers, especially men, have to come to terms with their lesser accomplishments, an adjustment made more difficult in a society where there is much upward social mobility. Boys who were their social inferiors at school can overtake their own status and wealth in adult life; and those schools which produce high achievers are enveloped in a culture of success. For those who have advanced little, or even slipped behind, Old-boy reunions are a painful lesson in their inadequacy. This is particularly so with Scotch College, where its size has ensured that it has a powerful and very visible 'old-boy aristocracy'. One Old Collegian described himself as: 'A very selfish person of limited achievements, limited ability, drive, energy and low social profile, who detests the "Public School image" as portrayed in *Great Scot*.[35] An over-reaction but am trying to be brutally honest'.[36] Not all who are less successful than they wanted project their frustration on to the school; for some, the high public profile of their former school-mates confers a sympathetic magic on those who were just one of the pack all those years ago. But the higher the status of the school, the more painful it can be for those who consider themselves to have fallen behind.

For women, marriage was even more important than career in measuring success. Those who never married sometimes suffered a sense of failure as well as of emotional loss, although it is not unknown for the

---

[33] Survey, No. 738: Scotch.

[34] Survey No. 739: Scotch.

[35] *Great Scot* is the quarterly magazine of The Scotch Family.

[36] Survey No. 794: Scotch.

single to see themselves as better off than their friends who married un-happily. And among those who did marry, the question was whether they 'married well', as not a few of their mothers had once wished for them. Some who 'married down' none the less adjusted well: a Genazzano school teacher returned to work and study after having seven children, and since doing so she has been 'less influenced by [her] husband's views'. Life has not quite turned out as she expected at eigh-teen: 'financially a lot worse than expected—no leisure time'. She has dealt with this well: 'Compared to my school friends, I haven't married well (in terms of money, power, status) and frankly I don't feel comfort-able now with that elitist group. However, compared with the majority of world citizens I and my family have enjoyed a comfortable life style for which I am thankful'.[37]

Among those who evaluated their social and financial position as be-ing worse off than their parents' in their prime, there were many from Genazzano who had 'married down', or for whom the raising of a large family had drained their financial resources. One doctor's daughter mar-ried a fitter and turner who became a mechanical plant supervisor, and had nine children. Yet in middle life, she was better off than her own mother had been after being widowed early. Clearly things have been difficult at times, but she is proud of her husband: 'He is a "workaholic" and was not fully appreciated—was retrenched. I have a good husband who has worked hard to provide us with a comfortable home and secu-rity. I am happy living in our suburb and have sincere friends'. They now live on the old-age pension.[38] Some Protestants had large families too. A Trinity pharmacist, who had been half-way through a medical degree when his father was killed and he was forced to leave university to run the family pharmacy business, became the father of six: 'My wife and I did not plan a large family of six children (quite unusual for an Anglican phar-macist!) Family and children have been a great satisfaction to me, espe-cially when my wife had twin sons (not identical) in 1968—gives us something "special" which cannot be attained by most families'.[39] Some have reached retirement age with insufficient capital and superannuation, and have never caught up on the years lost to building personal equity in the war and the 1950s. *Doug Gordon* is one of many doctors forced to keep working after sixty-five simply because they lacked adequate superannua-tion. Among the 'worse off' are those women who were widowed early,

---

[37] Survey No. 2: Genazzano.

[38] Survey No. 28: Genazzano.

[39] Survey No. 1041: Trinity.

were deserted or divorced. Loss of the male breadwinner imperilled financial security in the middle class, for as long as women suffered lower occupational opportunities and rewards; but those women who succeeded in raising their families alone are justifiably proud of their achievements. A number, like Elaine Corran, confess that they only acquired self-confidence after they lost their husbands and had to cope on their own. This generation had fully expected to be 'kept'—as one Genazzano woman admitted: 'At eighteen I hoped to get married, stay in one place and not have to go out to work again. Am now working full-time when I should be home'.[40] With others, businesses failed and careers went wrong, and guilt has been hard to avoid, especially when the business was a family one handed down in trust. And there are men who did poorly at school and who were ill-suited to jobs requiring literacy and numeracy. One 'escaped' from Trinity because he was 'too slow' and had 'developed an inferiority complex', but he counts himself as happy and fulfilled as a dairy farmer:

> I was never clever and I was not blessed with any skills: but I'm satisfied with what I've achieved with any abilities I have. My life has been simple and uneventful. At one stage during my farming life I leaned heavily on the local business community for credit. It was never refused and I only had to ask for time to pay and it was granted. The assistance given me at the time was, I thought, a tacit acceptance of my honesty and has always given me a great satisfaction and pleasure.
>
> As to the world—with the enormous increase in the human population in the last sixty years, and our frightening ability to destroy, I can't help feeling pessimistic about the future of the world as a nice place to live. I feel I've lived my life during the best period of human history.[41]

No amount of family wealth can protect you against the 'slings and arrows of outrageous fortune', especially those of war. If war service gave many men new confidence, new skills and new opportunities, there were still many for whom the war clouded the rest of their lives. Fully 68 per cent of the Trinity and Scotch men reported that the war had 'significantly affected the course of their lives'.[42] It was often a positive change, as testified by a highly successful accountant:

> At eighteen in 1935–6 my future life pattern appeared set in relation to study, career, environment, travel, personal and family relationships; my value judgements reflected limited exposure to the enormously complex and varied

---

[40] Survey No. 18: Genazzano.

[41] Survey No. 1023: Trinity.

[42] 'Did your war service significantly affect the course of your life?' Yes: Scotch, 67%; Trinity, 70%.

cultures and life patterns that existed throughout the world. Survival from air force service where the death rate was 50 per cent, has, I suspect, drastically changed my philosophical attitude to many of life's problems. A few years of life within an environment where a failure to consistently perform complex tasks with competence and exactitude would result in almost certain death certainly permanently changes behaviour patterns. I have been able to attain almost all personal goals I have set myself and I have many close friendships with people in very diverse areas of endeavour. So I suppose diverse personal relationships are my greatest satisfaction.[43]

But for another, now a Totally and Permanently Invalid pensioner who returned with both physical and mental disabilities, 'the effort of so many of us and sacrifices of thousands—1939–45 war—was a complete waste of the best part of our lives'.[44] A survivor of a Japanese prisoner of war camp said tersely: 'At 19.5 years became Japanese POW—changed my life completely' and his greatest satisfaction has been simply 'to survive war years and exist in later years'. By his fifties he was a pensioner.[45] The war left unexpected psychological legacies which lurked in the subconscious. *Dick Wallace* was greatly surprised by his occasional nightmares because in his opinion he hadn't had a bad war:

I had a few nasty bits—but most of it was just sheer boredom, yet I had a few nightmares and it hung around. But I went back to New Guinea—to see, as a matter of interest—and apparently I must have purged it.

This was at the Wewak airstrip, with the artillery and we'd dug into the side of a hill. And when I went back in 1978, I was sitting up with the pilot in the little aeroplane and I said, 'Good God—can we go over there? I think I lived there for a couple of months'. It was just a cavity in the side of a hill and it was still there and you could see that I'd dug there. Every time they'd fire a shell, you'd dig down another two or three feet. It wasn't particularly dangerous or anything—it was just uncomfortable. I hired a car and went up to Wewak on my own and I wanted to drive to a place called Brandi, which had been shelled pretty nastily. And I drove around the corner, sort of getting a bit emotional and I came around where we'd been shelled and blokes killed and so on—and it was a high school— Brandi High School. Kids playing all around the place—a sort of anti-climax. What I realized then was that I must have had some idea that places had a memory, or something showed. But no—I was delighted to see the kids.

---

[43] Survey No. 799: Scotch.

[44] Survey No. 1044: Trinity.

[45] Survey No. 1100: Trinity.

The actual disability rate suffered by the returned men from Trinity and Scotch is comparatively high, considering the ratio of those on active service to those in support services and those who remained in Australia. Between them, 36 per cent reported lasting disabilities, with three-quarters suffering from purely physical disabilities and the rest from mental disabilities, often mixed with physical ones; and 27.5 per cent are receiving disabled ex-servicemen's pensions. These figures are high first because of the high proportion who had been in the Air Force, and second because of the high incidence of tropical diseases which afflicted combatants and non-combatants alike.[46] The returned men also have not always received the sympathy and understanding they deserved, and much of the problem has been the public image of the R.S.L, in the opinion of *Ron Pearson*:

> One of the strange things I've found is that we've gone through a period where the young people just weren't interested—they couldn't care less. I'd try and sell poppies or Anzac Day tokens and they just weren't interested. Then, round about the 1970s, the young girls at the office used to come up and say, 'Can we sell any tokens for you?' and there seemed to be a great deal more interest in it. Previously there'd been this feeling that the R.S.L. get together and booze up. But one of the reasons why the R.S.L. attracts men is that they can talk there without being accused of boasting and they talk of experiences which they know other men will appreciate. But you talk to someone else and they'd say, 'Oh yes, it must have been terrible—then what's the price of eggs today?' They'd bring it back to the mundane.

The R.S.L. also attracts members because of the work it has done for ex-servicemen in fighting for their rights and benefits. Many of those who have had to apply for disability pensions have found it humiliating and frustrating. *Richard Stanton* began drawing a part pension in 1961 after his first breakdown, and by 1969 had qualified for a full one. But in 1986 he chose to go before the Administrative Appeals Tribunal, representing his own case for full T.P.I. status, despite his deafness and lack of legal training: 'It was an exhausting but successful day'. There are many stories of the difficulty returned servicemen have had in proving that their cancers and heart conditions are the long-term consequences of their war service. And as they grow older, those years in the jungles and deserts and prison camps begin to exact their final legacy. *Walters Rhodes*' long distant malaria predisposed him to the leukaemia which claimed his life in 1992, and

---

[46] Survey: 'Have you suffered any lasting disabilities from your war service?' Scotch: Yes, 34%, including physical disabilities, 74%, mental disability, 4% and both, 22%; Trinity, Yes, 38%, including physical disabilities, 74%, 24% both physical and mental disabilities, 2% N/A.
'Are you or your spouse receiving a disabled ex-servicemen's pension?' Yes: Scotch, 25%; Trinity, 29%; MLC, 24%; Genazzano, 22%.

for him Bruce Ruxton was 'a wonderful man—I don't believe in all that he believes in—but it's what he's done for the R.S.L.; and some of the old blokes he's employed down there in his business—he's a wonderful man for the returned bloke'. Almost 40 per cent of Scotch and Trinity men admire Bruce Ruxton, a number ringing his name on the questionnaire as their greatest hero in Australian public life. Many of these returned servicemen have been permanently marked by the war and stand apart from their school mates, both older and younger.

Minds and Manners

Those men who went to the war, especially those who went straight into the forces from school, are markedly more conservative, more angry and more disillusioned with modern Australian society than those who did not. From both Scotch and Trinity, those who left school in the late 1930s included the smallest proportion of Labor voters and leftward-swingers, and those who left school after the war the most. From Genazzano and MLC there were quite different patterns where the proportion of Labor and DLP voters and leftward-swingers rose slightly as the respondents became younger. The four school communities are, of course, predominantly conservative and consistent in their support for the coalition, but what is striking is the reluctance of the informants to apply political party labels to themselves. MLC had the most 'Liberals' (42.5 per cent) and the most 'Labor' (13 per cent)—a symptom of Methodist plain speaking perhaps, but it also had the fewest 'conservatives' (21 per cent) and the most who saw themselves as 'middle-of the-road' and 'small 'l' liberal (40 per cent). Many respondents chose both 'conservative' and 'Liberal' and hidden among the 'small 'l' liberals and 'middle-of the roaders' are many broken hearted long-time Labor supporters. This survey was made in September 1990, during the fall from grace of the Cain Labor government in Victoria, but even from Scotch, John Cain's old school, a quarter of the respondents admired him and he did far better than another old Scotch boy—Jeff Kennett. Looking carefully at the four school communities, MLC is the least conservative and Trinity, with its more ambiguous social status, the most conservative: but the differences are small. MLC has produced the most frequent Labor and leftward-swinging voters with 36 per cent, Scotch comes second with 35 per cent, Trinity third with 30 per cent and Genazzano far behind with 21 per cent. However, in Genazzano's case, another 25 per cent appear to have given the DLP some support before reverting, or converting, to voting Liberal

or National party. Moreover, 9 per cent of the Genazzano women still identify themselves as DLP and most would insist that the DLP has always had a
deep commitment to social justice. Therefore, in that sense 30 per cent of the
Genazzano women do not identify with the coalition and vote on social justice issues—a figure closer to the three Protestant schools. Among those who
left Scotch in 1950 fully 41 per cent appear to have voted Labor often—an
immense contrast with the mere 28 per cent of the 1938 school leavers who
have. And at Trinity the same pattern emerged.[47]

The post-war generation, of course, has been a lucky one. They
were too young for the war and there were Commonwealth scholarships
to take them to university, so they are better educated and more
materially successful than the 1934 and 1938 leavers. Not that the
successful do not have strong views: a Trinity doctor complained:

1 Socialistic trends appear to have weakened the work ethic,
2 Lack of morals in political people,
3 Poor teaching in state schools,
4 Vocal few get more attention than due to them—earlier they would have
   been dismissed as 'ratbags',
5 Biased news,
6 Misinformation rampant—eg. 'Greenies'.[48]

A successful businessman, who reported that he 'made [his] own success in
business' and did not use the 'old school tie', was critical of the media for its left-
wing 'indoctrination', of 'Labor and unionism being rife among State School
teachers', of working mothers not being 'good home makers' and that the
Public Service as well as 'Mr Hawke and his cohorts don't give a damn for ex-
servicemen and women'—'politics is at its lowest level in my lifetime'.[49] A
Scotch newsagent is deeply disappointed in the calibre of young Australia and
voted DLP 'when one of their platforms was conscription for all youth of
Australia, which in my opinion is absolutely essential from all angles'. He
believes that standards in the use of the English language and in everyday manners have deteriorated and 'shockingly so'. The former Labor Deputy Prime
Minister, Dr Jim Cairns, he condemns as a 'traitor' and he is deeply pessimistic:

I think that the Australian youth of today are generally speaking foul-
mouthed, mannerless, completely undisciplined and uncontrolled. Whilst
the so-called big business people and politicians are in many cases so cor-
rupt that unless decency is brought back on top our country will indeed
finish up a 'banana republic' or worse.[50]

---

[47] See Appendix II, tables 10, 11, 12 and 13.
[48] Survey No. 1160: Trinity.
[49] Survey No. 733: Scotch.
[50] Survey No. 719: Scotch.

This newsagent is among the 7 per cent from Scotch who nominated themselves as racist; Trinity came second with 5 per cent, MLC next with 2 per cent and Genazzano had a solitary offender. Genazzano and MLC have produced the most anti-racists—25 per cent and the men half that number.[51] Some of this middle-class racism comes from the war, but much of it is to do with a resentment towards multiculturalism and a fear of Asian immigration. No one mentioned Aboriginal land rights as a source of irritation; rather it is the retreat of their anglophile middle-class culture in the face of the new multi-cultural Australia that is regretted, even grieved over. If Genazzano is now the most staunchly Liberal of the four school communities, it is by far the least royalist and the least xeno-phobic—the Irish and European heritages, and the Catholic Church's consistent opposition to racism and support of multiculturalism have taken effect. But the distress at losing the world they inherited, cultivated and passed on to the next generation is powerful and moving; and it is this distress that animates Professor Geoffrey Blainey and accounts for his many admirers among the Protestants and somewhat fewer supporters from Genazzano.[52] A Trinity newsagent spoke for many when he declared: 'Multi-culturalism should be discouraged, the burning of an Australian flag recently was terrible. I don't think that using a radio station to broadcast Italian will help newcomers into our ways, if they don't like them, send them home'.[53] These discomforts with the times are of course not confined to men, and a woman from MLC wrote feelingly:

> I do not feel that the world is the happy one in which I grew up. The sexual attitudes of young people offend me and our governments seem not only to condone it but to encourage it. Also offensive is the attitude that the government should be responsible for so many extras. The old saying 'The Lord helps those who help themselves' might well be put into action now. We are too lenient on criminals. Our immigration policies have got out of hand. We lack support for our 'senior citizens' and our war veterans, the people who did so much to make this the 'Lucky Country'. Maybe I'm just a small town girl at heart.[54]

Another old collegian was angry that the deserving were no longer being rewarded:

> Sadly, somewhere in the early 1970s we lost the idea of giving a fair day's work for a fair day's pay. People seemed to think they really didn't need to work honestly, consistently and well, but should be rewarded with

---

[51] See Appendix II, table 10.
[52] See Appendix II, Table 12.
[53] Survey No. 1176: Trinity.
[54] Survey No. 404: MLC.

R.D.O.s, sickies, wage rises, leave loadings etc. The Protestant work ethic was scorned and the attitudes of most seemed to be—the world owed us a living. The payment of unemployment benefit without requiring work to be done for it was a great mistake. The welfare state has developed a nation of takers instead of givers. I don't think that the needy should suffer, but all who are physically able should contribute effort in return for sustenance.

[As for my husband and myself], we have never been materialistic, but the long hours of conscientious work—never taking days off and very rarely sick leave—was not rewarded with the salary and superannuation available today. I don't believe that today's workers know their jobs well or work nearly as hard as in earlier times.[55]

While critical of much in the 1980s, not all were bowed down with pessimism, as with this Scotch 'bank officer':

Quite obviously the world has changed enormously in my lifetime. I haven't caused any of the vast changes. Have I kept up with them? I think so—those which I have felt relevant to my situation. Which is not to say that I have not been happy with them all.

I regret the drop in standards of public and political morality, the clamour for rights with no thought of responsibilities as a necessary corollary, the bias against authority, the drift away from faith, and thereby from commitment and a sense of meaning in life.

The relentless Quest for Equality, though doomed to perpetual failure, has brought enormous benefits to great numbers of people and also to the community. The best of our young people are a great joy and a great sign of hope.[56]

A Trinity doctor, however, 'greatly deplores the cult of the mediocre and the economic and political trends to reduce everybody to be "average"— the failure to encourage the brilliant innovations and the paucity of funds for research and tertiary education will ensure that Australia will be always a backward country'.[57] This great struggle between the 'Quest for Equality' and the 'Pursuit of Excellence' lies at the heart of private schooling. Whether they feel comfortable about this or not, private schools, in addition to any religious commitments they espouse, are dedicated to the creation of social inequality. At the basest level this means superior social status to those who go to government or systemic Catholic schools; at the most refined level this means producing young people so trained in

---

[55] Survey No. 444: MLC.

[56] Survey No. 825: Scotch.

[57] Survey No. 1008: Trinity.

self-confidence, moral thought and intellectual skill that they are destined for leadership and to serve the nation from its highest positions. In other words, if going to a private school enables you to feel superior without ever having to achieve anything, then social privilege can only be justified if that privilege is returned to the community in some form of service: 'From those to whom much is given, much will be required'. The question to ask now is whether those of this generation which had the good fortune to attend these schools and others like them in the 1930s and 1940s really are different because of that opportunity and whether it has made a substantial difference to the outcome of their lives.

Of the four schools it is at Scotch and MLC that this 'duty of privilege' has been most debated and celebrated. John Blanch in every way personifies the highest ideals of Scotch: 'I've often tried to think of a justification for private schools, and I reckon that one of the major factors is the sense of community responsibility that most ex-public school girls and boys have. I think that in the state system we haven't seen it quite as strongly—some are good, but again there's much of the "nine to four" attitude'. Geoff Tolson has reflected for years on the 'magic' of Scotch, and for him it has always been not the academic achievements, but the production of 'good citizens'. He regrets the abandonment of school caps, for what they taught a boy and for what they symbolized to the outside world:

> The wearing and tipping of his cap automatically showed a boy's respect to his superiors and/or elders. It may sound infantile, but I assure you that it created a condition within oneself that showed a standard or respect that began to gain momentum as a boy got older.
>   The standard of boy that comes out of the school—the training of little things, all put together—turn out a superb finished product. You'll hear in football a coach say—'remember all the little things I've taught you, because when you get out there, you'll put all the little things together and we'll have success'. And that's what happened here—all those little things got put together so that the end product was good for society. I'm sure it happened in other schools, but I wonder whether generally in education today there aren't as many 'little things' as there were. That may be hard, but I see the Sixth formers here and I do see the superbness of the boy. Maybe I'm being a bit harsh, but I do feel there is a different standard in society in general, which emanates probably from when the person leaves school.

Alan Reid honours Colin Gilray for his teaching of moral responsibility: 'All that Scotch was giving you was the opportunity to live a life that could be responsible', and Alan was one of those receptive boys for whom Scotch was a spiritual and intellectual catalyst. Another was Hal Hallenstein, the Victorian Coroner:

It changed my life. It's a place where the theme running through every-thing is that you should serve your community. Scotch introduced an ability to be physically independent, to know how to read a compass and a map, put on old clothes and disappear into the bush. I see this as a very good basis for life in a young country which has a robust, youthful feel about it.[58]

But it was MLC under Dr Wood which made 'From those to whom much is given, much will be required' its own. Methodists envisaged Christ as 'the suffering servant', and the highest purpose in life was service, first to God and second to the world; and the idealism of the school touched many:

My life was greatly influenced by Dr Wood. Upon reflection I see my early childhood as very unsettled, as my mother died in my second year and many 'nurses' took her place until my father married a *very* acceptable substitute mother. Their sacrifice to send my sister and myself briefly to MLC raised my self-esteem even then, and the whole ethos of the school and the fact that Dr Wood always, even from day one, knew my name made a lasting impact! The values—Christian, effort because of privilege, music—have remained my philosophy of life. Teachers—Miss Kellaway, Miss Flockart, Miss Betty Jackson.[59]

These are sentiments echoed often in the survey and among old collegians everywhere.

Yet is this generation distinctive? What in the 1990s are the mental marks of being middle-class and private-school? First, they are well travelled and reasonably cultured. Eighty-five per cent have travelled overseas, with England and Scotland being the most popular destinations, with the addition of Ireland for Genazzano. (The Methodists have made more trips to Italy than the Catholics.) The men have made more trips to Communist countries, but still a good number from Genazzano have been to China. They have seen more of the outside world than any previous Australian generation and overseas travel has been one of their greatest life pleasures. They watch ABC and SBS television, with Genazzano being the keenest multicultural viewers—fully a quarter watch SBS regularly. Of the commercial channels, only Channel 9 reaches double figures, peaking with 24 per cent from MLC (MLC's SBS viewers are 19 per cent). All pale into insignificance next to the 78 per cent who watch the ABC. Those who live in Melbourne overwhelmingly read the *Age* (highest—MLC with 70 per cent, lowest Trinity with 58 per cent); of

---

[58] *Sunday Age*, 25 February 1990.

[59] Survey No. 379: MLC.

284 JOURNEYINGS

the few who read the *Australian* most are men, and around 20 per cent read the *Sun*. Women are the most regular readers of books (MLC 74 per cent and Genazzano 68 per cent) while just over half the men are. What is fascinating is that the men are not keener readers than their fathers were—their greater education making little impact on the family's 'habit of books'. Instead it is among the MLC women that there has been the greatest change in private reading habits over two generations. Music is another touchstone of private culture, and here gender was a deciding factor. Just over half of the MLC women play a musical instrument (87 per cent the piano, 6 per cent the violin) as do 38 per cent from Genazzano, where the piano is even more dominant. Twenty-two per cent of the men can play an instrument, but whereas just 2 per cent of MLC women play the organ, 27 per cent of the Anglican men do—a significant gender difference in church music. As for taste in music, 81 per cent of the men like classical music, and 93 per cent of the women do. This generation are active patrons of the arts, with only 30 per cent of the men, 24 per cent of the Genazzano women (many of whom live in the country) and 16 per cent of the MLC women never attending concerts, the opera, the ballet or live theatre. A quarter of the women attend all four. To the question 'Did your time at a church school foster in you a love for the arts?' the answers varied. At Scotch, despite the efforts of Colin Gilray and John Bishop, only 32 per cent said yes; at Trinity, with its cathedral choir boys, the answer was predictably higher at 42 per cent, but the women scored over 60 per cent—the acquiring of culture and accomplishments holding a higher place in the private school world of between the wars.[60]

If their tastes and leisure pursuits are different, what of their social attitudes? They were asked various questions about the role and character of 'church schools', and overwhelmingly they believe that church schools provide both a better academic and moral education than do state schools, and that they do have a special role in 'the preparation of young people for future leadership in society'.[61] Very few respondents added the qualification that such a role is the duty of all schools. They were then asked about their own values and behaviour. 'Have you ever felt you had a special duty to accept leadership, even though you might have preferred to stay on the sidelines?' to which two-thirds of the Protestants answered yes, as did almost as many from Genazzano. They were, in their senior

---

[60] Survey.
[61] Survey: 'Do church schools give a better academic education than state schools?' Yes: Scotch, 91%; Trinity, 76%.
'Do church schools give a better moral education than state schools? 'Yes: Scotch, 81%; Trinity, 83%.
'Do church schools have a special role in preparing young people for future leadership in society?' Yes: Scotch, 82%; Trinity, 72%; MLC, 83%; Genazzano, 83%.

years, comfortable with the quality and quantity of their contribution to the community and to their workplace: here MLC women were the least guilt-stricken (26 per cent) and Scotch men the most (36 per cent).[62] One who did suffer some sense of guilt was one of the most successful in business among the Scotch respondents, who of his satisfactions wrote:

> Good health in general for all my family and an interesting and rewarding life; gratitude for my good fortune, almost to the point of guilt feelings as my knowledge of the sufferings of so many people multiplies and my basic helplessness increases.

As for his contribution to the community:

> No outstanding contribution. I have been a good (in my opinion) citizen, helped neighbours etc. I have contributed financially each year to approximately twenty-five charities—above all every year of my working life I have paid income and other taxes many times in excess of the government services received by me and my family. In other words I have helped support a lot of people indirectly financially and am grateful to have been in this position.[63]

Few of this generation admired the capitalist achievers of the 1980s—Alan Bond, John Elliott or Rupert Murdoch—but such generosity from a high taxpayer was rare.[64]

Concern about personal goodness bothered only just over a third of both men and women—but whether the majority are morally complacent or simply emotionally mature is another, unanswered, question.[65] Certainly, the pursuit of personal goodness was impressed on them by the churches in their youth, but now only a minority are troubled by doubts about the quality of their moral life. The Genazzano women are the most prone to guilt (but only slightly so) but, since Vatican II, the decay of the weekly spiritual cycle of confesssion and repentance has relieved many of the nagging sense of personal sinfulness which clouded Catholic private life. Life experience had also taught the men that those educated in church schools did not have a monopoly on moral decency, for only 27 per cent still find it easier to trust the values of someone who also went to a church school.[66] But the telling test of whether these schools succeeded

---

[62] Survey: 'Have you ever felt a special duty to accept leadership even though you may have preferred to stay on the sidelines?' Yes: Scotch, 67%; Trinity, 66%; MLC, 69%; Genazzano, 61%.
[63] Survey No. 811: Scotch.
[64] See Appendix II, table 12.
[65] Survey: 'Do you worry much about being a "good person"?' Yes: Scotch, 34%; Trinity, 35%; MLC, 36%; Genazzano, 38%.
[66] Survey: Yes: Scotch, 26%; Trinity, 27%.

in producing people who accepted that privilege needed to be atoned for by service, is how they responded to the question: 'Has the motto "From those to whom much is given, much will be required" had any special relevance in your life?' Predictably, the affirmative was high from MLC (64 per cent), but it was also strong from Genazzano (57 per cent), despite their greater political conservatism and the onetime Catholic emphasis on personal spiritual improvement rather than on service to society. The Protestant men fell away however, particularly from Scotch, where just 37 per cent gave an unequivocal 'yes'.[67] In this sense, the boys' schools and, to a lesser extent, the girls' schools, had not quite succeeded in producing the moral citizens they had proclaimed as the justification for their existence. The men are little different from men from any section of society. If a vocal minority celebrate the public school virtues, this does not mean that most products of these schools practised them, nor that they were exclusive to the moral middle class. One man wrote eloquently of the Scotch ideal. He was one of that important but little-heard group who were at the school for only a year. He rose from being a clerk to being a factory manager. He also changed in his politics from 'confirmed conservative' to 'mostly Labor' and he considers that his one year at Scotch did change the course of his life:

> In retrospect, my family and school influences encouraged a strong work ethic, a sense of personal independence and self-responsibility, and some idea of service to others. No doubt also a habit of reticence and a feeling that displays of emotion should be avoided except in intimate and personal relationships. With all this went a feeling that ambition and striving for success was a good goal and that material objectives were a good measure of a person's ability to achieve; one should foster close and supportive family groups and maintain this without help from government or anyone else.[68]

These were fine values, but they were typical of the time and of the whole society, and not exclusive to middle-class products of church schools.

So what, in the final analysis, did their private schooling do for their adult lives and careers? To *Struggletown*'s eyes, the old school tie's magic smoothes the paths to success, affluence and status, but when asked whether the old school tie really 'does make a difference in business and

---

[67] Has the motto 'From those to whom much is given, much will be required' ever had any special relevance in your life?

	Scotch	Trinity	MLC	Genazzano
Yes	37%	40%	64%	57%
Yes, qualified	3%	2%		
No	54%	52%	29%	34%
N/A	6%	5%	7%	9%

[68] Survey No. 778: Scotch.

the professions', there was considerable ambivalence from these college men and women. Just over half the men agreed that it did but there were 12 per cent among those who gave only a qualified assent. The women were more confident of its magical powers with 70 per cent.[69] But when you analyse the occupations of those who replied 'no', many turn out to be those who are the most successful in business and the professions. When they were asked whether it had actually ever helped themselves, only 36 per cent from Scotch replied that it had, 30 per cent from Trinity, and 33 per cent from the women.[70] Comments from the questionnaires and oral evidence fleshed this out: the old school tie had done its bit for them many years ago—getting that first job as an office boy in the Depression, or a a bit of help when times were tough, or a commission during the war. In job opportunities it was mostly small beer—talent and experience were the qualities that mattered in later life. The 'old school tie' also became less significant as more and more young men and women acquired a tertiary education. One Scotch company secretary noted: 'it helped when I left school—probably less significant now'.[71] As for the professions, with the exception of obtaining articles for the law, most would consider appointing someone on the basis of the old school tie unethical. If the applicant happened to be good and suitable for the job, then the shared old school tie was a pleasant social bonus. Asked whether they had ever given preference to someone merely because of the old school tie, just 10 per cent of the men and 7 per cent of the women 'pleaded guilty'.[72] It needs to be remembered also that, even into the 1950s, people showed favouritism for other connections as well—church affiliation, membership of lodges and Friendly and Temperance societies and sporting associations. The most powerful networks of all were extended family and family friends. In a smaller, more intimate urban society, people moved in communities and maintained those connections when they moved into the outside world so that, in obtaining first jobs in

---

[69] 'Does "the old school tie" really make a difference in business and the professions?'

	Scotch	Trinity	MLC	Genazzano
Yes	42%	42%	55%	64%
Yes, qualified	11%	12%	16%	6%
No	41%	39%	20%	20%
N/A	6%	7%	9%	10%

[70] Survey: 'Has "the old school tie" ever helped you?'

	Scotch	Trinity	MLC	Genazzano
Yes	31%	23%	28%	32%
Yes, qualified	4%	7%	4%	3%
No	62%	68%	62%	55%
N/A	3%	2%	6%	10%

[71] Survey No. 810: Scotch.

[72] Survey: 'Have you ever given someone preference simply because of the "old school tie"?' Yes: Scotch, 11%; Trinity, 10%; MLC, 7%; Genazzano, 8%. Only Genazzano had a significant refusal to answer the question.

the 1930s, the local church and its extended 'family' would have played a much more important role than 'the old school'.

This is not to deny the power and richness of the old school networks and Scotch would have one of the most extensive and self-conscious networks in Australia. For Geoff Tolson, 'Scotch is a way of life in my book—and it comes down to one thing and that's what's called *values* and it's just what gets naturally taught'. He is deeply proud of 'the network':

> The success of the network depends on the quality of the boys a school produces—if they're not good citizens, then the network will have trouble in succeeding. The fact that we are the oldest school—a fact not mentioned in a way to be snobbish—but it makes the approach to the heritage of the school something of exceeding pride. And in so doing—like a Stawell Gift runner—'can you find another yard?' and our people seem to find that extra yard. They know that the heritage they are fulfilling is there because of the part *all* previous generations have played up till then. And we stress to each boy now, that irrespective of how successful he may be in the school, each individual boy plays a part in the heritage of the school. It might be miniscule, it might be great, but each boy is important to the school. Equally he could do damage to the school as well, but that doesn't often occur.
>
> So we have a base that makes our network work. And because we have a very old Old Boys' association, we're certain that we know the best things to do because of being able to correct our past mistakes. The network's not just the Old Boys—it's the whole Scotch family and that's an aspect that since the 1960s has been of tremendous importance to the school. The Old Boy working of the school is exceedingly strong. For instance, we don't only have a president of Old Scotch, but we have four vice-presidents, which means they have four years to become involved in just that step up from a Council member. And for those four years they are made responsible for a quarter of all activities associated with Old Scotch. And believe me, there are a multitude of activities. We have about 13 000 members.

Yet the great pride in the old school and the continuing social networks do not necessarily represent the debt of gratitude felt by the majority of their former students. The outstanding men and women are often deeply grateful to the teachers who inspired and guided them. Archie Crow:

> Just two years ago I was out at the annual dinner of the Mornington Peninsula branch of the O.S.C.A. I gave the toast to the school and on that occasion, the highlight of the night was the guest speaker, Sir Benjamin Rank, a pioneering plastic surgeon, who gave high praise to his schooling at Scotch a generation before mine. He said, 'I really owe

everything to my school and to those committed teachers who insisted that I reach certain standards, and they laid foundations of my professional life. Sir Zelman Cowen was several years ahead of me at Scotch and a number of others too went on to distinguished positions in the community—and not just money makers by any means. They were people of depth and integrity.

What of the troops? Only about half of these men claim that their education at Scotch College or Trinity Grammar made 'a real difference' to their lives. The women were quite different, with almost 80 per cent claiming that their time at Genazzano or MLC did change their lives— but this had more to do with hearts and souls than with minds and manners.[73]

Hearts and Souls

For *Marina Graham* her faith gives her comfort 'all of the time' and that faith was deeply affected by the nuns at Genazzano:

> I say my prayers every day. I'm the least pious person you could possibly meet. I don't have any pious practices. I do go to Mass every Sunday and I'm a regular communicant. I tune in avidly to any religious programme—I love Caroline Jones' 'The Search for Meaning'. I'm particularly interested in mysticism—though I don't claim to understand a lot, it holds an endless fascination for me.
>
> When I went to England last, I made a special trip to Norwich just to see the cell of Dame Julian. I went to Walsingham and I was a bit disappointed in it. I haven't been to Lourdes yet, because it sounds too commercialized, like a religious Stratford—I'm not decrying what is alleged to have happened at Lourdes. I'm not very interested in miracles and all that sort of thing *as such*, but I do love the old shrines. And I do think that this is part of the charm of England for me. In Canterbury Cathedral, down in the crypt, to hear that the Black Prince had left instructions that he be buried in the Lady Chapel—I thought that was beautiful. And then, as the greatest honour they could bestow on him, they buried him in the most important part up with St Thomas à Beckett and he wouldn't have wanted that. There's obviously a tremendous romantic side to my religious life.

If her religion has been a comfort, it has also forced painful decisions on her. Widowed at thirty, she might have remarried, but only to a man acceptable to the Catholic Church:

---

[73] Survey: 'Did your education at your old school make a real difference to the outcome of your life?' Yes: Scotch, 52%; Trinity, 47%; MLC, 76%; Genazzano, 80%. (N/A averaged 6%).

We were drilled in the Seven Sacraments—they were pretty hot on marriage and marriage was for life. At the sacrament of marriage you take the vows and they were absolutely indissoluble and so a marriage 'out of the Church' was out of the question. And it was sad because I wanted more children. A Catholic divorced friend used to say, 'You're luckier than me. If you meet an eligible man, you can marry him and I can't as long as my ex-husband is alive'. But not only was it my religious fears, there was also the fact that my parents were still alive and I could not have done it to them. It would have devastated them—their only child. I used to wish sometimes that I wasn't a Catholic. If you remember Sebastian in *Brideshead Revisited* saying, 'Oh dear, it's very difficult being a Catholic'. Charles said he didn't understand what difference it made and Sebastian said it made a difference 'all the time'.

If you're an old-time Catholic like me, it does make a difference to everything you do. Even when you've just told someone a marvellously scandalous story and then you think, 'Oh my God, a sin against charity'—it doesn't stop you doing it.

But she knows she is 'infinitely dear' to Christ and Catholicism is a faith that understands human frailty. The American writer Flannery O'Connor once wrote to a Protestant friend that the Catholic Church understands human nature, even the Pope has to go to confession and has sins to confess, whereas Protestants have to be good.[74] And *Marjorie O'Donoghue* insists that Catholics are not burdened by their church's rules: 'It's a very interesting proposition—people saying how difficult the Catholic Church's rules are for, say, married couples—sexual intercourse and all the rest of it, and yet you'll be meeting people while doing this book who've lived by the rules of the church and still aren't timid or crushed'. Quite the reverse:

That was one thing that Mother Winifred Dando used to say to us time and time again: work out what you believe in and have the courage of your convictions. Stick with what you believe in. And I think that might be the most valuable thing that you can give to anybody—to have that sort of feeling inside yourselves—that they know what they believe in, know what they're about and what this person feels is right for 'them'. And if each person has the courage of their convictions, they're a happier person inside.

What the nuns at Genazzano were simply very good at was inculcating in their pupils a structure of faith and practice which has stayed with them always. Fully 88 per cent of the survey women attend Mass regularly; 10 per cent occasionally and but two out of 120 never. Just three describe themselves as agnostic or atheist and one of those is *Helen Browne*:

---

[74] Sally Fitzgerald, ed., *The Habit of Being: Letters of Flannery O'Connor*, p. 346.

I believe in the ten commandments (except adultery—I'm very free thinking these days). I believe in God and my first thought is 'thank you God—you're doing awfully well by me—I've no complaints.

Mass now doesn't do anything for me. I know they say it's not what it gives you but what you give it, but that's a lot of nonsense. It doesn't do anything for me. I just see this priest—I've lived with these people and I know they're just human beings like myself, many of them haven't faith, but they're putting on a show like I put one on.

For a handful their faith faded late in life; for others the reforms of Vatican II brought a new intensity. Kate Morgan came from a devout family and three of her brothers entered religious life. When she was young it was something taught by her parents and teachers, but in later life she has found something 'that's deep':

It means so much to me. I have got that deep faith and trust. My brother who was a doctor was a very spiritual man. His acceptance of everything as the will of God was really quite extraordinary. We were very close— every night practically he came and had a drink with me, even when I lived in Parkville. And I said to him, not long before he died and he was very sick, 'Oh Frank I'm going to miss you terribly—what am I going to do—I'll be so sad and lost'. And he just looked at me and said, 'Kate, you put your trust in God and you'll be all right'. So that's what you do . . .

Many practise their faith with care and concentration, keeping the disciplines of weekly Mass, 'First Fridays' and retreats. Most pray daily. *Anne Sullivan* cannot conceive of a life without the moral structure and practice of her faith: 'I don't think I could cope if I couldn't say my prayers'. And some who left have returned. Josie Shields married a non-Catholic and practised birth control and became divorced. She was called to the bedside of her sister in Adelaide who was dying of cancer:

I was told she had twenty-four hours to live. I didn't have a home to go to there so I slept beside her and sat with her for two weeks. And every day we were told that her kidneys were not functioning—she won't last the night—but she did.

But while I was with her—I didn't talk to her much because she was semi-conscious a lot of the time—I just picked up books she was reading. And the first sentence in the first one I picked up was a book *Prayers for Pilgrims:* 'A thought becomes a prayer by just the act of the will in directing that thought to God'. When I left the hospital I'd walk to the cathedral and just sit there—not praying, because I'd got out of the habit of praying—I sort of felt I didn't quite belong. Then, when I read that sentence, the next day in church I began to talk to myself as you do when you're praying and I just thought—I'm allowed to pray. And that's how it began.

Then I came home. I hadn't sent my children to the Catholic Church or Catholic school because I didn't want them to be brainwashed as we were. Mostly I didn't want them to have the attitude towards sex that had been ingrained in us. I wanted them to grow up thinking that sex was a healthy, happy function of being a human being. So I just answered any of their questions and we talked religion in a down-to-earth sort of way. They'd never been to Mass.

My son was seventeen then and he'd been encouraged by one of his teachers at Melbourne High to become a born-again Christian. Peter was reading a lot of literature and his girl-friend was a church-going Catholic and he started going to Mass with her. So when I came home from Adelaide, I felt this change—I was saying to myself 'I *do* believe, I *do* believe and I'm *allowed* to believe'—it was like faith restored. But I decided I'm not going to say anything to the children—I'll just know my life has had this fundamental change. But my son button-holed me as soon as I got home and said, 'Mum—I've got something to tell you. I've been reading all that stuff that Caroline gave me and I don't see it from that point of view. But going to Mass with Theresa, seeing her family, I've thought it out and I think there's more reason for believing in God than *not* believing in God, so I'm a believer'. Peter and I started going to Mass together, then my daughter, Claudia, out of interest started going to Mass with us.[75]

Many of her fellow old girls from Genazzano would envy her her children, for the great sadness in the lives of quite a few is that their children do not share their faith, of if they do, they do not practise their religion fully. Just 41 per cent of their children share their religious beliefs without qualification; 43 per cent are Catholics but casual in their practice.

Genazzano has the most charismatic Christians of the four schools, with 4 per cent, but more representative have been those involved in the 'Renew' programme and the 'new communities'. Margaret Mary Martin:

In 1975 my husband and six children and I moved to Pymble, Sydney, where we then worshipped and attended Mass at Canisius College which is a Jesuit novitiate and tertianship—again the Jesuits playing a significant role in my faith life. Five years ago we joined a C.L.C. group which is a small community—Christian Life Communities, based on Ignatian spirituality and in this group I have changed from thinking about God and my fellow man in the head to feeling in my heart.

An example of this was a gospel at Mass recently where God cares and knows every hair on my head and everything about me. When I was at school I thought that was a frightening concept and it filled me with guilt; now I feel that this is explaining God's love for me and I feel very consoled by this reading.

---

[75] Interview with Josie Shields, 10 December 1990.

To sum up—my religion or my relationship with God is the central part of my life and I would say that this was begun in my home and my school. However, at home, the Irish Catholicism didn't lead to discussion about God or faith, to be a Catholic was basic and there was no room for argument. At school, the French influence of the F.C.J. nuns led to a more overt thinking and doing in my faith life—an interesting contradiction in the historical background of my Catholicism.

But if we cross the fearful sectarian chasm that once divided the girls of Genazzano from the girls of MLC, we find ourselves in the same spiritual country. *May Featherstone*'s inner spiritual life could easily be *Marjorie O'Donoghue*'s, for they both meditate and pray whenever they can be alone or silent:

I pray all the time. It's not necessarily words—a lot of it is silent meditation. I think we can be so full of words and thinking that we don't have time for God to talk to us. Then I do have a set—it sounds like a patter—of who I pray for and this grows all the time. And if I say to someone, when I know they're in need, that I'll include them in my prayers, it's surprising how often that will open up a deep relationship. And if I say that, I do it—every day. There's always your close ones, but there could be fifty or sixty others. I only present their name before the Lord and I'm just thinking of them at the moment.

I love retreats—I've only ever done two for a day at the Sisters of Charity. Our previous minister took me for a day and our family laughed when they heard that I was going for a day of silent meditation and they thought I couldn't cope with that. I think they don't really understand what it does mean to me—I really need time for myself.

I've just started reading the Bible through in two years—I have a large-print one. Before that I can't say I was regular. I'd open it—the Psalms and you would always find something, and in an hour of need I'd read it. I've been through phases. But I listen to every religious broadcast I can. I like the 10 past 7 of a morning—it's only short, but it sets a pattern for the day. And I've been very interested in the Caroline Jones' 'Search for Meaning'. I think she's got a very strong faith.

I think we can get too busy in life to develop that inwardness and I think the Church can get very busy. And I was going to have a chat to our minister—I think we need some quietness in our service. I really feel that I should be a Quaker only for my love of music.

The most dramatic social change to religion in the lifetime of this generation has been the decline of sectarianism—a new tolerance and affection that has come from both sides. For Geoffrey Serle it is simply 'one of the best things that has happened in my life'. The proportion of intermarriage has risen sharply since the war, with the Catholics being the keenest 'out-marriers'.[76]

---

[76] Survey: 'Has there been any intermarriage in your family between Protestants and Catholics?'

		Scotch	Trinity	MLC	Genazzano
Before 1940:	Yes:	14%	15%	17%	48%
Since 1940:	Yes:	34%	39%	42%	76%

For Protestants the decline in faith and Christian practice is an older and more familiar problem. This generation still overwhelmingly identifies itself as Christians, but only a minority participate in regular worship. The most agnostics and atheists come from Scotch with 23 per cent, Trinity is next with 19 per cent then MLC with a tiny 7 per cent. Eighteen per cent of them all called themselves 'humanists' and some of those were also Christians. Overall 69 per cent of the men and 78 per cent of the MLC women called themselves Christians, but only 27 per cent of the men and 48 per cent of the MLC women attend church regularly.[77] This is a generation in transition from the tight, sectarian, churchy society of their youth to the post-religious age. Hugh Stretton takes a long historical view of the decline in belief:

> I've always imagined that somewhere from about 1840, drifting slowly through the generations to somewhere about 1920, people stopped believing He was there. And you would expect, if that was true, that the people who stopped believing He was there would be some sort of self-selection of types of people and those who would be left *really* believing that He was there would be a rather odd personality set, to some extent. I've never had this thought for a moment about Anglicans, who in England, in particular, long ago came to terms with leaving it to Him if He was there.

An MLC woman described herself as 'Methodist—but shakily: Although still a firm believer in the basic principles of Christianity as a blue-print for living, I have progressively less faith in the theory of life after death. This probably came about after reading Darwin's theory of evolution, and it has become more positive in the last ten years when the acceptance of death after a good life seems to be a peaceful conclusion'. While having much to be thankful for, she ended on 'a pessimistic note—I believe that the eventual demise of the human race is inevitable'.[78] Robert Trumble's faith 'departed for a season' in that he ceased for some years to be an active member of a congregation: 'but I don't think I've ever departed from my Christian faith. I wandered off into the side alleys of philosophy for a while when I thought I might find truth in those areas'. James Austin has remained steady: 'I've always been a methodical Anglican' and apart from his war years, has been a continuous member of the choir since he was seven years old.

---

[77] See Appendix II, table 12.
Survey: 'How often do you attend religious services?'

	Scotch	Trinity	MLC	Genazzano
Never	23.3	22.9	8.9	1.7
Occasionally	50.4	47.6	42.1	10.0
Regularly	25.6	28.3	48.1	88.3
N/A	0.8	1.2	0.9	0

[78] Survey No. 471: MLC.

Alan Reid watches his congregation: observing those who are searching for something but who can never articulate it; only knowing what it is when they find it. He sees them 'confronted by one of the most friendly, welcoming congregations I've come across, who probably scare them because this is dragging them into a personal relationship'. Some come to church because of a personal God; others are searching for meaning; still others long for the church to be the centre of suburban community that it was in their youth—the place where you found your doctor, your plumber, your first job and your best friends and your life partner. He wonders how many really do have a powerful faith that illumines their lives. In the Uniting Church there are some who have been alienated by the politicization of the clergy and the church's radical public voice. Above all, there is the difficulty in believing in the supernatural in the last decades of the twentieth century. Even among the church-goers there are many who are in effect 'secular Christians'. Alan Reid cites the research of the Rev. Dr Philip Hughes which divides modern congregations into two groups—those who believe in a personal God and those who are involved in the faith because it gives them a moral-ethical structure. The struggle to believe the unbelievable has become perhaps the dominant struggle for those who would be Christians in the late twentieth century.

But for those whose faith remains strong, while they detect a new craving for meaning in the young and not too young, it is an undeniable sadness to see the great churches of the suburbs inexorably wither. Winsome Walklate is 'very sad' and quietly angry: 'In a way I would have thought better of girls I knew who gave the church away'. Older Catholics are now alarmed to see their community infected by the Protestant disease of doubt. *Marjorie O'Donoghue*:

> For us there was no doubt—there was certainty everywhere—it was very black and white. We believed in the 'Gift of Faith', and to keep that Gift firm, strong and alive, that we needed to nourish it with Grace, received through the continual practice or our religion in our daily life and at church. But for our children that hasn't come across at all and consequently there was a period when they were not in harmony with us. But now I feel they have great respect for us in our religion. They cannot practise it in our way themselves, but they would be very, very disappointed if we slipped out on one little thing of our standards.

Catholicism by generational proxy perhaps; and yet once the church *offered* the faith rather than implanted it, the seeds of doubt were sown.

If the majority of this generation of college men and women remain ethical Christians, the loss to middle-class life of the social and moral cement provided by the suburban churches is dramatic. And the fear and dislike of the Australian society they see taking over from their generation's leadership and stewardship is widely felt. Many feel anxious

for the future because they cannot trust the values of the generation that is succeeding them. They may be conservatives who believe in capitalism, but they
still deplore greed, materialism and waste. They may scorn socialist day-
dreams, but they are convinced that there has been a serious deterioration in
business ethics.[79] This is a society of their making—now run by their children—but they do not like it and do not trust it. They were a generation born
in the long shadow of the 1890s depression and shaped by that of the 1930s,
and their irony is to live to see their society swallowed up by the same greed
and selfishness and recklessness that brought 'Marvellous Melbourne' down.
They had relied on kindness and charity to amend poverty and social suffering
and make capitalism civilized and moral. Now kindness and charity have become old-fashioned. The champions of capitalism have their gaze fixed on
gloriously profitable level playing fields, self-regulated by the scientifically
beautiful natural laws of the market place. But there is another group of believers who have had their faith shaken to the core—the believers of the political Left. They long ago had to come to terms with the horror of the
'Communist experiment' but many still believed that a social democratic government could do much to right social wrongs. Now they feel betrayed by
Labor governments which have become indistinguishable in their economic
ideology from their opponents. And there are more neutral observers. One
old Scotch collegian who rose to some of the highest positions in the Australian Public Service is appalled as he witnesses the steady destruction of our
industrial base and national economic health by 'stupid government policies'.[80] But Left and Right have more in common than they have in differences as they contemplate the political wasteland of Australia in the 1990s. A
doctor from MLC echoed fears expressed by almost all:

> I worry for the future of my grandchildren's generation. There is so much
> corporate greed and financial mismanagement—degradation of the envi-
> ronment, too many greedy dictators (or would-be ones) and the impact of
> radical Islam in the Middle East.
> I pray daily for peace.[81]

In the final analysis it is the well-being of hearts that matters most.
People who enjoyed great success in the outside world still nominated
their marriage, children, partners or intimate friends as the source of their

---

[79] Survey: 'Do you believe that standards have fallen in business ethics?' Yes: Scotch, 90%; Trinity,
86%; MLC, 89%; Genazzano, 90%.
'Do you believe that standards have fallen in conscientiousness and attention to detail in the
workplace?'
Yes: Scotch, 83%; Trinity, 84%; MLC, 89%; Genazzano, 89%.

[80] Survey No. 808: Scotch.

[81] Survey No. 494: MLC.

greatest satisfaction; and people who had not done well still declared themselves happy and content because their hearts were. Some admitted, almost guiltily, to lives of peacefulness and love. One Genazzano woman felt it was 'unfair' of her to comment on the state of the world: 'because I have always lived in very pleasant places and I have not been in great need during my life'; and for her, the greatest satisfactions have been 'Beautiful views, colours, laughter, talking, music, loving, feeling peaceful, walking and "some people" '.[82] Men were just as likely as women to nominate their marriage and their children as the best things that have happened to them. And considering the difficult beginnings of so many marriages during or just after the war, they have done very well. With a divorce and separation rate of between 7 and 9 per cent for them all, their marriages have been durable indeed. Alan Reid sees his generation as 'the last which held together. Recently there was a 60th birthday party for me—forty or fifty people and all of them were still married—which was a strange thing after spending a lot of time with people whose marriages are breaking up—takes about 15 per cent of my time'.

These marriages have held together despite significant social change in the lifetime of the relationships. They have weathered the sexual revolution and the Women's movement and there is no doubt that these challenges to behaviour and gender have penetrated deep into the suburbs. While most agree that it was a man's world when they were young, more women, including almost half from Genazzano, believe that it has still not changed for the better.[83] Thirty-one per cent of the women described themselves as 'feminist', as did 8 per cent of the Trinity men and 13 per cent of the Scotch men—male feminists tend to have clever daughters. Many men appear to have greatly enjoyed their daughters, and a number of their girls have been high achievers, even in such male preserves as engineering—to the delight of their engineer fathers or grandfathers. But feminism does hit a raw nerve, because the questions about whether they thought the world would be a better place with more women in positions of power elicited almost more gratuitous comment than any other.[84] One Scotch man wrote savagely 'I can't handle angry or officious females'.[85]

What of those who are alone? These samples included a higher than normal proportion of women who have never married—11 per cent from

[82] Survey No. 60: Genazzano.
[83] Survey: 'When you were young, was it 'a man's world'?' Yes: Scotch, 85%; Trinity, 83%; MLC, 79%; Genazzano, 78%. Is it today? Yes: Scotch, 26%; Trinity, 31%; MLC, 38%; Genazzano, 48%.
[84] Survey: 'Would the world be a better place with more women leaders?' Yes: Scotch, 56%; Trinity, 45%; MLC, 66%; Genazzano, 53%.
[85] Survey No. 739: Scotch.

Genazzano and 14 per cent from MLC. Life has been easier for single women than single men of this generation, because people simply assumed that single women were 'respectable'—men they were more wary of. Some of the single men who happen to be homosexual have belatedly benefited from the growing sexual tolerance since the 1960s, a freedom very welcome after decades of genuine fear of prosecution, humiliation and ostracism. An Anglican priest listed as one of his life satisfactions, 'celebrating twenty-five years with my homosexual partner'.[86] A lawyer, now working as an AIDS counsellor, nominated 'The care of loving friends'. 'I have no regrets about my life—it has been very full, very interesting and very rewarding personally'.[87] Most of the single women indicated that they had wanted to marry, but few expressed grief that they hadn't: 'I had expected to marry and have children. Instead I have ended up a "Maiden Aunt"—although I am perfectly happy in that role', wrote one.[88] Another noted: 'My experience in bad times, often given uplift by pleasant manner of casual contacts—hope I do likewise'.[89] The single have led busy lives, filled with service to others—to their ageing parents, their siblings and their offspring, their friends, their church, their pupils and fellow workers. Some do regret the loss of sexual and reproductive life: 'I am grateful for good friends and happy memories. I regret never having experienced a happy love relationship with the opposite sex, or having children. I regret not having the courage or determination to pursue a career in fine art (portraiture) in my youth'.[90] For Dorothea Cerutty, her loss was her pupils' gain:

Why did I spend so much time with the weaker students? There's a funny little psychological quirk in myself that answers that. When I see a non-achiever I say—'She's a woman'—and I have never married and never had a child and this person—*Helen*, and I say the name with respect—4H, complete academic failure, married, three children—died of cancer aged thirty-six, and had given the world more in loving kindness as a wife and mother and friend than I've ever been able to give with all my scholarship and all my connections.

I feel with *Helen* that she gave in full what I've only given as a woman who's had a career but not a full life as a woman. And that's why I'm always so interested in the non-achievers because I say 'Who am I to say non-achiever?' What have I achieved—a degree, a long curriculum vitae, but not a woman.

---

[86] Survey No. 1101: Trinity.
[87] Survey No. 1117: Trinity.
[88] Survey No. 320: MLC.
[89] Survey No. 472: MLC.
[90] Survey No. 405: MLC.

I fight with my friend over this—he gets to the point of fury with me that I won't see that.

To me to pass academically or to achieve an accredited standard is only one side of living. Probably that's why I like men so much; that's why I'm so deeply attached to some very lovely men at my extreme age, because scholarship is only part of living—the full part is loving.

As Dr Wood so often said to his teachers and his girls: 'To give and give and give again what God hath given thee'.

This book has attempted to be the biography of a generation—of particular people from a particular place during a particular time—and it is the story of many fine human beings: people now full of wisdom; people who have taken great risks; people who have faced great personal danger; people who have changed with the times; people who have remained steadfast. They include people who have served their country in peace and war; people who have changed Australia. It has been one of the most creative generations in our recorded history—creative because it first knew stringency and war before it knew comfort and security. They were determined to make an end to war and injustice, so they were an idealistic generation—longing for magnificent new solutions and eager to serve. And they did serve, and did so with distinction. And yet while we are absorbed in them as individuals, we must not lose sight of our connectedness and our effect as social collectivities. If this book is to have more than local or individual significance, it must not shrink from examining the collective impact of this middle-class, privately-educated generation on Australia in the twentieth century.

The great ideological divide between the middle class and the working class—and the Right and the Left—in this country has been over the virtues of independence and the virtues of interdependence. Judith Brett sees Sir Robert Menzies' 'The Forgotten People' speech as encapsulating both the strength and weakness of Australian middle-class values. She contrasts with the virtues of independence and self-reliance those of charity—'those virtues in which the self is opened out to others and which express a sense of fellow feeling and implication with others' . . . and the strengths of dependence are 'of recognising, celebrating and drawing sustenance from people's interdependence with each other'. She goes on:

What I am calling the virtues of charity are all missing from the emotional register with which 'The Forgotten People' works. While this speech is concerned to bring out the strengths and pleasures of the virtues it celebrates, these virtues have a darker side and can be seen as defending against certain human experiences, even as they celebrate others. In particular they defend against the dangers of vulnerability to others. To be open, to be interdependent, is to be vulnerable. Others can drag you down with their insatiable demands, or they can fail you just when you need them most. Better to neither a lender or a borrower be and rely solely on oneself, however lonely and neglected that may leave you. The description 'forgotten' captures well the dangers of self-reliant individualism. If you give little or nothing to others, even though you ask for nothing in return, others are unlikely to recognise your virtues and to come to your aid when you are in difficulty. Your virtues will be unappreciated and your difficulties ignored. So Menzies, like the defenders of the middle class before him, praises it for its strengths and social contribution, even as he plays on its fears.[91]

The traditional middle-class frame of mind depended on a sense of personal righteousness—of believing oneself to be deserving, that one's life comforts and social position had been legitimately earned; and as Judith Brett has perceived, that the duty of independence and self-reliance is the essence of citizenship—one must provide for oneself and one's family and not be a burden on the community. And yet why should dependency be a burden—could it not be a life-stage which we all share? We all become old and helpless; we will all be bereaved and alone, and there are times in all lives when to be able to open out to others, to permit ourselves to be vulnerable, is necessary for survival. Many good people will protest that they do care for others—that they do participate in outreach in their churches, give generously to charities and are personally kind; but in a curious way, while they have learned to give—at least on an individual level—they have not learned to take. And because they are afraid to take, they unconsciously resent the takers. Along with other Anglo-Celtic societies such as New Zealand, Great Britain, the U.S.A. and Canada, we suffer from having a targeted welfare system rather than a universal one. We have never lost the charity model for old age pensions and public health and education, and we still believe that the backbone of the country is really the middle class, whose hard work, integrity and taxes hold the nation together. But societies which have universal pensions and health services and whose government schools possess the highest academic prestige enjoy a national unity that continues to elude us. In societies where the middle class see themselves as part of the whole—both as givers and takers—they are less resentful. Australians, by contrast, are very reluctant taxpayers—we have a tax phobia, even though we are among the most lightly taxed nations of the O.E.C.D. At a deep level, middle-class taxpayers see all their hard-earned cash being spent on hospitals they avoid, on people they would never have as friends, and on schools they will do everything they can to keep their children out of. And if they choose to send their own children to private schools, they resent their tax

---

[91] Brett, *Robert Menzies' Forgotten People*, pp. 71–2.

education dollars going only to state schools. They believe in user-pays services (we are yet to see how the user-pays principle can be applied to the unemployed). The moral middle class is also, therefore, a little mean—the danger to society for them lies in the 'insatiable demands' of trade unions and government services. Too few acknowledge that it is the taxes of the poor which pay for the universities that largely only their children can attend, for the education and protection of the workforce they employ, for the complex infrastructure which makes their whole existence possible.

The Lucky Country has never been a 'Workingman's Paradise' or a classless new society: it started and remains a deeply class-divided one, where even in eras of apparent consensus, resentments between the rich, the comfortable and the poor eat away at its commonweal. Children who are educated apart behind high walls can find it difficult in later life to become at one with those on the other side. Children who are told endlessly by their parents and teachers that they are fortunate, privileged, special, inheritors and examples of excellence, will find it difficult to be good democrats. Even if they are imbued with a sense of service and care 'for those less fortunate than themselves', they can still find it difficult to feel simply as fellow Australians. The middle-class Left has given the poor social workers; the poor simply wanted more money. For the younger generation now in power—who never knew the Depression nor served in the ranks in New Guinea—their psychic apartness from the common herd presents this country with one of its gravest dangers.

But we are all victims of history more than we are shapers of it. The historical forces which tossed about the lives of these young Australians from the 69 tram on that first day of school for 1934 were rarely of their own making. But their journeyings of the body, the heart, the mind and the soul speak to us of then, and now, and for evermore.

Appendix I
The School Cohorts

The following data have been extracted from the student records of the schools. MLC and Scotch College have the most detailed student records; Trinity has kept only final examination passes and Genazzano has no detailed student records for the period at all. The Melbourne Grammar School Cohort has been extracted from *Liber Melburniensis* (Melbourne, 1965). The cohorts of MacRoberston Girls', Melbourne Boys' and Essendon high schools referred to in the text have been extracted from the student records.

It needs to be emphasized that these records are not without error and are far from complete. For that reason these figures need to be read as 'trends' rather than as absolutes. The classification of occupations is loosely based on those of the Australian Census and in accordance with community perceptions of relative social status.

The Scotch 1934 Cohort consists of all those boys who entered the senior school of Scotch College in 1934.
MLC 1919–1920 Cohort consists of all the girls at the school who were born in 1919 and 1920.

TABLE 1: HOME ADDRESSES OF SCOTCH 1934 COHORT AND MLC 1919–20 COHORT
Note: the student records are not complete.

	Scotch		MLC
At school less than six months	3		0
Overseas	1		0
Country	43		62
'Top Drawer'			
Toorak	5	2	
South Yarra	1	0	

TABLE 1 (*cont'd*):

	Scotch		MLC	
Armadale	3		1	
Kooyong	1		0	
sub total		10		3
'Heartland'				
Hawthorn	27		36	
Malvern/East Malv.	25		19	
Kew	18		31	
Caulfield	11		25	
Camberwell	13		7	
Canterbury	13		19	
Surrey Hills	8		3	
Glen Iris	7		7	
Balwyn	3		3	
Mont Albert	3		0	
Deepdene	2		0	
sub total:		130		150
'Bayside'				
Brighton	11		1	
Hampton	2		1	
Black Rock	1		0	
Sandringham	0		1	
sub total:		14		3
'Sand belt'				
Elwood	7		1	
Elsternwick	2		5	
Glenhuntly	3		3	
Balaclava	1		0	
Ormond	0		2	
Murrumbeena	2		0	
sub total:		15		11
Inner suburbs				
City of Melbourne	4		1	
East Melbourne	0		1	
South Melbourne/Mid. Park	0		3	
Prahran/Windsor	1		3	
St Kilda/East St Kilda	5		7	
Carlton/North Carlton	1		2	
Fitzroy	1		0	
Brunswick	1		3	
Richmond/Burnley	1		2	
Newmarket	1		0	
sub total:		15		22
North and West				
Ivanhoe	4		1	
Moonee Ponds	6		2	
Essendon	3		2	
Footscray	4		4	
Preston/West Preston	2		1	
Sunshine	1		0	

TABLE 1 (*cont'd*):

	Scotch	MLC
Glenroy	1	0
Northcote/Westgarth	1	2
Moreland/Coburg	1	1
St Arnaud	1	0
Williamstown	1	2
Werribee	1	0
sub total:	26	15
Suburban fringe		
Forest Hill	1	0
Burwood	4	3
Box Hill	1	0
Doncaster	1	0
Blackburn	0	1
Mitcham	0	1
Ringwood	0	1
Dandenong	0	3
Oakleigh	1	2
Bentleigh	1	1
sub total:	9	12
TOTAL:	266	278

TABLE 2: SCOTCH 1934 COHORT: PARENTS' OCCUPATIONS BY BOYS' ACADEMIC ATTAINMENT

	Left without Intermediate	Left with Intermediate	Leaving Candidates	Honours Candidates	Total
Mothers					
home duties	8	5	6	1	20
shopkeeper	0	1	0	1	2
managing director	1	0	0	0	1
hotel owner	1	0	0	0	1
Chinese herbalist	1	0	0	0	1
grazier	2	0	0	0	2
sub total:	13	6	6	2	27
Fathers					
retired	0	0	4	0	4
Professional					
doctor	0	1	5	2	8
lawyer	0	1	2	1	4
clergyman	0	0	1	2	3
dentist	2	0	4	0	6

TABLE 2 (*cont'd*):

	Left without Intermediate	Left with Intermediate	Leaving Candidates	Honours Candidates	Total
engineer	3	2	5	4	14
pharmacist	2	1	3	0	6
analytical chemist	0	0	2	0	2
architect	0	0	1	0	1
teacher	1	0	2	1	4
surveyor	0	0	1	0	1
journalist	0	0	2	0	2
optician	0	0	1	0	1
sub total:	8	5	29	10	52
Commerce					
senior manager	10	6	9	7	32
accountant	4	3	0	0	7
merchants	5	1	0	0	6
importers/broker	1	4	1	0	6
investors/financier	1	1	1	0	3
bank manager etc.	0	2	2	2	6
sub total:	21	17	13	9	60
Business					
'business'	5	0	5	0	10
builder	1	0	1	0	2
Little Bourke St merch.	1	0	0	0	1
carrier	1	0	0	0	1
wireless merchant	1	0	1	0	2
confectioner	1	0	0	0	1
estate agent	1	2	1	0	4
butcher	1	0	1	0	2
hairdresser/tobac.	1	0	1	0	2
tailor	3	0	1	0	4
furrier	2	0	0	0	2
knitting manuf.	2	0	0	0	2
grocer	1	0	1	0	2
road contractor	1	1	1	0	3
garage proprietor	1	0	0	0	1
car dealer	1	0	0	0	1
plumber	1	0	0	0	1
printer	3	0	0	0	3
jeweller	1	0	0	0	1
storekeeper	0	1	0	0	1
manager-auto grinder	0	1	0	0	1
electrotyper	0	1	0	0	1
electrician	0	0	1	0	1
lead works	0	0	1	0	1
flour miller	0	0	1	0	1
dairy produce	0	0	1	0	1
publican	0	0	1	0	1
sub total:	29	6	17	0	52

TABLE 2 (*cont'd*):

	Left without Intermediate	Left with Intermediate	Leaving Candidates	Honours Candidates	Total
Commercial employees					
clerk	4	1	3	0	8
hotel manager	1	0	0	0	1
'collector'	1	0	1	0	2
warehouse manager	2	0	0	0	2
traveller	6	1	6	0	13
shop manager	0	1	0	0	1
warehouseman	0	0	0	1	1
sub total:	14	3	10	1	28
Public servants					
civil servant	4	1	4	0	9
railway employee	1	0	0	0	1
inspector of excise	0	0	1	0	1
sub total:	5	1	5	0	11
Armed services	1	0	3	0	4
Agriculture					
grazier	6	0	3	1	10
farmer	4	1	4	1	10
studbreeder	1	0	0	0	1
orchardist	0	1	2	0	3
sub total:	11	2	9	2	24
TOTAL:	102	40	96	24	262

TABLE 3:   ACADEMIC PERFORMANCE OF SCOTCH 1934 COHORT: 267 BOYS

> 3 were at Scotch for less than six months
> 40 failed sub-intermediate (year 9)
> 24 passed sub-intermediate only
> 2 were seriously ill
> 15 had no examination results recorded on their cards (sat no examinations?)
> 22 left with a partial Intermediate Certificate

106 or 40% left Scotch without the Intermediate Certificate

> 41 left with full Intermediate Certificate
> 16 left with failed or partial Leaving Certificate

57 or 21% left with the Intermediate Certificate only

80 left with the Leaving Certificate
24 attempted Leaving Honours
3 failed to obtain any honours
5 gained only one honour
7 gained two or more honours
9 gained at least one first class honour

83 or 31% left with the Leaving Certificate only
21 or 8% left with at least one honour

TABLE 4:   ACADEMIC PERFORMANCE OF MLC 1919–20 COHORT: 284 GIRLS

54 were designated as 'hopeless', having failed all year 9 subjects
17 failed sub-intermediate but passed some subjects
26 failed sub-intermediate but passed 'Special'
4 failed 'Special'
15 failed because of illness or family trauma
14 passed sub-intermediate but left MLC (five had good marks)
45 attempted Intermediate and failed

16 went into the Business Diploma only

170 left without the Intermediate Certificate
5 left despite good marks
175 out of 268 (i.e. less the 16 in the business course) or 65% left MLC without
the Intermediate Certificate

21 passed Intermediate and left (7 had good marks)
24 passed Intermediate and entered the business course (4 had good marks)
11 failed the Leaving Certificate.

56 out of 268 or 21% left MLC with the Intermediate Certificate

10 left with the Leaving Certificate (5 had good marks)
10 left with the Leaving Certificate and Business Diploma (2 had good
marks)

20 out of 268 or 7.5% left with the Leaving Certificate

17 attempted Leaving Honours
15 obtained some honours
4 obtained at least one first class honour

15 out of 268 or 5.5% left with at least one honour

WASTAGE: 2 able girls did Diploma after sub–intermediate
5 could have passed Intermediate but left MLC
7 left after good Intermediate results

TABLE 4 (*cont'd*):

> 4 able girls did the Business Diploma after the Intermediate
> 3 able girls left during the Leaving year despite good results
> 7 able girls did not attempt honours

28 out of 268 or 10% could have attempted more

> 170 out of 268 left without the Intermediate
> 15 failed because of illness or family trauma

155 out of 268 or 58% were 'poor' students

TABLE 5:   MLC 1919–20 COHORT: PARENTS' OCCUPATIONS

Note: occupations for the parents of only 200 of the 284 girls in the cohort were listed.

Mothers only: 23
(home duties 20, flower farmer 1, manufacturer 1, cinema owner 1)
Fathers
gentleman: 1

Professional: 46
(clergyman 22, doctor 3, solicitor 1, dentist 2, engineer/scientist 9, economist 1, school inspector 1, teacher 4, surveyor 1, optician 1, inventor 1)

Commerce: 33
(merchant/big business 7, company secretary 7, accountants 5, insurance 4, manager 5, bank manager etc 5)

Business: 50
(salesman/traveller 9, grain merchant 2, printer 2, electroplater 1, builder 5, leadlight manufacturer 1, hosiery manufacturer 1, tile manufacturer 1, mantle manufacturer 1, automotive engineer/garage proprietor 2, carrier 1, estate agent 3, furrier 1, magazine publisher 1, jeweller 1, draper 2, grocer 3, master baker 3, newsagent 2, hardware 1, general storekeeper 6, leather merchant 1)

Commercial employees: 10
(clerk 6, physical culture expert 1, window dresser 1, foreman 1, boot employee 1)

Public servants: 10
(civil servant 7, postmaster 1, superintendent of police 1, police constable 1)

Armed Services and uniformed: 5
(army officer 1, naval officer 2, ship's master 2)

Agriculture: 22
(grazier 3, farmer 14, orchardist 2, studbreeder 1, market gardener 1, landscape gardener 1)

TABLE 6:   ACADEMIC PERFORMANCE OF THE TRINITY 1919–20
COHORT: 118 BOYS

Note: the records at Trinity Grammar do not include parents' occupations or detailed examination results. There were 118 boys at the school who were born in 1919 or 1920. Thirty of these left Trinity before the age of fourteen so that they could proceed to other schools. A handful of these early leavers were St Paul's choristers returning to government schools once their voice broke, but most went on to finish their senior schooling at Melbourne Grammar or Scotch College. The academic performance has therefore been analysed of the 88 boys who remained at Trinity after year 8.

   38 out of 88, or 43%, left without the Intermediate Certificate
   22 out of 88, or 25%, left with the Intermediate or partial Leaving
   28 out of 88, or 32%, left with the Leaving Certificate
   15 of these, or 17%, attempted Leaving Honours

5 from the Leaving Honours class went to the university (medicine 2, law 1, theology 1, agricultural science 1)
4 from the Leaving class went to the university (medicine 1, arts 1, agricultural science 1, engineering 1)

TABLE 7:   WORLD WAR II RECORD OF SCOTCH COLLEGE, TRINITY GRAMMAR AND MELBOURNE GRAMMAR MEN

These records are far from complete, despite the efforts made by the schools during the war to trace the war service of all their old boys. This table consists of the total number who served from Scotch and Trinity, and of those from the Scotch 1934 Cohort and the matched Melbourne Grammar School 1934 Cohort. The sources are G. H. Nicholson, *First Hundred Years . . .* , the list of servicemen and war dead in the *Mitre*, December 1945, *Liber Melburniensis*, and the published list of war service for the Old Scotch Collegians Association. The three services include those who served in the British forces.

	Scotch	Scotch 1934	Trinity	M.G.S. 1934
Total served	3064	171	482	136
War dead	327 (11%)	28 (16%)	52 (11%)	18 (13%)
Commissions	1260+(40%+)	58 (34%)	112+(23%+)	62 (46%)
Navy	348 (11%)	21 (12%)	45 (9%)	19 (14%)
Commissions	?	13 (62%)	?	11 (58%)
died	?	1	?	0
P.O.W.	?	1	?	1
Army	1695 (55%)	99 (58%)	233 (48%)	73 (54%)
Commissions	?	21 (21%)	?	28 (38%)
died	?	11	?	4
P.O.W.	?	9	?	7
Air Force	1021 (33%)	51 (30%)	152 (32%)	44 (32%)
Commissions	?	24 (47%)	?	23 (52%)
died	?	16	24 (7 in training)	14 (5 in training)
P.O.W.	?	1	?	5

Appendix II
The 1990 'Journeyings' Survey

The survey results printed below and used throughout the text come from the '1990 *Journeyings* Survey' prepared by Janet McCalman and administered and tabulated by Mark Peel between June and November 1990. All the tables produced from the survey will be published separately in the Melbourne University History Department's History Research Series.

The survey asked some 140 questions. One series of questions asked respondents to reconstruct their school, work, marital and family lives and those of their parents and children, so providing information about three generations. Then followed questions concerning their views and experiences of emotional and sexual life, religious belief and values, educational ideas, social and gender relations and the changes in these over their lives. We then provided a list of public figures and asked people to indicate those whom they admired or deplored (Table 12) and a list of possible political and ideological identifications (Table 10). The respondents often tackled the terms and assumptions of these questions, adding in other 'admirable' or 'deplorable' people or providing alternatives and comments in their self-identifications. As ever, this kind of marginal comment was particularly useful. The concluding sets of questions in the survey covered first, the war and service experience of the respondents, their spouses and their fathers; second, leisure and cultural activities and travel; and third, questions asking whether their time at their respective church schools had affected the outcome of their lives and whether their lives had 'turned out' as they had expected. Finally, they were asked about their service to the community and about their reflections on the present and the future. This section elicited a rich cross-section of views, fears and hopes.

The survey form differed slightly according to the respondents' gender. Women were asked if they had ever been self-supporting, if they had expected to have to work for a living and for precise information on the duration of their paid employment; while men were asked about their wives' employment before and after marriage. Women were also asked about their attitudes to schoolwork and examinations, their achievement of self-confidence, their parents' attitudes to the education of girls and to 'marrying well', their own views on the importance of careers and girls' education and, finally, whether and how they had made a formal debut. Men were asked specific questions about their attitudes to marriage and their experiences of girls during and after their school years. There were also slight differences in questions asked of respondents from the three Protestant schools as opposed to women from Genazzano, who were asked about Vatican II and about the Catholic Church's rules on contraception, abortion and I.V.F. They were also questioned about their involvement in Catholic Action and their reading of the Catholic press. The respondents from MLC and Genazzano were asked about the incidence of religious intermarriage in their extended families both before and after 1940 and about sectarianism. Finally the Genazzano women were questioned about their ethnic origins and identifications.

The survey form was posted to former students, using addresses provided by the schools. In the case of Genazzano, a much smaller school than the others, a questionnaire was sent to almost all of the 285 women who had left the school before 1950 and with whom the school was still in contact. For Trinity and MLC, forms were sent to a sample of people who had left before 1950. Because Scotch College was, and is, so large, a more precise sampling was practised, and forms were sent to men who had left the school in the years 1934, 1938 and 1950. We made no other attempt to 'select' respondents. The only restriction on our sample group, therefore, was whether or not the school still had an address for the person. This would obviously rule out those who were unwilling or unable to remain in contact with their old school. One result may be that those who did poorly at school, who hated the place or who were there for only a short time might be less likely to appear within our potential response group. The school results of our respondents (Table 6a) bear this out: in general, those we could contact and probably those who returned their forms were more likely to be those who had been more successful at the school, from the evidence of general examination records. This does not mean that our response group was uniform in their attitudes to the school or to the education they received and, as Table 6a notes, the fact that these were more likely to be the 'achievers' makes many of the survey results even more interesting.

We sent the survey, along with a covering letter inviting people to participate and an addressed envelope for return, to a total of 1235 people. Overall, 633 people, or 51 per cent of those contacted, returned the survey, a rate far above expectations. The very high return rate is even more remarkable given that the survey was lengthy, demanding and intrusive. There were variations in the return rate according to school. The highest—62 per cent (214 out of 350)—was of former MLC students. Among the men 55 per cent (166 out of 300) of those from Trinity and 44 per cent (133 out of 300) of those from Scotch replied. The return rate for Genazzano was 42 per cent, or 120 out of the 285 sent out. Given that our 'sample' for Genazzano was almost *every* woman who had left the school before 1950 and for whom the school had an address, a 42 per cent return rate is a significant achievement.

We began the project on the principle that a good rate of return would be around 20 per cent. This, indeed, was somewhat optimistic, as many surveys struggle to achieve 10 per cent. A return rate of over 50 per cent was testimony to the interest of our respondents in the project and to their willingness to give time and effort in completing the form. Certainly these hundreds of men and women have provided this book with an unusually rich and dense body of material. Moreover, both here and in the separate book tabulating all the results, they have provided historians and observers of Australian society with a rare series of insights into political views and ideological identifications, as well as the remembered processes of family formation and mobility, intermarriage, educational achievement and failure, the building of careers and all the aspirations and disappointments of life in a turbulent period of recent history. We are grateful to the men and women who were so willing to share their memories and experiences and who have fulfilled the historians' search for good stories.

Mark Peel,
Canberra

TABLE 1a: TYPE OF SCHOOL ATTENDED BY FATHER

	Scotch	Trinity	MLC	Genazzano
	133	166	214	120
Church only	26 (19.5%)	34 (20.5%)	23 (10.7%)	—
State only	74 (55.6%)	93 (56%)	151 (70.6%)	27 (22.5%)
Mix of both	31 (23.3%)	30 (18.1%)	34 (15.9%)	—
Catholic	—	—	—	71 (59.2%)
Protestant (Gen.)	—	—	—	19 (15.8%)
Not/Answered	2 (1.5%)	9 (5.4%)	6 (1.6%)	3 (2.5%)

TABLE 1b: TYPE OF SCHOOL ATTENDED BY MOTHER

	Scotch	Trinity	MLC	Genazzano
Church only	33 (24.8%)	49 (29.5%)	45 (21%)	—
State only	61 (45.9%)	85 (51.2%)	130 (60.7%)	18 (15%)
Mix of both	32 (24.1%)	22 (13.3%)	33 (15.4%)	—
Catholic	—	—	—	98 (81.7%)
Protestant (Gen.)	—	—	—	4 (3.3%)
Not answered	7 (5.3%)	10 (6%)	6 (2.8%)	0

TABLE 2a: AGE FATHER LEFT SCHOOL

	Scotch	Trinity	MLC	Genazzano
	133	166	214	120
	%	%	%	%
By age 14	24.8	38.5	36.4	10.8
Aged 15–16	42.1	29.6	36.0	30.0
Aged 17 or over	30.8	26.0	20.1	42.5
Unknown/Not given	2.3	6.0	7.5	16.6

TABLE 2b: AGE MOTHER LEFT SCHOOL

By age 14	18.8	24.1	32.7	13.4
Aged 15–16	43.6	36.2	34.2	35.0
Aged 17 or over	27.1	23.5	20.6	40.0
Unknown/Not given	10.5	16.3	12.6	11.7

Note: The respondents were invited to 'guess' the age their parents left school if they did not know exactly and it seems that many have done so, and with considerable optimism. If 71 per cent of the MLC fathers attended state schools only, then only 33 per cent of them cannot have left school by the age of fourteen.

TABLE 3:   FATHERS' AND MOTHERS' POST-SCHOOL QUALIFICATIONS

		Scotch 133	Trinity 166	
	Fathers	Mothers	Fathers	Mothers
Ph.D.	1	1	1	0
Masters degree	4	0	2	0
Bachelor of Arts	2	0	0	0
Bachelor of Science	1	1	1	0
Bachelor — professional	10	3	10	1
TOTAL UNIVERSITY (per cent):	13.5	4	8	0.6
Diploma	16	7	1	9
certificate/training	16	16	24	13
apprenticeship	6	0	9	0
TOTAL OTHER (per cent):	28.5	17.2	28	13.2
NONE (per cent):	58	78.9	63	86.1

TABLE 4a: OCCUPATIONS OF FATHERS IN THEIR TWENTIES

	Scotch	Trinity	MLC	Genazzano
	133	166	214	120
Learned professions				
doctor	2	2	2	6
lawyer	4	1	1	3
clergyman	2	2	5	0
TOTAL:	(6%)	(3%)	(4%)	(7.5%)
Other professionals				
dentist	1	2	1	1
engineer	4	4	15	3
scientist/researcher	1	2	3	0
architect/surveyor	2	1	3	0
missionary/religious officer	1	0	2	0
teacher	6	2	10	1
pharmacist	4	4	0	0

TABLE 4a (cont'd):

	Scotch	Trinity	MLC	Genazzano
journalist/editor	1	1	0	0
musician/artist	1	2	3	1
TOTAL:	(16%)	(11%)	(18%)	(5%)
Commercial				
large factory owner	0	0	2	0
company director	1	0	1	0
company secretary	1	0	2	0
'proprietor'	0	0	0	2
property developer	0	0	1	0
merchant/exporter/importer	1	3	3	4
small factory owner	1	1	1	5
accountant/actuary	9	10	10	5
supervisor/consultant	0	0	0	1
bank manager	1	1	2	1
owner of small business	8	6	11	7
real estate	0	0	0	1
factory manager	1	0	0	0
TOTAL:	(18%)	(13%)	(15%)	(22%)
Public servants				
senior rank	0	0	0	1
middle rank	2	2	2	1
low rank	8	7	7	5
TOTAL:	(7.5%)	(5%)	(4%)	(7.5%)
Uniformed occupations				
armed services officer	1	2	2	5
armed services lower rank	0	2	2	2
master mariner	1	0	3	0
TOTAL:	(1.5%)	(2%)	(3%)	(6%)
Tradesmen				
printer/publisher/photo'er	2	3	4	0
contractor/builder	4	0	6	1
electrician	1	1	1	0
carpenter/cabinetmaker	3	5	3	1
shoemaker/saddler	2	0	4	0
fitter & turner/painter	4	3	4	0
watchmaker/jeweller	1	1	0	0
plumber/bricklayer/potter	2	1	1	0
trade instructor/technician	0	3	1	1
draftsman	0	5	0	0
butcher/baker/chef	0	1	1	3
hatter/tailor	0	1	1	0
mechanic	0	1	0	2
TOTAL:	(14%)	(15%)	(12%)	(7%)
'White collar'				
petty manager	2	4	5	4

TABLE 4a *(cont'd)*:

	Scotch	Trinity	MLC	Genazzano
bank employee	1	11	10	4
insurance employee	1	1	2	0
law clerk	0	2	3	1
book keeper	0	0	2	0
union official	0	0	1	0
petty clerical/sales	25	27	31	11
employee of company	1	0	3	1
TOTAL:	(22%)	(27%)	(27%)	(17.5%)
Manual workers				
transport worker/train driver	1	1	1	0
factory operative	2	3	1	0
labourer/casual work	1	3	1	0
fisherman	1	0	1	0
storeman/packer	0	2	0	0
hotel worker	0	2	1	0
miner	0	0	1	0
TOTAL:	(4%)	(7%)	(3%)	0
Agriculture				
farmer/grazier	8	16	16	22
orchardist/vintner	1	2	1	0
farm worker	2	1	0	0
TOTAL:	(8%)	(11%)	(8%)	(18%)
Retired/gentleman	0	1	0	0
Student:	1	1	3	7
Not given	3	6	9	4
TOTAL	(3%)	(5%)	(6%)	(9%)

TABLE 4b: OCCUPATIONS OF FATHERS IN THEIR FIFTIES

	Scotch	Trinity	MLC	Genazzano
	133	166	214	120
Learned professions				
doctor	2	1	1	10
lawyer	4	2	2	5
judge/magistrate	1	0	1	0
clergyman	1	5	15	0
TOTAL:	(6%)	(5%)	(9%)	(12.5%)
Other professionals				
dentist	1	2	1	2
engineer	1	7	12	2
scientist/researcher	1	1	1	0
architect/surveyor	1	2	2	0
missionary/religious	0	0	1	0
teacher	5	2	7	0

TABLE 4b (cont'd):

	Scotch	Trinity	MLC	Genazzano
pharmacist	3	4	0	2
journalist/editor	0	1	0	0
musician/artist	0	2	2	0
psychologist	0	1	0	0
librarian/curator	1	0	1	0
TOTAL:	(10%)	(13%)	(13%)	(5%)
Member of Parliament	1	1	0	2
Commercial				
large business owner	0	1	2	1
company director	9	4	1	1
company secretary	3	3	6	1
property developer	0	0	2	0
'proprietor'	1	0	0	9
merchant/export	1	3	6	4
senior manager	2	1	6	4
small factory owner	2	3	7	3
accountant/actuary	8	8	8	3
supervisor/consultant	1	2	3	1
bank manager	1	6	7	3
small business owner	13	9	21	12
real estate	1	2	1	0
factory manager	1	1	0	0
senior clerical	0	1	0	0
TOTAL:	(33%)	(26.5%)	(37%)	(42%)
Public servants				
senior rank	1	2	5	4
middle rank	6	8	5	5
low rank	5	6	7	3
TOTAL:	(9%)	(10%)	(8%)	(10%)
Uniformed occupations				
armed services officer	1	1	0	1
armed services	0	1	0	0
master mariner	1	0	3	0
TOTAL:	(1.5%)	(1%)	(1%)	(1%)
Trades				
printer/publisher	1	2	3	0
contractor/builder	4	0	8	2
carpenter/cabinet'er	1	4	1	1
fitter & turner	2	2	0	0
watchmaker/jeweller	1	1	0	1
plumber/bricklayer	0	1	0	0
technician/instructor	1	4	1	0
draftsman	0	0	0	1
butcher/baker	1	1	1	1
hatter/tailor	0	0	1	0

TABLE 4b (*cont'd*):

	Scotch	Trinity	MLC	Genazzano
mechanic	0	0	0	1
TOTAL:	(8%)	(5%)	(7%)	(5%)
'White collar'				
petty manager	10	13	9	3
bank employee	1	2	1	0
insurance employee	2	2	2	0
law clerk	0	1	0	0
petty clerical/sales	8	11	9	1
TOTAL:	(16%)	(17%)	(10%)	(3%)
'Blue collar'				
transport/train driver	3	1	1	0
miner	1	0	0	0
storeman/packer	0	0	2	0
fisherman	0	0	1	0
hotel worker	0	0	1	0
TOTAL:	(3%)	(1%)	(1%)	0
Agriculture:				
farmer/grazier	9	11	9	9
orchardist/vintner	1	2	1	1
TOTAL:	(7.5%)	(8%)	(5%)	(8%)
Unemployed/invalid	0	3	0	0
Retired	1	3	1	1
Deceased	5	10	10	13
Not given	1	2	6	0
TOTAL:	(5%)	(11%)	(8%)	(12%)

TABLE 5a: 'DID YOUR MOTHER EVER WORK FOR A LIVING?'

	Scotch	Trinity	MLC	Genazzano
	133	166	214	120
Yes	78 (57%)	103 (62%)	139 (65%)	82 (68%)

TABLE 5b: MOTHERS' OCCUPATION

Professional				
doctor	1	0	0	0
dentist	1	1	0	0
teacher	11	7	18	7
architect/planner	1	0	0	0
pharmacist	0	1	1	1
missionary	0	1	1	0
companion/governess	2	1	2	0
paraprofessional	1	2	0	0

TABLE 5b (*cont'd*):

journalist	1	1	1	0
nurse	6	5	3	11
physio/speech ther'st	0	1	0	0
music teacher	3	2	6	3
musician/singer	1	0	1	1
artist	0	1	0	1
commercial art/print	0	1	1	0
teacher aide	0	1	1	0
TOTAL:	(36%)	(24%)	(25%)	(29%)
Owner of small business	4	2	0	1
Proprietor	0	3	0	0
TOTAL:	(5%)	(5%)	0	(1%)
Clerical work				
secretary	7	6	10	10
stenographer	4	10	6	10
accountant/book'er	2	1	5	3
low rank public serv't	1	3	1	4
bank/insurance empl't	0	1	3	0
petty clerical/sales	10	8	28	9
TOTAL:	(31%)	(28%)	(38%)	(44%)
Trades and unskilled				
shop assistant	2	11	6	4
dressmaker etc.	4	14	20	4
milliner	6	3	9	5
machinist/spinner	3	1	3	0
bookbinder	0	1	1	0
factory operative	0	1	2	1
hostess	0	1	0	0
waitress/hotel work	2	3	1	1
domestic servant	0	3	4	0
transport worker	0	0	0	1
TOTAL:	(22%)	(37%)	(33%)	(20%)
Agriculture				
farmer/grazier	0	1	0	0
orchardist/vintner	1	0	0	0
farm worker	1	0	1	0
Unknown/not given	5	4	4	5
TOTAL:	(6%)	(4%)	(3%)	(6%)

TABLE 6a: RESPONDENTS' SCHOOL QUALIFICATIONS: PER CENT

	Scotch	Trinity	MLC	Genazzano
None/not given	2.3	7.2	8.4	8.3
Merit only	1.5	4.8	0.9	0.8
Sub–intermediate	1.5	0.6	0	2.5

TABLE 6a *(cont'd)*:

	Scotch	Trinity	MLC	Genazzano
Intermediate only	28.6	30.7	18.7	26.7
Intermediate & Business Dip.	—	—	11.7	1.0
Leaving only	18.8	24.7	16.8	30.8
Leaving Honours/Matric.	47.4	31.9	43.5	30.0

These school results reveal how very different the 'Survey' sample is from the cohorts of students at the four schools in the 1930s. The matriculation rate is boosted by those who left school 1940–50, when retention rates and pass rates improved in most schools, especially after the reforms of 1944. The sample collected very few of the unhappy and unsuccessful at school, which makes some of the following results all the more interesting.

TABLE 6b: POST-SCHOOL QUALIFICATIONS

	Scotch	Trinity	MLC	Genazzano
Total	133	166	214	120
None (per cent)	45 (33.8%)	48 (28.9%)	99 (46.3%)	45 (37.5%)
University degree	28 (21.0%)	38 (22.9%)	37 (17.2%)	15 (12.5%)
Ph.D.	5	4	3	1
Masters	5	6	6	1
B.A.	2	4	14	6
B.Sc.	2	2	3	1
bachelor-prof.	14	22	11	6
Diploma	21 (15.8%)	28 (16.9%)	29 (13.6%)	17 (14.2%)
Certificate/training	39 (29%)	49 (29.5%)	48 (22.4%)	42 (35%)
Apprenticeship	0	3	1	1

TABLE 7a: MEN'S OCCUPATIONS IN THEIR TWENTIES
(excluding military service)

	Scotch	Trinity	MLC (husbands)	Genazzano (husbands)
TOTAL:	133	166	185	107
Learned professions				
doctor	6	5	5	9
lawyer	2	2	3	8
clergyman	2	2	2	0
TOTAL:	(7.5%)	(5.4%)	(5.4%)	(15.9%)
Other professionals				
academic	0	2	1	0
dentist	1	2	2	0
engineer	7	7	13	8

TABLE 7a (*cont'd*):

	Scotch	Trinity	MLC (husbands)	Genazzano (husbands)
scientist/researcher	5	10	14	2
architect/surveyor	4	2	3	2
missionary/religious	1	0	0	0
teacher	3	9	8	2
pharmacist	5	1	1	1
psychologist	0	1	0	1
journalist/editor	1	1	0	0
musician/artist	1	2	2	1
TOTAL:	(21%)	(22.3%)	(23.8%)	(15.9%)
Commercial				
manager of large bus.	0	0	1	1
supervisor/consultant	2	2	1	2
owner of small bus.	1	6	15	5
proprietor	0	0	0	2
merchant	0	0	2	0
accountant/actuary	9	7	13	1
bank manager	1	1	0	0
real estate	0	1	2	0
wool broker	0	0	0	1
senior clerical	4	1	0	0
TOTAL:	(12.8%)	(10.8%)	(18.4%)	(11.2%)
Public servants				
middle rank	1	2	1	4
low rank	5	9	4	6
TOTAL:	(4.5%)	(6.6%)	(2.7%)	(9.3%)
Uniformed occupations				
armed services officer	1	1	2	0
armed services	1	0	2	1
master mariner	1	0	0	2
TOTAL:	(2.2%)	—	(2.0%)	(2.8%)
Tradesmen				
printer/photog.	0	2	4	0
contractor/builder	0	0	1	0
carpenter/cabinet'er	1	0	1	0
fitter/turner/painter	0	2	1	1
watchmaker/jeweller	1	0	1	0
plumber/bricklayer	0	0	1	0
technician/instructor	1	5	1	0
draftsman	3	4	2	2
butcher/baker/chef	0	0	0	1
mechanic	0	2	0	1
TOTAL:	(4.5%)	(9.0%)	(6.5%)	(4.7%)
'White collar'				
petty manager	5	1	3	7

TABLE 7a *(cont'd)*:

	Scotch	Trinity	MLC (husbands)	Genazzano (husbands)
bank employee	13	17	5	1
insurance employee	2	6	4	2
law clerk	1	0	1	0
petty clerical/sales	26	34	29	9
TOTAL:	(35.3%)	(34.9%)	(22.7%)	(17.8%)
'Blue collar'				
employee/operative	0	2	2	1
transport/driver	0	0	1	1
forester/ranger	0	0	1	0
TOTAL:	0	(1%)	(2%)	(2%)
Agriculture				
farmer/grazier	8	5	8	16
orchardist/vintner	1	2	0	0
gardener	0	0	1	0
farm worker	1	1	0	1
TOTAL:	(7.5%)	(4.8%)	(4.9%)	(15.9%)
Student	4	6	12	4
Not given	2	1	8	1
TOTAL:	(4.5%)	(4.2%)	(10.8%)	(4.7%)

TABLE 7b: MEN'S OCCUPATIONS IN THEIR FIFTIES

	Scotch	Trinity	MLC (husbands)	Genazzano (husbands)
	133	166	185	107
Learned professions				
doctor	7	9	8	12
lawyer	2	3	0	7
judge/magistrate	0	0	2	1
clergyman	3	3	3	0
TOTAL:	(9.0%)	(9.0%)	(7.0%)	(18.7%)
Other professionals				
academic	4	6	6	0
dentist	3	2	3	0
engineer	5	7	11	5
scientist/researcher	4	3	9	1
architect/surveyor	4	4	4	2
teacher	2	11	7	1
pharmacist	5	1	0	1
journalist/editor	2	1	0	0
musician/artist	0	2	2	1
psychologist	0	0	0	1
computer skills	0	1	0	0
TOTAL:	(21.8%)	(22.9%)	(22.7%)	(11.2%)

TABLE 7b (cont'd):

	Scotch	Trinity	MLC (husbands)	Genazzano (husbands)
Member of Parliament	0	0	1	0
Commercial				
large business owner	1	0	1	0
company director	6	12	9	6
company secretary	3	4	1	0
merchant/exporter	1	2	3	1
senior manager	8	13	5	5
small factory owner	0	3	2	1
accountant/actuary	6	9	6	0
supervisor/consultant	6	5	5	2
bank manager	5	6	2	1
small business owner	8	8	12	4
real estate	1	2	0	1
factory manager	1	0	0	0
senior clerical	1	0	1	0
TOTAL:	(35.3%)	(38.6%)	(25.4%)	(19.6%)
Public servants				
senior rank	3	0	2	2
middle rank	6	3	2	5
low rank	0	2	1	4
public admin.	0	2	3	0
TOTAL:	(6.8%)	(4.2%)	(5.4%)	(10.2%)
Uniformed occupations				
armed forces	0	1	2	0
master mariner	0	0	0	1
Trades				
printer/publisher	0	2	2	0
contractor/builder	1	0	2	1
carpenter/cabinet'er	2	0	0	0
watchmaker/jeweller	0	0	1	0
technician/instructor	1	5	4	3
draftsman	0	1	1	1
TOTAL:	(3%)	(4.8%)	(5.3%)	(4.7%)
'White collar'				
petty manager	11	15	16	8
bank employee	6	4	0	0
insurance employee	1	1	2	1
law clerk	1	0	0	0
fundraiser	0	0	1	0
petty clerical/sales	5	3	10	1
TOTAL:	(18.4%)	(13.9%)	(15.5%)	(9.3%)
'Blue collar'				
transport	0	1	2	0
factory operative	0	0	1	0

TABLE 7b (*cont'd*):

	Scotch	Trinity	MLC (husbands)	Genazzano (husbands)
forester/ranger	0	0	1	0
TOTAL:	0	(1%)	(2.2%)	0
Agriculture:				
farmer/grazier	7	5	4	14
orchardist/vintner	0	2	1	0
gardener	0	0	1	0
TOTAL:	(5.3%)	(4.2%)	(3.2%)	(13.1%)
Retired/gentleman	0	2	2	2
Deceased	0	0	9	7
Not given	0	0	8	4
TOTAL:	0	(1.2%)	(10.3%)	(12.1%)

TABLE 8a: WOMEN'S OCCUPATIONS AT AGE TWENTY/BEFORE MARRIAGE

	MLC	Genazzano	Scotch wives	Trinity wives
	214	120	125	157
Professional				
doctor	0	0	1	1
dentist	0	0	0	1
scientist/researcher	3	0	3	1
teacher	13	5	12	27
pharmacist	0	0	3	0
paraprofessional	1	1	2	1
physio/speech ther'st	1	1	2	1
social work/psych.	0	0	1	1
librarian/archivist	3	1	2	2
journalist	0	0	1	0
nurse	18	31	18	28
radiographer	0	0	1	0
lab tech./paramedic	6	1	2	4
music teacher	1	0	0	2
musician/singer	1	0	1	3
artist/commercial art	1	0	1	0
designer	3	0	1	1
TOTAL:	(23.8%)	(33.3%)	(42.4%)	(45.5%)
Owner of small business	0	1	0	0
Charity worker	0	0	1	0
Clerical work				
secretary	26	11	23	16
stenographer	19	7	13	22
accountant/book'er	5	1	2	2

TABLE 8a (*cont'd*):

	MLC	Genazzano	Scotch wives	Trinity wives
pub. serv.	3	2	2	1
bank/insurance	4	2	5	7
petty clerical/sales	33	8	17	22
TOTAL:	(42.0%)	(25.8%)	(49.6%)	(44.6%)
Trades and unskilled				
shop assistant	2	1	1	3
dressmaker etc	1	2	1	5
hairdresser	1	0	3	0
bookbinder	0	0	1	0
factory operative	2	0	1	1
hostess/air hostess	0	0	1	0
cook/caterer	0	0	0	1
waitress/ hotel work	0	2	0	0
domestic servant	1	0	0	0
TOTAL:	(3.3%)	(4.2%)	(6.4%)	(6.4%)
Uniformed workers				
armed forces	2	1	1	1
Agriculture				
orchardist/vintner	0	0	1	0
farm worker	0	1	0	1
Student	51	26	1	0
Home duties	7	7	0	0
Not given	6	6	0	3
TOTAL:	(29.9%)	(34.1%)	(1%)	(1.9%)

TABLE 8b: WOMEN'S MATURE CAREERS

	MLC	Genazzano	Scotch wives	Trinity wives
	214	120	75	101
Professional				
doctor	6	1	1	1
dentist	1	0	0	0
nun	0	2	0	0
academic	3	2	2	1
scientist/researcher	4	4	0	0
teacher	33	7	15	16
architect/town pl'er	2	0	0	0
pharmacist	2	1	3	0
paraprofessional	0	1	2	1
social worker/psych.	5	1	2	2
physio/speech ther'st	5	3	2	1
librarian/archivist	4	5	1	3
journalist	1	0	1	0

TABLE 8b (cont'd):

	MLC	Genazzano	Scotch wives	Trinity wives
nurse	19	30	8	12
lab technician etc	3	1	0	1
childcare/teach. aide	1	0	1	0
music teacher	1	1	0	4
musician/singer	1	1	0	3
artist/comm. artist	3	0	2	1
designer	1	0	1	0
media	1	0	0	0
computer tech.	1	0	0	0
TOTAL:	(45.3%)	(50%)	(54.7%)	(45.5%)
Owner of small business	1	4	1	2
Real estate	1	0	0	1
Travel agent	0	0	1	0
Clerical work				
consultant/executive	2	0	0	4
secretary	20	8	7	19
accountant/book'er	4	2	2	5
senior clerical	0	0	0	1
public servant/admin	5	2	3	2
petty managerial	2	0	0	2
bank/insurance empl.	1	0	0	2
petty clerical/sales	9	2	11	8
TOTAL:	(20.1%)	(11.7%)	(18.7%)	(42.6%)
Trades and unskilled				
hostess	1	0	0	0
dressmaker	0	1	0	0
cook/caterer	0	0	1	1
shop assistant	1	0	2	5
Agriculture				
farmer/grazier	0	0	0	1
orchardist/vintner	0	0	1	0
Charity worker	1	0	2	2
No career/not given	68	40	0	4
TOTAL:	(31.8%)	(33.3%)		

TABLE 9:   FAMILY SIZES OVER THREE GENERATIONS: PER CENT

	Scotch	Trinity	MLC	Genazzano
	%	%	%	%
Averages of grandparents' families, born 1870–1900:				
3 or fewer children	35	27	29	26
4 or 5 children	24	31	30	26
6 or more children	41	42	41	48

TABLE 9 (*cont'd*):

	Scotch	Trinity	MLC	Genazzano
Parents' families, born 1910–1940:				
3 or fewer children	77	71	80	44
4 or 5 children	18	24	16	39
6 or more children	5	5	4	17
Respondents' families, born 1935–60:				
one child	5	5	6	2
2 or 3 children	74	66	69	28
4 children	13	20	19	17
5 children	3	7	2	18
6 children	3	1	2	14
7 children	0	1	1	7
8 children	1	0	0	7
9 children	0	0	0	5
10 children	0	0	0	1

TABLE 10:   PERSONAL IDENTIFICATIONS

In this section of the questionnaire the respondents were invited to circle those labels which they believed applied to themselves. There was wide variation in the number of labels chosen and while some chose many, at times, seemingly contradictory ones, others scarcely chose any. The results are as percentages. This survey was made in September 1990.

	Scotch	Trinity	MLC	Genazzano
Jewish	1.5	0	2.8	0
Christian	68.4	69.9	78.0	86.7
orthodox	6.8	8.4	5.6	8.3
liberal	40.6	34.3	31.3	29.2
evangelical	3.8	3.0	7.9	0.8
charismatic	1.5	1.8	1.9	4.2
agnostic	15.0	10.2	5.6	1.7
atheist	7.5	8.4	1.4	0.8
humanist	20.3	16.9	15.9	6.7
Liberal	39.4	34.3	42.5	35.0
Labor	8.3	10.8	13.1	8.3
DLP	0	0	0	9.2
Australian Democrat	4.5	0.6	4.7	0.8
conservative	28.6	31.3	20.6	25.0
small 'l' liberal	22.6	19.9	18.2	14.2
'middle-of-the-road'	13.5	15.1	21.0	21.7

TABLE 10 (*cont'd*):

	Scotch	Trinity	MLC	Genazzano
Christian Socialist	2.3	0.6	1.4	2.5
socialist	4.5	1.8	2.3	0.8
marxist	0	0.6	0.5	0
apolitical	3.0	0	1.9	0.8
swinging voter	12.0	12.0	10.3	13.3
royalist	51.9	49.4	55.6	35.0
republican	5.3	5.4	3.3	7.5
Australian nationalist	34.6	41.6	30.8	30.8
Empire loyalist	20.3	15.7	17.3	6.7
Irish nationalist	0	0	0.5	3.3
internationalist	13.5	12.0	11.7	9.2
pacifist	4.6	7.2	14.0	12.5
feminist	12.8	7.8	29.9	31.7
anti–feminist	4.5	4.2	9.3	10.8
radical feminist	0	0	0	0
conservationist	34.6	28.9	47.7	25.8
greenie	3.0	1.2	7.5	4.2
racist	6.8	4.8	1.9	0.8
anti–racist	13.5	12.0	23.8	25.0
conformist	30.1	33.7	31.8	30.0
rebel	10.5	5.4	2.3	6.7

TABLE 11:   'HAVE YOU UNDERGONE ANY MAJOR CHANGES IN POLITICAL ALLEGIANCE?

	Scotch	Trinity	MLC	Genazzano
	%	%	%	%
Yes	21.0	25.3	19.7	25.00
No	74.5	72.9	75.2	70.8
Not answered	4.5	1.8	5.1	4.2

TABLE 12:   ATTITUDES TO PUBLIC FIGURES
              Admire/Deplore

The respondents were asked to circle the names of those they had admired in their
lifetime, and to cross out the names of those they deplored. A number objected to the
language of the question, finding 'deplore' too strong a term. The figures are expressed
in rounded percentages. Remember also that these attitudes applied in September 1990;
some may well have changed their minds.

	Scotch	Trinity	MLC	Genazzano
Sir Robert Menzies	76/11	81/4	77/7	79/4
Malcolm Fraser	32/16	34/11	33/10	47/6
Dr John Hewson	36/5	45/1	39/3	31/3
John Howard	38/5	40/7	42/2	31/3
Andrew Peacock	14/23	16/23	15/15	11/15
Sir Henry Bolte	69/9	65/7	57/9	56/6
Sir Rupert Hamer	29/11	41/5	37/5	28/6
Lindsay Thompson	35/6	39/2	50/2	38/2
Jeffrey Kennett	17/19	19/16	21/12	21/8
Roger Pescott	7/17	6/12	6/7	2/9
John Curtin	55/3	52/4	39/3	53/1
Ben Chifley	50/7	52/4	43/2	58/2
H. V. Evatt	14/33	14/28	13/14	5/28
E. G. Whitlam	19/38	22/37	22/28	11/40
Dr J. F. Cairns	11/50	12/42	15/28	8/42
R. J. Hawke	18/32	24/28	19/30	8/33
Paul Keating	13/47	9/49	8/42	6/37
John Button	42/8	43/7	38/5	38/5
Brian Howe	11/20	10/13	11/8	7/6
John Cain	24/25	19/24	21/19	12/24
Joan Kirner	11/32	9/30	15/19	8/25
John Halfpenny	5/55	7/54	5/41	2/47
Sir Roderick Carnegie	26/2	33/2	22/2	26/3
Alan Bond	5/53	7/47	4/35	8/29
John Elliott	5/44	8/36	3/40	3/30
Rupert Murdoch	17/30	15/24	7/23	10/18
Robin Boyd	38/2	36/2	37/2	38/0
Bruce Ruxton	38/24	37/19	32/26	29/30
Professor Geoffrey Blainey	55/3	52/8	56/5	42/5
Archbishop Mannix	14/25	8/30	6/22	61/3
B. A. Santamaria	13/31	16/27	10/21	44/7
Denys Jackson	2/6	1/2	1/2	34/2
Father Jeremiah Murphy SJ	4/4	1/4	1/3	56/2
Professor Max Charlesworth	12/3	10/2	18/2	27/6
Senator Frank McManus	10/17	6/19	1/13	27/2

TABLE 12 (*cont'd*):

	Scotch	Trinity	MLC	Genazzano
A. A. Calwell	29/17	24/18	16/11	17/8
Dr W. S. Littlejohn	54/2			
Colin Gilray	53/5			
Rev. Alec Fraser	50/2			
Rev. Stephen Yarnold	30/5			
Frank Shann		71/1		
Alfred Bright		55/2		
Rev. Dr W. H. Fitchett			50/0	
Rev. John Grove			50/1	
Rev. Dr A. H. Wood			70/3	
Mother Philomena Douglas				66/3
Mother Gerda Prytz				39/3
Mother Bernadette Fitzgerald				74/1

TABLE 13:   VOTING TENDENCIES

The respondents were not asked directly how they had voted over the years, apart from the one question as to whether they had ever voted Labor, even if only once. The voting tendencies have therefore been extracted from their personal identifications, the public figures they admired or deplored and any additional information provided in comments. Many of the questionnaires were heavily annotated. The majority have voted for the Liberal/National Coalition for most of their lives, so this small analysis is of those who did not do so. As in so much in the survey, the differences between the schools are small to the point of insignificance; the interesting variation with the Protestant schools is between the generations. Genazzano is a special case.

		Liberal/Nat.	ALP/leftward swingers—per cent		
Scotch	1934 school leavers	26	15	=	36.6%
133	1938 school leavers	35	13	=	27.1%
	1950 school leavers	24	17	=	41.5%
	TOTAL:			=	34.6%
Trinity	Year left Trinity				
164	1930–1934	25	11	=	30.6%
	1935–1939	48	16	=	25.0%
	1940–1944	28	13	=	31.7%
	1945–1950	12	11	=	47.8%
	TOTAL:			=	30.1%
MLC	Year of birth				
213	1908–1918	46	24	=	34.3%
	1919–1925	53	29	=	35.4%
	1926–1934	37	24	=	39.3%
	TOTAL:			=	36.15%

TABLE 13 (*cont'd*)**:**

Genazzano	Year of birth	Liberal/Nat	ALP	DLP	Dem	Non LCP
122	1909–1927	32	9	15		42.9%
	1928–1937	31	17	15	1	51.6%
	TOTAL ALP left swingers:					21.3%
	TOTAL DLP:					24.6%

The Genazzano figures are not clear. Many appear to have swung between Liberal and DLP, and ALP and DLP. Some swung from Liberal to ALP in the late 1960s and have stayed there; others have swung from ALP>DLP>LCP. It remains true, however, that about the same proportion as at the Protestant schools are steady Liberal voters.

The 1990 Journeyings Survey by Janet McCalman and Mark Peel and *Who Went Where in Who's Who 1988* by Mark Peel and Janet McCalman are both published by the History Department of the University of Melbourne in its History Research Series. They can be purchased by mail order from

    History Department
    University of Melbourne,
    Parkville, Vic., 3051

Appendix III
Who Went Where in Who's Who 1988

The tables which appear below are reproduced from *Who Went Where in Who's Who 1988: the Schooling of the Australian Elite*, a book written jointly by Mark Peel and Janet McCalman and published by the History Department, University of Melbourne, in 1991. The book is an account of where the almost nine thousand people listed in *Who's Who 1988* went to school and focuses particularly on the interesting differences between the patterns of schooling in the various states of the Commonwealth over time. There are significant contrasts, for instance, between New South Wales—where government schools have dominated the training of the élite—and Victoria, which is mostly taught, healed, ruled and judged by men from a small group of private and especially Protestant schools. The book also traces the differing educational histories of various professional groups, the collective educational history of the relatively few women who appear in *Who's Who*, and the residence patterns of members of the élite in each capital city.

One of the most important findings of the project, beyond these variations, was the quality and significance of *Who's Who* as a research aid. The authors performed various 'tests' of its coverage of Australia's leaders and found that, in general, it performs very well as a register of the national and state élites. While its view of the élite is somewhat old-fashioned—it tends to miss, for instance, some significant actors in the public service and therefore some potential women leaders—it nevertheless achieves an excellent coverage of leaders in such fields as medicine, law, the universities, business, the senior public service and government.

Mark Peel
Canberra

TABLE 1:   *WHO'S WHO 1988:* TYPE OF SCHOOL ATTENDED BY ALL VICTORIAN-EDUCATED MEN

Type of School	number	per cent	cumulative
Greater Protestant	852	41.2	41.2
Lesser Protestant	222	10.7	51.9
Greater Catholic	156	7.6	59.6
Lesser Catholic	140	6.8	66.4
Jewish*	2	0.1	66.4
Selective state high	300	14.5	80.9
Older state high**	79	3.8	84.8
Other state high	231	11.2	95.9
State technical	47	2.3	98.2
Primary school only	26	1.3	99.5
Unknown	11	0.5	100.0

SOURCE: *Who's Who in Australia 1988*
*We have not studied Jewish schools as a special category. The two Victorian men from Jewish private schools—lawyers from Mount Scopus and Yeshivah colleges—have been included in the non-Catholic private sector for the purposes of analysis. The extremely small number means that this omission of a significant religious difference does not affect our findings.
**We defined 'older high schools' as those built and operating as full high schools before World War II. The schools included Northcote Boys', Essendon, Ballarat, Bendigo, Coburg and Williamstown high schools.

TABLE 2:   The 'Greater Protestant' Schools in 1962, 1980 and 1988

School	Total			Medicine			Academic			Judiciary*			Business			Public Service			Law
	1962	1980	1988	1962	1980	1988	1962	1980	1988	1962	1980	1988	1962	1980	1988	1962	1980	1988	1988
Scotch College	287	309	247	54	46	26	21	38	43	18	31	12	38	53	57	31	24	12	11
Melbourne Grammar	228	252	222	14	28	25	16	30	35	23	32	19	48	59	53	10	14	8	18
Geelong Grammar	103	185	178	17	14	14	3	12	20	2	9	4	27	49	52	0	7	7	5
Wesley College	186	155	142	31	20	20	17	15	14	9	17	9	22	24	27	27	13	7	10
Geelong College	49	61	63	13	9	8	3	9	12	3	6	4	7	10	15	0	0	3	3

* Judiciary includes law in 1962 and 1980.

SOURCE: *Who's Who in Australia 1962, Who's Who in Australia 1980, Who's Who in Australia 1988*

TABLE 3: Selected schools in 1980 and 1988

School	Total		Medicine		Academic		Judiciary*		Business		Public service		Law	
	1980	1988	1980	1988	1980	1988	1980	1988	1980	1988	1980	1988	1980	1988
Selected Catholic schools														
Xavier College	84	87	17	15	5	9	16	16	11	10	1	6	12	6
Sr Patrick's East Melbourne	22	16	4	1	1	1	5	0	1	0	3	1	0	6
St Kevin's CBC	47	34	2	4	3	6	5	4	2	3	13	3	4	2
De La Salle	24	19	0	0	2	4	6*	5*	3	2	3	3	0	0
CBC St Kilda	15	12	0	0	2	3	3*	3*	2	2	5	2	0	0
All Lesser Protestants	242	233	10	12	23	41	15	7	45	48	15	12	0	9
Selected Lesser Protestants														
Trinity Grammar	42	38	2	0	3	6	1	1	10	9	3	1	0	1
Caulfield Grammar	54	50	4	5	7	10	3	2	12	8	2	2	0	1
Carey Baptist Grammar	26	30	2	1	3	7	1	2	14	8	1	2	0	2
Selected High Schools														
Melbourne Boys' High	228	209	16	9	38	48	7	9	28	35	37	16	4	7
University High	90	91	14	16	18	22	4	1	5	6	13	10	0	8
Essendon High	26	28	1	0	2	4	1	0	4	5	5	4	0	1

* Judiciary includes law

SOURCE: *Who's Who in Australia 1962*, *Who's Who in Australia 1980*, *Who's Who in Australia 1988*

Bibliography

Adams, Dorothy *et al. Memories of Darling Road Uniting Church.* Spectrum Publications, Melbourne 1985.

Archer, Fred. *The Treasure House.* Self published, Melbourne 1974.

Austin, A. G. (ed.). *The Webbs' Australian Diary 1898.* Pitman, Melbourne 1965.

Australian Student Christian Movement. *Report of the Industrial Service Camp.* Melbourne 1950.

Badger, C. R. *The Reverend Charles Strong and the Australian Church.* Abacada Press, Melbourne 1971.

Barrett, Sir James. *Eighty Eventful Years.* Self published, Melbourne 1945.

Barrett, John. *We Were There: Australian Soldiers of World War II.* Viking, Melbourne 1987.

Bate, Weston. *Light Blue Down Under: the History of Geelong Grammar School.* Oxford University Press, Melbourne 1990.

Bean, C. E. W. *Here My Son: An Account of the Independent and Other Corporate Boys' Schools of Australia.* Angus and Robertson, Sydney 1950.

Bell, Sister Maria, F.C.J. (ed.). *And the Spirit Lingers . . . Genazzano—One Hundred Years, 1889–1989.* History Committee for the Genazzano College Centenary Celebrations, Melbourne 1988.

Benson, C. Irving. *A Century of Victorian Methodism.* Spectator Publishing Co., Melbourne 1935.

Blainey, Geoffrey. *A Centenary History of the University of Melbourne.* Melbourne University Press, 1957.

Blainey, Geoffrey. *A Land Half Won.* Sun Books, Melbourne 1982.

Blainey, Geoffrey, Morrissey, James, and Hulme, S. E. K. *Wesley College: the First Hundred Years.* Wesley College, Melbourne 1967.

Blake, L. J. (ed.). *Vision and Realisation: A Centenary History of State Education in Victoria.* 3 vols. Education Department of Victoria, Melbourne 1973.

Bossence, W. H. *Epping Street.* Hawthorn Press, Melbourne 1978.

Bradshaw, F. Maxwell. *Rural Village to Urban Surge: A History of the Presbyterian Congregation at Hawthorn, Victoria.* Hawthorn Presbyterian Church, Melbourne 1964.

Bradshaw, F. Maxwell. *Selbourne Chambers Memories.* Butterworths, Melbourne 1975.

Brennan, Niall. *John Wren: Gambler.* Hill of Content, Melbourne 1971.

Brett, Judith. *Robert Menzies' Forgotten People.* Macmillan, Sydney 1992.

Bunting, Sir John. *R. G. Menzies: a Portrait*. Allen and Unwin, Sydney 1988.

Butlin, N. G. 'Some Perspectives of Australian Economic Development, 1890–1965', in Colin Forster (ed.), *Australian Economic Development in the Twentieth Century*. Allen and Unwin, London 1970, pp. 266–327.

Byard, Trevor. *The Merriment of Parsons*. Neptune Press, Geelong 1982.

Campbell, Ruth, *A History of the Melbourne Law School*. Faculty of Law, University of Melbourne 1977.

Campion, Edmund. *Rockchoppers: Growing Up Catholic in Australia*. Penguin Books, Melbourne 1982.

Cannon, Michael. *The Land Boomers*. Melbourne University Press, 1966.

Cathcart, Michael. *Defending the National Tuckshop: Australia's Secret Army Intrigue of 1931*. McPhee Gribble, Melbourne 1988.

Chartier, Roger (ed.). *The Passions of the Renaissance: The History of Private Life*, vol. III, trans. by Arthur Goldhammer. Harvard University Press, Cambridge Mass. 1989.

Chisholm, A. H. *History of the Royal Caledonian Society of Melbourne*. Angus and Robertson, Sydney 1950.

Clarke, Patricia. *The Governesses: Letters from the Colonies, 1862–1882*. Hutchinson, Melbourne 1985.

Clowes, E. M. *On the Wallaby Through Victoria*. Heinemann, London 1911.

Coleman, Robert. *Above Renown: the Biography of Sir Henry Winneke*. Macmillan, Melbourne 1988.

Colles, O. G. A., and Dew, M. *History of the Hawthorn Jubilee Year, 1910*. Hawthorn 1910.

Comettant, Oscar. *In the Land of Kangaroos and Goldmines*. Paris 1890, trans. by Judith Armstrong. Rigby, Adelaide 1980.

Coulthard-Clark, C. D. *Duntroon: the Royal Military College of Australia, 1911–1986*. Allen and Unwin, Sydney 1986.

Courbin, Alain. 'Backstage', in Michelle Perrot (ed.). *From the Fires of the Revolution to the Great War, The History of Private Life*, vol. IV, trans. Arthur Goldhammer. Harvard University Press, Cambridge Mass. 1990.

Crawford, R. M. *An Australian Perspective*. Melbourne University Press 1960.

Croll, R. H. *I Recall: Collections and Recollections*. Robertson and Mullen, Melbourne 1939.

Crow, the Rev. Archie. 'The Triple Farewell', text of speech given on the occasion of his retirement as the chaplain of Scotch College, 15 November 1985. MS.

Darian-Smith, Kate. *On the Home Front: Melbourne in Wartime, 1939–1946*. Oxford University Press, Melbourne 1990.

Davies, A. F. *The Human Element*. McPhee Gribble/Penguin Books, Melbourne 1988.

Davies, A. F. *Skills, Outlooks, Passions: a Psychoanalytic Contribution to the Study of Politics*. Cambridge University Press, Cambridge 1980.

Davison, Graeme. *The Rise and Fall of Marvellous Melbourne*. Melbourne University Press 1978.

Davison, Graeme, 'An Urban Context for the Australian Legend', in *Historical Studies*, no. 71, October 1978, pp. 191–209.

Davison, Graeme, and Dunstan, David, 'Images of Low Life', in Graeme Davison, David Dunstan, and Chris McConville (eds). *The Outcasts of Melbourne*. Allen and Unwin, Sydney 1985, pp. 29–57.

Dean, Arthur. *A Multitude of Counsellors: A History of the Bar of Victoria*. F. W. Cheshire, Melbourne 1968.

Dening, Greg. *Xavier: a Centenary Portrait*. Xavier College, Melbourne 1978.

de Serville, Paul. *Pounds and Pedigrees: the Upper Class in Victoria, 1850–1880*. Oxford University Press, Melbourne 1991.

Dickinson, S. R. *The Essential Basis of a New Order for the Education of the Young as Social Units*. Melbourne 1945.

Dow, Hume (ed.). *Memories of Melbourne University*. Hutchinson, Melbourne 1983.

Eagle, Chester. *Play Together, Dark Blue Twenty*. McPhee Gribble, Melbourne 1976.

Falk, Barbara. *No Other Home: An Anglo-Jewish Story, 1833–1987*. Penguin Books, Melbourne 1988.

Faull, Jim. *The Cornish in Australia*. A. E. Press, Melbourne 1983.

Feith, Betty, 'What are the Spheres Open to Women? The Methodist Deaconess Order, 1942–1974, and its Implications for the Ordination of Women'. MS., 1982.

Fitzgerald, Sally (ed.). *The Habit of Being: the Letters of Flannery O'Connor*. Vintage Books, New York 1980.

Fitzpatrick, Brian. *The Australian People 1788–1945*. Melbourne University Press, 1946; 2nd edition 1951.

Fitzpatrick, Kathleen. *P.L.C. Melbourne: the First Century*. Presbyterian Ladies' College, Melbourne 1975.

Fitzpatrick, Kathleen. *Solid Bluestone Foundations, and other Memories of a Melbourne Childhood, 1908–1928*. Macmillan, Melbourne 1983.

Foster, John (ed.). *Community of Fate: Memories of German Jews in Melbourne*. Allen and Unwin, Sydney 1985.

Frederick, W. H. 'Components of Failure', in E. L. French (ed.), *Melbourne Studies in Education, 1957–1958*. Melbourne University Press, 1958.

Freeland, J. M. *Architecture in Australia*. F. W. Cheshire, Melbourne 1968.

Galbraith, J. K. *The Great Crash, 1929*. Penguin Books, London 1975.

Gilbert, Alan. 'The Roots of Australian Anti-Suburbanism', in S. L. Goldberg and F. B. Smith (eds), *Australian Cultural History*. Cambridge University Press, Melbourne 1988, pp. 33–49.

Grimshaw, Patricia, and Strahan, Lynne (eds). *The Half-Open Door: Sixteen Modern Australian Women Look at Professional Life and Achievement*. Hale and Iremonger, Sydney 1982.

Gronn, Peter. 'Schooling for Ruling: the Social Composition of Admissions to Geelong Grammar School, 1930–1939'. *Australian Historical Studies*, no. 98, April 1992, pp. 72–89.

Gullett, Henry ('Jo'). *Not as a Duty Only: An Infantryman's War*. Melbourne University Press, 1976.

Hazlehurst, Cameron. 'The Advent of Commercial T.V.', *Australian Cultural History*, no. 2, 1982/3, pp. 104–19.

Healy, Mary. *Railways and Pastures: the Australian O'Keefes*. Spectrum Publications, Melbourne 1988.

Hellier, Donna. ' "The Humblies": Scottish Emigration to Nineteenth Century Victoria', in Patricia Grimshaw, Chris McConville, and Ellen McEwen (eds), *Families in Colonial Australia*, Allen and Unwin, Sydney 1985.

Hilliard, David. 'God in the Suburbs: the Religious Culture of the Australian Suburbs in the 1950s', *Australian Historical Studies*, no. 97, October 1991, pp. 401–2.

Hocking, Patricia. *Stormy Petrel: a Biography of Albert Edward Hocking, 1885–1969*. Hyland House, Melbourne 1990.

Hohne, H. H. 'Success and Failure in Scientific Faculties of the University of Melbourne'. Australian Council for Educational Research, Melbourne 1955.

Howard, Frederick. *Kent Hughes: A Biography*. Macmillan, Melbourne 1972.

Howe, Renate. *New Houses for Old: Fifty Years of Public Housing in Victoria, 1938–1988*. Ministry of Housing and Construction, Melbourne 1988.

Hughes-Jones, R. N. *Wm Noall and Son*. Self published, Melbourne n.d., *c.* 1959.

Jackson, Hugh. *Churches and People in Australia and New Zealand, 1860–1930*. Allen and Unwin, Sydney 1987.

Jackson, Hugh. 'Fertility Decline in New South Wales', *Australian Historical Studies*, no. 92, April 1989, pp. 260–73.

Jacobs, P. A. *A Lawyer Tells*. F. W. Cheshire, Melbourne 1949.

Johnston, George. *My Brother Jack*. Collins, London 1964.

Kennedy, Sally. *Faith and Feminism: Catholic Women's Struggles for Self-Expression*. Sydney 1985.

Kingston, Beverley. *Glad, Confident Morning: the Oxford History of Australia, 1860–1900*. Oxford University Press, Melbourne 1988.

Knight, F. F. *These Things Happened*. Hawthorn Press, Melbourne 1975.

Lambert, Moira. *A Suburban Girl: Australia 1918–1948*. Macmillan, Melbourne 1990.

Larmour, Constance. *Labor Judge: the Life and Times of Judge Alfred Foster*. Hale and Iremonger, Sydney 1985.

Lee, Jenny. 'The Marks of Want and Care', in Verity Burgmann, and Jenny Lee (eds), *Making a Life*. McPhee Gribble/Penguin Books, Melbourne 1988.

Lewis, Brian. *Our War*. Melbourne University Press 1980, Penguin Books, Melbourne 1980.

Lewis, Brian. *Sunday at Kooyong Road*. Hutchinson, Melbourne 1976.

Little, Graeme. 'Whitlamism and the Whitlam Years', in Bruce Grant (ed.), *The Whitlam Phenomenon*. Fabian Papers, Melbourne 1986.

McCalman, Janet. Respectability and Working-Class Politics in Victorian London, 1850–1990. Ph.D. A.N.U. 1975.

McCalman, Janet. *Struggletown: Public and Private Life in Richmond, 1900–1965*. Melbourne University Press 1984, Penguin Books, Melbourne 1988.

McCarthy, John. *A Last Call of Empire: Australian Aircrew, Britain and the Empire Air Training Scheme*. Australian War Memorial, Canberra 1988.

McConville, Chris. 'At Home with Sandy Stone', in John Rickard and Peter Spearritt (eds), *Packaging the Past*, Melbourne University Press, 1991.

McInnes, Graham. *Goodbye Melbourne Town*. Hamish Hamilton, London 1968.

McNicol, N. G. 'St John's Presbyterian Church, Elsternwick, 1887–1962' MS., Melbourne 1962.

Mac-Ormiston. *A Pageant: One Hundred Years of Presbyterianism, 1837–1937*. Presbyterian Church of Victoria, Melbourne 1937.

Manne, Robert. *The Petrov Affair*. Pergamon Press, Sydney 1987.

Marshall, Norman. *The Yooralla Story: A History of the Yooralla Hospital School for Crippled Children, 1918–1977*. Self published, Melbourne 1978.

Matenson, Winsome. *From Open Fields: A History of the Trinity Uniting Church, 1941–1991*. Trinity Uniting Church, North Balwyn, Melbourne 1991.

Matenson, Winsome. *Sullivan Bay and Beyond: A Short History of Two Port Phillip Bay First Fleeters and Some of their Descendants*. Self-published, Melbourne 1988.

Melbourne Grammar School. *Liber Melburniensis: Centenary Edition*, Melbourne 1965.

Merrett, D. T. 'The School at War: Scotch College and the Great War', in Stephen Murray-Smith, (ed.), *Melbourne Studies in Education 1982*. Melbourne University Press, 1983.

Miller, Rhys. *Calling and Recalling: One Minister's Pilgrimage into the Uniting Church*. Melbourne Uniting Church, Melbourne 1984.

Moloney, David. *From Mission to Mission: the History of Sacred Heart Parish, West St Kilda, 1887–1987*. Self published, Melbourne 1987.

Morton, Francis H. *My Guardian Angel*. Self published, Melbourne *c*. 1987.

Muir, Barry. *Bolte from Bamganie*. Hill of Content, Melbourne 1973.

Murphy, Rev. J. M., S.J., and Moynihan, the Rev. F. (eds). *The National Eucharistic Congress, Melbourne 1934*. The Advocate Press, Melbourne 1936.

Murray, James. *The Paradise Tree*. Allen and Unwin, Sydney 1988.

Nicholson, G. H. (ed.) and Alexander, D. H. (asst ed.). *First Hundred Years: Scotch College Melbourne, 1851–1951*. Scotch College, Melbourne 1952.

Nicholson, Joyce. *The Heartache of Motherhood*. Penguin Books, Melbourne 1983.

Norris, Ada. *Champions of the Impossible: A History of the National Council of Women, 1902–1977*. Hawthorn Press, Melbourne 1978.

O'Brien, Kate. *Land of Spices*. Heinemann, London 1941.

O'Connor, Sister M. Clare, F.C.J. *The Sisters, Faithful Companions of Jesus in Australia*. F.C.J., Melbourne 1982.

O'Farrell, Patrick. *The Irish in Australia*. New South Wales University Press, Sydney, 1987.

Ollif, Lorna. *Women in Khaki*. Self published, Sydney 1981.

Osmond, Warren G. *Frederic Eggleston: An Australian in Politics*. Allen and Unwin, Sydney 1985.

Owen, J. E. *The Road to Peace*. Melbourne 1954.

Peel, Mark, and McCalman, Janet. *Who Went Where in Who's Who in 1988: the Schooling of the Australian Elite*. Melbourne University History Research Series No. 1, 1992.

Poynter, J. R. *Russell Grimwade*. Melbourne University Press, 1967.

Prentis, Malcolm. *The Scottish in Australia*. A.E. Press, Melbourne 1987.

Prior, Tom. *A Knockabout Priest: the Story of Father John Brosnan*. Hargreen, Melbourne 1985.

Pyke, A. D. *The Gold, the Blue: A History of Lowther Hall*. Council of Lowther Hall, Melbourne 1983.

Rawson, D. W. *Australia Votes: the 1958 Federal Election*. Melbourne University Press, 1961.

Reiger, Kereen M. *The Disenchantment of the Home: the Modernization of the Australian Family, 1880–1940*. Oxford University Press, Melbourne 1985.

Rennick, Elizabeth (ed.). *Sketched from Memory*. Self published, Melbourne 1982.

Robertson, J. Gray. *Golden Jubilee History of St John's Presbyterian Church, Elsternwick, 1887–1937*. Melbourne 1937.

Robinson, W. S. *If I Remember Rightly*, ed. Geoffrey Blainey. F. W. Cheshire, Melbourne 1967.

Robison, L. L. *A Century of Life: the Story of the First One Hundred Years of the National Mutual Life*. National Mutual Life, Melbourne 1969.

Russell, K. F. *The Melbourne Medical School: 1862–1962*. Melbourne University Press, 1977.

St Stephen's Caulfield, *History of St Stephen's Presbyterian Church, Caulfield, 1910–1960*. Melbourne 1960.

Santamaria, B. A. *Against the Tide*. Oxford University Press, Melbourne 1981.

Scates, Bruce. 'A Struggle for Survival'. *Australian Historical Studies*, no. 94, April 1990, pp. 41–63.

Scotch College. *Diamond Jubilee, 1851–1911*. Melbourne 1911.

Scotch College. *Prospectus, 1934*.

Serle, Geoffrey. *From Deserts the Prophets Come*. Heinemann, Melbourne 1973.

Serle, Geoffrey. *The Golden Age*. Melbourne University Press, 1963.

Serle, Geoffrey. *The Rush to be Rich*. Melbourne University Press, 1971.

Sheehan, Mary. *Victories in Camberwell: A History of Catholics in Camberwell*. Pakenham Gazette, 1989.

Sinclair, Keith. *A History of New Zealand*. Penguin Books, London 1960.

Sinclair, W. A. 'Capital Formation', in Colin Forster (ed.), *Australian Economic Development in the Twentieth Century*. Allen and Unwin, London 1970, pp. 11–65.

Southey, Robert. *Life of Wesley and Rise and Progress of Methodism*. 2 vols, London 1820.

Speed, F. W. *Esprit de Corps: the History of the Victorian Scottish Regiment and the Fifth Infantry Battalion*. Allen and Unwin, Sydney 1988.

Stewart, D. Macrae. *Growth in Fifty Years: the Presbyterian Church of Victoria Jubilee History, 1859–1909*. Presbyterian Church, Melbourne 1909.

Strahan, Lynne. *Private and Public Memory: A History of the City of Malvern.* Hargreen, Melbourne 1989.

Stretton, Hugh. 'The Quality of Leading Australians', in Stephen R. Graubard (ed.), *Australia: the Daedalus Symposium.* Angus and Robertson, Sydney 1985.

Strong, Charles, D.D. *Christianity Re-Interpreted and Other Sermons.* George Robertson and Co., Melbourne 1894.

Sugden, Mary Florence. *Edward H. Sugden.* Lothian, Melbourne 1941.

Taylor, Fairlie. *Bid Time Return.* Alpha Books, Sydney 1977.

Tennison, Patrick. *The Marriage Wilderness: A Study of Women in Suburbia.* Angus and Robertson, Sydney 1972.

Terrill, Ross. *The Australians: In Search of an Identity.* Bantam Press, London 1987.

Theobald, Marjorie R. *Ruyton Remembers.* Hawthorn Press, Melbourne 1978.

Thompson, E. P. *The Making of the English Working Class.* Penguin, London 1968.

Tisdall, Constance. *Forerunners: the Saga of a Family of Teachers.* F. W. Cheshire, Melbourne 1961.

Trumble, Robert. *The School on the Hill: A Book of Trinity Grammar School, Kew.* Trinity Grammar School, Melbourne 1987.

Turner, Henry Gyles. *A History of the Colony of Victoria.* 2 vols, 1904, Heritage Edition, Melbourne 1973.

University of Melbourne Schools and University Examinations Board. *Examiners' Reports.*

Vaughan, W. D. *Kew's Civic Century.* Kew City Council, Melbourne 1960.

Victoria, Government of. *Reports of the Ministry of Public Instruction.* 1932–37.

Victoria, Government of. *Education in Victoria.* Government Printer, Melbourne 1973.

Walker, Alan. S. *Clinical Problems of War.* Australian War Memorial, Canberra 1952.

Ward, Russel. *A Radical Life.* Macmillan, Melbourne 1988.

Watson, Don. *Brian Fitzpatrick.* Hale and Iremonger, Sydney 1979.

Wesley, John. *The Works of John Wesley.* Vol. 1. London 1872.

Whitlam, Nicholas, and Stubbs, John. *Nest of Traitors: the Petrov Affair.* Jacaranda Press, Brisbane 1974.

Wickert, Rosie. *No Single Measure: A Survey of Australian Adult Literacy.* Sydney College of Advanced Education, Sydney 1989.

Williams, Thos. *Memoir of Mr James Wood.* Geelong 1883.

Wischer, John (ed.). *The Presbyterians of Toorak: A Centenary History of Toorak Presbyterian Church, 1876–1976.* Toorak Presbyterian Church, Melbourne 1975.

Zainu'ddin, Ailsa G. Thomson. *They Dreamt of a School: A Centenary History of the Methodist Ladies' College, 1882–1982.* Hyland House, Melbourne 1972.

Index